SECOND
ACTS

SECOND ACTS

Presidential Lives and Legacies After the White House

MARK K. UPDEGROVE

THE LYONS PRESS
Guilford, Connecticut
An imprint of The Globe Pequot Press

The Lyons Press is an imprint of The Globe Pequot Press.

10 9 8 7 6 5 4 3 2 1

Printed in the United States of America

ISBN-13: 978-1-59228-942-4
ISBN-10: 1-59228-942-8

Library of Congress Cataloging-in-Publication Data is available on file.

To my Evie, and our Charlie
And to my parents

TABLE OF CONTENTS

ACKNOWLEDGMENTS

There are a number of people I am indebted to in the writing of this book.

Presidents Gerald Ford, Jimmy Carter, and George Bush generously gave of their time to provide me with firsthand perspectives on their lives after the White House, and Penny Circle, Deanna Congileo, Jean Becker, and Tom Frechette helped to arrange those meetings. I am grateful to them and to all the others who agreed to be interviewed for this project (see page 297).

As it happens, the seed for the book was planted at a reception in President Bill Clinton's Harlem office, where Cathy Saypol encouraged me to put these stories into words and later introduced me to publishing contacts to vet the concept. It grew with the help of my sister; Susie Crafford, Rachel Ginsburg, Adam Bellow, and Don Carleton; my agent Ed Knappman, and, at The Lyons Press, Gene Brissie, Melissa Hayes, Chris Mongillo, Michelle Patterson, Jane Reilly, Jane Sheppard, Jessie Shiers, Jennifer Taber, Scott Watrous, and my outstanding editor, Rob Kirkpatrick.

Through the years, I have had the good fortune of having many people in my life who have been supportive of my efforts, including friends—David Hume Kennerly, whose brilliant photograph of five U.S. presidents standing together for the first time in history graces this book's cover; Steve Bez, John Bryant, Michael and Arla Campus, Helen Chang, Richard and Elaine Duran, Larry Goodman, Steve Huestis, Pam and Paul Machemer, John Moore, Kathi Perea, Jimmy Popkin, Mike Purcell, Dick Raskopf, Lee Rosenbaum, Nick Segal, Anne Sidey, Sarah Simpson, Lizzy Smith, Rich Stalzer, Hal Stein, Matt Turck, Jeff van den Noort, Peter Varley, Ray Walter, and Brett Wilson—and family—Marj, Jeff, Cindy and Mike Kaskey, Herbert Krombach; Jim and Nancy Krombach; my in-laws Peter Cundill and Roger and Kay Wiewel; and my faithful siblings Susie and Glenn Crafford, Randall Updegrove, and Stuart and Christine Updegrove.

The late Hugh Sidey, my friend and former *Time* colleague, died shortly before the manuscript for this volume was finished, and before he could write the book's foreword. Through long letters and conversations, Hugh gave me invaluable guidance in writing about the men in these pages, all of whom he knew and covered with the exception of Truman. For my money, he was the best of his breed. I will miss him.

Finally, to my parents, Jake and Naomi Updegrove, whose love and sacrifices for their children are the stuff American dreams are made of; to my son Charlie who patiently waited to play Spiderman or go to "the wood park" while his daddy hunched over his keyboard for "just one more minute" (which often turned into many more); and to my wife, Evie, whose love, encouragement, advice, and support every step of the way made all the difference in the world—my thanks and love.

—MKU

New York, New York

I n the annals of legend, Cincinnatus, a wealthy farmer who worked his own land in ancient Rome, was called upon to lead his country in battle when a horde of barbarians threatened attack. Unhesitatingly, he took up arms as the leader of the army and triumphed over the enemy after several days of fierce battle. Upon achieving victory, foregoing glory and fame, he returned to his farm where he humbly laid down his sword and once again took up his plow.

George Washington, who emulated Cincinnatus throughout his life, did much the same upon leaving the presidency after two terms in 1797. He gave the office over to his vice president, John Adams, who had won it in his own right, and returned to Mount Vernon, his Virginia farm on the banks of the Potomac River. There he tended to his tobacco, corn, and wheat crops until his country beckoned him once more. At Adams's behest, the duty-bound first president served briefly as the commander in chief of the American military when skirmishes with French ships in the Atlantic meant possible war. When the storm passed, he returned to his fields where he lived his remaining days as a gentleman farmer before passing on to the ages in 1799. Like so much in the American ideal, Washington set the precedent for his successors, quietly leaving office without meddling in the affairs of the incumbent president, heeding his country's call back to service, and doing nothing to compromise the dignity of the office he had left.

Prior to American democracy, the world was primarily made up of monarchies where kings and queens gave up power only in death, by natural or more sinister forces. While we may take it for granted in the new millennium, a man relinquishing power over his countrymen and systemically giving it over to another was a radical concept when Washington did it on the eve of the nineteenth century. Just as novel was the notion of a supreme ruler in open retirement, relieved irrevocably of the power he once wielded. In other times and places, kings were celebrated as the very symbols of fertility. The idea of a king rendering himself impotent by willingly giving his crown over to another was as foreign as democratic principles in general. Even well into the twentieth century, the bulk of the world's most powerful leaders were appointed for life—unless they were overthrown. But in America, where power is transferred peacefully as a matter of course—no daggers to the heart, no tanks in the street—a president giving up the power he fought so vociferously to acquire is just part of the bargain.

Forty-three men have taken the presidential oath of office; thirty-four have lived to realize a post-presidency, a natural by-product of the democratic process. At the very least, former presidents provide institutional memory and are powerful symbols, if not of fertility, then of American unity and continuity. Though living succession is no longer unique to the American model, former U.S. presidents, by virtue of the exalted office they held, are a breed apart from their peers in other places in the world. Most presidents who followed Washington into retirement returned to their homes to venerably, if uneventfully, live out their twilight years. There were, however, a number whose lives after the White House were more than just anticlimactic epilogues. In many cases, the lives of ex-presidents have provided a clear glimpse into their character, and have served to underscore their legacies.

John Adams and Thomas Jefferson both survived long after leaving office and had a direct and profound influence on those who followed them—Jefferson as a mentor and friend to his immediate successors, fellow Virginians James Madison and James Monroe, and Adams as the father of Monroe's successor, John Quincy Adams. After sneaking out of Washington just after midnight on the last day of his presidency, rather than bearing witness to the transfer of executive authority to Jefferson, the elder Adams retired to his native Quincy, Massachusetts, where he lived modestly for a quarter of a century, most of which was spent with his wife Abigail who died in 1818. Jefferson went on to achieve one of his proudest accomplishments: conceiving, designing, and overseeing the University of Virginia, which was established in 1819. His lavish lifestyle presented an enigmatic contrast to his frugal fiscal policy as president. Expensive French wines and the upkeep of Monticello, his beloved home and architectural masterpiece, threw him into debt, which he alleviated by selling off many of his precious books—until he could take it no more.

In earlier years, during the heady days of the American Revolution, Adams and Jefferson forged an intimate bond and, of course, did much to shape the breakaway colonies into a fledgling republic, including overseeing and drafting the Declaration of Independence. But they were long estranged as a result of bitter political differences by the time Jefferson followed Adams into retirement in 1809. Feeling that they owed it to themselves—and perhaps, to history—to repair their faded friendship, they exchanged a series of remarkable letters beginning in 1813, in which they delicately "explained" themselves to each other as they watched the nation they helped create move forward in the hands of the next generation. As if by divine providence, the withered revolutionaries died on the same day—July 4, 1826—fifty years to the day after the Declaration of Independence was signed, inspiring Daniel Webster to write, "They took their flight together to the world of spirits."[1]

John Quincy Adams had a far more significant post-presidency than his father. After being voted out of office in 1828, he too enjoyed a quiet retirement in Quincy until he was voted into Congress as a representative of the Plymouth district just two years later. The fact that Adams was not a candidate for office did not deter voters, who more or less drafted him into the role. Adams bowed to the wishes of the electorate, serving nine consecutive terms before his death after a stroke on the House floor in 1848. A mediocre president, Adams, "Old Man Eloquent" as he came to be known, went on to become a powerful abolitionist voice in the congressional debates on slavery that defined the times and portended the future.

With the marked exception of his tenure as a heroic Civil War general, Ulysses S. Grant did not achieve much success in the endeavors he pursued in his life. He was elected president in 1868 and served two undistinguished terms that were marred by scandal. After stepping down from office, Grant faced financial ruin, selling many of his presidential possessions as souvenirs to keep creditors at bay. Bankrupt in his last years and bankrolled by Mark Twain, Grant hurriedly wrote his memoirs while battling throat cancer in order to keep his family solvent after his imminent death. The two-volume *Personal Memoirs of Ulysses S. Grant* generated $450,000 for the Grant family, providing them some measure of financial security, and remains one of literature's great autobiographies.[2]

Theodore Roosevelt left office the youngest ex-president in history at just fifty, choosing to step down instead of running for a second full term in office, which the wildly popular twenty-sixth president would almost surely have won. He chose as his heir, his loyal secretary of war, William Howard Taft, who succeeded him in 1909. The idea of a quiet retirement—or anything quiet, for that matter—was anathema to Roosevelt, and the public remained fascinated by him—so much so that a full-time reporter was posted outside Oyster Bay, Roosevelt's home on Long Island, in the event Roosevelt had something to say. In 1912, he had a lot to say. After becoming disillusioned with Taft's growing conservatism, Roosevelt created the progressive "Bull Moose" Party and challenged Taft and the Democratic nominee, Woodrow Wilson, for the presidency. But Roosevelt's presence in the race split the Republican Party vote, ensuring Wilson's victory and leading to two terms of Democratic rule in the White House.

As in earlier chapters in his life, Roosevelt's retirement was full of adventure. With his son Kermit, he went on safari in Africa where he zealously hunted the local wildlife but spared the life of a small bear, creating a legend that spawned the "Teddy Bear" industry. Later the pair took a disastrous journey up the uncharted River of Doubt in the heart of the Brazilian jungle, which nearly turned fatal for Roosevelt, who returned thirty-five pounds lighter after battling fever and dysentery.[3] The death of his youngest son, Quentin, in the First World War took the will out of the formerly jingoistic "Rough Rider," who died brokenhearted at age sixty, a decade after leaving office.

Like John Quincy Adams, William Howard Taft played a prominent public role after leaving the White House. He had been ambivalent about the presidency when Roosevelt chose him as his successor, preferring an appointment to the Supreme Court. After Wilson took the White House, he served as a law professor at Yale University, but when the Republicans won back the presidency in 1920, the incumbent, Warren Harding, made Taft the court's chief justice. Taft had not enjoyed his one term as president, but relished the days he spent on the high court, which he considered his greatest honor. By the time of his death after heading the court for nine years, Taft had all but forgotten about his term in the White House.[4]

Herbert Hoover, who passively presided over the nation when the Depression hit in 1929, left the White House, if not in disgrace, then acutely unpopular. Americans blamed him for the country's economic crisis and overwhelmingly voted him out of office in favor of Franklin Roosevelt. Embittered by his defeat, Hoover became a vocal critic of Roosevelt's popular New Deal, stressing his concern that it would lead to widespread socialism. But when Harry Truman took over after Roosevelt's death, he turned to Hoover, a former mining engineer who had helped feed war-torn Europe in the wake of the First World War, to do the same after World War II. Truman's gesture touched Hoover, leading to a close friendship cherished by both. The relief effort Hoover orchestrated was enormously effective in staving off famine in the areas hardest hit by the war. If compassion was not a hallmark of Hoover's presidency, his humanitarianism before and after his term was indisputable.

He also made other contributions: In 1947, Truman appointed him to a commission to reorganize federal executive departments. Hoover was selected by his colleagues to chair the committee, which saved millions in federal monies through the economies they identified. Dwight Eisenhower reestablished the commission during his administration, with Hoover once again at its helm, and it achieved similar results. By the time Hoover died in 1964, at the age of ninety, he had redeemed himself in the minds of many of the Americans who had angrily voted him out of office in 1932, exacting the ultimate revenge on his critics. As he put it, "I outlived the bastards."[5]

After arriving back in his native Independence, Missouri, upon leaving the White House, Truman was asked by a member of the press what he was going to do first. Truman, referring to the suitcases he and Mrs. Truman would have in tow, replied humbly, "Take the grips up to the attic," a remark that set the tone for the modest post-presidential chapter he had begun.[6] There is little doubt that what came after he stowed his bags securely away was as uncertain to him as it was to anyone wondering what a man does after descending from the pinnacle of power.

Clearly, the post-presidency has evolved in ways that may have been unimaginable to Truman when he left the White House more than half a century ago. In contrast to their predecessors, "formers" are living longer, doing more, and in a position to wield greater influence on U.S. policy, effect change in the U.S. and abroad, accumulate wealth, and shape their legacies. In effect, the post–White House years have become a new phase of presidential privilege. The stories of presidents Truman through Clinton in their post-presidential years are revealing not only of the character of those men, but of the growing importance and influence of ex-presidents in the U.S. and abroad in an increasingly small world. Indeed, since the middle of the last century, the magnitude of the post-presidency has grown in tandem with the presidency itself.

Like the American population at large, former presidents are leading longer, healthier lives and remaining active in their "retirement" years. Before Truman, the longevity of a president out of office averaged eleven years. From Truman to Clinton, the average has increased to fifteen and counting, with four formers still alive. Gerald Ford, active into his nineties, could easily break Herbert Hoover's record of living the longest—thirty-one years—after his term in office. Jimmy Carter, still swinging hammers for Habitat for Humanity into his eighties, could outdistance Hoover and Ford, and Bill Clinton, just into his sixth decade, threatens to overtake them all.

Prior to Ronald Reagan's passing at ninety-three, there were as many former presidents living as when Lincoln took office in March 1861, when, for just under a year, a record five ex-presidents were alive—Martin Van Buren, John Tyler, Franklin Pierce, Millard Fillmore, and James Buchanan—following a long string of single-term presidencies. Just one day into his second term in office, Richard Nixon became the only living president after the passing of Lyndon Johnson. Before Nixon's death in 1994, he was one of five former presidents who consecutively preceded the incumbent, Bill Clinton.

In the past quarter century, ex-presidents have been used collectively to lend symbolism to significant occasions or causes. In 1981, Nixon, Ford, and Carter represented the U.S. at the state funeral of the assassinated Egyptian president Anwar Sadat, when the climate in Egypt was deemed "too dangerous" for President Ronald Reagan or Vice President George Bush to attend. Sending a delegation Secretary of State Alexander Haig called "the presidential hat trick" prevented a major breech of protocol on the part of the U.S. as the world's reigning leaders descended on Cairo for the proceedings.[7] Thirteen years later, Ford, Carter, and Bush stood shoulder to shoulder with President Clinton at the White House, to show their support of the controversial North American Free Trade Agreement, forming a united presidential front. More recently, in the wake of the September 11th terrorist attacks in 2001, they reunited with former president Clinton and President George W. Bush in Washington, for the memorial service at Washington's National Cathedral, symbols of American endurance and continuity. In 2005, after the tragic tsunami swept over coastal areas of Southeast Asia, leaving untold thousands victimized in its path, Bush dispatched his father and Clinton on a fund-raising and humanitarian mission as a symbol of America's generosity and compassion. Bush tapped them once again to generate relief for the victims of hurricanes Katrina and Rita, which devastated New Orleans and other parts of the Deep South.

Those gatherings and others, including reunions around presidential library openings and funerals, have brought the fraternity of presidents closer than ever—and the bonds they share as members of "the world's most exclusive trade union" have led to unlikely friendships. Overcoming the election of 1976 in which they were bitter rivals, Ford and Carter have formed not only an intimate friendship, which Carter has described as "almost like brothers," but on occasion, an effective bipartisan alliance.[8] Through the years they have co-chaired conferences at each other's libraries, monitored the 1989 national election in Panama, and offered joint statements advocating, among other things, free trade, Israel's recognition of the Palestinian leadership, and a congressional censure of Clinton over the Monica Lewinsky scandal in lieu of impeachment. Bush and Clinton, who squared off as opponents in the 1992 election, have also become close, traveling the world together like a mismatched pair in a buddy movie, in the name of relief for the Asian tsunami and hurricanes Katrina and Rita and for the funeral of Pope John Paul II. Their bond was manifest in Bush's invitation to Clinton to visit the Bush family compound in Kennebunkport, Maine, in the summer of 2005 for a weekend of golf and powerboating. Bush has called their friendship "a dividend in my life."[9]

While formers relinquish power, they have always retained influence. In the past, the influence of an ex-president—unless he went back into public service like John Quincy Adams or Taft—came primarily in the form of playing the role of elder statesman, acting as counselor, mediator, or ambassador for those in power, or for those seeking it. James Polk was greatly influenced by the aging Andrew Johnson in his handling of the Mexican War and in America's standoff with England over the Oregon Territory. When John Kennedy dealt with the aftermath of the Bay of Pigs fiasco early in his term, he turned to his predecessor, Dwight Eisenhower, for advice. The oldest president to be elected to office (up to that point) and the youngest met at Camp David, where Ike publicly supported his successor and privately took him to task for his mistakes in the matter, counseling him on how to move forward.

Until recent years, the ability of a former president to make a direct impact on the nation and the world was largely contingent on his relationship with the incumbent president. Before Truman tapped Hoover to help feed Western Europe after World War II, Franklin Roosevelt's advisors suggested that he call Hoover into service in anticipation of the war's end. FDR's reply—"I'm not Jesus Christ. I'm not waking him from the dead"—all but assured that Hoover would remain on the sidelines despite his desperate desire to make a contribution.[10] Truman's magnanimous gesture in bringing Hoover back into service effectively resurrected him. Like Hoover, Truman would have liked to avail himself to those in power after leaving office, but an acrimonious relationship with his own successor, Eisenhower, meant that his role would be limited largely to that of partisan critic.

Today formers are still called upon by the sitting president and others in power to play the traditional role of elder statesman, but they now often have their own agendas and aggressively pursue them independent of those in power. With the advent of globalization in a world dominated by the U.S., the opportunity for formers to make their marks has increased significantly. Ex-presidents are international celebrities, sought out in all parts of the world, where they can readily have an effect on policy by acting as American ambassadors, emissaries, and conduits to the current U.S. administration—or by pursuing their own agendas.

Richard Nixon and Jimmy Carter are not the first ex-presidents to actively seek to influence American foreign policy based on their own deeply held views. Theodore Roosevelt harangued Woodrow Wilson for his reluctance to get the U.S. involved in the First World War, and was able to hold sway largely because of his enormous popularity and credibility—neither of which Nixon or Carter had in abundance after their presidencies. But by drawing on the relationships they established with foreign leaders while in office, or by virtue of their status as former presidents, both Nixon and Carter were able to successfully pursue foreign policy goals left unfinished when they were driven from office. Today, globalization and America's position as the world's lone superpower make it easier for former presidents to make their mark on foreign policy than it would have been for say, Grover Cleveland or Calvin Coolidge.

Nixon traveled throughout the world, meeting with heads of state and other leaders, shooting off memos to the State Department, writing books on foreign policy, and sharing his perspectives on world affairs with the media. Despite his tarnished image when he left office, he became a respected, sought-after foreign policy advisor to Ronald Reagan and George Bush, and even formed a surprising alliance with Bill Clinton toward supporting Russia in the wake of the Soviet Union's collapse. Ultimately, through his activist agenda to improve America's position in the world, he was largely rehabilitated in the public's eye.

Carter has actively practiced "track-two diplomacy," establishing and maintaining dialogues with high-level contacts in foreign governments decidedly outside formal "track-one" diplomatic channels.[11] Though he has often worked at odds with incumbent administrations to push his own agenda, Carter has nonetheless been called upon by the White House to intercede on its behalf on several occasions, due to the influence he holds. In 1994, when leadership of a military dictatorship in Haiti refused to cede power to its first democratically elected president, the exiled Jean-Bertrand Aristide, Carter worked out an agreement with the leaders to step down. Though Clinton was wary of involving the freelancing Carter, he bit his lip and allowed him to broker a settlement as a last resort to avert military action. Carter's self-appointed role as a world peacemaker has prompted criticism from those who see him as a reckless would-be secretary of state—and has helped earn him a Nobel Peace Prize, making him only the third U.S. president to be so honored, along with Theodore Roosevelt and Woodrow Wilson, and the first to win it as a former president.

George Bush is, of course, a direct link to the incumbent president and his influence is indisputable. Father and son are, in Bush's words, "closer than the public realizes," and while he has kept himself at arm's length with the president on matters of state, he is most certainly his most trusted advisor when tapped, and hopes that the legacies of Bush "41" and Bush "43" are intertwined.[12]

Clinton has used Carter's activist post-presidency as a model for his own and has ambitious aims, in partnership with Nelson Mandela, to relieve sub-Saharan Africa and Caribbean nations of the AIDS epidemic that has gone mostly unchecked in those regions. His relative youth, popularity, ambition, and political ties make it likely that he will have ample time and opportunity to leave a deep impression in his post–White House years. In the wake of Al Gore's loss to George W. Bush, Clinton continued to be called on by the Democratic Party to define its principles at a time when it was in a state of ideological disarray. Like his friend the elder Bush, he has a chance to extend his legacy through a member of his family as his wife, New York senator Hillary Clinton, emerges as a prospective presidential front-runner, aided by her husband and the family brand name.

Mrs. Clinton is not the only former first lady to make her mark after leaving the White House. Like their husbands, former first ladies have also successfully used their prominent positions to bring attention to causes and issues. Betty Ford, in dealing candidly with her own struggles with addiction to pain medication and alcohol, has raised awareness about addiction while lessening its stigma. The Betty Ford Center, in Rancho Mirage, California, which she co-founded and served as chairman, has treated almost 70,000 patients for drug and alcohol dependence since she cut its ribbon in 1982.[13] Rosalynn Carter has been a full partner with her husband in his efforts through The Carter Center, and has become an acknowledged expert in issues relating to mental health, an area she has championed since 1971 when she began as first lady of Georgia. And Nancy Reagan has been a powerful advocate for the federal funding of embryonic stem cell research, which offers the prospect of a cure for a number of deadly diseases including Alzheimer's, the illness that tragically afflicted her husband.

Another aspect of the post-presidency that has changed markedly since the days when Jefferson and Grant worried about mounting debt in their retirements is the ability for former presidents to make money after their time in the Oval Office. In 1958, Congress enacted a law that, for the first time, provided a pension and other entitlements for outgoing presidents.

After Truman left office in 1953, his only income was a World War I veteran's pension of $110 a month.[14] The government offered no financial assistance for his transition, no administrative aides, no office space, and no Secret Service protection. The financial well-being of Truman and his predecessors was primarily a function of their means prior to running for public office. Now, ex-presidents are well taken care of through congressional provisions that have escalated disproportionately through the years, but given the abundant opportunities they have to make money after their presidencies, those emoluments are a mere pittance.

In fact, the current crop of ex-presidents has aroused criticism for their willingness to trade in on their years in office for ready cash. The "anything goes" behavior of several recent former presidents stands in contrast to their deceased predecessors, most of whom simply didn't have the opportunity to use the office to make money or consciously chose not to commercialize the presidency.[15] Truman even refused to use expensive brand-name pens at book signings because he feared it might be construed as his endorsement of their brands.

The writing of White House memoirs, autobiographies, and other literary endeavors has been a long-accepted form of making money from the presidency. Every former president since Coolidge, and many who went before him, have drawn substantial paychecks for presidential tomes. Truman, Nixon, and Carter, like Ulysses S. Grant, all used book contracts to stave off debt. The sums they earned, however, pale in comparison to the reported $12 million Clinton recently earned for penning his memoir. In addition, Eisenhower, Nixon, and Ford all struck lucrative television deals to tell their stories through another medium.

Likewise, the practice of giving speeches in exchange for hefty honoraria is nothing new; in addition to making money from his prolific efforts as an author, Theodore Roosevelt commanded handsome sums for his speaking engagements. Today, opportunities to generate income both at home and abroad abound. There is no shortage of offers from U.S. and foreign corporations willing to pay big money to have an ex-president behind their podium. Ford became a regular on the lucrative "mashed potato circuit," making $15,000 to $50,000 per engagement, followed by Reagan, who pulled down a whopping $2 million for an eight-day trip to Japan sponsored by a Tokyo-based communications company that required only a few appearances, speeches, and interviews. Supplementing his huge literary payday, Clinton has made up for a career of collecting paltry checks as a public servant by raking in six-figure speaking fees for appearances that require no more than a few hours of his time.

Additionally, Ford unapologetically sat on well over a dozen corporate boards, including American Express and 20th Century Fox, claiming it was his right as a private citizen. Since Ford's departure from the White House, cashing in on the presidency has become standard practice for ex-presidents, allowing them to amass considerable wealth and live far more extravagantly than many of their predecessors.

Modern former presidents also have a greater chance to shape their own legacies through the eponymous presidential libraries and museums that have been built for every president since Hoover. Maintained by the National Archives under the provisions of the Presidential Libraries Act, they give former presidents a lens through which they would like history, and current and future generations, to view them and their accomplishments. The only catch is that the former presidents themselves, through the foundations they establish, are on the hook to raise the necessary funds needed to build the institutions, a burden that Ford confided to Carter was "the most difficult task" of his life.[16] Truman built most of his post-presidential life around his library in Independence, Missouri, going there almost every day he was in town to tend to his correspondence, lead tours, and lecture visiting high school students on the office he once proudly held. Plans for Carter's library led to The Carter Center, which, in partnership with Emory University, is "committed to advancing human rights and alleviating unnecessary human suffering."[17] Among the center's remarkable accomplishments are the monitoring of over fifty democratic elections worldwide, and the eradication of the Guinea worm and river blindness, once widespread diseases that afflicted impoverished parts of Africa, Asia, and South America.

The deeds of an ex-president provide an opportunity to burnish their most important contributions in the presidency. Nixon's tireless efforts to influence American policy abroad helped to dim Watergate and spotlight foreign policy as the focal point of his presidential tenure. And if not for his active post-presidency, Carter would likely be remembered simply as a failed one-term president. His contributions as a humanitarian and peacemaker in the years following his presidency—most of which have been made through the auspices of The Carter Center—are an important addendum to his legacy, and give his presidency greater legitimacy. As it stands, he may be the first president since John Quincy Adams—or perhaps William Howard Taft—to be of greater historical significance as a former president than for his tenure in the White House. Should Clinton's activities as an ex-president resonate, they may help lessen the stain of impeachment and scandal that currently blight his presidential record.

With all that is available to and possible for a former president, the notion of retreating quietly and uneventfully into retirement seems as foreign today as that of living succession might have been to Henry VIII. One wonders what George Washington would think of Carter's global peacekeeping agenda, occasionally in opposition to the White House, or of Nixon's tenacious attempts to affect U.S. foreign policy. How would he react to the six-figure speaking fees former chief executives earn for an hour or so behind a podium, or to the score of corporate board appointments accepted by Ford? And what would he make of Clinton's confessionary memoir and the $12 million he earned to pen it? Would he pass judgment on the interloping, avarice, and lack of dignity demonstrated by his latter-day successors, or would he accept these things as part of the evolution of the post-presidency in relation to America and the world?

A natural leader among men, Washington probably would have sympathized with their transitions back to private life, despite his own ostensible eagerness to leave politics for the "more rational pursuits of cultivating the earth."[18] It may have been easier for him. He, like few others, left the presidency on his own terms. A third term could have been his for the asking, and he had largely achieved the things he set out to do as president. Some weren't so lucky. Ford, Carter, and Bush left office dejectedly after hard-fought elections to remain in power. Nixon was compelled to resign the presidency in the face of scandal, and Johnson opted against running for a second full term rather than risk almost certain defeat due to the unpopularity of the war in Vietnam, which he had escalated in his tenure as commander in chief. All left the White House with unfinished agendas and faced the prospect of an unwelcome retirement. While it may have been easier for Eisenhower, Reagan, and Clinton, who left knowingly in accordance with the 22nd Amendment, giving up the most powerful position in the world was not without its challenges. Post-presidential lives are still, as in Truman's day, rife with uncertainty—though they hold more promise and potential than ever before.

In one of the nineteen letters Jefferson sent in his winter years to Adams in far-off Quincy, the Sage of Monticello wrote, "I believe in the dreams of the future more than the history of the past."[19] Almost two hundred years later, despite the uncertainty he faces, a former president more than ever before has the opportunity to shape the future—his own, and that of America and other countries—and, in so doing, enhance his legacy in the eyes of history.

In contrast to F. Scott Fitzgerald's famous assertion, the lives of these former presidents prove that there are indeed second acts in American lives.

I.

HARRY S. TRUMAN:
BACK TO INDEPENDENCE

The tradition had stood for 142 years, since Thomas Jefferson gave the presidency over to his secretary of state, friend, and protégé, James Madison, in 1809. On the last day of an outgoing president's term in office, the president-elect would arrive at the White House by midmorning to be received by the man he would soon succeed. Together along with their families, they would repair to the mansion for coffee or tea and small talk before riding up Pennsylvania Avenue to the Capitol, where, as the last grains of sand fell to the bottom of the hourglass of his tenure as chief executive, the incumbent would watch the president-elect swear into office at 12:00 noon. It wasn't always a comfortable ritual—many an outgoing president had been forced into retirement by the man he was graciously greeting—and often tensions were palpable. But it had always been observed, symbolic of the peaceful transfer of power ensured by the American way of government.

Either out of ignorance of inaugural custom or animosity between himself and Harry Truman, or both, Dwight Eisenhower ignored tradition. Ike, who would succeed Truman, requested that on Inauguration Day, the president pick up him and his wife, Mamie, at the Statler Hotel, where they had spent the night. The apoplectic Truman refused. So it was that the Eisenhowers arrived at the White House on the morning of January 20, 1953. Truman and his wife, Bess, awaited them in the Red Room, where they had planned a small reception, along with members of Truman's cabinet and their wives. But after Eisenhower's motorcade pulled up to the South Portico, Truman received word that his successor was awaiting him outside; President-elect and Mrs. Eisenhower would not be calling on the Trumans. The first couple let the awkward moment pass before setting out into the crisp, clear winter morning, where the Eisenhowers got out of their cars to greet them. The president and president-elect got into an open Lincoln, gleaming black in the sun, as their wives boarded the next car in the motorcade, and journeyed up Pennsylvania Avenue where huge crowds gathered on either side.[1] The trip began with light observations on the day, until Eisenhower, who had been a five-star general when Truman was inaugurated four years earlier, informed his former commander in chief, "I did not attend your inauguration in 1948 out of consideration for you, because if I had been present I would have drawn attention away from you." In response, Truman snapped, "You were not here in 1948 because I did not send for you. But if I *had* sent for you, you would have come."[2] The passengers were largely silent for the remainder of the ride.

Things hadn't always been so bad between the two. For most of Truman's term in office, when Ike had been commander of Allied Forces in Europe in World War II, and after retiring from the army, returning as supreme commander of NATO forces in 1951, they had enjoyed a cordial relationship. Eisenhower even claimed that Truman offered to support him as the Democratic presidential nominee in 1948—though Truman denied it—before the opposing party had successfully courted Eisenhower. But soon after Eisenhower announced his Republican candidacy for the presidency in 1952, politics got in the way.

While stumping for office, Eisenhower made a Milwaukee campaign stop in the home state of Senator Joseph McCarthy, who attended the rally. McCarthy's truculent Communist witch hunt had put many innocents in its crosshairs, including General George Marshall, who had been army chief of staff and secretary of state for Truman, and had been responsible for much of Eisenhower's rise through the army's ranks. Despite the advice of his political advisors who thought it unwise, Eisenhower had planned to use the occasion to pay tribute to Marshall in repudiation of McCarthy's attacks. In the end, however, in deference to the powerful senator, Eisenhower left out the tribute—not realizing that the text of the original speech had been distributed to the press in advance.[3] The conspicuous omission left many lambasting Eisenhower for his political opportunism, including the president. Truman held Marshall in the highest regard and eviscerated Ike for abandoning his principles for the sake of his campaign. "I thought he might make a good president," he said of Eisenhower at an Indiana campaign stop for Adlai Stevenson, the Democratic presidential candidate he had handpicked, in one of many derisive comments he would make after the incident. "But that was a mistake. In this campaign, he has betrayed almost everything I thought he stood for." Ike was stung by the ferocity of Truman's rebukes and vowed then not to ride down Pennsylvania Avenue with him if and when he was inaugurated.[4]

If Eisenhower had turned a cold shoulder toward Truman, so, too, for the most part had the country. Almost eight years earlier, as World War II raged abroad, Truman had had the monumental task of succeeding Franklin Roosevelt after the ailing thirty-second president died of a brain hemorrhage shortly into his fourth term. The prosaic Truman was dwarfed by FDR's formidable legacy, but he hung on and made some of the most difficult decisions in the history of the American presidency. He saw the war to its conclusion, presiding over the nation as victory gave way in Europe, and giving the okay to drop nuclear bombs on the Japanese cities of Hiroshima and Nagasaki, which prompted an end to the war in the Pacific. In the wake of the war, he instituted the Marshall Plan, named for George Marshall, which lifted up war-torn Western Europe economically. As the Cold War emerged out of the ashes of the war, he established the Truman Doctrine to beat back the Soviet threat in Greece and West Germany. He also gave Americans the Fair Deal, an expansion of FDR's New Deal that created social programs to benefit the underclass, including the GI Bill, which gave veterans of every class the chance to pursue an affordable college education. Still, as the election of 1948 neared, Truman stood little chance of beating his Republican rival, New York governor Thomas Dewey. Truman's tireless campaign efforts—now the stuff of political legend—won him favor across the nation. In the face of long odds and low expectations, he prevailed by a razor-thin margin.

His reward was a second term fraught with difficulty. After Communist North Korea—with the aid of neighboring China—invaded South Korea, the U.S. led United Nations forces to drive the enemy back over the 49th parallel. Americans, weary of war, grew frustrated with the lack of military progress from allied forces and blamed Truman for the stalemate. Much to the relief of Mrs. Truman, he opted early on not to run for a second full term in office. Lightning was not likely to strike him a second time at the polls. The public had tired of the controversial Mr. Truman, who was so much a reflection of them, and was eager to move forward and cast its image in the personage of the immensely popular and heroic General Eisenhower. As Truman left office, his 32 percent public approval ratings were among the lowest in modern presidential history.[5]

Tensions notwithstanding, Truman and Eisenhower made it up to the Capitol together. As President Eisenhower gave his inaugural address, Truman did his best to listen to his words to the nation, but his mind wandered.[6] It may well have been that he was thinking of the uncertain future before him, one that would take him back to the small Midwestern town of Independence, Missouri, where he had spent his entire life with the exception of his two-year military service, before his election to the Senate brought him to Washington in 1935, and fate landed him in the White House ten years later.

To the Trumans' surprise, nine thousand souls saw them off at Union Station as they boarded the *Ferdinand Magellan*, the presidential railroad car on loan from Eisenhower for their journey back home. The crowd, which four policemen and three Secret Service men held back so the former first couple could board the train, delighted the Trumans, who would see similar receptions along the rails all the way back to Missouri. Truman reckoned it was a payoff for the "thirty years of hell and hard work" he had put into public service.[7] In Cincinnati, he took advantage of a fifteen-minute stop to go into the station to buy a newspaper, queuing up at the newsstand to pay just like everyone else as news photographers captured one of his first acts as a private citizen. The trip culminated with the warm reception they received upon arrival in Independence. Nearly a quarter of the town's 40,000 citizens turned out as they pulled into the station, the biggest such event in the proud history of Independence. A band played "The Missouri Waltz" (a song Truman actually disliked) and the mayor gave them an official welcome. Truman expressed his appreciation to the townspeople, saying the reception was "more to the heart than I expected. We are back home for good. I have joined the army of the unemployed," he laughed, then added with some pride, "but it's a small army." Mrs. Truman, eyes glazed with tears and lips quivering, was too overcome with emotion to address the crowd.[8]

"When you get to be president, there are all those things, the honors, the twenty-one-gun salutes, all those things, you have to remember it isn't for you," Truman told Merle Miller in his oral autobiography, *Plain Speaking*, years into his retirement. "It's for the presidency, and you've got to separate yourself from that in your mind."[9] As he settled back into life in Independence, it was clear that Truman was indeed separated from the presidency. He and Mrs. Truman returned to their fourteen-room Victorian home, white clapboard with green trim, at 219 North Delaware Street. The "old Wallace place," as it was known to their neighbors, had been built by Mrs. Truman's grandfather in 1867. The newly married Mr. and Mrs. Truman lived there with Bess's mother, Madge Wallace, after their wedding in 1919. The "temporary" arrangement lasted until their departure for Washington sixteen years later. After Mrs. Wallace's death in 1952, they bought shares of the property left to Mrs. Truman's three brothers for $25,000.[10]

Upon their return to Independence, Mrs. Truman remained housebound for three days as she devoted herself to the chore of unpacking bags and putting the house, "quite upset" from all the activity, back in order.[11] Several members of the news media kept watch outside, with Truman giving periodic updates upon entering and leaving.

Truman's liberation from the office kicked in as he took his first walk through Independence, five days after his return. At 9:20 on a Sunday morning, as most of the townspeople gathered in church—the Trumans decided to forego church until their return wouldn't cause such a fuss—he strolled through the familiar streets of town at his brisk 120-steps-per-minute clip, his left hand clutching one of his American Legion convention canes. It was the first time in seven years he had taken a walk without a cadre of Secret Service agents and aides in tow. His entourage consisted of only a few reporters who struggled to keep pace with the soon-to-be sixty-nine-year old ex-president. Occasionally another pedestrian or a driver in a passing car would call out, "Good morning, Mr. President. Good to have you home," or words to that effect. "Good morning," he would say in return. "Mighty nice to be home."[12] "More than any single thing," he wrote later of the half-hour, fifteen-block turn, "this marked the abrupt change in my life."[13]

Truman's Secret Service detail was relieved of the responsibility of keeping watch over him just after Eisenhower took the oath. The federal government did not provide Secret Service agents for ex-presidents, and wouldn't until the fall of 1963, over a decade later, when they were granted protection through a congressional act passed quickly in the wake of John Kennedy's assassination. In his first weeks out of office, Truman's sole protection came from a state patrolman appointed by the Missouri governor, and later, for many years, in the form of a burly, middle-aged police detective named Mike Westwood, who was paid by the town.[14] Westwood acted as his bodyguard, companion, and sometime chauffeur—despite his questionable driving skills.[15] The only thing separating the Truman house from a curious public and intrusive souvenir hunters was an iron fence that had been erected when Truman was in office. He never liked the fence and upon returning home contemplated its removal—Who cares about an old ex-president and first lady, anyway?—but thought better of it after a steady stream of tourists began coming by, mostly out-of-towners who drove by in cars or tour buses with the hope of spotting a genuine former president of the United States.[16] For the most part, though, the townspeople of Independence took their return home in stride, much to the Trumans' relief.

Just as the government provided no Secret Service protection, neither did it extend any of the benefits taken as a matter of course by more recent former chief executives. Transition budgets, presidential pensions, office space and expenses, travel expenses, administrative assistants and aides— none of it was awarded in Truman's day. On January 21, 1953, the thirty-third president was on his own. To a large extent, the modest—albeit upper-middle class—lifestyle the Trumans returned home to was a function of their limited economic means. Truman's only income came from the pension he drew as a World War I veteran, which added up to little more than $1,300 a year. Thirty years as a public servant had not garnered much in the way of savings, and earlier in life, a failed Kansas City men's clothing store he had established with an army buddy after the war had racked up $28,000 in debt, which he faithfully paid down throughout the twenties and into the thirties. As president, Truman earned an annual $75,000 in his first term and $100,000 in his second, but the more draconian tax schedule of the time required that almost half of it went back to the federal government. And the tax-free $50,000 federal grant he was given yearly went to pay White House operating expenses for which he was on the hook.[17] While Truman tried to put as much of his White House income away, it probably wasn't a sizable sum.[18]

A few members of Congress recognized that something needed to be done for ex-presidents to guarantee their financial security. Several of those who went before Truman, like Jefferson and Grant, faced the prospect of financial ruin. Senator Robert Taft and Representative Franklin Roosevelt, both sons of presidents of more than ample financial means, proposed a bill that would award an annuity of $25,000 to former presidents, in addition to extending other benefits. Their cause was supported by *The New York Times*, which, in an editorial written a week after Truman left office, wrote that not doling out a presidential pension "contrasts strikingly with the generous provision we make for five-star generals and fleet admirals who receive full salaries and other emoluments for life." *The New York Times* further prevailed upon Congress to provide an ex-president with an office, a staff, and a nonvoting seat in the Senate to "insure the continuing prestige which it seems should automatically be his due."[19] But Congress heeded neither the admonishment of the *Times* nor the proposal from Taft and Roosevelt.

Truman could have easily alleviated financial worry by accepting one of the many jobs dangled before him, some of which would have had him earning $100,000 or more each year. But the jobs—including a sales management position—weren't in keeping with Truman's criteria for post–White House employment: that is, that the position was of undisputable propriety, immune to the charges that he was cashing in on his years in office, and a good use of his talents.[20] None of the jobs offered fit the bill. He did agree to a $600,000 contract with *Life* magazine to write a memoir of his years in office, and looked forward to the task of putting the story of his administration on paper. *Life* would publish installments of the book, which would later be released by Doubleday. But while the paycheck seemed ample, expenses, taxes, and the time needed to complete the project would drain much of the venture's profitability.[21]

After a week or so, when the bags were all unpacked, the Trumans began settling back into private life. Mrs. Truman fell easily into old and familiar routines, spending time with family (her two brothers and their wives lived in separate bungalows behind the Truman home), gathering with friends she had known throughout her life for bridge club on Tuesdays, and going to weekly appointments at the beauty salon in town.[22] There had been some continuity for her during the White House years, during which she spent summers in Independence with their daughter Margaret while her husband braved loneliness and the stresses of being president back in Washington.

Like her husband, Mrs. Truman was much attached to the town. She had been born there of well-to-do parents in 1885, a year after her future husband came into the world in nearby Lamar. Young Harry met "Bess" Wallace in Sunday school in 1890, shortly after his family moved to Independence, and remained classmates with the girl with the "golden curls" through high school.[23] After graduation, they courted for years, but Truman refused to propose until he had made something of himself. Clerical jobs and a career as a farmer didn't add up to much. Their engagement in 1917 was prompted not by Truman's professional success, but by his call to serve in World War I after his National Guard unit was mobilized.

Truman returned after serving as the captain of Battery D in the field artillery in faraway France for two years, and at the age of thirty-five, he married his sweetheart. His professional lot got no better when his haberdashery went belly-up. By the time Margaret was born in 1924, Truman had launched into public life as an elected judge for Jackson County. Politics agreed with him, and success, which had been so elusive, came to him as an honest, hardworking public servant. However, Mrs. Truman was not suited to public life. Just as he was drawn to the attention like a moth to a porch light, she shunned it. When Democrats at the 1944 convention implored Senator Truman to accept the number-two spot on the ticket in FDR's reelection bid, Mrs. Truman was less than supportive. After initially hedging, Truman accepted. As the Truman family walked across the convention floor while party members cheered and flashbulbs popped, Mrs. Truman asked her husband, "Are we going to have to go through this for the rest of our lives?"[24] In the White House, of course, the lights got brighter. Mrs. Truman zealously protected her privacy, giving reporters little firsthand grist for their columns, and rarely even smiling for the cameras. Solace came in her summer sabbaticals from Washington when she could return to her Independence roots, even if her husband missed "the Boss" terribly.

It may have been a bit more difficult for Truman to return to private life, but he quickly established his own routines. Keeping the hours he had known years before as a farmer, he rose every morning before daylight, enjoyed a light breakfast, looked through his morning mail, and read the morning papers. Then, weather permitting, he would take his daily walk early in the hopes of "avoid[ing] interference."[25] Truman had long used the constitutionals as a form of exercise and a way to gather his thoughts, though now as a private citizen they were often interrupted by fans staking out his route to meet him. Truman always gave them his time, his train of thought broken, knowing that they may have traveled far for the simple privilege of shaking his hand.

Several weeks into his retirement, impressed by its gadgetry, he bought a black '53 Chrysler. After breakfast, he or a driver would back it out of the garage and motor ten miles to his office in the Federal Reserve Bank Building at 10th and Grand in downtown Kansas City, where he would arrive before nine o'clock. Suite 1107 consisted of four corner offices that housed him and a staff of three, who helped him with administrative needs. No guards stood at the door; anyone could drop by and see him. Initially, he was faced with the task of sorting through the 72,000 letters he had received upon his homecoming. He felt strongly that he should respond to each one, and every morning he would bring an aluminum suitcase filled with newly arrived correspondence that needed attention.[26] Each reply was signed by Truman himself, and he also paid for the postage on every envelope. Later in the day, Truman—accompanied by Tom Evans, a drugstore magnate and Truman's friend of forty years—would go to the Kansas City Club, dubbed the "822 Club" for the suite it occupied. There he would have lunch, play a few hands of poker, and a have a nap before returning home for dinner.

On weekends Mr. Truman typified the suburban husband, feeding the parking meter while doing his errands in town, scrambling to put his newly washed car in the garage before an ominous spring sky turned to rain, and doing his best to get out of weekend yard work. When the frugal Mrs. Truman got after him to mow the lawn, he deliberately did so on a Sunday morning as many of their neighbors were setting off to church, drawing their attention. Mortified, Mrs. Truman demanded he stop, thereafter relieving him of the duty.[27]

But despite his best efforts, Truman complained to a friend that he couldn't "seem to get from under that awful glare that shines from the White House," declaring it a nuisance to the people around him.[28] "I try to live the way I did before I went to Washington, try to live like I always did, but it's a hard thing to do," he said.[29] Most nights found Mr. and Mrs. Truman alone at 219 North Delaware Street, eating dinner together, telephoning Margaret in New York, reading and turning in before 10:00 P.M. Susan Chiles, a retired schoolteacher, sometime writer, and friend of the Trumans summed up the attitude of many who had known them long before their White House years: "Almost nobody goes to see them," she explained. "I think people would go to see them, but when a man . . . when a couple has been a president and the first lady, you hesitate to just go and call. They've met so many people, kings and queens, and . . . people just don't seem to call the way they might otherwise."[30]

Tom Evans recalled that Truman had changed too: "He was utterly lost. After all those years in the White House with somebody around to do everything for him, he didn't know how to order a meal in a restaurant. He didn't know when to tip. He didn't even know how to call a cab and pay for it."[31]

The reality that the spotlight would always shine upon him became evident in March after he and Mrs. Truman loaded up the Chrysler and drove due east to visit friends in Washington, and then on to New York to see Margaret. They had made the journey to the capital often during Truman's ten years in the Senate, and initially felt the thrill of once again being just two ordinary folks on the road. But when they stopped to top off the tank at the Shell station in Decatur, Illinois, which they had frequented during those earlier trips, the old attendant recognized him as "Senator Truman." At his recommendation they spent the night at a nearby motel. Before long it seemed that all of Decatur knew not only that the Trumans were in town, but where they were staying as well. The local police chief worried about their safety, whereupon he assigned four of his men to their care. They took the former first couple to dinner and an early breakfast before escorting them back to the highway and out of town, according to

Truman, "with a sigh of relief."[32] Similar episodes occurred across the Midwest and up the eastern seaboard. A highway patrolman stopped them simply to shake hands; diner patrons and waitresses asked for autographs as they tried to eat; and motorists honked their horns and waved as they passed. Although Truman often enjoyed the attention—even if his wife didn't—they were never again going to be just ordinary folks.

Truman stayed "busy as the proverbial bee" with work on his book.[33] The project provided him with an opportunity to tell his story and answer his critics. He had a reverence for history, which he had read voraciously since his youth. "There's nothing new in the world," he said, "except the history you don't know."[34] He lamented the fact that more of his predecessors hadn't recorded the stories of their lives and administrations, and was determined to do his part for history—and to shape its image of him. Historians couldn't always be trusted, but he wrote, "When the lives of great men are studied from [their] records they leave some idea of what happened."[35]

A number of people assisted him in the task. By his own admission, Truman was no writer, and he enlisted the services of William Hillman and David Noyes, White House speechwriters and Truman loyalists, to ghostwrite the work. Their job was to transcribe Truman's responses to questions posed by a series of interviewers from academia, several of whom were let go during the course of the project. Additionally, many of Truman's White House staff and cabinet members were interviewed. While the material proved abundant, it hardly constituted the makings of a good historical memoir. No one knew this more than Truman himself who, after reviewing the manuscript, wrote his own critique at the top of one of the pages: "Good God, what crap!"[36] Eventually, the material added up to two million words, considerably more than the 300,000 words that were contracted.[37] An agreement was reached with Doubleday to produce two volumes, allowing for 580,000 words, but the daunting task of editing the work and meeting looming deadlines meant Truman often worked as many as seventeen hours a day in his Kansas City office. A number of other cooks were asked to weigh in on the broth, including the editors of *Life* and Doubleday, Dean Acheson, Truman's friend and secretary of state, and additional writers.

Eventually, the volumes were delivered on time; *1945: Year of Decisions*, an accounting of his first year in office, was in print by the fall of 1955.

It was followed in the winter of 1956 by *Years of Trial and Hope*, which covered the balance of his presidency. Though the books sold well, both lacked the author's authentic and unique voice. The work didn't sound much like it came from Truman due to the number of writers involved in the project and Truman's reverence for the office. Although the result was a dry work, it was important by virtue of its author and its comprehensive documentation of the times.

While Truman readily agreed to sell the story of his presidency, he drew the line at other financial opportunities to commercialize it. The former president railed against the idea of selling an autographed limited edition of the books that would be priced at thirty-five dollars. "I cannot possibly enter into a program which would look as if I were selling autographs instead of a book. I want the book sold on its merit," he wrote the editor in chief at Doubleday. "I have a very strong feeling about any man, who has the honor of being an occupant of the White House in the greatest job in the history of the world, who would exploit that situation in any way, shape, or form."[38] However, he did agree to sign copies of *1945: Year of Decisions* for any and all takers at a launch party in the grand ballroom of the Muehlebach Hotel in Kansas City, happily autographing as many books as were put in front of him. In a feat of endurance, he signed four thousand copies during a session that lasted nearly six hours. Those who waited were treated to Truman's angular signature on the title page, written with one of several $1.75 fountain pens he had equipped himself with in a conscious effort not to offer an implied endorsement for a brand-name pen.[39]

The release of the memoirs brought forth an appreciation for Truman that would grow over time. The public had always maintained a certain affection for him, controversial as he was, but the memoirs, despite poor reviews, inspired a reevaluation of the Truman years, and with it, an acknowledgment of his contributions in office. But while the memoirs served his burgeoning legacy, they did little for his bank account. By his own estimation, the $600,000 he grossed for the work netted just $37,000 in profit after office and personnel expenses (which added up to $153,000) and taxes.[40] The 67 percent bite the government took could have been eased by President Eisenhower, who had the option to deem the work exempt from federal and state taxes and treated as a capital gain, as Truman was not an author by trade. Truman had done as much for him when his World War II memoir, *Crusade in Europe*, was published during Truman's presidency, which meant that the $635,000 Ike earned for the book was taxed at only 25 percent. Truman's appeal for reciprocity under the same conditions drew no response from the White House, a manifestation of the chill between the two men that would last throughout the Eisenhower years.[41]

Another came at the end of Truman's book itself. While most presidential memoirs end on an upbeat, reflective note, the last words of Truman's were reserved to cast doubt on his successor. At the close of *Years of Trial and Hope*, Truman recalled the tense transition meeting he had held with Eisenhower during his last days as president, which left him "troubled" by the president-elect's "frozen grimness." "He may have been awestruck by the long array of problems the President has to face," he wrote in the book's final paragraph. "But it may have been something else. He may have failed to grasp the true picture of what the administration had been doing because in the heat of partisan politics, he had gotten a badly distorted version of the true facts. Whatever it was, I kept thinking about it."[42]

Truman biographer Alonzo L. Hamby put Truman's harsh feelings toward his successor this way: "The Eisenhower presidency gnawed at [Truman] in a way that was not altogether healthy."[43] But his attitude was certainly not without reason. As the distinct air of McCarthyism permeated the political climate in late 1953, Ike's attorney general, Herbert Brownell, resurrected charges—albeit, ill-founded—that Truman had appointed a Soviet spy to the board of directors of the International Monetary Fund six years before. The claim was accompanied by a subpoena for Truman to appear in front of the House Un-American Activities Committee. Truman's response came in the way of a nationally televised rebuttal in which he lambasted the incumbent administration for "shameful demagoguery" and "McCarthyism."[44] Brownell's zeal clearly irked Eisenhower and the matter fizzled, but not Truman's anti-Eisenhower rhetoric. He kept the jabs coming. In the presidential campaign of 1956, in which he stumped for the once-again ambivalent nominee, Adlai Stevenson, he was no kinder than he had been in 1952. For a country that "liked Ike," the vitriol fell mainly on deaf ears, and may have served to reinforce Truman's image as a hot-tongued, less-than-presidential partisan—a view shared by Ike himself.

Eisenhower easily won reelection, ensuring Truman the agony of watching him at the helm for another term. In an unsent letter of "congratulations" to Ike on his win—a cathartic exercise by Truman to vent his ill feelings—Truman wrote, "Best of luck, and may honest Democrats and liberal Republicans save you from disaster."[45] Eisenhower may have been less vocal in his opinion of Truman, but as with his refusal to enter the Truman White House in its waning hour on Inauguration Day, his actions spoke volumes. When Truman called the president's Kansas City hotel to see if he could pay his respects when Eisenhower was in Missouri on presidential business—Ike was, after all, still the president—his call went unreturned. (The aide who answered the phone claimed he thought it was a crank call.) Perhaps most insulting, though, was that he never sought Truman's advice or perspective on matters of state, which rendered Truman all but irrelevant throughout the Eisenhower era.

Herbert Hoover, the country's only other living former president, knew all about that. When Franklin Roosevelt beat him out of the White House in 1932, Hoover, like Truman, was relegated to the political wilderness during his successor's tenure, which stretched more than a dozen years, though he would have liked nothing more than to continue to serve the public after getting his presidential pink slip. As a young mining engineer, Hoover had made his fortune in the diamond mines of Africa, amassing millions before turning thirty. As World War I raged, he oversaw the Commission for Relief in Belgium, when the food supply was cut off after German occupation. His success in staving off famine won him fame and a future in public service, which led to the White House in 1929. Just six months after taking office, the stock market crash triggered the economy's downward spiral, and Hoover's laissez-faire response made him a magnet for culpability. Over a decade into his own presidency, FDR rejected the notion of calling Hoover back to service in anticipation of food shortages at the end of World War II. Instead, it was more politically expedient to have Hoover remain the Republican scapegoat New Dealers blamed for the Depression and the economic strife that had come since the crash.

After Roosevelt's death, Hoover's chance for redemption and further input came in the unlikely form of Harry Truman. The new president, just two months into office, invited Hoover (whom he barely knew) to the

White House to discuss the food shortage in Europe and Asia as World War II drew to a close. The reason was simple enough: if there was anyone "who knew about hungry people, it was [Hoover]." But there may have been another reason too. Truman was thrust into the role of chief executive with no notice and preparation, and was forced to accept the position's inherent loneliness. As the only living former president at the time, Hoover was the one man in the world who understood the burden Truman carried. Overcoming his instinct to tell the Democrats summoning him to "go to hell" for his vilification over the years, Hoover accepted. For the first time since leaving office, he entered the White House; and although he was suspicious of Truman's motives, by Truman's own account, Hoover was moved to be there. As Truman began to discuss the situation, Hoover's eyes flooded with tears. He excused himself for a moment and returned to the conversation after regaining his composure. "I knew what was the matter with him," Truman recalled. "It was the first time in thirteen years that anybody had paid attention to him."[46]

Hoover was gone in less than an hour with a request from the president to draft some thoughts on food relief. Nine months later, Truman called upon him to offer his name and expertise as the honorary chairman of the Famine Emergency Committee, which would work to feed much of Europe and Asia, hungry and bleeding from the ravages of war. Hoover threw himself into the task, journeying some 50,000 miles on an army transport plane dubbed *The Sacred Cow*, calling upon Americans and heads of state abroad to lend a hand in the crisis, and orchestrating solutions that equaled the success of his earlier triumph over famine three decades earlier.[47]

After the war's end, Republicans in Congress formed the Commission on Organization of the Federal Branches of Government, with the goal of restructuring federal departments in the name of efficiency. The bipartisan panel of twelve, including Joseph Kennedy and Dean Acheson, was to be headed by Hoover in an agreement reached by both parties. When some congressional Democrats blanched at the thought of the conservative Hoover chairing the committee, Truman held firm that he was the right man for the job. "You politicians leave him alone and we'll have organization in the government," he told Sam Rayburn, the Democratic Senate majority leader who opposed Hoover's selection. "Now, Sam, that's all—you help!"

When the commission's work was done, the Truman White House had accepted over two-thirds of its recommendations, resulting in taxpayer savings of untold billions of dollars over the years.[48] Hoover's latter-day vindication was almost entirely due to Truman bringing back the old engineer to the national and world stage, allowing him to reclaim a legacy that had been all but eclipsed by his ill-fated term in the White House. In addition, Truman saw to it that the portrait of Lou Hoover, the thirty-first president's wife, hung in the White House, and that the erstwhile Hoover Dam—built on the Colorado River during Hoover's term in office and renamed Boulder Dam at the behest of the Roosevelt administration—was once again to be known by its original name through an act of Congress in 1947.

While their party affiliations and differences kept them on opposite sides of the political spectrum, the men developed an esteem and affection toward each other that extended well beyond Truman's term in office. As former presidents, they maintained a close friendship, though their lives were as different as their politics. Hoover, wealthy and urbane, lived in New York's Waldorf Towers and became a venerated Republican elder. While afternoons might find Truman playing poker with his cronies at the 822 Club or having "H_2O with a little bourbon" at the nearby Muehlebach Hotel with some of the boys of Battery D, his Republican peer might be found with members of the business establishment in New York, or in retreats to the Bohemian Grove among northern California's redwoods with the fellow Bohemian Club members who comprised much of the country's elite conservative power base. But they understood each other in ways neither might have anticipated, even given their shared experience at the height of power.

For his part, Hoover never forgot Truman's generosity. In a letter to his friend two years before his death in 1964, he openly summed up his gratitude:

Yours has been a friendship which has reached deeper into my life than you know. I gave up a successful profession in 1914 to enter public service. I served through the First World War and after for a total of about eighteen years. When the attack on Pearl Harbor came, I at once supported the President and offered to serve in any useful capacity. Because of my various experiences, I thought my services might again be useful;

however, there was no response. My activities in the Second World War were limited to frequent requests from Congressional committees. When you came to the White House, within a month you opened a door to me to the only profession I know, public service, and you undid some disgraceful action that had been taken in prior years.[49]

The letter remained one of Truman's prized possessions.

In 1957, Hoover was on hand to honor his friend when the Truman Library was dedicated. Asked by a woman in attendance what former presidents did with their time, he replied, "Madam, we spend our days taking pills and dedicating libraries." Hoover, of course, did far more, and Truman made it so.[50]

The Truman Library would become the greatest and most meaningful post-presidential accomplishment for Truman. With the memoirs out of the way, he devoted himself to the library's construction and development. The project had been much on his mind since his arrival home. Just a few days after returning to Independence, Truman led a handful of chilled reporters through the cornfields of the 600-acre Truman family farm in Grandview, now operated by the former president's brother Vivian and his wife, Luella. After sampling Luella's homemade coffee cake, the group, incongruously attired in fedoras, business suits, and overcoats, slogged through the snow to see the plot the Truman family was prepared to donate as the site for the library. While they walked, Truman reminisced about the days he had spent working the fields, and discussed the importance of the library as a place of study for historians.[51]

The notion of building the library on the farm soon fizzled, however, when Vivian Truman led another group—including an architect and Truman's staff assistant, George Elsey—to survey the site. The architect questioned the parcel of land that Vivian had suggested for the library, an area at the bottom of a small hill that was swampy in one corner. Instead, he proposed an elevated site with vistas in every direction. "Ain't no use wastin' good farmland on a dang library," Vivian replied.[52]

Other locations were discussed. The campus of UCLA was rejected by Truman as quickly as it was offered, as he was no fan of either Los Angeles specifically or California generally.[53] Eventually, the ideal situation presented itself. The town of Independence offered thirteen acres in what had been Slover Park and part of a residential neighborhood before the city bought the private properties and tore down the homes. The location was just a mile from the Truman home.

The architectural plans for the library changed several times too. Truman had in mind a colonial design, something that resembled Philadelphia's Independence Hall. But while the structure would bear his name, his design preference was overruled by the project's architects and the trustees of the Harry S. Truman Corporation. Charged with raising the $1.75 million needed for the library, the group decided to go with something a bit more modern and therefore un-Truman-like. The plans called for an arc-shaped Indiana limestone and New Hampshire marble structure with a large, plain, six-pillar portico at its center. Disdainful of the contemporary twentieth-century style epitomized by Frank Lloyd Wright, Truman remarked, "It's got too much of that fellow in it to suit me."[54]

The groundbreaking for the library took place in 1955, the second facility to be built under the Presidential Libraries Act of the same year, which allowed for the National Archive's management and maintenance of institutions for every president since Hoover. (Franklin Roosevelt's library, on the grounds of his estate in Hyde Park, New York, was the first.) In accordance with the act, the Truman Library was built with private funds—much of which Truman secured himself through speaking engagements and selling written pieces to newspapers—and would be given to the government upon completion.[55] Among other things, the act was designed to provide a repository for the papers of a president's administration.

Prior to the act, the papers of the nation's past presidents were scattered to the winds, mostly in private hands if they could be found at all. The only exception was one-term president Rutherford B. Hayes, whose library, found in Fremont, Ohio, and funded by the state, houses his entire presidential archive. Since the days of Washington, the papers of a president have been considered the president's private property to do with as he wishes upon leaving office. However, none of the beneficiaries of the Presidential Libraries Act have failed to turn them over to the government through their libraries, excepting Richard Nixon, whose legal battle against the government over possession of his papers in the wake of Watergate lasted over two decades.

The summer of 1957 saw the dedication of the Truman Library, as several thousand people gathered on the unfinished grounds to watch a host of VIPs give praise to the thirty-third president. Supreme Court Chief Justice Earl Warren—the Republican vice-presidential nominee who had been defeated by Truman and his running mate Alvin Barkley in the election of 1948—presided over the occasion, which also included Eleanor Roosevelt, House Speaker Sam Rayburn, Senate minority leader William Knowland, and, of course, Hoover. Truman enjoyed it all with a bright-eyed smile, looking every bit the former haberdasher who had left office five years before: trim and dapper, he wore a double-breasted suit, with a squared handkerchief jauntily peeking from the pocket of his jacket like bread from a toaster. Just over five years since he had left office, history was beginning to take note of the importance of Truman's administration, which, Warren pointed out, was "already recognized as one of the most momentous periods of our country and the world."[56] Hoover was pleased to see that history was being brought "closer and closer" to the American people, not concentrated in Washington. That pleased Truman too, who saw the library as the Midwest's foremost place of study for the presidency.

In addition to the convenient location, the library offered Truman another advantage: office space. No longer would he incur rental charges for his Kansas City offices. For the remainder of his days, he would have a suite of offices at the library expressly for his use, including his own, which, like the one he had left at the White House, looked out onto a rose garden. The benefit offered from the library helped to alleviate the substantial financial burden Truman had carried since leaving office. Additional financial aid came from the sale of some of the land at the Truman family farm in Grandview, for which a developer paid the family handsomely to develop a shopping center. If not for the income generated from the sale, he wrote House majority leader John McCormack, "I would practically be on relief, but with the sale of that property I am not financially embarrassed."

Insisting he wasn't asking for a pension, Truman lobbied McCormack for a subsidization of office expenses—70 percent, he suggested. In fact, a pension is what Truman ended up getting. McCormack took the matter up with House Speaker Sam Rayburn and Senate majority leader Lyndon Johnson, who worked their congressional magic, leading to a law that granted a yearly payout of $25,000—comparable to the annual salaries of heads of industry at the time—as well as allowances for other amenities such as staff, travel benefits, and franking privileges for nonpolitical mail. The latter alone was a huge benefit for Truman, who estimated that he was spending $30,000 a year responding to all the letters and offers he received.[57] As the country's other living former president, Hoover was entitled to the same emoluments. He instinctively resisted accepting the package, worrying that it would lead to the kind of criticism he had endured in the early years of his post-presidency, but out of loyalty to his friend of more limited means, Hoover accepted the money.[58]

His financial concerns behind him, Truman settled into a comfortable routine for the remainder of his active years, much of which revolved around the library. He went there almost every day he was in town, including weekends, arriving at 6:30 in the morning or shortly thereafter, working until he returned to 219 North Delaware Street for a lunch break, and returning to the library to resume work until dinner.[59] He played a hands-on role there, often leading tour groups through the library himself and answering phones before business hours, disclosing his identity as "the man himself." He told a visitor that he wanted the institution to be "a storehouse for the presidency, and I aim for it to be used that way."[60] He even added his own artistic flourish, at the artist's request, to a mural depicting the migration of settlers in the Midwest plains by Thomas Benton, which stood in the library's entry hall.

At least several times a week, he would speak about the presidency before an audience of high school students in the library's auditorium. Standing behind a podium, he presided over the sessions like a genial schoolteacher, encouraging their interest in learning more about their country and the world and, by many accounts, getting as much from them as they did from him.[61] By his own estimation, he addressed more than 200,000 students, patiently answering the questions he was asked repeatedly.[62] One question that almost invariably arose was why Truman chose to drop atomic bombs on Hiroshima and Nagasaki at the end of World

War II. Truman's answer, while not rehearsed, was consistent. "The atom bomb was no great decision," he told a group of Columbia University students when asked the question at a seminar on the university's campus in 1959. "It was used in the war, and for your information, there were more people killed by firebombs in Tokyo than dropping the atom bombs accounted for. It was merely another powerful weapon in the arsenal of righteousness. The dropping of the bombs stopped the war, saved millions of lives. It is just the same as artillery on our side. Napoleon said that victory is always on the side of the artillery. It was purely a military decision to end the war."[63]

Occasionally, travels took him away from his life in Independence. President and Mrs. Truman could often be found on New York's Upper East Side, visiting Margaret, who had moved to Manhattan during her father's second term in office to pursue a career in music, where her earnest attempt at a singing career led to only modest success. While in New York, she met and began a clandestine relationship with Clifton Daniel, a foreign correspondent for *The New York Times*, and later, its managing editor. They married in April 1956 in Independence, and produced four children for the Trumans to dote on, all boys: Clifton, William, Harrison, and Thomas.

On three separate occasions the Trumans vacationed in Western Europe. The first, a seven-week trip in 1956, was initiated by an honorary degree Truman was to receive at Oxford University. Attired in ceremonial garb, Truman walked through the university grounds after the ceremony. Students trailed him, crying out "Give 'em hell, Harricum," which put a tear in Truman's eye. The trip marked the last time he would see his old friend and peer, Winston Churchill. He and Mrs. Truman visited Winston and Clementine Churchill at Chequers, their home outside London. They spent the better part of a day with them, even touring Churchill's painting studio. It was a "very pleasant visit and a happy one" but "was all over too soon," Truman wrote in his diary of the fleeting afternoon.[64] (Several years later, President Eisenhower would invite Truman to a White House stag dinner in honor of Churchill. Despite the fact that he was in Washington at the time, the bad blood between him and Eisenhower caused him to send his regrets.) The European escapade was heavily scheduled and largely ceremonial, not the relaxing vacation they had dreamed about earlier in their lives. Like their car trip earlier in the decade, the first couple would enjoy little peace and quiet.

While Truman's popularity grew during his retirement, his influence in his own party waned. After tapping Adlai Stevenson as his successor in 1952, he soon became disillusioned with him and his moderate voice, which had come to dominate the party's platforms. Stevenson lacked Truman's common touch and waged an uninspired, and ultimately failed, campaign. In 1956, his man was Averell Harriman, who had been elected two years earlier (by a slim margin) as governor of New York. But despite a public endorsement from Truman, the delegates at the Democratic National Convention in Chicago renominated Stevenson as their standard-bearer. In the fall, Stevenson was once again defeated handily by the immensely popular Eisenhower.

As the presidential campaign of 1960 heated up, Truman threw his support to fellow Missourian, Senator Stuart Symington. He was less enthusiastic about another of the candidates for the nomination, Senator John F. Kennedy, an undistinguished backbencher whom Truman deemed too inexperienced for the job. But while he may have had reservations about the senator from Massachusetts, it was his imperious father, Joseph Kennedy, who gave him greater pause. "It's not the Pope I'm afraid of," Truman said, referring to the initial controversy over Kennedy's Catholicism, "it's the pop."[65] He refused to attend the Democratic National Convention in Los Angeles that summer, and, in a national press conference, charged that Kennedy's nomination was a foregone conclusion managed by Kennedy forces—privately, he felt Joseph Kennedy has bought his son the nomination—and questioning Kennedy's readiness for the presidency.[66] The remarks only served to make Truman appear bitter and out of touch with his party. When the Democrats crowned Kennedy as their nominee, though, Truman rallied to his cause just as he had for Stevenson four years earlier. Kennedy reached out to Truman during the campaign, visiting him at the library to solicit his advice in gaining victory over his Republican rival for presidency, vice president Richard Nixon. Truman eventually warmed to the Democratic candidate, aiding in his cause by taking to the stump. By the end of the campaign, the seventy-six-year-old Truman had made thirteen speeches in nine states across the country.[67]

Truman's growing fondness for Kennedy and party loyalty may have only been part of the reason for his support, for he viewed the Republican challenger with utter contempt. At a low moment in the 1952 campaign, when Nixon played hatchet man as Eisenhower's running mate, Nixon accused Truman, Dean Acheson, and Adlai Stevenson of being "traitors of the high principles in which many of the nation's Democrats believe," and further condemned them for their "toleration of and defense of Communism in high places."[68] Harry Truman did not take kindly to that kind of smear tactic. Thereafter, he loathed Nixon for his opportunism and demagoguery, in addition to his politics. While he never stooped to those kinds of tactics himself, he did often refer to Nixon privately, and at least once publicly, as "squirrel head."[69]

Another low moment for Nixon came in the 1960 campaign, in the third of the televised Nixon-Kennedy debates, when he responded to a zealous campaign appearance by Truman. While stumping for Kennedy in the South, Truman had claimed that southerners who voted for the GOP could "go to hell," a befitting example of the "give 'em hell" rhetoric for which he was known. Nixon was indignant over Truman's use of profanity. "When a man is president of the United States, or former president," Nixon said in the debate, "he has an obligation not to lose his temper in public . . . It makes you realize that whoever is president is going to be a man that all the children of America will look up to, or will look down to. All I can say is that I'm very proud that President Eisenhower restored dignity and decency, and frankly, good language to the conduct of the presidency of the United States."[70] Kennedy's only response was that Nixon should take up Truman's language with Mrs. Truman. (Nixon's objections to Truman's language became ironic when transcripts of tapes released from the Nixon White House years later were rife with "expletive deleted" references where Nixon's profane language had been removed.)

Kennedy's victory in November was a tonic for Truman, who had endured eight years of the Eisenhower-Nixon administration. In January, he, along with Mrs. Truman, attended Kennedy's inauguration, smiling broadly when the new president asked him to sign his menu at the luncheon that followed. The next day, at 10:00 A.M., as Kennedy's first official visitor, Truman entered the White House for the first time since he had left it as a resident, and gave the president gentle counsel on the responsibilities he had just assumed.[71] Kennedy remained cordial toward Truman during his presidency, occasionally soliciting his advice and inviting the Trumans, including Margaret and Clifton Daniel, to spend the night at the White House, throwing a dinner in their honor. But the president didn't go beyond that. "You are making a contribution. I am not. Wish I could," Truman wrote to Dean Acheson, who was being drawn upon to counsel Kennedy on Vietnam and other matters as one in a group of sage "Wise Men."[72] It was a great disappointment to Truman, who longed to be called on by the administration, but would remain an outsider.

On November 20, 1963, along with the rest of the world, Truman got word that Kennedy had been assassinated in Dallas. The news left him physically ill, unable to leave his home, or give a statement to the press.[73] He had grown quite fond of the young president, who had measured up better than he had expected. The day after the assassination, the newly inaugurated Lyndon Johnson called Truman, who gave him advice as another former vice president who had been thrown unexpectedly into the presidency, and two days later he and Mrs. Truman arrived in Washington for Kennedy's funeral. Eisenhower was there too, prompting a temporary thaw in their relationship. Truman, staying at Blair House, received an unexpected call from Eisenhower, who was staying at the Statler Hotel. Speaking to a Truman aide, Ike asked if he and Mamie could pick up the Trumans to take them to the memorial service. "Certainly," Truman replied, and reciprocated by asking the Eisenhowers to join them for drinks and coffee at Blair House after the service, where they talked comfortably for the better part of an hour.[74] Both of them were appalled by the opulence of the funeral and the chaos that ensued at the gravesite at Arlington, where they had trouble getting to their cars through the crowds. Truman resolved that when his time came the funeral and gravesite would be at the library.[75]

When the Trumans returned home to Independence, Secret Service agents, by government order, were once again fixtures in their lives. Mrs. Truman was initially reticent about allowing the agents, reminders of the confines she had endured as first lady, inside the gates of the house. But a personal entreaty from President Johnson, who put in a call to her from the White House, convinced her otherwise.[76] At $182,000 per year, the cost of the Secret Service detail substantially dwarfed the $25,000 annual pension Truman received.

Lyndon Johnson's ability to get his own way was not limited to former first ladies. His prodigious skills as a legislator, much admired by Truman, were manifest in a flurry of laws he put into effect as Senate majority leader during the Eisenhower years, unmatched by any of his twentieth-century predecessors. As president he used his power to pass programs the martyred Kennedy had championed; then, after winning election in his own right by a landslide in 1964, he set about creating The Great Society. His efforts brought forth several programs dear to Truman's heart, including low-income housing, enhanced civil rights legislation, a peace center in Israel, and the passage of Medicare.[77] When Johnson signed the latter into law in 1965, it was at the Truman Library with the aging Truman, who had tried and failed to pass Medicare during his administration, beaming beside him as Johnson presented him with the pen he used. Proclaiming Truman "the real daddy of Medicare," LBJ also awarded President and Mrs. Truman the first two Medicare cards, numbered one and two. All told, Johnson's Great Society looked a lot like Truman's Fair Deal, further enhancing Truman's growing legacy.

Truman's physical condition took a turn for the worse in 1964, at age eighty, when a fall in his bathroom resulted in two broken ribs and cuts to his forehead. He was rushed by ambulance to a nearby hospital after a maid discovered him lying unconscious on the floor. He slowly recovered, but was never quite the same again. The cheerful vitality that had always characterized Truman faded. He went to the library only sporadically, and often his attention wandered.

In 1966, his health went into further decline. Afterward, he would be largely confined to his home, where he spent much of his time in his small, book-lined study reading history, or occasionally, one of the mysteries that Mrs. Truman favored. He visited the library only twice before his death. The last time was in 1969, when Richard Nixon, now president, visited the library to donate the piano that had been in the White House when Truman was in residence. Truman, lean and bent with age, was respectful toward Nixon; even if his loathing of the man had not mellowed with age, he revered the presidency. As part of paying his respects to Truman, Nixon sat at the library's piano and played "The Missouri Waltz," perhaps an awkward tribute given Truman's aversion to the song. Truman lasted several more years before old age finally caught up to him in the last month of 1972, in his eighty-eighth year. On December 5, he was admitted to Kansas City Research Hospital and Medical Center, suffering from heart irregularity, kidney blockage, and failure of the digestive system. It was somehow fitting that the cost of his treatment—$59.50 a day—was paid for in part by Medicare.[78] Feisty as ever, Truman hung on until the day after Christmas, when he died of heart failure at 7:50 A.M.

Like most former presidents, Truman approved plans for his burial well in advance of the event itself. It was to be an elaborate five-day state funeral, with Truman's body being flown to Washington to lie in state at the Capitol before returning home to Independence where he would rest in perpetuity. "Damn fine show," Truman remarked. "Sorry I'm going to miss it."[79] But true to form, Mrs. Truman toned it down. The simple ceremony—no eulogy, no hymns—was held in the library's auditorium. Due to lack of space, only 242 people attended, including presidents Nixon and Johnson and their wives. Mrs. Truman watched the ceremony with Margaret and her family behind a green curtain, which veiled her from the attendees. Truman was buried in the library's courtyard, just yards away from his office, so he could "get up and walk into [his] office if [he] want[ed] to."[80] Mrs. Truman would live another ten years at 219 North Delaware Street before dying at the age of ninety-seven. She was laid to rest next to him at the library.

Sometime after leaving office, Truman was bounding down Highway 40 toward Jefferson City, with Mike Westwood at the wheel. After spotting a woman trying to corral some pigs that had strayed by the side of the road, Truman asked Westwood to pull over, whereupon he hopped out of the car to lend her a hand. When he arrived in Jefferson City, a reporter who had heard rumor of his good deed asked him if it were true. Yes, he admitted, adding that he had been a farmer long before he had been president.[81] Truman once remarked, "I tried never to forget who I was and where I'd come from and where I was going back to."[82] As surprised motorists who cast eyes on the thirty-third president herding swine on a random stretch of Missouri road may have attested, Harry Truman never did.

II.

DWIGHT D. EISENHOWER:
ELDER STATESMAN

The morning was bitter cold. A winter blizzard that had begun the day before gripped the mid-Atlantic, dumping as much as twenty-nine inches of snow in parts of northern New Jersey and southeastern New York. Eight inches fell on Washington. By just after noon, as northeast winds careened down the streets of the capital, the snow tapered off and the mercury reached its peak at 22 degrees Fahrenheit. Presently, on the East Wing of the Capitol Building under a blue sky with clouds pushed across by icy gusts, the old guard of the Eisenhower administration gave way to John F. Kennedy's New Frontier.

Dwight Eisenhower, wrapped up in a dark overcoat and white scarf, watched the man, twenty-seven years his junior, who had just minutes before taken his place. The transfer of power and the new beginning was as visibly symbolic as at any presidential inauguration. At age seventy, Ike, the outgoing Republican icon, had been the oldest president in the history of the American republic. Kennedy, of the opposing party, became the youngest elected president at forty-three, the very picture of youthful vigor. The old general had steered the allied powers through World War II as supreme commander, orchestrating the planning of D-Day, while Kennedy and those of his generation were on the front lines. "Let the word go forth from this time and place, to friend and foe alike, that the torch has been passed to a new generation of Americans," Kennedy's voice rang out from the inaugural platform in his distinctive Boston cadence, "born in this century, tempered by war, disciplined by a hard and bitter peace, proud of our ancient heritage—and unwilling to witness or permit the slow undoing of those human rights to which this nation has always been committed, and to which we are committed today at home and around the world."

While Eisenhower presided over the country for eight prosperous years, his most significant contribution may have been the peace his successor referred to, "cold" and "bitter" though it may have been. "The peace we seek," Ike had said, "is more than an escape from death; it is a way of life."[1] At a time when tensions between the U.S. and the Soviet Union were rising, the steady-handed Ike kept the Cold War from becoming hot. The hostility between the two superpowers belied the halcyon facade of America in the 1950s, as the threat of the hydrogen bomb loomed. According to opinion polls at the time, the majority of Americans thought there would be a nuclear exchange in the near future, and a fear of Communism and Russian aggression pervaded the nation and defined the Eisenhower era.[2]

After promising "I will go to Korea" in his campaign for president in 1952, Eisenhower saw the war to its end with a truce that divided Communist North Korea from neighboring South Korea at the 38th parallel—roughly where it had been before the conflict began. Around the same time in the U.S., the Communist "witch hunt" led by Wisconsin senator Joseph McCarthy, which ostensibly outed Communists and Communist sympathizers, raged in Washington and Hollywood. Eisenhower's strategy had been to ignore McCarthy, to "never admit he [had] damaged me, upset me," eliciting criticism from those who felt his passivity allowed McCarthy to continue his damaging crusade long after it could have been stopped.[3]

The space race was initiated with the launch of *Sputnik*, a Russian satellite that caught the U.S. off guard and had many accusing Eisenhower of being asleep at the wheel. The U.S. countered with the creation of NASA and played a hapless game of catch-up during the remainder of his administration. In Cuba, just ninety miles from the U.S., Communist Fidel Castro led revolutionary forces to overthrow the U.S.-friendly Fulgencio Batista, resulting in huge economic losses for the U.S. and introducing Soviet-style Communism in the Western Hemisphere. Eisenhower strived toward achieving détente with his Russian counterpart, the mercurial Nikita Khrushchev, offering to allow "facilities for aerial photography to the other," that would allow the monitoring of military buildup as a first, though ultimately fruitless, step toward disarmament. Ike ended his presidential term with his last speech to the nation in which he presciently warned of the "the acquisition of unwarranted influence, whether sought or unsought, by the military industrial complex," which had "the potential for the disastrous rise of misplaced power."

It now fell to Kennedy to deal with the Cold War. Despite Kennedy's bold inaugural rhetoric, Khrushchev would test the new president in ways he hadn't with Eisenhower, hoping his youthfulness and inexperience would mean weakness and opportunity. Among other media outlets, *The Dallas Morning News* reminded Kennedy of the shoes he was filling in an editorial that ran on the eve of his inauguration. "No man in universal history has amassed so much influence or power without taking one more step: assumption of an imperial diadem or the trappings of dictatorship," its editors wrote. "It behooves JFK to remember as we think he does, that neither the U.S. nor the rest of the world is through with Dwight Eisenhower."[4] Neither, for that matter, was Kennedy, who as president would carefully court Ike, seeking his counsel and support often in the turbulent days ahead.

On two occasions prior to the inauguration, Kennedy had visited Eisenhower in the White House for the traditional transition meeting between the incoming and outgoing presidents. The two had met only once before, a brief encounter in Potsdam during World War II, which Eisenhower could not recall. Remarkably, Kennedy, a senator from Massachusetts during Eisenhower's White House tenure—a backbencher by many accounts—had not had any personal interaction with him in all those years.[5] One of four agenda items in the second White House meeting, decided upon jointly by the Eisenhower and Kennedy camps, was "trouble spots."[6] Among them was the Far East, which dominated their discussion.[7] Eisenhower expressed concern that Laos might fall to the Communists, opening the way for a domino effect in South Vietnam, Cambodia, and Burma. "This is one of the problems I'm leaving you that I'm not happy about," he told Kennedy. "We may have to fight."[8] The subject briefly turned to Cuba. Prior to the meeting, Kennedy had been informed by the CIA about a plan involving the training of anti-Castro guerrillas in Guatemala who would attempt to sabotage and overthrow the Castro government. "Should we support guerrilla operations in Cuba?" Kennedy asked Eisenhower. "To the utmost," came the president's reply, adding his view that the training in Guatemala be "continued and accelerated."[9]

Eisenhower liked the young man well enough—he was impressed by his warmth and humility in their meetings, arriving alone in the back of a limousine for their meetings without a phalanx of aides surrounding him—but he had reservations about him in the job he was about to assume.[10] Eight years earlier, Truman had worried that Eisenhower didn't understand the enormity of the task before him. Now Ike had the same concerns about JFK.[11]

Among Eisenhower's few regrets upon leaving the presidency was that he was not able to pass the torch onto another young man on the inaugural platform that day: Richard Nixon, his forty-seven-year-old vice president, who had been his number-two throughout his two terms. Nixon had nobly battled Kennedy for the presidency in 1960, losing by one of the slimmest margins in history. As Eisenhower would put it later: "One of my greatest disappointments was the defeat of Mr. Nixon. I thought he was highly qualified to take over the office of the presidency."[12] The loss, he believed, reflected on him as much as Nixon; when voters elected the candidate from the other party, he felt it was a repudiation of his administration and leadership. "All I've been trying to do for eight years has gone down the drain," he told his son John after Kennedy's victory. "I might just as well have been having fun."[13]

Shortly after Kennedy's inauguration ceremony, Dwight and Mamie Eisenhower retired through a side exit to discover they were, as Eisenhower would later write, "free—as only private citizens in a democratic nation can be free."[14] They attended a small luncheon at the F Street Club in downtown Washington with Richard and Pat Nixon, a few close friends, and members of the former president's cabinet. Then they made their way by car to Gettysburg Farm, the 189-acre property they had bought in 1950 for $23,000, with proceeds generated from Eisenhower's World War II memoir, *Crusade in Europe*.[15] As befitting the five-star general, it abutted Gettysburg's hallowed Civil War battleground, featuring sweeping views of Pennsylvania's rolling hills and South Mountain in the distance. It was also close to a piece of land Eisenhower's grandfather had called home before uprooting the family and moving west to Kansas. Gettysburg Farm's spacious white colonial farmhouse, which had been renovated while the Eisenhowers were in the White House, was the first real home they had ever had, and the only one they ever owned in Eisenhower's nomadic career spent mostly in the military. It was the ideal place to settle into the serene retirement they had both longed for.

"Leaving the presidency was no chore, for Eisenhower had done his best and the time had come," wrote historian Robert Farrell.[16] The thirty-fourth president was tired. For fifty years he had been in command—of his regiment, the allied armed forces in the European theater in World War II, NATO, Columbia University, and in his two terms in the White House. He had made daily decisions that would have put Solomon to the test, and he was more than ready to pack it in.

A nearly fatal heart attack he had suffered in 1955 illustrated the frustration Eisenhower had always felt with the constant demands on his time as a public servant. He had been enjoying a day of golf, when on the eleventh hole he was summoned to the clubhouse to discuss an urgent matter with Secretary of State John Foster Dulles. He took the call, but in the interim, another emergency came up that the State Department needed to see to. Could Dulles call him back in an hour or so? Eisenhower agreed, and stopped his game again later to take the call, discussing a situation that he felt was "not all that important."[17] Then another call came from State from someone not realizing that Eisenhower had already addressed the issue. "And by this time—I always had an uncertain temper—I had gotten completely out of control," Eisenhower recalled. "One doctor said he had never seen me in such a state and that's the reason I had a heart attack."[18]

Now the burdens of power were all behind him. But as he would soon realize, the reality of retirement for a former president—let alone a popular one—was far busier than his ideal. He would comment often in the days ahead that he was more in demand as a former president than he had been as president.[19]

After getting a sense of the demands that would be made on her husband, Mrs. Eisenhower would comment that she thought retirement was just a word in the dictionary. Nevertheless, life outside the White House gave the Eisenhowers considerably more time to spend together, after enduring the long domestic separations inherent in army life. Nineteen-year-old Mamie Geneva Doud had met the twenty-five-year-old Second Lieutenant Eisenhower in 1915, at Fort Sam Houston in San Antonio, where he was stationed on his second tour of duty. Eisenhower was immediately taken by the "vivacious and attractive" girl from Denver, and four months later they were married.[20] Two sons followed. Doud Dwight, or "Icky" as he was called, was born in 1917. His death from scarlet fever three years later would become "the greatest disappointment and disaster" in Eisenhower's life, and "the one [he was] never . . . able to forget completely."[21] John was born a year later in 1922, and would eventually follow his father's path into the army.

For years, while Eisenhower threw himself into his career, climbing slowly but steadily up the army's ranks, Mrs. Eisenhower tended to John and kept the house in order for her husband. "I have only one career, and his name is Ike," Mrs. Eisenhower said on more than one occasion.[22] Still, it was an active career. By Mrs. Eisenhower's calculations they had lived in twenty-seven places during Ike's thirty-seven years in the army, moving across the U.S., and to France, the Panama Canal, and the Philippines.[23] After moving up to the rank of five-star general, he resigned from the army in 1948 to become president of Columbia University, a move that took them to New York. Two years later he was reinstated in the army to oversee the establishment of military forces under the auspices of NATO. Now they could both settle into life on the farm without worrying about having to pack their bags for another post in another place, unless it meant heading west to Palm Springs to their second home, where they spent the winter months.

The whole Eisenhower family was now together in Gettysburg. John and his wife Barbara lived in a small house just a mile from the farm. John, an aide to his father in his second term, had resigned his commission in the army to work for Doubleday as an editor on his father's presidential memoirs, a project both father and son embarked upon soon after leaving Washington. Having John and Barbara nearby also meant the Eisenhowers could be full-time grandparents to their five grandchildren, David, Barbara, Anne, Susan, and Mary Jean, who provided them with immense pleasure in their latter years.

Two weeks into his life as an ex-president, John was "shocked" by the change he saw in his father's demeanor. "His movements were slower, his tone less sharp, and he even [had time] for casual conversation," he recalled.

At first he worried about his father's health, until he realized he had "simply relaxed."[24] But adjusting to the life of a retiree in the 1960s posed its challenges for a former president and five-star general, who had spent almost all of his adult life being waited on by an attentive staff, ready to ensure that his every need was met. While he was glad to leave the burdens of power behind, he initially found the prosaic activities and necessities of everyday life troublesome. On his last evening in the White House, he tried to give John a telephone call without the aid of a secretary. The last time he had done so was almost two decades earlier, at which time he had picked up the receiver and told the operator on the other end the number he wanted. This time he tried to do the same, but heard only a dial tone on the other end. He yelled for an operator, clicked the receiver button repeatedly, and fiddled with the rotary dial—all in vain—resulting in a tantrum. He growled for an aide, who gave him a lesson in how to properly operate the instrument. "Oh, so that's how you do it," he said with some relief after the tutorial, marveling at the technology and thereafter able to master the task.[25]

Attempts to learn how to drive ended up with him deciding he would be better off continuing to be chauffeured by an army sergeant he had on staff, who took on the responsibility most of the time.[26] He was more successful at learning to do things like mix frozen orange juice, adjust the picture on his television set, and order train tickets—once he learned where to buy them. He also had to learn to carry and handle money, something unnecessary during his army and White House years. Only once since his days in power had he actually entered a retail establishment when, in 1958, he took his grandson David into a store in Gettysburg for fishing supplies. On that occasion he walked out without any thought of paying for the goods. A reporter covering the president assured the owner that if he sent a bill to the White House, it would be paid. It was.[27]

Though Eisenhower may have had to remind himself to keep money in his pocket, at least he did have ample funds in his bank account. Eisenhower received a presidential pension of $25,000 per year and an office budget of $50,000.[28] His World War II memoir, *Crusade in Europe*, published in 1948, was a critical and commercial success, netting $476,000. He added to his wealth with a lucrative deal he would strike with Doubleday for the writing of his White House memoirs.[29] His lifestyle was subsidized considerably by his "gang" of friends, ten or so wealthy businessmen who gave him lavish gifts and often picked up his travel tabs and other expenses. Though offers to trade in on his name and office came pouring in once he became a private citizen, he adamantly turned down anything smacking of commercialism, refusing to exploit the presidency or his own celebrity.[30]

By a special act of Congress passed just after he left the presidency, Eisenhower was reinstated in the military in his former rank as a five-star general (albeit a retired one), and accordingly was eligible to receive benefits and retain members of his White House staff who were enlisted in the military. It was fitting for a man who was known as "General" (not "Mr. President") in his post-presidential years, and who would often be called back into his country's service as an advisor on military issues. Congress had invoked the act only once before when it honored Ulysses S. Grant in a similar fashion after he left the office in 1877.[31]

Like General Washington before him, Eisenhower as an ex-president became a gentleman farmer of sorts, aided in his efforts by nine field hands. "I wanted to take a piece of ground like this that had been sort of worn out through improper use and try to restore it," he said of the place. His goal before he died: "to leave it better than I found it."[32] He buzzed around the grounds on a golf cart tending to his crops of corn, oats, barley, soybeans, and hay, and overseeing a herd of thirty Aberdeen-Angus cattle that roamed the property, along with several horses and dogs.[33] The operation became a successful cattle business, though Eisenhower sometimes wondered aloud whether it supported him or he supported it.[34]

Life after the White House gave Eisenhower considerably more time to spend on his hobbies. Oil painting was one. In 1947, while having his portrait painted by Welsh painter Thomas Stephens, one of twenty-three he would do of Eisenhower through the years, he told the artist, "By golly, I'd like to try that." Stephens turned over his brush to the general, who took an immediate liking to it. His first subject was Mrs. Eisenhower, followed by other canvases when time allowed, although most were discarded, some with X's painted on top.[35] At Gettysburg, he frequently painted in the sun-filtered, glassed-in porch where he and Mrs. Eisenhower spent much of their time reading or watching television.

Golf was another great passion. While in the White House, Eisenhower had a putting green installed not far from the Oval Office. "Look at what that son of a bitch did to my floor," Kennedy said as he showed a visitor the scratch marks Eisenhower's golf cleats had left in the Oval Office.[36] Gettysburg Farm also boasted a putting green, though Ike was never quite able to master his short game. Poor putting and a signature slice usually meant a score in the eighties or low nineties, though he did manage to break eighty on occasion, always marching determinedly to his next shot and striking the ball anxiously. His favorite venue was Augusta National, home of the Masters, where he became a dues-paying member in 1948. He would visit the famous course forty-five times throughout his life, making several trips a year in his post-presidential days. Ike's "gang" built him a seven-room cottage for his frequent trips—white with green shutters—just off the tenth tee. The cottage, dubbed "Mamie's Cabin" by the members, sat next to one used by famed golfer Bobby Jones, with whom Eisenhower had played years earlier. Around back was a pond where Ike would indulge another passion, often fishing after a day on the links.[37] He was also able to spend time with his closest friends, playing long hours of bridge and swapping stories.

The "uncertain temper" that had resulted in Eisenhower's cardiac arrest in 1956, mellowed in Ike's post-presidential years, but when it flared on occasion aides around him had no compunctions about reining him in for the sake of his fragile heart. After topping his drive and loudly fuming about it during a round at Augusta, his Secret Service agent Richard Flohr dressed him down. "Now, you cut that out right now, Mr. President," Flohr instructed the boss. "And I mean cut it out, or I'm going to put you in that cart and take you right back to the cottage and lock you in!" A deflated Eisenhower continued his round, his anger in check.[38]

The man who took the White House with the help of the irresistible campaign slogan "I like Ike" continued to be enormously popular throughout his post-presidency, typically showing up in annual opinion polls as the most admired American.[39] A *Life* magazine article published just several months after Eisenhower left the White House reported that as Eisenhower drove his golf cart to close the farm's front gate, tourists bounded out of five separate cars, "running at him with cameras and autograph books."[40] Visitors of the Gettysburg battlefield almost invariably made the farm another stop on their tour, with the hope of catching a glimpse of Gettysburg's most famous resident. *Newsweek* wrote: "[I]n his later years, Ike—though still a Republican as an icon of unity—became less a political figure than a sort of prized antique."[41] But his enduring appeal remained a great asset for the GOP. As the party's most prominent member, he was constantly fielding requests to campaign on behalf of candidates or to participate in fund-raisers. Though he was concerned about the party's drift to the right, veering off the moderate trail he had blazed after twenty years of Democratic rule in the White House, he was glad to do what he could. "I figure that when the time comes that a person can't do good, he might as well die," he said. He was far busier than he wanted to be. "I don't know if I am relieved to some extent or dismayed to a large extent to discover that there seems to be little cessation from the constant stream of demands upon my time," he wrote to Winston Churchill.[42] But as Mrs. Eisenhower often reminded him, it beat being forgotten.[43]

Mrs. Eisenhower also remained popular with the public, though her retirement years were spent a bit more restfully then her husband's. As in her days in the White House, she seldom rose from bed before 10:00 A.M., and rarely left her room before noon, which she maintained was one of the privileges of a woman over fifty. She still made sure Ike was well taken care of and he in turn doted on her. Whenever possible they traveled by train or car instead of by air, owing to her fear of flying. Guests at the farm were more likely to be served breakfast by the general than by Mrs. Eisenhower, who didn't cook. Though she shared none of his pastimes—she didn't fish or play bridge or golf—they enjoyed many happy hours together on the sunporch or spending time with the grandchildren. The former president became more demonstrative toward his wife in his later years, often declaring, "The luckiest thing I ever did is marry that girl."[44]

During their first transition in early December, Kennedy asked Eisenhower if he would be willing to "serve the country in such areas and in such manner as may seem appropriate." "Of course," Eisenhower replied, adding that he hoped it would be as a consultant on matters "on which I have some experience," and not to run "errands" on behalf of the president necessitating extensive travel.[45] On April 21, just three months after he left office, Eisenhower got a call from Kennedy requesting his counsel on a matter of some urgency—and on which he had some experience. The only travel required was a short hop by military helicopter from Gettysburg to Camp David, in the Catoctin Mountains of Maryland, where the president met his predecessor to discuss a botched military invasion of Cuba at the Bay of Pigs.

Eisenhower, of course, had been aware of the CIA's plot to overthrow Fidel Castro, involving the training of Cuban exiles in Guatemala, which Eisenhower had briefly covered with Kennedy in their second presidential transition meeting. The CIA and the exiles believed that the invasion would draw the support of Cubans who would help their cause, driving the Castro regime out. Neither the CIA nor the exiles understood the widespread support Castro had from the masses that benefited from his reforms. Kennedy had been wary of the plan from the start, as had a number of his aides, but eager to show America's might under his watch—particularly to the ambitious Russians who he feared might see him as callow—he gave it the go-ahead. None could have foreseen the operation's utter failure. Within seventy-two hours after the incursion began, Cuban forces had killed four hundred of the invading exiles and captured the rest. Kennedy's first major test as president on the world stage had ended in ignominy.

The call to Eisenhower was a symbolic move on Kennedy's part, a chance to show the world America's unity in a time of crisis—and to mitigate the partisan political fallout at home. Kennedy consulted other prominent Republicans by phone, including Richard Nixon, Nelson Rockefeller, and Barry Goldwater. (As a fellow Democrat, Harry Truman required only the attention of vice president Lyndon Johnson, who called him on the matter.)[46] But only the consultation with Eisenhower was done in full view of the media.

The president was there to greet his predecessor when the helicopter landed at Camp David. It was Kennedy's first visit to the presidential retreat, which had been called Shangri-la by FDR but was renamed Camp David for Eisenhower's grandson. They had lunch at Aspen Cottage, where they consulted privately on the terrace, and slowly walked the grounds of the compound as Kennedy gave Eisenhower a full, candid debriefing on the failed operation. Eisenhower listened intently, observing later that Kennedy was "more than a little bewildered" in the aftermath, but pleased that he had taken full responsibility without casting blame.[47] Then, like a stern father, he took him to task for his mistakes in the matter, drilling him with a series of questions.

"Mr. President," he demanded, "before you approved this plan, did you have everybody in front of you debating the thing so you got the pros and cons yourself and then made your decision, or did you see these people one at a time?"

Kennedy confessed that he had not had a meeting with the whole National Security Council staff to fully debate the plan, adding, "No one knows how rough this job is until after he has been in it a few months."

Eisenhower snapped, "Mr. President, if you will forgive me, I think I mentioned that to you three months ago." Eisenhower continued the questioning, asking why the mission did not include air support.

"We thought that if it was learned that we were really doing this rather than these rebels themselves, the Soviets would be very apt to cause trouble in Berlin," Kennedy responded.

"Mr. President, that is exactly the opposite of what really would happen," Eisenhower informed him. "The Soviets follow their own plans, and if they see us show any weakness, then that is when they press us the hardest. The second they see us show strength and do something on our own, that is when they are very cagey. The failure of the Bay of Pigs will embolden the Soviets to do something they would not otherwise do."

"Well, my advice was that we must try to keep our hands from showing in the affair," the president said naively.

Again Eisenhower shot back, "Mr. President, how could you expect the world to believe that we had nothing to do with it? Where did these people get the ships to go from Central America to Cuba? Where did they get the weapons? Where did they get all the communications and all the other things that they would need? How could you possibly have kept from the world any knowledge that the United States had been assisting the invasion? I believe there is only one thing to do when you go into this kind of thing. It must be a success."

"Well," Kennedy said, "I assure you that hereafter, if we get into anything like this, it is going to be a success."

"Well, I'm glad to hear it," said Ike.

With that, Kennedy's trip to the woodshed had ended.[48]

Both men were all smiles as they greeted the forty members of the press who waited for them outside Aspen Cottage. Kennedy told them he had asked Eisenhower to come and brief him on "recent events, and to get the benefit of his thoughts and experience." After commenting, "It's very nice to be in a position not to be expected or allowed to say anything," Eisenhower added, "I'm all in favor of the United States supporting the man who has to carry the responsibility of our foreign affairs." As Hugh Sidey would later write in his book, *John F. Kennedy, President*, "It was the only endorsement that Ike could give Kennedy for the mishandled matter. But it was almost enough. At the moment it meant a lot."[49]

However, Eisenhower's concern with the Bay of Pigs did not end with his lukewarm backing of Kennedy at Camp David. While Kennedy had squarely taken the blame for the foreign policy blunder, his aides in the ensuing weeks hinted that the operation was also a failure of the Eisenhower administration, which had conceived of and approved the plan before Kennedy took office.[50] With an eye toward history, Eisenhower wanted to set the record straight—even if it meant altering that record. He wrote to aides in his inner circle asking for their recollections on conversations relating to the plan, confident that no notes had been taken upon his instruction.

But one aide *had* taken notes. Gordon Gray, Eisenhower's special assistant for national security affairs, told Eisenhower that he had made notations in meetings relating to Cuba that he had attended with Eisenhower. In June, upon his father's instructions, John obtained Gray's records, which had been housed at Fort Ritchie in Maryland, along with other classified material from his administration. Eisenhower then asked Gray to come to Gettysburg to review the documents. Eisenhower agreed with what he read until he came to a passage indicating his approval of a four-point CIA recommendation that included "planning a paramilitary force outside Cuba for future guerrilla action."[51] "This is wrong," he told Gray, adding that he had not, as Gray had indicated, used the word "planning" in relation to the guerrilla action, and that he had given no such approval. "With your permission, I'm going to have the page rewritten to reflect the facts," he told Gray, who agreed. The word "planning" was expunged from the memorandum. In exchange, Gray received his former boss's "cheerful forgiveness" for taking notes in the first place.[52]

A year and a half later, Cuba was on Kennedy's mind again. The Bay of Pigs fiasco had solidified a strategic and economic relationship between Cuba and the Soviet Union, which led to the Soviets' aggressive posture in the region. In October 1962, they began shipping nuclear warheads to Cuba, just ninety miles off the coast of Florida, attempting to bolster their military position in the Western Hemisphere. U.S. warships formed a blockade around the island to prevent the delivery of the missiles, resulting in a standoff and triggering the threat of a nuclear war. Eisenhower advocated the blockade plan, a position he had made clear when the CIA asked him to come to Washington on October 20 to discuss military options. Two days later, on a Sunday morning, just before the darkest hour of the showdown—and perhaps the Cold War—Kennedy called Eisenhower at Gettysburg to discuss the very real possibility that Nikita Khrushchev would give the order to launch a nuclear attack. Kennedy was cool and unemotional, and Eisenhower used the garbled syntax for which he had become known.

"General," asked Kennedy, "what about if the Soviet Union— Khrushchev—announces tomorrow, which I think he will, that if we attack Cuba that it's going to be nuclear war? And what's your judgment as to the chances they'll fire these things off if we invade Cuba?"

"Oh, I don't believe they will," Eisenhower replied confidently.

"In other words, you would take that risk if the situation seemed desirable?"

"Well, as a matter of fact, what can you do? If this thing is such a serious thing, here on our flank, that we're going to be uneasy and we know what thing is happening now. All right, you've got to [do] something. Something may make [the Soviets] shoot [their nuclear missiles] off. I just don't believe this will. In any event, of course, I'll say this: I'd want to keep my own people very alert."

"Yeah," Kennedy laughed, perhaps nervously, at the situation's gravity, "well, we'll hang on tight."[53]

Eisenhower chuckled in return, and then left it to the president to make his decision.

Kennedy held firm, the Russians backed down, and a crisis of unimaginable proportions was averted.

Thirteen months later, on November 22, as he attended a luncheon in New York at the UN, Eisenhower got word that Kennedy had been assassinated. The following morning, he and Mrs. Eisenhower were driven to Washington to mourn his loss. The same day, Lyndon Johnson, newly sworn in as president, asked Eisenhower to meet him in his vice presidential office in the Old Executive Building next to the White House. Johnson had been the powerful Senate majority leader during Eisenhower's presidency, and though they shared a cordial relationship, Eisenhower judged Johnson to be "the most tricky and unreliable politician in Congress."[54] They consulted for almost an hour. Afterward Eisenhower adjourned to Johnson's outer office where he wrote out a confidential memo to the new president on several pages of a yellow legal pad.

The "Notes for the President" recommended that Johnson enlist the help of three men who had aided him as president: Robert Anderson, as an advisor on fiscal matters; and Andrew Goodpastor and Gordon Gray, as advisors on foreign policy. He also recommended that Johnson make a brief speech to a joint session of Congress, adding a four-part outline of what he should cover. "Point out first that you have come to this office unexpectedly and you accept the decision of the Almighty," he advised, "who in His inscrutable wisdom has placed you in the highest responsibility of this nation."[55] The two men would confer often in the years ahead, during which the general's advice to Johnson on the central trial of his administration—Vietnam—would become "an unfailing source of strength."[56]

In the early 1960s, Eisenhower remained active and began to put together the cornerstones of his legacy. In the spring of 1962, he and Mrs. Eisenhower took a train from Palm Springs, where they had wintered, back to Gettysburg Farm. Along the way they stopped at Eisenhower's boyhood home, Abilene, Kansas, for the dedication of the $3 million Eisenhower library.

The Eisenhower Center, which comprised thirteen acres, would include the library, Eisenhower's restored boyhood home, and a museum which had been built eight years earlier, attracting some 200,000 tourists a year. Twenty-five thousand people—more than three times Abilene's population of 7,136—descended on the town to join in the celebration, including then vice president Lyndon Johnson, five cabinet members, and longtime friends and benefactors. (Eisenhower's own vice president, Richard Nixon, sent his regrets, as did Harry Truman, who had planned to attend but for the death of a cousin.) Three of Ike's seven brothers—Edgar, Earl, and Milton—were also on hand for the dedication. The day marked the one hundredth anniversary of the birth of their mother, Ida, whom the former president recognized for "her strength and her refusal to admit defeat in small or great things."

Ida and her husband David, both Kansas natives, had moved briefly to Denison, Texas, after David failed in the grocery and banking businesses. Dwight David Eisenhower, the future president and the Eisenhowers' third son, was born there in 1890, before the family returned to Abilene two years later where David found work as a mechanic in a creamery. The family lived in a small house on a two-and-a-half-acre farm. Growing up, the Eisenhower boys all did chores on the farm—milking their cow, planting corn, tending to the chickens—and sold the farm's products door to door.[57] Although Eisenhower had left Abilene as a twenty-year-old in 1910, after his appointment to West Point, he remained connected to his Midwestern roots well after fame and glory had boosted him up the military ranks and into the White House. It was in Abilene that he chose to announce his candidacy for the presidency on a rain-soaked morning in the winter of 1952.

He used the occasion of the library dedication to wonder aloud about the declining state of "beauty and decency and morality" in America, which hadn't kept pace with American developments in industry and the sciences. He cited the dance craze "the Twist" and modern art ("looks like a broken-down tin lizzie loaded with paint has driven over [the canvas]") as examples of how far the country had strayed from the beauty of the minuet and the works of Michelangelo. He reserved singular contempt for "the vulgarity, sensuality, and indeed, downright filth," in the promotion of movies, theater, books, and magazines. But he expressed faith that the U.S. would not "suffer the fate of Rome," and that the American people would "see to it that our spiritual strength, that the morale of this country, is as strong" as it was in the days of Washington and Lincoln.[58]

Throughout 1963 CBS paid the general generously to do a series of four one-hour specials on his life and career, in which Walter Cronkite held conversations with Eisenhower at Gettysburg, Palm Springs, Abilene, West

Point, and Normandy.[59] One of them, "D-Day Plus Twenty Years," commemorated the twentieth anniversary of D-Day, perhaps Eisenhower's finest hour. Cronkite accompanied him on the beaches of Normandy as he recounted the invasion that turned the tide of the Second World War. Eisenhower had been back to the battlegrounds several times since the war, but bound by official or ceremonial occasions, he had been unable to linger and reminisce. This time he drove the beaches in a jeep with Cronkite and, as Cronkite recalled, "mused upon what the Wehrmacht lookouts must have thought when, on that morning of June 6, 1944, they saw that great armada of battlewagons and landing craft emerging from the dawn's haze."[60]

Cronkite spent long hours with Eisenhower on the project, including a week at Gettysburg where they recorded thirteen hours of interviews. Prior to doing the specials, Cronkite had shared the prevailing view among the press that Ike had been a mediocre president, lazy and removed from day-to-day operations which he left to his staff, and generally more concerned with his golf score than governing. In the time he spent with him, Cronkite realized he had been wrong.

"I did not ask him about a single incident during his eight years in the White House of which he did not have intimate knowledge," Cronkite recalled in his memoirs.[61] Others would come to the conclusion that they had been wrong about him as well, though it would take some time. Just a year after Eisenhower left office, a panel of seventy-five noted historians ranked him twenty-second of the thirty-four U.S. presidents they considered.[62] By the 1980s, as the list of presidents grew longer, his name would be among the top ten.

In 1963, Eisenhower published the first installment of his memoirs, entitled *Mandate for Change: 1953–1956*, which covered his first term in office. The second volume, recounting his second term, *Waging Peace: 1956–1961*, would be published the following year. Eisenhower didn't relish the task of chronicling his years in the White House, but felt duty-bound to future generations. "Very few of my predecessors left definitive volumes," he said. "What wouldn't you give now to have a definitive memoir by Johnson, who succeeded Lincoln—reconstruction and all that?"[63] Most days he would work on the project in his second-floor office in a small, two-story brick building that had formerly been a part of Gettysburg College, aided by his son John, who did much of the historical fact-checking. The office was spartan: a simple desk angled at the window, and behind it an American flag, three leather chairs for guests, a bookcase, several Steuben glass figurines, and a light pink rug.[64] The office's entrance was a glass door marked by five stars, not so much to reflect the general's rank as to prevent guests from walking into it.

He worked diligently at writing the books, dictating to or having his notes transcribed by one of his three secretaries, but frequently other things got in the way. There was always mail to attend to—at least one hundred letters a day, a number that would spike after a speech or television appearance—and guests who would visit.[65] When *Mandate for Change* hit bookstores on November 9, 1963, it got an eager reception from consumers, if not from all critics. The book quickly advanced up *The New York Times* best-seller list to the number-two spot, before stalling and quickly falling off the list after Kennedy's assassination just two weeks later.[66]

The presidential election of 1964 presented a quandary for Eisenhower. A number of prominent Republicans tried to convince him to block the nomination of lead candidate Barry Goldwater, whose conservatism stood in contrast to Ike's moderation and threatened to split the party. Eisenhower, however, while himself concerned about the party's rightward drift, resisted their pleas; he remained publicly neutral, which he believed was in order for a former party standard-bearer and president, a position he maintained as a paid commentator for ABC during the GOP Convention in July. Though he was less than pleased with the party's choice, Eisenhower dutifully supported Goldwater as the GOP nominee. A television special in which Eisenhower and Goldwater held a discussion at Gettysburg Farm, rejecting the notion that Goldwater was an extremist, did little to help the candidate's chances in November. The GOP vote split, and Johnson won reelection in a landslide.

By the middle of the decade, just several years into the retirement he had dreamed of, Eisenhower was beset by illness. In the fall of 1965, during a three-week golf vacation at Augusta, the general was awakened by severe chest pains and quickly rushed to a nearby army hospital that held a five-room suite kept vacant for him during his visits. Thirty-six hours later, he suffered a new wave of pain in his chest, which his doctors diagnosed as another heart attack. It happened, Eisenhower observed, exactly a decade after he had experienced his first heart attack while he was president.[67] At seventy-five, he recovered remarkably well and was released after several weeks of convalescence at Walter Reed Army Hospital where he had been flown by a White House Jetstar shortly after his initial hospitalization. His doctors gave him strict orders to slow down, including a reduction in his golfing outings, all of which he obeyed. Even so, his health would remain under siege in his remaining years.

In 1967, sensing the end was near, Eisenhower got his house in order.[68] A year later, he approved a fifty-four-page plan that outlined his state funeral in exacting detail, a plan that had his body lying in state at the Capitol before being transported to his final resting place at the library. He ordered the body of his son Icky to be moved from the Doud family cemetery in Denver to Abilene, where he was buried next to the plots reserved for the former president and Mrs. Eisenhower. He also arranged to donate the farm to the U.S. government as a national historical site after their deaths, causing Mrs. Eisenhower to quip, "Well, we're back in government housing again."[69] And perhaps he could go a bit more peacefully having achieved the perfect score on at least one turn at the tee when he hit a hole-in-one at a par-three golf course in Palm Springs, a feat he pronounced "the thrill of a lifetime."[70]

Eisenhower's final memoir, *At Ease: Stories I Tell to Friends*, was published the same year. The book reflected the voice of Eisenhower and an informal, personal tone that served its subject better than the White House memoirs. It also sold more briskly and generally yielded more favorable reviews than those earlier works.

At a time when Americans were divided and defined by their stance on Vietnam—hawks and doves—Eisenhower fell decidedly in the former camp, advocating the escalation of the war to beat back the Communist North Vietnamese. Such was the advice he fed Lyndon Johnson, who solicited his opinion and sought his support on every major military decision on the war. Every other week Johnson would dispatch an aide to brief Eisenhower on the war's developments in meetings that would last three hours or more.[71] Given Eisenhower's unequaled stature as a military hero and elder statesman, he was a powerful ally for the beleaguered Johnson, whose support in the war effort was fast eroding.

The general's views on the war were not shared only with the president. In a nationally televised interview at the farm, Eisenhower—along with Omar Bradley, the only other living U.S. five-star general—jointly campaigned for a foray into North Vietnam to take out the enemy's artillery positions. It wasn't an invasion in Eisenhower's view, "just removing an annoyance."[72] Dismissing the threat of China entering the war, and the "hippies" and "kooks" who advocated withdrawal, he also supported raids into Laos and Cambodia—countries that were much on his mind in his second transition meeting with Kennedy—to pursue Communist troops.[73] He went so far as to advocate enemy planes in China.[74] Eisenhower's hawkishness was a paradox for the man who as president had so steadfastly avoided war, and had opposed sending American troops into a major war on the Asian mainland. A *New York Times* editorial appearing in November 1967, entitled "Eisenhower vs. Eisenhower," pointed out the contradiction. Citing its view that escalation wasn't the solution and that there was no assurance the Chinese wouldn't enter the war, the *Times* wrote that Eisenhower's proposal was "untimely, unsound, and not characteristic of a revered national leader who is best remembered for his prudent restraint."[75]

One wonders what advice the Eisenhower of ten or twenty years earlier might have given on Vietnam, and on Southeast Asia in general. What accounted for his changed outlook on war in Asia remains a mystery. It seems to have begun as he neared the end of his presidential term; he was clearly and uncharacteristically preoccupied with the threat of a Communist takeover of Laos in his second transition meeting with Kennedy. Was it an increased fear of the encroachment of Communism? Or could the physiological ravages of prolonged heart ailments have had an effect on his frame of mind?

Eisenhower became disillusioned when Johnson announced a stop to the bombings in Vietnam in 1968, after which he angrily cut his ties to the administration. Regardless of the abrupt change in policy, Vietnam ultimately proved to be Johnson's undoing. As support for the war slipped, he took himself out of the 1968 presidential race, leaving the field open for aspiring Democrats to seek the party's nomination. On the Republican side, one candidate immediately drew Eisenhower's support, despite his previous position of never endorsing a contender before his nomination. After losing the presidency in 1960 and the California governorship in

1962, Richard Nixon had emerged from the political wilderness as his party's front-runner, aided in part by his former boss's enthusiastic support.

Eisenhower's feelings toward Nixon in their long association were marked by ambivalence. In 1952, as Eisenhower took his first run at the presidency, the thirty-nine-year-old Nixon was one in a short list of vice-presidential candidates he would entertain for the ticket. Soon after Nixon was chosen, it was alleged that he had received $18,000 in illegal campaign contributions in his senatorial bid two years earlier. Rather than rally around Nixon, Eisenhower said he was going to judge the case on its merits.[76] Only after Nixon's famous "Checkers" speech, in which he defended his position in a maudlin but effective address on national television, did Eisenhower publicly support him. Ike was impressed by Nixon's ability and potential, but often remarked that he didn't feel Nixon had matured as vice president and wondered at his lack of popularity. They were not close personally; Ike's gregariousness contrasted with Nixon's aloofness. When he ran for reelection in 1956, Eisenhower suggested repeatedly that "it might be better" if Nixon drop off the ticket to take a cabinet position, which would surely have had an adverse effect on his political future.[77] He toughed it out and remained on the ticket, continuing to work hard for Eisenhower, playing the partisan hatchet man while the president remained above the fray, though he was continually disappointed by Ike's lack of gratitude. As the 1960 election came around, Eisenhower maintained his neutrality during the Republican primaries, refusing to endorse his loyal vice president, and when Nixon won the nomination Eisenhower gave what appeared to some to be lukewarm support.

Despite the mixed feelings he had about Nixon, there appeared to be no one else he preferred. Nixon was it. And perhaps Eisenhower looked on his election to the presidency in 1968 as a bit of unfinished business from 1960. "Dick," Eisenhower told Nixon on the eve of the Republican National Convention, "I don't want there to be any more question about this. You're my choice, period," a position he made clear in an unambiguous statement of endorsement he gave to reporters.[78]

In May of 1968, after suffering his fourth heart attack—this time on a golf course in Palm Springs—Eisenhower's health went into a precipitous state of decline. He was admitted to Walter Reed Army Hospital where he would spend his remaining days in a three-room suite, with Mrs. Eisenhower spending most nights just down the hall. Another heart attack followed in June, and a sixth and seventh in August. His last appearance before the GOP occurred when he addressed the delegates at the National Convention in Miami by television from his hospital bed. The aging general, looking frail after losing twenty pounds, got a thunderous reception. He was still hospitalized in November when word came that Nixon had won the presidency over the Democratic candidate, Hubert Humphrey, news that "elated" him. In the days running up to the inauguration Eisenhower would interview and advise all of Nixon's future cabinet members, each of whom came to Ward Eight at Walter Reed to visit him.[79]

By December the Eisenhower and Nixon families were linked not only politically but by marriage as well. Earlier in the year, David Eisenhower and Nixon's daughter Julie, college students at Amherst and Smith colleges respectively, announced that they were engaged to be married, a development that pleased both of their families. The ceremony took place in New York at Manhattan's Marble Collegiate Church, where the bride's "something blue" was a thin garter Mamie Doud had worn when she wed Eisenhower fifty-two years earlier. The Eisenhowers had to settle for watching the ceremony through a closed-circuit television hookup at the hospital. Before the wedding, Eisenhower offered David a hundred dollars to cut his shaggy hair. Though David got a trim and had a shorter style than his groomsmen and many college students at the time, it wasn't enough to earn his grandfather's bounty or approval.[80]

The end was near early in 1969. Eisenhower had shown remarkable resilience after every medical setback. "He is a soldier," a hospital spokesman said of the patient. "He is used to the discipline of a soldier."[81] But persistent complications ensued and his condition continued to deteriorate. Mrs. Eisenhower, as always, made sure all his needs were met. On at least one occasion she went without sleep for thirty hours as he rallied for his life.[82] When Nixon visited Eisenhower on March 26, two months into his presidency, he sensed it would be the last time he would see him alive. After a fifteen-minute visit, doctors gave him a sign that he should let the patient rest. Before leaving, he turned to Eisenhower. "General, I just want you to know how all the free people of Europe and millions of others in the world will forever be in your debt," he said. "You can always take great pride in the fact that no man in our history has done more to make America and the world a better and safer place in which to live."

"Mr. President, you do me great honor in what you have just said," Eisenhower replied as he lifted his hand to salute him.[83]

Two days later, on the morning of March 28, the general issued his last orders. With Mrs. Eisenhower, John, David, his doctors, and a nurse at his bedside, he commanded that the shades be lowered, which John did hastily. "Pull me up," he asked, upon which John and one of the doctors pulled him up on the bed. "Two big men," he snapped. "Higher." They obliged. He then looked at John and softly spoke his last words: "I want to go. God take me."[84] With that Eisenhower fell asleep, never to regain consciousness.

Operation Kansas, the code name the army had given for Eisenhower's state funeral, began the following day. After a three-hour processional through the streets of Washington, Eisenhower's body lay in repose in the Capitol Rotunda, where it rested on a velvet-draped catafalque that had held the bodies of Abraham Lincoln, John Kennedy, and Herbert Hoover. Fifty-five thousand mourners came through the halls of the Capitol to pay tribute. Among them was Nixon who, upon hearing of Eisenhower's death, had cancelled five days of appointments to get his thoughts in order. In his eulogy to his former boss and mentor, Nixon called him "one of the giants of our time . . . an authentic hero," and shared the last words Eisenhower had spoken to his beloved Mamie: "I have always loved my wife. I have always loved my children. I have always loved my grandchildren. And I have always loved my country."[85]

The body was then placed in the baggage car of a ten-car funeral train pulled westward by three engines, which brought the general back to the heartland, to Abilene. A simple eight-minute service held all the military trappings owed a man who had served his country honorably: flags at half-mast, a twenty-one-gun salute, a flag folded neatly into a triangle and presented to the widow, veiled in black. "His battles have all been fought and his victories are all won," the reverend presiding over the ceremony said, as the eighty-five-dollar, standard-issue, metal soldier's casket the general had requested was lowered into the Kansas soil of his youth.[86]

III.

LYNDON B. JOHNSON:
EXILE

"The golden coin is spent," thought Lady Bird Johnson on January 20, 1969, her last morning in the White House. After a restless night, she rose at 6:00 A.M. as her husband slept, and walked the mansion's hallways, among the boxes, rolled-up carpets, stacks of pictures, and workmen preparing for the day's move, peering into the rooms that had been home for the last five years.[1]

Lyndon Johnson was awakened an hour later by a knock on his bedroom door from his two military aides. Usually just one of the aides took on the task of waking Johnson, but this morning was special. At midday, their commander in chief would hand the office over to Richard Nixon, lifting the awesome burden that had been Johnson's since John F. Kennedy's assassination in the tragic fall of 1963.

The president and first lady had breakfast together in the family quarters overlooking the great South Lawn and the Washington Monument in the distance before Johnson went downstairs to the Oval Office to attend to last-minute business. At 10:15, he joined his wife and daughters, Luci and Lynda, to welcome President-elect Nixon, his wife Pat, and their daughters, Tricia and Julie, for the traditional coffee between incoming and outgoing first families. Johnson's last order of business was to sign letters he had dictated to his two sons-in-law, Chuck Robb and Pat Nugent, both serving in Vietnam, saying how proud he and Mrs. Johnson were of them.[2]

At 10:30 sharp, the Nixons arrived by limousine through the White House's North Gate and were met by the Johnsons at the South Portico. They repaired to the Red Room, where the two families were joined by the incoming and outgoing vice presidents, Spiro Agnew and Hubert Humphrey, and their families, and members of the congressional leadership.

The group sipped coffee and talked amiably while Johnson and Nixon made their way to a corner of the room, where they had a moment to talk alone. Nixon told him he appreciated the relationship Johnson had established with former president Eisenhower while Johnson was in office, and he, Nixon, intended to maintain the same kind of relationship with Johnson. Shortly afterward, the Johnson and Nixon families boarded limousines for the two-mile drive up Pennsylvania Avenue to the Capitol for Richard Nixon's inaugural ceremony. As they walked out the front door of the White House for the last time as residents, Mrs. Johnson whispered in her husband's ear that she had no regrets.[3]

A little after noon, Richard Nixon took the oath of office to become the thirty-seventh president. It didn't take Nixon long to take aim at the Johnson administration. "We are caught in war, wanting peace. We are torn by divisions, wanting unity," he said in his inaugural address, referring to Vietnam, the war Johnson could not stop. Then he struck the first blow at the "Great Society" Johnson had labored to build during his tenure, a preview to the dismantling that would begin under Nixon's regime: "In these difficult years, America has suffered from a fever of words; from inflated rhetoric that promises more than it can deliver."

After the inauguration, the Johnsons attended a luncheon in their honor at the Georgetown home of Clark Clifford, Johnson's secretary of defense, to whom Johnson had awarded the Medal of Freedom earlier that morning. The mood was light and festive, full of toasts and tributes to Johnson from the small group of cabinet members and aides in attendance. Finally, it was on to Andrews Air Force Base for the trip back home. A crowd of well-wishers was there to see them off, including longtime friends and aides, and at least two Republicans—Congressman George Bush and his wife Barbara—on hand to bid farewell to their fellow Texans, a bipartisan gesture that touched Johnson.[4] "He's my president, and he's leaving town," Bush said. "And I don't want him to leave without my being out here and paying my respects to him."[5]

At Andrews, Johnson boarded Air Force One—a last vestige of presidential power that President Nixon had loaned him for the four-hour trip home—with Mrs. Johnson, Luci, his grandson Lyn, and a small retinue of aides. Shortly after takeoff, Johnson convened his aides in the bedroom of the aircraft. There he outlined the major projects he wanted to complete in the time he had remaining:

1. Write and edit his memoirs.
2. Complete a series of televised interviews with Walter Cronkite of CBS News.
3. Build and staff the LBJ Library on the campus of the University of Texas in Austin.
4. Build and staff the LBJ School of Public Affairs, also at University of Texas.
5. Assist Mrs. Johnson, if needed, with her memoirs.
6. Get his estate and various business interests in order.[6]

Tellingly, Johnson's plane flew to Bergstrom Air Force Base rather than the Austin Airport where antiwar protestors would almost certainly have congregated. Instead a crowd of five thousand military personnel and their families enthusiastically greeted him, yelling out warm sentiments.[7] At Bergstrom, Johnson parted from Air Force One—but not before he ordered the removal of its amenities. Almost everything with a presidential seal was taken as a keepsake, including china, silverware, blankets, towels, toilet paper, and the president's swivel chair, which was liberated from its bolted base.[8]

Finally, an LBJ Corporation King Air turboprop carried them on the last leg of their trip, home to the 330-acre LBJ Ranch on the Pedernales River, sixty miles west of Austin. Fifty or so friends and neighbors, some of whom had known Johnson since childhood, were at the hangar to welcome the Johnsons back to Texas. After thirty-two years of public service in Washington, they were back home in Johnson City, in their beloved Hill Country, where, as Johnson's father put it, "the people know when you're sick and care when you die."[9]

Darkness had descended by the time the Johnsons arrived at the ranch, and the weather, warm and mild, was a welcome contrast to the harsh winter they had left in Washington. Mrs. Johnson had seen to it that a fire was burning in the living room and that the televisions were set up so the former president could watch all three network news broadcasts simultaneously, as was his habit.[10] Also awaiting them was a pile of luggage direct from the White House that had been unceremoniously stacked in the carport. For years the Johnsons had had attendants who handled the bag-carrying duties, but now the responsibility rested squarely in their hands. Mrs. Johnson looked at the pile and laughed. "The coach has turned back into the pumpkin," she told her husband, "and the mice have all run away."[11]

Later, when Nixon asked Johnson what it was like to no longer be president, Johnson replied, "The most pleasant words that ever came into my ears were 'So help me God' that you repeated after the oath. Because at that time I was no longer the man who could make the mistake of involving the world in war."[12] But the world *was* involved in a war—even if it wasn't entirely Johnson's doing—and the U.S. was in the thick of it. And there was little doubt that if not for the quagmire of Vietnam, Lyndon Johnson would have wanted to be the one on the inaugural stand taking the oath that afternoon. As it was, he left Washington without fulfilling his promise to the nation or to himself, and it weighed on him terribly.

Just ten months earlier in a televised address to the nation, Johnson shocked by announcing that he would "not seek" and would "not accept the nomination of my party for another term as your president." Severely weakened by the U.S.'s involvement in Vietnam, which he had escalated as commander in chief, and challenged by members of his own party—including Robert Kennedy—for the presidential nomination, Johnson resolved to give up the presidency to concentrate on a peaceful settlement to the war. He slipped the unscripted announcement into the end of his speech.

It was not supposed to be that way. Johnson had desperately wanted to carve out his place in history by lifting up the poor, uneducated, elderly, and disenfranchised, and by curing the ills of racism and discrimination. Taking over for Kennedy in November 1963, Johnson succeeded in passing the Civil Rights Act and the tax cut his martyred predecessor had fought for before his death. After winning the presidency in his own right a year later, by the biggest margin in American history, Johnson sought to create "The Great Society," in which "the meaning of a man's life matches the marvel of a man's labor." Along with it came an ambitious legislative agenda that he pursued with remarkable effectiveness, employing the legendary tactics he had used in his eight years as the most powerful Senate majority leader of the twentieth century. He prodded, threatened, charmed, cajoled, flattered, and bullied his opponents—an approach well known as the "Johnson treatment"—and more often than not, they came over to his way of thinking.

In the first several years of his presidency, his prodigious drive had fueled spectacular achievements: He signed the Medicare bill into law; increased government aid to fund public schools and college student tuition; put in place more effective safeguards to protect black voting rights; enacted environmental laws to prevent air and water pollution; reformed immigration laws; passed beautification measures (the chief crusade for Mrs. Johnson as first lady); and boosted the minimum wage and funding for antipoverty programs. He also appointed African Americans to unprecedented heights of federal power; Thurgood Marshall sat on the Supreme Court as its first black justice, and Robert C. Weaver became the first black to hold a cabinet post as secretary of Urban Development (later, Housing and Urban Development).

Had it not been for Vietnam, Johnson might have inherited the mantle of his hero, Franklin Roosevelt, who was serving as president when Johnson was elected to Congress. But his inability to stem the tide of Communism in a small Southeast Asian country proved his undoing; all his persuasive powers could not convince dissenters that America's presence in Vietnam was of urgent national importance—or a winnable campaign. Antiwar protestors became ubiquitous for Johnson during his last years in office, and their relentless chant, "Hey, hey, LBJ, how many kids did you kill today?" haunted him. "People think you're isolated in the White House," Luci Johnson said later. "But [we] could hear it every day. We heard it late at night, and in the morning it was our wake-up call."[13]

As support for the war eroded, so did Johnson's clout with Congress and his popularity with the American people. His approval rating fell as low as 36 percent.[14] The nation that had rallied around him after Kennedy's assassination was sharply divided on the war—and Johnson himself—when he relinquished power. For Johnson, who craved approbation, the rejection was devastating. "My daddy committed political suicide for that war," Luci Johnson told her father's biographer, Robert Dallek. "And since politics was all he had, it was like committing actual suicide."[15]

Though Johnson left the problems of the war on Richard Nixon's desk, the tragedy of Vietnam followed him home. In an interview at the ranch just days after Johnson's return, a journalist asked him if he would have done anything differently as president. Johnson paused, then quietly said he couldn't answer until he looked back at his diaries . . . if he looked back at March 5, 1965, he might . . . His barely audible voice then trailed off. March 5, 1965, was the day Johnson had committed 35,000 marines to Vietnam, leading to the U.S.'s direct involvement in the war.[16]

For almost thirty-five years in Washington—as a congressional aide, congressman, senator, vice president, and president—Lyndon Johnson had devoted himself to the acquisition and use of power to the exclusion of any activities that may have afforded him a more balanced life. Everything in his world revolved around politics; he had no pastimes, hobbies, or outside interests that didn't have some political end attached to them.[17] Few who knew him thought he would make the transition to private citizen easily. "He's basically not constituted to assume [the] new posture," said a former aide, reflecting the thoughts of many others. Johnson himself put on a brave face. The ex-president was physically and mentally drained and looked forward to relaxing, sleeping late, and spending time with his wife and family. He admitted that it would be difficult to leave public life, but added, "I want to miss it. I want it to hurt good."[18]

Predictably, the first few months after his homecoming were difficult for Johnson, and just as hard for those around him. He was shrouded in depression and groused about how he had been wronged in self-pitying monologues. The press, the Democratic Party, the Kennedys, even his own advisors—all were culprits that had led to his demise. Mrs. Johnson tried to cheer him up by having old friends over, urging them to steer clear of subjects like Vietnam and to talk of life at the ranch. For some, it may not have mattered. One friend remembered that Johnson "didn't want to talk about anything that was less than twenty-five years old." When Mrs. Johnson suggested they watch movies of their time in the White House, Johnson said, "That's all past and done with." When she insisted, he refused to watch, and then fell asleep. Eventually the dark cloud lifted and he seemed to enjoy himself at times, but bouts with depression would recur often throughout his winter years.[19]

Mrs. Johnson, as always, was a stabilizing force. She alone could quiet his storms and her presence gave him genuine comfort, particularly in the difficult transition back to private life. The two had met in the summer of 1934, when the twenty-six-year-old Johnson returned to Austin from Washington, where he had worked as a congressional aide to Texas congressman, Richard Kleberg. Claudia "Lady Bird" Taylor, twenty-one years old, was immediately taken with the ambitious, take-charge Lyndon Johnson, who epitomized the "young man in a hurry."

The two came from different upbringings: While Johnson grew up humbly in the Hill Country (though his family was not as poor as he often implied), Lady Bird was raised in relative prosperity in East Texas. After her mother died when she was five, she was brought up by her aunt and father, a successful merchant and farmer who became the wealthiest man in the county. As a student, Lady Bird, sensible but adventurous, had designs on a career in journalism. After meeting Johnson, however, her life took an unexpected turn. He asked her to marry him on their first or second date—Lady Bird could not remember which—and put his proposal in writing several days later in the form of an ultimatum. "If you say no, it means that you don't love me enough to marry me," he wrote on the train back to Washington. "We do it now or we never will." After worrying that she would lose her dashing suitor, she said yes. They wed in November of 1934.[20]

Mrs. Johnson's considerable charm, sound advice, and wealthy background made her an ideal political wife. Together they began a partnership that saw Johnson rise to congressman, senator, vice president, and president in the course of twenty-nine years. From the beginning, their roles were clearly established. Johnson threw his formidable energies into fulfilling his political ambitions, while "Bird" took care of him, raising their daughters and managing the details of their lives. "I only think about politics eighteen hours a day," Johnson once said. It fell to Mrs. Johnson to think of almost everything else. With "steel magnolia" stoicism, she endured much pain in their marriage: a series of miscarriages before giving birth to Lynda in 1944 and Luci in 1947; her husband's frequent infidelities, dark moods, and verbal abuse; and the general difficulties inherent in the Faustian pact made by political wives. Still, they had an unusually close union. Mrs. Johnson described it this way: "Ours was a compelling love.

Lyndon bullied me, coaxed me, at times even ridiculed me, but he made me more than I would have been. I offered him some peace and quiet. Maybe a little judgment."[21]

In their retirement years, Johnson was more reliant on his wife than ever. Mrs. Johnson's role was as much mother as wife, determining what he ate and wore and closely monitoring his diet and activities to make sure he was not overtaxing his weak heart. As in all other parts of their lives, their entire world revolved around him; everything else was an afterthought. That was part of the bargain. She was glad to be out of Washington and "on our own time," and gladder still that her husband had left the office that had taken so much out of him.[22] She looked forward to many happy years with him at the ranch—but his mercurial nature and restless energy was simply not suited to an idle life.

The question was: What would he do? The projects he was obligated to tackle—fulfilling his contract with Holt, Rinehart and Winston to write his memoirs and overseeing plans for his presidential library and museum and the LBJ School of Public Affairs—did not stir him. He entertained the possibility of being a lecturer at Texas universities, and even accepted an offer from the University of Houston to do so in the spring, but then declined at the last minute, as he had received many other offers for speaking engagements.[23] He also turned down lucrative offers to join boards of major corporations and rejected the notion of becoming a full-time businessman, neither of which he felt was in keeping with the role of a former president, though he did join the board of the Mayo Clinic.[24]

Money was not an issue anyway. The Johnsons had amassed considerable wealth, even by Texas standards, with assets totaling some $20 million. (Johnson himself did not own a single share of stock in the LBJ Company. Mrs. Johnson held 48 percent of the stock, Luci and Lynda both held 24 percent, and the remaining shares were spread between longtime general manager Jesse Kellam, and general sales manager Bob Bobbitt, Johnson's brother-in-law.)[25] Chief among them were the ranch holdings they had bought over time, which added up to 15,000 acres in Gillespie County, where the LBJ Ranch was located, and in neighboring counties and Mexico, and included six ranch houses. They also held the majority interest in KTBC, a CBS affiliate based in Austin that brought in $100,000 to

$200,000 in profits every year, and had significant investments in several Texas banks.[26]

As a former president and congressman, Johnson drew annual pensions of $25,000 and $20,000 respectively. And even though Johnson no longer held the office of the presidency, he still enjoyed many of its privileges. As an ex-president, free military transport was at his beck and call, and the government provided five thousand square feet of office space—including a teak-paneled office suite for Johnson—on the ninth floor of a federal office building in Austin. He was given a $375,000 "transition" budget to draw from in his first eighteen months out of office, and an annual office budget of $80,000 a year. The budget allowed for a staff of twelve who attended to his needs, in addition to the nine or so Secret Service agents assigned to him who often played servant roles far beyond their responsibilities as protectors.[27]

As it turned out, Johnson had little interest in anything outside the borders of his ranch, including, to the surprise of many, the political life he had left behind. Despite his hard work and best intentions, the outside world had been cruel to him. He felt his presidency had been sabotaged, and his legacy was largely in the hands of highbrow, Ivy League intellectuals who didn't understand him and were unlikely to be kind to his presidency. All were beyond his control. But he could be the master of his ranch, which, nestled in the Hill Country where he was born and raised, gave him great solace. As Robert Caro concluded in his biography of Johnson's early years, *Path to Power*, "all the patterns of his life were rooted in that land."[28] Johnson spent nearly a fifth of his 1,887 days as president on the ranch's grounds, going there, as a friend said, "to recharge his batteries."[29] The land that had nurtured him as a boy and buoyed him as president now helped sustain him in his twilight years. In return, he resolved to "put my energies into the one thing they can't take away from me."[30]

"What he did was go to work . . . on the ranch," recalled Tom Johnson (no relation), who was a special assistant to Johnson in the White House and returned with him to Texas as part of his executive staff. "He ran [it] the way he ran his presidency—involved in every inch of it."[31] Johnson threw himself into the role of cattleman, playing it with as much urgency and importance as he had his role of chief executive. He rose most mornings by

6:00 A.M. and convened a meeting with his foreman Dale Malechek and four or five ranch hands. The group was subject to exhortations from the boss to do more and do better.

"Now, I want each of you to make a solemn pledge that you will not go to bed tonight until you make sure that every steer has everything he needs," he would say. "We've got a chance to produce some of the finest beef in the country if we work at it, if we dedicate ourselves to the job. And if we treat those hens with loving care, we should be able to produce the finest eggs in the country. Really fresh. But it will mean working every minute of every day." He kept a running list of priorities for them to attend to, and demanded memos on subjects like egg production, a request that may have been a bit misguided. "Cowboys don't write very good memos," Malechek's wife Jewell pointed out. "When you're really busy it's kind of hard to come in at night . . . and write a memo to President Johnson about what you're going to do the next day."[32]

Throughout the day he would patrol the ranch grounds on horseback or in his Lincoln convertible, micromanaging every aspect of its operation. He "became one of them," said Malechek, helping to carry and lay heavy irrigation pipes in the Pedernales and working his Beresford cattle, each of which he knew by name. "I never worked harder for a man in my life. If you did the work, he'd stand behind you, but if you didn't you had hell to pay." Often he literally stood behind them. One early morning at six o'-clock, Malechek was milking the cows only to find Johnson there in his pajamas, asking, "How are the dairy cows? Do the fences need to be fixed?" "Gee," Malechek confided to a guest at the ranch afterward, "I hope he runs for president [again]."[33]

At night, dirty and exhausted from a full day's labor, he would return home where his guests would invariably hear the prosaic concerns of his new life. "He's become a goddamn farmer," an old friend complained. "I want to talk Democratic politics and he talks only hog prices."[34] When he went to bed, he took the problems of the ranch with him, worrying about how to improve his herd and grow better Bermuda grass.[35]

The ranch took on a monumental importance in Johnson's life. Its success and output were a reflection on him. "All my life, I've wanted to enjoy this land," he told Doris Kearns (later Doris Kearns Goodwin), who had been an aide to Johnson in his last year in the White House and followed him to the ranch to help him write his memoirs. "I bought it. I paid it off. I watched it improve. It's all I have left now."[36]

Johnson's immersion in the ranch meant that he evaded working on his memoirs. The book may have been an unwelcome reminder of the life he had left in Washington, and it was clear from the start that his heart was not in the project. After months of procrastination, however, he began to dabble at it, dictating his thoughts on the events of his administration into a tape recorder. But the voice Johnson used to recount events was tailored to what Johnson thought a presidential voice should be, not his own. It proved a frustration for Kearns, who, against Johnson's wishes, tried to sneak stories he had told informally into the manuscript to add color and authenticity to the narrative. When Johnson read one anecdote about Congressman Wilbur Mills he insisted on its removal. "Goddamn it, I can't say this," he snapped. "Get it out right now; why, he may be Speaker of the House someday. And for Christ's sake, get that vulgar language of mine out of there. What do you think this is, the tale of an uneducated cowboy? It's a presidential memoir, damn it, and I've got to come out looking like a statesman, not some backwoods politician."[37]

Kearns was compelled to help Johnson with the book. He implored her to return to Texas with him, despite her desire to return to her native Boston to work with the poor and teach. They eventually reached a compromise, with Kearns commuting to the ranch to work with Johnson on weekends. A number of Johnson's collaborators on the book were surprised that Johnson brought the twenty-five-year-old on to work on the project, though as she herself recognized, "I was young and from Harvard, two constituencies whose approval he desperately wanted."[38] As their relationship evolved, Kearns played the role of confidante for her employer as he reflected extensively on his life and career. The man she saw in those years was melancholy, insecure, and worried about his place in history. *That* Lyndon Johnson does not appear in the memoir, but would be thoroughly explored in her book, *Lyndon Johnson and the American Dream*, published several years after his death.

Other projects occupied Johnson's time too. The construction of the Lyndon Johnson Library had begun, part of an $11.8 million LBJ complex on the University of Texas's Austin campus. Johnson actively participated in all decisions surrounding the eight-story building, as well as determining the direction of the Lyndon B. Johnson School of Public Affairs, which would be housed in an adjacent building.

In his first year back home, Johnson seldom strayed far from the ranch and, when he did, was soon anxious to get back. He took short vacations to Florida and Bermuda with his family but declined to go on a trip to France with Mrs. Johnson and Lynda. His most high-profile outings included the funeral of Dwight Eisenhower, who died in March of that year, and the launch of *Apollo 11* at Cape Kennedy, Florida, in July. The latter proved particularly unsettling for Johnson, who remembered it as an excruciating ordeal. As he recalled to Kearns in vivid detail, he was relegated to a seat in the bleachers under a glaring sun with a thousand other VIPs. Along with everyone else in the crowd, he waited for President Nixon, who arrived by helicopter looking cool and comfortable as "Hail to the Chief" was played.

"I hated every minute of it," he complained. "All I kept thinking was how much I wanted to be home, walking through my fields, looking after my cattle." While the story may have captured Johnson's feelings that day, it also reflected his bent for historical revisionism: President Nixon watched the liftoff of the moon-bound *Apollo 11* from the comfort of the Oval Office; it was Vice President Agnew who was on hand at Cape Kennedy that day.[39]

If the public had seen little of LBJ since he left office, in December they had a chance to see him as they never had before. The first of a series of three television interviews aired on CBS with veteran anchorman Walter Cronkite talking to the thirty-sixth president about his life and presidency. Johnson earned $300,000 for the interviews, which contained some surprising—and scarcely believable—revelations. He cast himself improbably as a humble man of modest ambition who wielded power reluctantly. He never really wanted to be president, he told Cronkite, a dubious claim since he had run hard for the Democratic presidential nomination in 1960 before losing to John Kennedy, who he would then join as running mate on the Democratic ticket. Upon becoming president after Kennedy's death in 1963, he claimed he did not want to run in 1964, and had even written a statement taking himself out of the running and recommending Hubert Humphrey or Robert Kennedy as standard-bearer. Persuasive memos from Mrs. Johnson helped change his mind. She did, however, agree with his decision not to run again in 1968. If he had run, though, he was confident he would have won reelection.

"Now you can call that egotistical . . . or arrogant if you want to," he said, "but I call it professional evaluation." Johnson suggested that "the men who have power, are generally people who don't want power," implying he was among them. "I always felt that every job I had was too big for me," he added, a suspect notion for a man of legendary ego.[40]

In the second interview with Cronkite, which aired in April 1970, Johnson further strained credibility. Discussing Vietnam, he presented himself as the catalyst for the de-escalation in the war that occurred in his last year as president. He claimed that he and Dean Rusk, his hawkish secretary of state—not his dovish secretary of defense, Clark Clifford, as was commonly believed—had initiated the stop to the bombings in North Vietnam.

The last interview contained one revelation that was lost to editing before it aired in May. In discussing his views on the Kennedy assassination, Johnson said, "I can't honestly say that I have ever been completely relieved of the fact that there might have been international connections. I have not completely discounted it." After seeing a tape of the interview later, he exercised a long-established right among presidents to order the removal of material they felt might compromise national security. CBS fought him on it, claiming he had missed the deadline for invoking the privilege. The network eventually acquiesced, but Johnson would go on the record with similar comments later.[41]

The doubt that lingered over many of Johnson's comments after the specials aired further bruised Johnson, reminding him of how misunderstood he was. It may have also explained why, with the noted exception of the paid Cronkite interviews and a few others, he turned his back on the press during his retirement years. Since Johnson had always been available to the news media in the past, and because he offered such good copy, his elusiveness fueled rumors that he was depressed. Whether he actually was or not depended on who in Johnson's circle was asked.

On some days Johnson seemed content with his new bucolic life outside of Washington. He had ample time to spend with his family, which had been all but impossible during his political life. Luci and Pat Nugent lived in Austin, and Lynda and Chuck Robb were in Charlottesville, Virginia. Luci thought retirement would be like putting her father "in a tomb."[42] But he discovered the joys of spending time with his family, including hours of play with his grandchildren.[43] A "loving, doting" grandfather, he spent hours patiently playing with his grandchildren, Lyndon Nugent and Lynda Bird Johnson Robb. "He got the grandfather thing down," remembered Lyn Nugent, who was born in 1967. "He wanted to make up for lost [family] time and I got the most benefit from it." Johnson often included Lyn on his inspection tours of his ranch holdings in Texas and Mexico, sharing his passion for the cattle business. Time with his grandfather meant "planes, helicopters and horses . . . it was like Disneyland, twenty-four/seven."[44] LBJ said of his life after the White House, "I've got exactly what I want right now: a wonderful wife, two wonderful daughters, and two beautiful grandchildren. I am happy, very happy."[45]

Continuity may have made the transition a bit easier than it might have been otherwise. In addition to Tom Johnson, at least a dozen members of Johnson's presidential staff made the move to Texas to remain with their boss, including Harry Middleton, a staff assistant, who came back to collaborate on the memoirs and run the LBJ Library, and Yolanda Boozer, a member of Johnson's senate and presidential staffs, who became a member of his post-presidential staff. Others settled in Austin and found jobs in the private sector. Walt Rostow, Johnson's top advisor on national security, taught at the University of Texas, and Larry Temple, a White House counsel, began his own private practice.[46] There was also a steady stream of visitors at the ranch ensuring that Johnson, who hated to be alone, always had company and a ready audience. George Bush, still a Texas congressman, paid a visit in 1970 as he was weighing a decision to run as a Republican candidate for the U.S. Senate. He found Johnson as he was in Washington, "bigger than life." Quirky, too. Along with sound advice, he gave Bush a tour of his closet to show him, among other things, his vast collection of pants—"I never saw so many clothes," Bush recalled—while barking orders to Jake Pickle, another Texas congressman who tagged along, to make sure Bush was well taken care of. Bush went on to lose the election to the Democratic challenger, Lloyd Bentsen, but valued Johnson's counsel.[47] An article in *U.S. News & World Report* nine months after Johnson left office portrayed him as a "busy man," satisfied with the serenity of his ranch, and another in April 1971 said, "[H]e might not stay that way, but so far Lyndon Johnson seems content with a quiet life."[48]

But there were disturbing signs that may have provided a clue to Johnson's diminished sense of purpose. A needlepoint pillow at the ranch that read THIS IS MY RANCH AND I DO AS I DAMN WELL PLEASE reflected Johnson's post-presidential state of mind. He indulged his gargantuan appetites with abandon, much to the consternation of family and friends who worried about his health. After a massive, near-fatal heart attack sidelined him for six months in 1955 at the age of forty-seven, he had adhered to doctor's orders, altering his lifestyle and, under Mrs. Johnson's watchful eye, carefully monitoring his health. He quit his three-pack-a-day smoking habit, cut down on alcohol, watched his diet, exercised regularly, and reduced his workday from fourteen hours to eleven or twelve.

In retirement, Johnson resumed his bad habits and often seemed bent on self-destruction. He started smoking again on the plane ride home from Washington. When his daughter Luci remonstrated him for lighting up, he erupted, "For fourteen years I've wanted to smoke when I've wanted to smoke, and for fourteen years I've had a country to serve, children to raise, and a job to do. Now, the job is done, and the children are raised. Now it's my turn."[49] By 1971, he was smoking up to two packs daily and drinking the Cutty Sark whiskey he favored more liberally than ever. Dispensing with calorie counting, he enjoyed the fatty foods and sweets his doctors had warned him about. While eating lunch with Johnson at the ranch during his interview sessions, Walter Cronkite recalled, "With each course, and particularly dessert, he kept a sharp eye on Lady Bird, and whenever her attention was directed elsewhere, without apology, he would sneak a forkful of food from the guests' plates on either side of him."[50]

His physical activity, limited mostly to daily swims in the ranch's pool and occasional golf outings in which Johnson played three balls at once and didn't keep score, were not enough to ward off the effects of his indulgences. His weight climbed as high as 235 pounds, where it had been when he had had his heart attack in 1955. Mindful that his father had died of a heart attack at just sixty, he seemed resigned to an early death himself; the notion that he didn't have many years left was never far from his mind.[51] Years earlier he had had his family's medical history entered into a computer, which spat out a prediction that he would die at age 64.[52] "I'm going to enjoy the time I have left," he told a friend. "When I go, I want to go quick. I don't want to linger the way Eisenhower did."[53]

Doctors had also warned him against reckless drives in his Lincoln convertible—also in vain. For years he raced down highways and through the fields on or near the ranch as the speedometer climbed to ninety miles an hour or more. Guests were often given hair-raising tours of the ranch with Johnson at the wheel. While president, he had drawn fire from critics for taking reporters on a wild drive around the grounds as he slurped from a beer on the dashboard and gestured toward local points of interest. In retirement, the only thing that changed was that reporters were seldom invited on those joy rides.

As Johnson settled into retirement, he bore less and less resemblance to the man who had occupied the White House just several years before. The creases in his weathered face deepened with increased exposure to the strong Texas sun, and his added weight thickened his once lanky six-foot-two-inch frame. But perhaps the most striking difference in his appearance was his hair. The tightly cropped cut he had worn, commonly found atop the heads of members of the establishment, had given way to a decidedly shaggier look. His hair, now white and wavy, fell almost to his shoulders and curled slightly at the back, and his sideburns dropped almost the full length of his long ears. He bore an uncanny resemblance to the hippie, antiwar protestors who had picketed on college campuses and outside the White House on any given day late in his presidency. The unkempt style was paradoxical for the once-meticulous Johnson, who while in Washington had maintained a drill sergeant's insistence on well-shined shoes and had berated his secretaries for not having their hair done, or for the slightest runs in their stockings. A neighbor who spotted Johnson at a county fair noted that he "needed a haircut and it looked like he had on an old shirt."[54] Was the new hairstyle simply the look of a mellowed Texas rancher who was going to do whatever he damn well pleased? Or was it the tacit gesture of a man who desperately wanted to be loved, reaching out to those who had most vocally opposed his presidency?

By March of 1970, Johnson's weak heart began to catch up with him. Complaining of chest pains, he was taken to the Brooks General Hospital in San Antonio, where the Johnson family went through what Mrs. Johnson described as "four anxious days [when] his condition was nip and tuck."[55] Johnson was suffering from angina pectoris, the result of deficient blood flow to his heart muscle. After two weeks, when doctors could find no evidence of a heart attack, he was released with strict orders to rest and limit his activities. Angina would afflict him for the rest of his life. The chest pain it caused was combated by the nitroglycerin pills he stuffed in his pocket and popped often in his remaining days.

Despite his recent illness, he and Mrs. Johnson returned to Washington several weeks later to attend a wedding and extended their brief visit by five days. A pleasant dinner at the Georgetown home of *Washington Post* owner and publisher Katharine Graham led to an invitation to have lunch with *Post* and *Newsweek* editors the following day. Johnson used the occasion to make a case for his actions in Vietnam. Tom Johnson, his administrative assistant, joined him, armed with two briefcases of top-secret files, a paper trail to the decisions LBJ had made in Vietnam during his administration. As Johnson presented his defense, Tom Johnson handed him documents which he used as exhibits to support the claims he made. Any signs of his illness dissipated as he pleaded his case. Richard Harwood, an editor for the *Post*, remembered Johnson's transformation as he spoke. "All of a sudden," Harwood said, "you were sitting with a vigorous, strong man whose mind was so clear, so well organized, so quick that you became aware of the power of that personality, of the ability to dominate and persuade and overwhelm."[56]

The luncheon turned into a "tour de force" by Johnson. Katharine Graham recognized it as the "Johnson treatment" as he looked deeply into the eyes of his audience and gesticulated wildly to make his points. After he talked about Vietnam, he spoke about his love-hate relationship with the press and his life and times before bidding farewell to his "friends at the *Post*." By the time he was done, four hours had elapsed, during which time Mrs. Johnson had called to inquire about her husband's whereabouts, demanding unsuccessfully that he come home and rest. As he stood to leave, the editors around the table, many of whom were harsh critics of Johnson, rose with him and burst into spontaneous applause, some with tears in their eyes. It was the only time Graham could recall her editors responding to a visitor with such emotion.[57]

While the visit may not have changed minds about Johnson's Vietnam policy, it may have changed perceptions about the man himself. "We thought we may never see his likes again," said Haynes Johnson, another *Post* editor in attendance. "And maybe we were right."[58] The following week, *Newsweek* ran an article about Johnson's Washington visit. "He may be a simple Texas rancher now instead of President of the United States," it read. "But when Lyndon Johnson cast his formidable presence upon the city of Washington last week, even the cherry trees burst into bloom."[59]

In the summer of 1970, Johnson's birthplace, just a mile down the road from the ranch on the Pedernales River, opened its doors as a national monument operated by the Department of the Interior. The actual house had been knocked down in 1964, and carefully reconstructed under Johnson's supervision. Occasionally, it was used during his presidential years to house the overflow of guests visiting the ranch. Now the public could walk through the small five-room clapboard house resembling the one in which LBJ was born and raised as Mrs. Johnson provided audiotaped commentary through speakers in each room. In June, the month it opened, 16,000 tourists paid to take the fourteen-minute tour.[60]

The birthplace gave Johnson a quantifiable measurement by which to gauge his popularity as he micromanaged it with the same intensity that he managed his ranch, always wanting more than the day before. Weekly memos were drafted for his review, providing a detailed account of attendance, admission receipts, gift shop sales, and expenses.[61] His goal was nothing short of having the most-visited presidential birthplace in America, and he drove its eight-person staff to make it so. Each day became a referendum on Lyndon Johnson and every paid visitor and dollar spent was a vote for his validation. When he wasn't at the ranch, he could often be found at the birthplace in his work clothes, working the crowds like the old politician he was, shaking hands and talking with visitors, conducting tours and, after his memoirs were published, stirring book sales. "Aren't ya going to buy one of my books? If you do I'll sign it right here—give me a pen," he would say as lines formed and wallets opened.[62]

Less than a year later, Johnson would have not only another vehicle to quantify his popularity but one that would house his legacy. The dedication of the Lyndon Johnson Library at the University of Texas in Austin took place on a warm, blustery Friday afternoon in late May of 1971. President and Mrs. Nixon joined a crowd of three thousand invited guests, a who's who of Johnson's Washington years, for the unveiling of the $18.6 million complex which housed thirty-one million pages of documents and half a million photographs spanning Johnson's thirty-two-year political career. "It's all here: the story of our time—with the bark off," Johnson told the crowd, his favorite tan suit contrasting with Nixon's in navy blue. "There is no record of a mistake, nothing critical, ugly, or unpleasant that is not included in the files here."[63]

The travertine marble building, windowless and boxlike, was a monstrosity by presidential library standards. A 1955 Presidential Libraries Act ensured that every president starting with Herbert Hoover would have a memorial and archive in the form of a presidential library and museum, but the Johnson Library one-upped those relatively modest structures by a long shot. The oil-rich University of Texas funded the project, which was much in keeping with the Texan fixation with "bigness" and the outsized personality of the library's namesake.

Not all of those who came to the dedication were welcome. Twenty-one hundred antiwar demonstrators, most in their early twenties, were kept several blocks away from the ceremonies by 1,200 highway patrolmen and Texas Rangers. Their "No more war!" chants, however, carried by twenty-five-mile-an-hour winds and accompanied by the pounding of trash-can lids, could be heard clearly by the speakers on the podium and guests in the audience. Twenty-four protestors were arrested.[64]

If Vietnam was not on Johnson's mind during the proceedings, he was reminded of it at a barbecue after the ceremonies upon seeing General William Westmoreland, his army chief of staff who had overseen the war during his administration. As guests dined on pork ribs, coleslaw, and other Texas cuisine, Johnson put his arms around Westmoreland and said, "Some have said that people misinformed me," referring to allegations that

Johnson had been too dependent on the poor information his military team had given him. "I said, 'No. Whatever mistakes I made, *I* made.'"[65]

But generally, the day was a triumph for Johnson. It had "all the ingredients of a golden wedding celebration, a twenty-fifth alumni reunion, and a Sunday school picnic," one guest remarked.

The library, soon to be known as "Johnson's Pyramid," was frequently visited by the Johnsons. President and Mrs. Johnson both had offices there—a replica of the Oval Office, constructed almost to scale, was open to visitors when it wasn't being used by Johnson himself—and would commute from the ranch by helicopter, descending on a landing pad atop the library's roof. As with the birthplace, Johnson aimed to make the LBJ Library and its museum the most popular of its kind, and monitored attendance figures carefully to ensure it. To appease the boss and prevent angry outbursts, library employees learned to inflate attendance figures over time, increasing them slowly week over week.[66] Johnson himself fashioned strategies to drive more people through its doors. After a Longhorns football game at the university, he asked the library's director, Harry Middleton, to have the game's announcer use the public address system to invite the crowd to "come to the library for some cool water and to use the can," disregarding the fact that the library had only one water fountain and one restroom each for men and women.[67]

Johnson's memoir, *The Vantage Point: Perspectives of the Presidency*, hit bookstores in the fall of 1971. Originally planned as two volumes, the book sold poorly and fetched tepid reviews. The voice of a "statesman" Johnson used throughout its 636 pages captured neither its author nor, in the view of many of its critics, its readers. *Time's* Hugh Sidey called the book "a nervous bow to the Harvard faculty and thus not very Johnsonian."[68] The colorful Texas storyteller who could hold his audience spellbound with tales of Washington politics and the personalities surrounding them never came through. There were, however, some familiar Johnson themes. As in the Cronkite interviews, he made a number of dubious claims: He admitted no mistakes or regrets in the war he waged in Vietnam and confessed to few overall, and held to the claim that he had had no intention of running for president in 1964. Johnson's revisionism, like the voice he used, was tailored to what he thought would cast him in the most flattering historical light—

no matter how far it fell from the truth. Criticism and poor sales disappointed the book's publisher, Holt, Rinehart and Winston, which had paid the author a hefty $1.5 million in anticipation of a receptive public. If Johnson was stung by the criticism, it likely came as no surprise, thinking as he did that the eastern-establishment press was out to get him.

The albatross of Vietnam would remain with Johnson throughout his post-presidency. His sons-in-law, Chuck Robb and Pat Nugent, were both in Vietnam when Johnson left office. Robb, a career officer, and Nugent, a national guardsman who volunteered for duty in Vietnam, served in the war for a year, overlapping most of the time. They both returned within months of Johnson's retirement, but the war continued to be a part of LBJ's regimen as an ex-president. Every Friday, Nixon dispatched a White House Jetstar that would touch down on the ranch airstrip with a pouch of classified briefing papers offering the latest developments on the war. Johnson also received a weekly call from a cabinet member with regular updates. Nixon sent members of his staff to the ranch—including national security advisor Henry Kissinger and chief of staff Alexander Haig—to brief Johnson personally, and they frequently called Johnson to seek counsel on the war.[69] As long as the war raged on, it was a living obstruction of Johnson's legacy. "I knew from the start that if I left the woman I loved—the Great Society—in order to fight that bitch of a war," he confessed to an aide after leaving office, "then I would lose everything . . . all my hopes . . . my dreams."[70]

For his part, Nixon made good on his inaugural-day pledge to reach out to Johnson. He kept in frequent touch directly or through friends, and extended himself on occasion.[71] For Johnson's sixty-first birthday, he flew the Johnson family to his home in Southern California for a small party during which a mariachi band played as Nixon led the guests in singing "Happy Birthday" and a chorus of "The Yellow Rose of Texas." When Johnson became involved in the building of a model nursing home near the ranch, to be named for his mother, members of Nixon's administration began to leak stories that the Department of Health, Education and Welfare was going to conduct an investigation into the project to route out alleged improprieties. Johnson went directly to Nixon asking him to intervene, insisting that "nobody's getting anything out of this except old folks," whereupon the problem went away and the project went on.[72]

Nixon was also gracious during Johnson's few Washington visits, inviting him to the White House to discuss foreign affairs, and Vietnam in particular. Johnson reciprocated by consistently voicing public support for Nixon on foreign policy and expressing his belief that Nixon was doing everything he could to stop the war. He refrained from the kind of public criticism that Harry Truman had exacted on Dwight Eisenhower. Before leaving office, he assured Nixon that he would "let you know privately if I disagree with you. But you can be sure I won't criticize you publicly."[73] Still, he said of Nixon's domestic policy, which put the Great Society directly in its crosshairs, "Nixon has plenty up here," pointing to his temple, "but nothing in here," thumping his chest.[74]

Nixon, conversely, wrote in his White House diary that Johnson's Great Society programs were the product of a man "motivated by the heart, not the head." Indeed, Nixon's cordiality stopped at the foot of Johnson's proudest accomplishment. Upon taking office, he "moved to reorganize, reduce, or abolish the remaining behemoths of the Great Society that had done little to aid the poor." Nixon thought Johnson knew he had overextended American resources by giving it both guns and butter—Vietnam and the Great Society—but had done so to satisfy his own need for approval. After all, Johnson had never asked him to preserve any of the Great Society programs that he, Johnson, had put in place.[75] But there was little doubt that Johnson's heart was in the Great Society during and after his presidency, and he anguished over its fate at Nixon's hand. It was only a matter of time before it was all gone. "And when she dies," he told Doris Kearns, "I too will die."[76]

An article in *Look* magazine's November 1972 issue painted a grim picture of Johnson's last full year. "Seemingly invincible in 1964," it read, "[Johnson] is all but invisible in 1972—an ailing and retired politician living in self-imposed exile on his ranch." The piece had Johnson in physical pain from angina, reeling over criticism of his memoirs, and unable to establish with Nixon the kind of warm relationship he had had with Eisenhower. It also maintained that the regard the public had for Harry Truman as an elder statesman, which took at least a decade, was "nowhere in sight" for LBJ.[77]

Though *Look* may have overstated it, the year was full of pain and disappointment for Johnson. In April, he was stricken by a heart attack while he and Mrs. Johnson were visiting Lynda and her family in Charlottesville, Virginia. After complaining of severe chest pains early one morning, he was rushed to a local hospital where he was treated by the doctor who had attended him after his first heart attack in 1955. He convalesced for a week before demanding to return to Texas in defiance of doctors' orders and Mrs. Johnson's protests. "You stay here if you want," he told Lady Bird. "I'm going home." Johnson bolted to the Charlottesville Airport with his wife in tow, much to the surprise of hospital workers whose only notification of his departure was Johnson's empty and idle wheelchair in the hospital parking lot.[78]

Angina became a daily reality for Johnson during his last year. The chest pains he had suffered in the past intensified in his remaining days and often made breathing difficult. "I'm hurting real bad," he would tell friends of his condition, which slowed him down, forcing him to take long afternoon naps and give up driving (which undoubtedly pleased his doctors).[79] His condition was monitored by specialists at the Mayo Clinic and in Houston, who rejected him as a candidate for open-heart bypass surgery, which was in its infancy at the time.[80]

Politically, Johnson was fading into oblivion. The party he had fought for most of his life had largely turned its back on him by 1972. His political protégé, former Texas governor John Connally, who sat on Nixon's cabinet as secretary of the treasury, had defected from the party, taking a number of prominent members with him. Johnson's views, which had pervaded the party's platform less than a decade before, were largely out of step with the Democratic ideology by the early seventies. Perhaps sensing the end was near, Johnson had planned to attend the Democratic National Convention in Miami, "if only to stand up and take a bow," but it was not to be. Aides talked him out of it, citing the probability of demonstrations and the possibility of a repeat of the violence that had overrun the party's 1968 convention in Chicago.[81] In fact, he may not have been particularly welcome. The views of the Democratic presidential nominee, the stridently antiwar candidate George McGovern, reflected those of most Democrats. Johnson settled for watching the convention on television at the ranch. His name was absent from the proceedings save for a brief reference to him in a speech by Ted Kennedy.

Johnson did, however tepidly, support the party's nominee—perhaps out of force of habit. As he put it, he had been sucking at the tit of the Democratic Party for years and couldn't let it go, even though the milk might have gone a bit sour because of what the cow was eating.[82] He quietly met with McGovern at the ranch. "Now, on the war. You think I'm crazy as hell," he told McGovern, "and I think you're crazy as hell. So let's not talk about that. Let's talk about America and this election." He dispensed a little political advice—"It doesn't hurt to tell folks you love your country. I wish I had done it more," he told McGovern—and assured him that he had always supported the Democratic nominee and it would be no different this time.[83] But casting his ballot for McGovern, who was as foreign to him politically as many staunch Republicans, must have been a bitter pill to swallow. His only public endorsement came in the form of a weakly written piece that appeared in *The Standard*, the local paper in Fredericksburg, a small town twenty miles from the ranch. Published a full month after the convention, the article hardly mattered; McGovern went on to get trounced in November in a Nixon reelection landslide reminiscent of Johnson's own lopsided victory over Barry Goldwater in 1964.

When the LBJ Library planned a series of symposiums to be held at the facility soon after its dedication, Johnson insisted that one of them address the topic of civil rights.[84] The two-day meeting took place in mid-December as a thousand participants braved a rare ice storm to take part. Many of the old warriors of the movement were on hand—Hubert Humphrey, Roy Wilkins, Clarence Mitchell, and Earl Warren—along with a body of African Americans representing a new crop of black leadership. After the assassination of Martin Luther King in 1968, no unifying leader emerged in his place. The movement stumbled and groped for direction and soon split up into factions, several of which were represented at the meeting. Though Johnson played no speaking role on the first day, he attended the day's events, followed by a guest reception; battling angina, he labored to make it through the evening. Mrs. Johnson and his doctor tried to sideline him the next day. "I was determined that he wasn't going to attend," Mrs. Johnson recalled, "and the doctor insisted that he absolutely, positively could not go—but he went."[85]

Johnson showed up the following morning looking more like a president and less like a rancher in a navy blue suit and well-shined shoes, ready to address the gathering.[86] Luci worried when she saw her father take the stage at noon. "He walked out a very old man—it was frightening—he was obviously not well," she recalled.[87] But there he was, bigger than life, giving a moving twenty-minute oration on the plight of blacks in America: "I didn't want this symposium to spend two days talking about what we have done. The progress has been much too small; we haven't done nearly enough. Until we overcome unequal history, we cannot overcome unequal opportunity. But to be black in a white society is not to stand on equal and level ground. While the races may stand side by side, whites stand on history's mountain and blacks stand in history's hollow. It's time we get down to the business of trying to stand black and white on level ground . . . And if our efforts continue and if our will is strong and if our hearts are right and if courage remains our constant companion, then, my fellow Americans, I am confident we shall overcome."[88]

The speech was clearly a strain on Johnson, who at one point popped a nitroglycerin pill to keep his chest pains at bay. After the applause died down, black leaders began arguing. One read an indictment of President Nixon, claiming that racism had escalated under his watch, before Johnson unexpectedly bounded back up the stairs to the podium. "Now I want you to go back, all of you, and counsel together," Johnson told the group. "Let's try to get our folks reasoning together and reasoning with the Congress and with the cabinet! Reason with the leadership and with the president. There's nothing wrong with—as a matter of fact, there's everything right—about saying, 'Mr. President, we would like you to set aside an hour to let us talk.' And you don't need to start off by saying he's terrible, because he doesn't think he's terrible. Start talking about how you believe that he wants to do what's right and how you believe this is right, and you'll be surprised [by] how many who want to do what's right will try to help you . . . While I can't provide much go-go at this point in my life, I can provide a lot of hope and dreams and encouragement, and I'll sell a few wormy cows now and then and contribute."[89]

Afterward, Luci rushed to the greenroom where her father had retreated after the speech. Knowing the doctor had warned him not to attend, Luci demanded, "Why did you come?"

"My darling," he replied, "because if I had died, I would have died for what I had lived for—and what more could a man want?"[90]

That day, Johnson reclaimed a rightful part of his legacy that had been obscured by Vietnam. The old lion could still roar.

Death cast a shadow over Lyndon Johnson's last weeks. Despite his weak condition, he was compelled to attend three funerals over the course of December. Mrs. Johnson said that her husband "was very upset by going to funerals, but he made himself go . . . And each one was a particularly harrowing experience."[91] The first was for Hale Boggs, a Democratic congressman from a New Orleans district whom Johnson had appointed to the Warren Commission investigating Kennedy's assassination. Boggs had died in a plane crash in Alaska and was never found. The second, the most upsetting, was for a busload of schoolchildren who had died in an accident on the way to a church outing in humble, working-class south Austin. When Lady Bird suggested he did not need to attend, he reminded her of his loyalty to them and their grieving families: "These people are my people. When they hurt, I hurt. Nothing, nothing, nothing is ever going to keep me away from them at times like they're going through."[92] The final service was for Harry Truman, who had passed on just after Christmas. He was given a state funeral at the Truman Library in Independence, Missouri, with the Nixons and Johnsons in attendance. Those ceremonies further strained Johnson and, no doubt, reminded him of his own mortality.

Mrs. Johnson told a friend her husband wasn't well enough to attend Nixon's inauguration ceremonies on January 20, 1973—four years to the day after he had left office. He remained at the ranch instead. Early that morning, he called Doris Kearns in Boston, despondent over the uncertainty of his legacy. He had been reading Carl Sandburg's biography of Abraham Lincoln and just couldn't seem to get a sense of the sixteenth president despite Lincoln's stature and Sandburg's prose. "If that's true for me, one president reading about another," he told her, "then there's no chance the ordinary person in the future will ever remember me. No chance. I'd be better off looking for immortality through my wife and children and their children in turn instead of seeking all that love and affection from the American people. They're just too fickle."[93]

Two days later, while lying down for his usual afternoon nap, Johnson placed an urgent call to the switchboard at the ranch asking for Mike Howard, one of his Secret Service agents, to come up to his room immediately. Howard was out in a car, but the switchboard operator sent two other agents, who rushed to the room with a portable oxygen unit. Johnson lay unconscious beside the bed. His skin had turned blue. The agents tried in vain to revive him through mouth-to-mouth resuscitation and then, when Howard arrived, through heart massage. They scrambled to get Johnson into a Beech King Air family plane and, along with Jewell Malechek and two doctors who had been summoned from nearby hospitals, flew to Brooke Army Medical Center in San Antonio. The plane touched down in San Antonio at 4:33 P.M., when one of the doctors aboard the plane pronounced the former president dead. He had died at age sixty-four, just as a computer prediction based on the Johnson family's medical history had foretold years earlier. Mrs. Johnson was in a car in Austin, just a block from the LBJ Library where she had an office, when she got the call at 4:05. She was rushed by helicopter to meet the plane and her fallen husband in San Antonio.[94]

Flags across America were still at half-mast—the nation had been mourning the passing of Truman the month before—when the shocking news broke that Johnson had died. He had gone quickly, as he had wanted: no lingering illness, no reporters standing deathwatch vigil on his lawn, and having accomplished everything he had outlined on Air Force One the day he left office. And he must have derived great comfort from knowing that peace was at hand in Vietnam. Nixon had announced a cease-fire agreement, drawn up in Paris earlier in the month, the morning after Johnson's death. Although Johnson wasn't alive to hear the announcement, he had received word that the bombs had stopped and peace was imminent through his regular briefings from the administration. "No one would have welcomed peace more than he," Nixon told the nation.

A day later, Johnson's body lay in state at the LBJ Library where some twenty thousand mourners lined up to pay their respects. Echoes of history resounded as Air Force One carried Johnson's body back to Washington. A decade before, the same plane had brought the martyred John F. Kennedy from Dallas back to Washington, as Johnson was inaugurated on board with his wife and Kennedy's widow flanking him. The following day, forty thousand people, many of them black, filed past the silver-gray, flag-draped coffin in the Capitol Rotunda, paying tribute to Johnson.[95] One of the mourners was Richard Nixon who, with Johnson's death, became the only living man to have taken the presidential oath of office—only the sixth time in American history when the one living president was the incumbent. After a memorial service at the National City Christian Church, the body was flown back home to Texas.

In his tours of the ranch, Johnson would often show visitors the small burial plot surrounded by a stone wall, located about four hundred yards from the house, where his mother and father and other family members rested. Among those he took there was *Newsweek* journalist Sam Schaeffer. "Sam, this is where I'm going to be buried," the earthy LBJ said as an arc of urine streamed from his open fly to the sacred ground below.[96] On January 26, Johnson was lowered into the earth in the same spot, near a twisted old oak tree, rugged and beautiful, much like the Hill Country itself.

The Reverend Billy Graham and John Connally offered eulogies. "It is fashionable among some to refer to Lyndon Johnson as a tragic president," Connally said. "But I believe history will describe his presidency as tragic only in the sense that it began through tragedy, for his service to this nation and to the world and to the people he loved was not one of tragedy, but of triumph." At the close of his remarks, he added, "Along this stream and under these trees he loved, he will now rest. He first saw light here. May he now find peace here."[97]

Mrs. Johnson, stoic as always, held up well under the strain, personally greeting hordes of mourners who showed up in Austin and Washington. Privately, in the company of Lynda and Luci the evening of her husband's death, she allowed herself to cry along with them. But at the funeral she and her daughters were strong. As Luci put it: "[My daddy] wanted his women to have their hair combed, their lipstick on, and to be strong and brave. That's what we tried to do today."[98]

Enigmatic to the end, Johnson left many wondering whether he simply died as a result of a weak heart, or if disappointment in a destiny unfulfilled played a role. "I think that Lyndon Johnson died of a broken heart physically and emotionally," Richard Nixon wrote in his memoirs. "He was an enormously proud and able man. He desperately wanted, and expected, to be a great president. Above all, he wanted to be loved—to earn the approval but also the affection of every American." Johnson still longed for that approval when he left office, Nixon contended, but it eluded him.[99]

The slow pace of retirement may also have been a factor in his early death. Cardiologists reviewing the circumstances of his condition concluded that the stress of leaving a high-pressured life in politics for a quieter existence may have been greater for him than the strains of political life itself.[100] Regardless, few would argue that Lyndon Johnson was a giant among men and led a life that was just as big. His titanic ups and downs were all part of the ride.

Maybe Johnson would have gotten some satisfaction in knowing that in a 2003 C-SPAN poll on presidential greatness, conducted among ninety historians and presidential experts, he ranked tenth among the forty-one presidents measured, and that in "Pursued Justice For All," one of the ten categories contributing to the overall ranking, he placed second, just behind Abraham Lincoln. (Not surprisingly, in another of the categories, "Foreign Relations," he placed thirty-sixth, behind Warren Harding.) But it likely would have disappointed him that among C-SPAN viewers responding to the same poll, his ranking dropped to nineteenth overall.[101] One can't help wondering if, somewhere up in the cosmos, LBJ had already tracked those results with the undying hope of doing better tomorrow.

IV.

RICHARD NIXON:
REHABILITATION

I t happened in the skies of Missouri, thirteen miles southwest of Jefferson City. On August 9, 1974, as the minutes brushed past 12:00 noon Eastern Standard Time, Air Force One—lumbering from Andrews Air Force Base toward Southern California with Richard Nixon on board—became simply Special Air Mission 7000.[1] Back in Washington, Gerald R. Ford became the thirty-eighth president of the United States. And Richard Nixon became just another American on his way home.

Two hours earlier, President Nixon had been in the East Room of the White House, bidding farewell to embattled staff members who, for the last twenty-six months, had endured the scourge of Watergate. The scandal took its toll as it unraveled, but its biggest casualty was standing before them—the first president in American history to resign the office. Flanked by his wife, Pat, daughters Julie and Tricia, and their husbands, David Eisenhower and Ed Cox, Nixon, for perhaps the first time in public, spoke from the heart. Fighting back tears, he talked about his father—"He was a great man because he did his job"—and his mother—"No books will be written about her, but she was a saint." He read a quote from Theodore Roosevelt, who as a young man despaired over the death of his first wife. "He thought the light of his life had gone out forever," he said. "But he went on . . . We think that when we suffer a defeat, that all has ended. Not true. It is a beginning, always." He alluded to the volatility that had been consistent throughout his political career: "Greatness comes when you take some knocks . . . because only when you have been in the deepest valley can you know how magnificent it is to be on the highest mountain."

"Always remember," he concluded, "others may hate you, but those who hate you don't win, unless you hate them, and then you destroy yourself."

Vice President and Mrs. Ford were waiting for the Nixons in the White House Diplomatic Room. Had Nixon listened to his own advice, Ford thought upon hearing the speech that evening, this day may never have come.[2] Even then, though, Ford did not blame Nixon entirely for the downfall, believing that Nixon lieutenants John Ehrlichman and Bob Haldeman, who had helped to set the paranoid tone that pervaded the White House, were just as culpable for his demise.[3]

The Fords greeted the Nixons shortly after their farewell to the staff, and together the two couples walked through the doors to the South Portico and to the green army helicopter that would take the Nixons to Air Force One and on to private life. "Drop us a line if you get a chance. Let us know how you're doing," Ford said as they parted, a request that struck Nixon as odd in its banality, given the circumstances.[4]

Pat Nixon had not slept in forty-eight hours and the strain was evident on her face. "My heavens," she said to Betty Ford, "they've rolled out the red carpet for us. Well, Betty, you'll see many of these red carpets and you'll get so you hate 'em."[5] She climbed the stairs and entered the helicopter followed by Nixon who, arms outstretched skyward, incongruously flashed his trademark victory sign before waving a final goodbye and boarding himself. After her husband boarded, Mrs. Nixon said to no one in particular, "So sad. So sad."[6] At least several of those who watched the helicopter ascend from the immaculate South Lawn grounds didn't think Nixon would last more than a year.

By noon, Gerald Ford was in the East Room somberly reciting the presidential oath of office. There was no pomp and circumstance, no "Hail to the Chief," no jubilant smiles. The seats had been rearranged from Nixon's farewell speech to face another direction, symbolizing a new beginning.[7] Shortly after taking the oath, Ford spoke to the nation. "My fellow Americans," he said. "Our long national nightmare is over."

Ford's speech—"a little straight talk among friends," he called it— struck the right tone for a nation tired of deception from the White House. "Our Constitution works. Our Republic is a government of laws and not men," he reassured Americans. "Here, the people rule." It was as though the sun had finally broken through storm clouds. Jerry Ford seemed open, uncomplicated, comfortable in his own skin—in marked contrast to the man he succeeded. Toward the end of his remarks, he referred to Nixon. "May our former president who brought peace to millions," he said, "find it for himself."

If America's nightmare was over, Nixon's was just beginning. When he returned home to San Clemente, California, the peace Ford had wished for him would prove elusive. And it would continue to elude him for a long time to come.

"One after another," Nixon later wrote of his first weeks out of office, "the blows rained down."[8]

Following Nixon to San Clemente were legal and financial problems—with severe health problems not far behind. Upon arriving home, he confined himself largely to Casa Pacifica, his Spanish-style home on a twenty-nine-acre estate overlooking the Pacific Ocean, and to the Coast Guard station adjacent to the property where the office to the former "Western White House" was located. There he withdrew from the world. As phones rang unanswered and well-wishing friends were politely rebuffed, he languished in self-pity, carping bitterly over former supporters in Congress who had "deserted" him, brooding over whether he had made the right decision in resigning, and wondering what his immediate future would hold.[9] Nothing was certain.

Nixon's diminished staff was now composed of twenty assistants, mostly former White House staffers, including Ron Ziegler, Ray Price, Frank Gannon, Diane Sawyer, Jack Brennan, and Rose Mary Woods. Eighteen Secret Service men were assigned to his detail. All would remain for a six-month "transition" period, after which most would move on. Except for the Nixon family and close friends like Charles "Bebe" Rebozo and Robert Abplanalp, few others would enter through Casa Pacifica's foreboding gates.

The reality of being a disgraced ex-president sunk in immediately. Gone were all of the trappings and inherent respect that came from occupying the office. The insularity of being president offered some protection from the invective directed at him as Watergate unfolded. Now he was alone, vulnerable and irrelevant. That became evident when Nixon called the White House and talked to a former aide who had been loyal to him during his darkest hours as president. Now, caught up in the new administration, he told Nixon, "Those who served you best hate you most."[10]

Hanging over Nixon's head as an "unindicted co-conspirator" of Watergate was the threat of prosecution and jail. As it stood, he was almost certain to be indicted by Leon Jaworski, the White House special prosecutor. He was consumed by the thought of being tried for criminal acts and could think of little else. Occasionally he was stoic about his fate, talking pragmatically about imprisonment, pointing out that Gandhi and Lenin used their time in jail to write and think; he could do the same.[11] But more often he was deep in depression, mentally lethargic, and emotionally spent. The one man who could save Nixon was Ford—as president, he alone had the constitutional power to grant a full, unconditional pardon that would relieve him from legal action.

If Nixon had his way, his successor would have been John Connally, the former Democrat who had been governor of Texas and went on to become Nixon's secretary of the treasury as a Republican. Nixon thought Connally had the stuff to be a good president. Like his mentor Lyndon Johnson, he was brash, self-confident, and decisive. Henry Kissinger recalled that Connally was the one person Nixon had never openly derided.[12] When Nixon's vice president, Spiro Agnew, resigned in 1973 in the wake of a bribery scandal dating back to his tenure as governor of Maryland, he first considered Connally to replace him. But Connally didn't have the widespread support of either the Democrats from whom he had defected or the Republicans he had joined—and he had legal problems of his own. (Connally was implicated in a "milk-price" scandal in Texas but was later acquitted in federal court.)

Nixon had also considered Ronald Reagan and Nelson Rockefeller. Neither was likely to get through the nomination process without a fight in Congress, and it was doubtful that Nixon, already weakened by Watergate, had the political clout to win. Congressional leaders let it be known that their choice to succeed Agnew was one of their own, House minority leader Jerry Ford. Ultimately, Nixon chose the path of least resistance in selecting Ford, but not without reservations. Nixon had known Ford since Ford had arrived in Washington as a freshman congressman in 1948, and while the two had established an easy friendship, Nixon thought Ford lacked the gravitas to ascend to the presidency. "Can you imagine Jerry Ford in this chair?" he asked an aide from his Oval Office desk.[13] After signing the nomination papers, he sent one of the pens he had used to an aide. A note from Nixon accompanying it read, "Here's the damn pen I signed Jerry Ford's nomination with."[14]

Al Haig, Nixon's chief of staff, made Ford aware of a president's power to grant a pardon in a conversation on August 1, just before Nixon's resignation. He suggested that some on Nixon's staff thought Nixon would be inclined to resign if he knew Ford would subsequently grant a pardon. Upon learning of the conversation, Ford's aides were furious at the notion of a deal. The following day, Ford called Haig and read a carefully written response to his statement. "I want you to understand," he said, "that I have no intention of recommending what the President should do about resigning or not resigning, and that nothing we talked about yesterday afternoon should be given any consideration in whatever decision the President may wish to make." Haig agreed. There would be no guarantee of a pardon; Nixon would have to take his chances.[15]

Upon taking office, Ford was forced to face the issue of a pardon head-on. The White House was swept clean of Nixon, but the problems surrounding him lingered. The press and the country were preoccupied with Nixon's fate, and Watergate still hung thick in the air. Ford's position on Nixon was clear: He had suffered enough. Nixon's resignation, he felt, "was an implicit admission of guilt," which in itself was a life sentence. He also worried about Nixon's health. Those close to Nixon felt sure that he would not get through a trial without grave physical and psychological consequences. Members of the administration were particularly worried about Nixon's mental state after hearing reports that he was sending bizarre letters to foreign leaders.[16] Ford's bigger concern, though, was for the country. The prospect of Nixon fighting to stay out of jail would continue to divide the nation and dominate the headlines. Urgent matters, like a foundering economy, needed attention without being overshadowed and subordinated by Watergate. America needed recovery, he thought, not revenge.[17] Ford's aides and friends in Congress advised against the pardon, which was sure to hurt him and the Republican Party. Ford didn't doubt they were right, but he also knew that pardoning Nixon was the right thing to do.[18]

The White House wrangled with Nixon over the statement he would release upon accepting the pardon. Ford discreetly sent Benton Becker, a private criminal attorney and longtime friend, along with Nixon's Washington attorney, Jack Miller, to San Clemente to show Nixon a draft of Ford's statement that would grant the pardon, and to discuss his public response. Ford was sticking his neck out, and wanted some assurance from Nixon that there would be contrition on his part. Benton was also asked to come to terms with Nixon on gaining access to Nixon's tapes and presidential papers for future cases involving Watergate, which Nixon saw as his property, while the government wanted it in its hands.

Becker and Miller met with Ron Ziegler, Nixon's White House press secretary and now the senior member of his staff. The meeting did not go well. Ziegler told Becker that Nixon would not issue any statement regarding Watergate, pardon or no pardon. After Becker threatened to leave, Miller got the two to agree to meet the next day to discuss a statement and sort out the matter of the papers and tapes. After several drafts, they agreed on a short statement in which Nixon expressed deep regret over the mistakes he had made. It was not the "full confession" Ford had sought, but given Nixon's stubbornness and perhaps, denial, the best they could have expected.[19] They also came to an agreement on the papers and tapes: They would go into the hands of the General Services Administration and be stored close to Nixon in Southern California until a legal decision on the matter could be reached. That decision was made in 1997 when the Supreme Court ruled that Nixon, unlike other presidents, could not retain possession of the material since his resignation placed him "in a different class from all other presidents." For thirteen years the case remained in the courts as Nixon's lawyers fought—ultimately in vain—against their release. The National Archives won the right to begin making the papers available to the public in 1987, and soon after secured the same rights to the tapes. (In 1998, lawyers working for the Nixon estate did win a battle to keep the Archives from releasing tapes of private conversations Nixon had had while in office.)

Before heading back to Washington, Becker met briefly with Nixon and was taken aback by what he saw. Nixon was drawn and tired, his clothes were too big for him, his handshake was weak. He looked like a man who had given up. There were no pictures on the walls of his office, no personal touches. He sat behind his desk; an American and presidential flag stood behind him. As Benton stated his purpose for being there, Nixon seemed indifferent. When he learned that his guest came from Washington, he asked how the Redskins were doing; he said little else as Becker explained that the White House saw his acceptance of the pardon an admission of guilt, and cited a legal precedent dating back to the Wilson administration. Becker left after twenty minutes, feeling great pity for the man he had just met. When he returned to Washington, he briefed Ford on his trip, telling him he wondered whether Nixon would be alive by the next election.

"Well," Ford said, "1976 is a long time away."

"I don't mean 1976," Becker responded. "I mean 1974."[20]

On September 8, a quiet Sunday morning, Ford applied his left-handed signature to a "full, free and absolute pardon" that would relieve Nixon of direct legal entanglements and put an end to the Nixon family's "American tragedy in which we have all played a part." Nixon's statement expressed his "regret and pain at the anguish my mistakes over Watergate have caused the nation and the Presidency." The press and public were unmoved and their response was resounding. Ford's approval ratings plummeted from 71 percent to 49 percent, and Nixon was once again the object of scorn.[21]

While the pardon set Nixon free—or at least, allowed him to remain free—it came at a cost. Aside from his resignation, accepting it was the most difficult decision of his life.[22] He had spent the better part of his years campaigning for Republican candidates and causes, but with Watergate and the pardon clouding the political horizon, he believed his parting legacy to the party would be the disastrous state of the GOP. Their showing in the midterm elections of 1974 just two months later confirmed his fears. The Democrats picked up forty seats in the House and four in the Senate. The "Class of '74" would change the face of Congress and bring a whole new breed of congressmen to Washington, who got there largely by campaigning against the Republican establishment epitomized by Nixon.

The pardon also did irreparable damage to Ford; the public opposed it, two to one.[23] His brief honeymoon with the American people was over. The man who toasted his own English muffins in the morning, the antidote to the imperial Nixon, would forever be associated with letting him off the hook. Public sentiment seemed to be summed up in a picket sign Ford spotted at a rally shortly after the pardon. It read NIXON, FORD—SAME OLD SHIT.[24]

During the midst of the fallout, Nixon called the White House and spoke briefly to Ford to express his gratitude for putting himself on the line. "I'm convinced that it was the right decision," Ford replied. "And I think history will prove me right."[25] Then he got off the phone—a little too abruptly, Nixon thought.[26]

Compounding Nixon's anguish was his dire financial situation; he was nearly broke. His lawyers' fees alone would run as much as $500,000, in addition to the $446,000 he owed in back taxes accrued in his first term. There was also a $260,000 "balloon" payment due on Casa Pacifica, and the mortgage owed on his second home in Key Biscayne, Florida.[27] His only cash flow was an annual presidential pension of $60,000, replacing the $200,000 yearly salary he had earned until his resignation, hardly enough to abate the mounting debt.[28] Congress balked at the $850,000 Ford requested for Nixon's transition expenses—almost twice the amount allowed by a law providing for a president's moving expenses after leaving office. The sum was debated in Congress, where once again Richard Nixon aroused controversy. Eventually they arrived at a figure just over $200,000, significantly less than the $375,000 budget allotted to Lyndon Johnson five years earlier.

Nixon's best chance to mitigate his financial situation was by selling his memoirs. Acting as his literary agent was Irving "Swifty" Lazar, the legendary Hollywood agent who represented a number of well-known authors, as well as many of Hollywood's elite. Lazar, who boasted that Nixon's would be one of the "greatest stories of all time," claimed he could fetch over two million dollars for the book—as long as Watergate was dealt with at length.[29]

In late September, Lazar got a buyer. Warner Books was willing to put up $2.5 million for Nixon's story and the chance to publish the inside account of Watergate from the man it brought down.[30] Revisiting his presidency so soon after leaving office, and having to delve deeply into the mud of Watergate, would be daunting and painful, but it was not an offer Nixon could refuse.

If, as Nixon believed, one's mental and physical states are directly related, what came less than a week after accepting the pardon was more than just a chance development.[31] In the midfifties while serving as vice president under

Eisenhower, Nixon had developed a mild case of phlebitis, a vein inflammation often resulting in blood clots in the legs. Two decades later, in the summer of 1974, the condition recurred shortly before a scheduled trip to the Middle East. At the time the swelling and acute pain were relieved by hot and cold compresses, and the problem was forgotten in the ensuing days leading up to the resignation. Now, however, the symptoms were back, and Nixon's doctor expressed concern that the clots in his legs would become lethal by breaking apart and spreading to his lungs. He advised immediate hospitalization. Nixon balked. "If I go into the hospital," he told the doctor, "I'll never come out alive."[32] After a week of medicine failed to relieve the problem, he finally relented.

He entered Long Beach Hospital for twelve uneventful days, sleeping very little and vowing never to go to a hospital again. When he was released, he dutifully followed his doctor's prescribed regimen of anticoagulant drugs and limited exercise, but five weeks later, when his doctor discovered the problem had recurred, he was back in the hospital. This time the clot was serious enough to warrant immediate surgery. A little before dawn on October 24, 1974, doctors inserted a plastic clip into his left leg designed to prevent the clot from fatally spreading to his lungs. The operation was successful, but shortly afterward complications arose. At 12:45 that afternoon, he was back in the operating room bleeding internally and in shock. As he hovered near death, his blood pressure plunging as low as sixty over zero, an intensive care unit fought to bring him back. A nurse slapped his face in a desperate attempt to revive him. "Richard," Nixon could hear her call. "Pull yourself back." Three hours later, he came out alive. Now, he had consciously decided on the operating table, was not the time to die.[33]

For the next several days, with his wife and daughters by his side, he slowly stabilized and the bleeding stopped. Three days later, he received his first visitor outside of family. Gerald Ford had debated making the trip. If he did, he would be linked with Nixon anew; if not, it might have been construed as a cruel snub. In the end, decency prevailed. Ford called Pat Nixon to see if a visit would help. "I can't think of anything that would do him more good," she said.[34]

In the midst of a California campaign swing, Ford arrived at Long Beach Hospital's room 706. When he turned the knob to enter, he found the door was jammed shut. For five tense minutes, he waited as attendants pried the door open, wondering what would happen if Nixon's condition suddenly took a turn for the worse. When the door was finally opened, he entered the room and saw Nixon for the first time since he had left the White House. Nixon's condition took him by surprise. "I had never seen so many tubes, or anyone in such condition," Ford recalled. Nixon was propped up on pillows, looking very much like a man who had nearly died; Ford wondered if this was the last time he would see Nixon alive.[35] For five minutes they talked, mostly about foreign policy, before Ford patted his hand. "Be well," he said, and left his predecessor to his recovery.[36]

Shortly after returning to Casa Pacifica to convalesce, Nixon summoned his White House communications director, Kenneth Clawson, a loyalist who had seen him through his last days in power in Washington. Clawson found his former boss bitter and reflective. "They'll never give us credit," Nixon said, his ailing left leg raised on his office desk. "Even now they try to stomp us, you know, kick us when we're down. They'll never let up, never, because we were the first threat to them in years. And, by God, we would have changed it all, changed it so they couldn't have changed it back in a hundred years, if only. . . ."[37]

He continued, "What starts the process really, are the laughs, the slights, and the snubs when you are a kid . . . But if you are reasonably intelligent and if your anger is deep enough and strong enough, you learn you can change those attitudes by excellence, personal gut performance, while those who have anything are sitting on their fat butts . . . So you are lean and mean and resourceful, and you continue to walk on the edge of the precipice because over the years you have become fascinated by how close to the edge you can walk without losing your balance. This time there was a difference. This time we had something to lose."[38]

Nixon's spectacular downfall had been precipitated by his battle of Us versus Them—political enemies, the press, the Eastern establishment, the liberals and other anti-Nixon forces as he saw them—but even then it was being waged with a vengeance.

By the end of 1974, Pat Nixon, in a letter to Julie, described herself and her husband as "two broken people."[39] While Nixon's health slowly improved, there were constant reminders of his political demise. The Watergate grand jury disbanded in December after handing down sentences to those caught up in the wrong side of the scandal. The new year had barely begun when Nixon, a rabid football fan, learned in a news update during the Rose Bowl that three of his top White House lieutenants, John Mitchell, Bob Haldeman, and John Ehrlichman, had received prison terms of two and a half to eight years. This may have been the moment when he hit rock bottom.[40]

While mental anguish may have brought on Nixon's illness and depression, mental toughness and tenacity brought him back. He had always prided himself on not being a quitter, and throughout his political career—with the exception of the resignation—he had proven it. He had faced more than his share of setbacks and defeats that could have ended his political career. There was the "Fund Crisis" of 1952, when allegations that friends of his had formed an illegal slush fund for his benefit threatened his position on the Republican ticket as Eisenhower's running mate. Then there was his narrow defeat against Kennedy in the presidential election of 1960, and his decisive loss in the California gubernatorial election two years later. Through extraordinary resolve and self-discipline, he always came back. He gave the famous "Checkers" speech that won the favor of the American people and got him back on the Republican ticket—and led to two terms as vice president. He conceded defeat gracefully after losing to Kennedy. And after being humiliated in the gubernatorial election and giving his "last press conference," he made his way back to become the thirty-seventh president in 1968. In just six years, he had emerged from the wilderness to win the ultimate political victory.

As he would later recount in his book, *In the Arena: A Memoir of Victory, Defeat, and Renewal*, he learned three valuable things during those years of tribulation: Never give up. Get perspective on your weaknesses and learn how to get beyond them. And tap into strength you never knew you had until you found yourself dealing with adversity.[41]

As a devout student of history, he was also secure in the knowledge that many great leaders had spent time in the wilderness before him and had come back to fulfill their destinies and rise to greatness. In particular, he drew inspiration from two men he had known in his own political career: Winston Churchill and Charles de Gaulle. Both had been on the outs politically before being summoned back into public service to lead their nations out of crisis.

Surviving his own hardships and knowing of great leaders who had done the same may have provided some comfort to Nixon in 1974, but as he later noted, "residing in the deepest valley is far different from passing through the wilderness. There was no precedent for what faced me in the 1970s. No one had ever been so high and fallen so low. No one had ever resigned the presidency."[42]

There was also another difference. When he had suffered defeat before, he had always had something to live for that was greater than himself: the prospect of another shot at a prized political office, and the chance to lead the nation. This time the only thing at stake was his own survival.[43]

But there were signs that he would get through this crisis too, even in the first weeks after returning to private life. He stuck rigidly, perhaps instinctively, to presidential routines, rising every morning at six o'clock, dressing in business attire, and adhering to a schedule that noted his availability or unavailability. He demanded formal briefings from his aides, who generated summaries and memos for his review, even if it was on the upcoming football season.[44] And there was another positive sign: Just two weeks after leaving Washington, he began asking them for strategies on how he would restore his position in public life.[45]

His wife and daughters also helped sustain him. "Dick, I don't know how you keep going," his wife said to him when things were at their worst. "I get up in the morning just to confound my enemies," he responded.[46] Without her, Tricia, and Julie, he may not have gotten up at all. As a friend later recalled, when things were at their worst, "he found enormous solace in his family, and it changed his perspective."[47]

Like her husband, Pat Nixon also came from hardscrabble Southern California beginnings, and she faced life's travails with her own toughness and resolve, which helped bolster Nixon during the most difficult of times. The twenty-six-year-old Nixon met Patricia Ryan, one year his senior, when both were acting in a community theater production of *The Dark Tower* in 1939, just after he had returned to Whittier, California, from law school at Duke University. "You shouldn't say that," he told her when she cited a busy schedule after he had asked her out for a date, "because someday I'm going to marry you."[48] They laughed and eventually she gave in. They courted for two years, Nixon sometimes driving her to dates with other suitors, before marrying in 1941. Tricia was born in 1946, followed by Julie in 1948.

Six years into their marriage, Nixon won a seat in Congress and quickly moved up the ranks of the Republican Party, becoming a senator in 1950 and vice president just two years later at the age of thirty-nine. Though Mrs. Nixon was initially excited about a political career for her husband, it did not last long. Nonetheless, she supported his ambitions and stoically endured the scrutiny and false smiles of public life. After his defeat in the 1960 presidential election, she had had enough and asked for Nixon's promise to bow out of politics. But just over a year later he was back in the arena, running unsuccessfully for governor and eventually winning the presidency. Life in the fishbowl atmosphere of the White House did not suit her, but she gracefully fulfilled her duties as first lady with quiet dignity.

The Nixons' marriage often appeared awkward and strained. Never demonstrative, Nixon often humiliated her by his remoteness. One of the only times the public saw the tenderness between a husband and wife was when the Nixons danced at Tricia's White House wedding in 1972. Even privately he kept his distance. At Nixon's behest, it was his secretary, Rose Mary Woods, who informed the first lady of her husband's intention to resign the presidency. When the president told several members of the congressional leadership of his decision in an Oval Office meeting, he tried to put on a brave face. "I have a supportive family," he said, "and a pretty good wife." Nixon's guests looked at each other quizzically over the comment.[49]

Yet they remained committed to each other, held together by the mysterious bonds of marriage and family. When they returned to San Clemente, Mrs. Nixon tried to ease the transition for Nixon as much as possible through small gestures. The day they left the White House, she had packed up the pictures and trinkets in his office and carefully rearranged them in his office at Casa Pacifica. After he took ill, she rarely left the side of his hospital bed. "When he was defeated," Julie wrote, "Mother upheld him." If he had taken her for granted before, he now sought refuge in her strength.[50]

Tricia and Julie staunchly supported "Daddy" at every turn, urging him to fight for his presidency even when Ed and David thought it was a lost cause and impeachment was inevitable. When their parents returned home to San Clemente, the two rallied around them, frequently leaving their East Coast homes to be with them for long stretches, especially when illness struck.

Nixon spent the next several years building himself back up. In early 1975, the White House asked Nixon to dispense some much-needed political advice to Ford in his bid to win the office he currently held under the provisions of the 25th Amendment. It was Ford's first national election; his campaign experience to that point had been limited to Michigan's fifth congressional district. Through the White House liaison to former presidents, Nixon secretly passed on suggestions to the president under the code-name "The Wizard." Though the Ford team remained receptive to his guidance, Nixon grew frustrated by Ford's lackluster campaign performance. Well before the election, he had scribbled the names of the fifty states on a yellow legal pad with predictions on whether the state would fall to Ford or his Democratic challenger, Jimmy Carter. In November, the Wizard's predictions—without exception—rang true.[51] Carter eked out a 2 percent margin of victory and won the White House. The pardon played a significant role in the election's outcome; 7 percent of voters said it was the reason they did not vote for the incumbent.

The year before Ford's defeat, Nixon told the president he would keep himself out of the public eye. It was not a promise he would keep. In February of 1976, President and Mrs. Nixon returned to the scene of his foreign policy triumph, accepting an invitation from Chairman Mao Tse-tung to visit China. The trip would mark the fourth anniversary of the historic reopening of U.S.-Chinese relations. Nixon received the invitation two months after it was extended by Mao to Julie and David during their own excursion to China, and Nixon readily accepted without informing the White House. When word got back to the president of Nixon's impending trip, Ford and his aides seethed. Ford was battling for the Republican presidential nomination against an insurgent Ronald Reagan, the former governor of California, who was gaining ground among the party faithful. Nixon would arrive in China just two days before the all-important New

Hampshire primary, guaranteeing that Nixon—and reminders of the pardon—would appear in the headlines. In an attempt to mollify the White House, Nixon told Henry Kissinger, Nixon's and now Ford's secretary of state, that the Chinese had extended the invitation just thirty-six hours before the trip. Kissinger would have none of it. "The Chinese don't do business that way," he assured Ford.[52]

The Nixons, with eighteen aides and twelve American journalists in tow, spent just over a week in China. While the constant scrutiny of the press spoiled the trip for Mrs. Nixon, Nixon himself reveled in being back on the international stage, talking with government leaders about the issues affecting their two countries, and greeting the tens of thousands of Chinese who welcomed him throughout his travels. Back in the U.S. Ford went on to win in New Hampshire—just barely—securing 49 percent of the vote and edging out Reagan by a single percentage point.

That summer Nixon was back in the news, but not by choice. Bob Woodward and Carl Bernstein, the *Washington Post* reporters who broke the Watergate story and followed it through to Nixon's resignation, had published *The Final Days*, which chronicled Nixon's last harrowing weeks in office. It presented a portrait of a psychologically unbalanced and possibly suicidal president who soliloquized to the paintings of the presidents in the White House corridors in drunken, late-night wanderings. Its worst allegation, however, may have been that the Nixons' marriage was loveless and that they had not been intimate since the early sixties.

Among the many who read the book was Pat Nixon who, against her husband's wishes, borrowed a copy from one of his secretaries. While reading it she suffered a stroke that landed her in Long Beach Memorial Hospital the next day. She was released after just over a week, but her left arm and leg and the left side of her face would remain partially paralyzed for the next year, a painful reminder of the toll the savage press had taken.[53]

The following summer, Nixon gave his own version of the events surrounding Watergate. David Frost, the flamboyant British talk-show host, had offered Nixon $600,000 and 20 percent of net profits for a series of interviews that would be televised in the U.S.[54] Nixon and Frost had prepared for the sessions like prizefighters going for a shot at the title, determined to outmaneuver each other in "intellectual combat," but when Nixon arrived at the first taping he threw the first jab, disarming his host by asking, "So, did you do any fornicating this weekend?"[55] Twenty-six hours of prodding by Frost was edited down to four ninety-minute prime-time specials on Nixon's life and presidency. Fifty million viewers tuned in to the first special, which dealt exclusively with Watergate. For many, Nixon was more forthcoming than expected, admitting, "[I] let the American people down and I have to carry that burden for the rest of my life. I brought myself down." But, as always, the contrition was tainted by self-pity and intimations that his foes played a major role in his downfall. Of course, he himself didn't subscribe to the notion that his enemies were out to get him, but others had told him "there was a conspiracy." Alluding to the unnamed conspirators, he conceded, "I gave 'em the sword and they stuck it in and they twisted it with relish. And, I guess that if I'd been in their position, I'd have done the same thing." Still, he maintained he had committed no crime or impeachable offense, insisting that "when the president does it, that means it's not illegal."[56]

Viewers, for the most part, didn't buy it. As an ABC/Harris poll conducted after the first show revealed, 74 percent believed Nixon knew he had obstructed justice, and 58 percent said they felt no more sympathy for him than before the broadcast.[57]

The ratings of the remaining three specials steadily eroded, but afforded Nixon some auspicious moments. In particular, he shined when holding forth on international affairs and the leaders with whom he had shared the international stage while in office. With the exception of Stalin, Nixon had known and dealt with all the major postwar leaders—Churchill, de Gaulle, Mao, Chou En-lai, Nikita Khrushchev, and every American president since Truman. When talking about them, he was relaxed and self-assured; his eyes brightened and his speech cleared. Nixon was the only living person with that kind of experience, and when he talked about it he looked downright presidential.

Nixon's memoirs provided another chance to directly address Watergate. The project became a painstaking process that took three and a half years to bring to completion. Writing itself was hard enough—Nixon referred to his first book, *Six Crises*, as his "seventh crisis"—but revisiting Watergate again so soon after his resignation would prove doubly difficult. Frank Gannon, Ken Khachigian, and Diane Sawyer conducted the hours of research necessary for a presidential memoir. Sawyer took on the task of learning all the intricacies of the Watergate affair. It often proved a sticky situation with Nixon, who dictated to her on the subject as she grilled him for more. Sometimes, tired of the interrogation, he would retreat for several days before returning as though nothing had happened.[58]

But looking back wasn't all bad. He enjoyed recounting his foreign policy accomplishments. To ensure accuracy he called Brent Scowcroft, who had served as military advisor in his administration, and invited him to San Clemente to review the book's foreign policy content. Scowcroft's week-long visit allowed Nixon to hold forth on foreign policy for hours on end, an opportunity he relished. Scowcroft pored over Nixon's manuscript, correcting some of the foreign policy passages that weren't consistent with his memory of events. When he brought several of the erroneous passages to Nixon, Nixon told him they were correct, as they were consistent with the diaries he kept as president, material he relied on for the book but didn't allow Scowcroft to read. Eventually Scowcroft came to the conclusion that the president's chronicle was a "Walter Mitty diary" of sorts, in which Nixon recorded things he wished had happened but that didn't necessarily reflect the whole truth.[59]

Despite the pain of having to revisit Watergate, Nixon came to see the project as a catharsis. In addition to forcing him to engage mentally, it gave him a chance to understand and come to terms with everything that led up to his resignation—and to begin to put it behind him.[60]

Though critics panned it, *RN: The Memoirs of Richard Nixon*, was an instant best-seller, selling 330,000 copies in the first six months. By Nixon's count, almost one-third of its 1,106 pages were devoted to Watergate, a decision he would later regret as being dramatically out of proportion with the events and accomplishments in his life that he felt were of equal or greater significance.[61] But for all its coverage, Nixon once again fell far short of admitting full culpability for the scandal, or of granting the apology that many thought they deserved.

As difficult as they may have been for Nixon, the memoirs and the Frost interviews were important because they unburdened him of the debt he had accrued since the early 1970s. He paid off his legal fees, back taxes, and mortgages, and had enough left over to achieve some measure of financial security.[62]

Shortly after his illness, Nixon sought physical rehabilitation through an unlikely outlet: golf. Before becoming vice president, he had tried his hand at the sport a handful of times, yielding less than spectacular results. After becoming vice president, he used it as a means of getting closer to the boss. Ike was an ardent duffer, though his outings with the hapless Nixon proved frustrating for both. Golf suited neither Nixon's lack of physical grace nor his temperament. He saw it as a frivolous waste of time. Now, in need of exercise—and perhaps a diversion—he threw himself into the game with characteristic self-discipline and intensity. With his administrative assistant Jack Brennan as his tutor, he made strides to break 100, and, playing twice a week or so, gradually brought his scores down.

By 1978, he had broken 90, a respectable achievement particularly for one of limited athletic ability, but as with many ambitious golfers, his goal was to break 80. That year, on an "easy" course in San Clemente, he claimed to have scored a 79. After the triumph, he rarely picked up his golf clubs again and gave them away several years later. There were now, as before, more important things to do.

Later that year, Richard Nixon took the first steps on his remarkable comeback trail. He had survived the resignation, the pardon, financial ruin, and near death. What's more, he had addressed the misdeeds of Watergate in the living rooms of America through the Frost interviews and in "cold print" in the memoirs.[63] A new administration was in place, supplanting the remaining Nixon holdovers on Ford's team, and with it a new political breeze blew through America. It was time to move on.

In mid-January, he returned to Washington for the first time since his resignation, attending the funeral of his rival for the White House in 1968, former vice president Hubert Humphrey. A light snow fell as he landed by commercial airline at Dulles International Airport. He evaded the reporters, cameramen, and a handful of picketers who awaited his arrival, slipping into a car that took him to a friend's house in Virginia.[64] The following day, looking disheveled and uncomfortable, with Tricia on his arm, he entered a reception in the Senate office of Howard Baker, the Senate minority leader from Tennessee, where many of Washington's elite—past and present—had congregated. "Nobody would get near him," Baker recalled. "Everybody was afraid of him."[65] Nixon quickly retreated to the corner of the room. It was Jerry Ford who broke the ice, affably greeting Nixon as "Mr. President." Kissinger and Nelson Rockefeller soon joined their conversation before the sitting president, Jimmy Carter, approached, shook Nixon's hand, and welcomed him.

After his historic handshake with Chou En-Lai upon landing in Beijing to "open" China in 1972, Chou told Nixon, "Your handshake came over the vastest ocean in the world—twenty-five years of isolation."[66] Nixon's handshake with Carter was far less significant but no less symbolic. After three and a half years in exile across the continent, it represented an easing of tension and an opening for Nixon to make his way back into the Washington mainstream. It marked a new beginning.

That same month, when he turned sixty-five, Nixon resolved to rededicate himself "to the causes that had always inspired my actions."[67] He would strive to once again make a difference in foreign policy. His new sense of purpose was summed up in a speech he made to students at Oxford University the following November. Speaking without notes, he shared his views on geopolitics for ten minutes before taking questions from the audience. One student asked what he planned to do with the rest of his life. "So long as there is breath in my body," he responded, "I am going to talk about the great issues that affect the world. I am not going to keep my mouth shut. I am going to speak for peace and freedom."[68] Quite unexpectedly, he left the room to a standing ovation.

By the beginning of the new decade, and after five and a half years behind the gates of Casa Pacifica, the Nixons were ready to trade sedate Southern California for a new life in New York. They sold "the Western White House" and bought a three-story brick townhouse on East 65th Street near Lexington Avenue, for $750,000. It was a calculated move that put Nixon directly in the center of American culture, media, business, and political thought, and "closer to the people and the whole public arena." Besides, he reasoned, "any town that would support the Mets is for an underdog."[69]

Now more active after her stroke, Mrs. Nixon was also eager to escape California for a new life. "We're just dying here slowly," she told Julie. In New York she could roam about more freely despite her celebrity, and she and her husband could readily play "Ma" and "Pa" to their nearby grandchildren. Tricia and Ed lived just blocks away with their son, Christopher, and Julie and David and their daughter, Jennie, were on Philadelphia's Main Line, two and a half hours south of New York.[70] (By the late eighties, Julie and David would give the Nixons two additional grandchildren, Alex Richard and Melanie.) Nixon, who seemed to relish his role as a doting grandfather, observed that Mrs. Nixon's priority was her grandchildren, and "after that, there are no priorities."[71]

Suddenly, Nixon was a fixture in the city. Undeterred by the "recognition factor," he took brisk, early-morning walks, a Secret Service man trailing behind him, shaking hands and talking with the proprietors opening their coffee shops and newsstands, and waving to taxi drivers. Afterward—seven days a week when he was in town—the Secret Service would drive him downtown to his fifteen-room office complex in a nondescript federal building on Foley Square, near City Hall. There, assisted by a staff of six, he would tend to his mail, make phone calls, autograph his books and pictures, toil on his newest book, and receive select visitors. He would usually be back uptown for dinner with Mrs. Nixon by six and in bed by ten.[72]

The move galvanized Nixon's social life. While he shunned the "trendies, sophisticates, beautiful people, and Henry [Kissinger]'s crowd," he often saw old friends and associates who lived nearby, his former law partners, Robert Abplanalp, Alexander Haig, and Kissinger himself, whom he breakfasted with several times a week.[73] Every other week or so, he would host a dinner, usually stag affairs featuring free-flowing French wine, exquisite Chinese cuisine, and off-the-record—and often ribald—conversations. The guests, all Nixon-friendly, depended on the evening's topic. Alan Greenspan would be among those selected to discuss the economy, or Richard Holbrooke would be invited when the issue was the Soviet Union. There were even a few members of the press who received invitations. He sought out journalists he thought might eventually offer more broad-minded evaluations of his presidency. And he was keen on courting a dozen or so younger members of the media who were beginning to make their marks.

After a little over a year of running on "the fastest track in the world," as Nixon called New York, the Nixons moved to Saddle River, New Jersey, a tranquil bedroom community where they could be close to the glow of

Manhattan without being subjected to its relentless pace.[74] The Nixons would spend their remaining years in suburban New Jersey, in their home in Saddle River, where they lived until 1988, and in their final home in neighboring Park Ridge.

Sitting presidents are measured by the power they wield. Former presidents are gauged by their legacies and the influence they have out of office. Nixon spent his last years zealously cultivating both. He believed twentieth-century presidents would be remembered primarily by the boldness and effectiveness of their foreign policy and, if his presidency was evaluated evenly and fairly, he belonged in the pantheon of the presidential greats: Washington, Jefferson, Lincoln, Theodore Roosevelt, Wilson, and Franklin Roosevelt. If Watergate was put in its proper perspective, he felt, historians would see it that way too.[75]

But when told that he would be remembered favorably, he would often reply, "That depends on who writes the history."[76] If he trusted history, he did not trust the left-leaning historians who often penned it. Churchill once said, "I know history will be kind to me, for I shall write it." Nixon did much the same thing. While writing came no easier than it had with earlier literary endeavors, he was enormously prolific. From 1979 to 1992, he wrote nine books that served up his views on foreign policy while burnishing his own accomplishments as president. They were: *Real War; Leaders; Real Peace: A Strategy for the West; No More Vietnams; 1999: Victory Without War; In the Arena: A Memoir of Victory, Defeat, and Renewal; Seize the Moment: America's Challenge in a One-Superpower World; Six Crises;* and *Beyond Peace.* Most quickly became best-sellers, and while critics recognized his self-serving tactics, they also had to concede that he had a firm grasp of the matters at hand.

As acceptance of Nixon's views grew, so did his influence. Shortly after Nixon's arrival back on the East Coast, Ronald Reagan became president, creating an opportunity for Nixon to provide advice to a like-minded Republican. Reagan often telephoned, seeking his counsel on political and global issues. "As far as this White House is concerned," a senior aide to Reagan said shortly after Reagan's second term, "[Nixon's] rehabilitation is complete. There is tremendous respect for him around here."[77] Nixon's offers to help were often unsolicited. Staff members could expect lengthy memos from him when he had a view to share. When Don Regan became a liability to the administration as Reagan's chief of staff, incurring the ire of Nancy Reagan among many, Nixon offered Mrs. Reagan his services to give Regan a push out the White House door.[78]

Nixon liked and respected Reagan and felt, in many ways, responsible for his rise in American politics.[79] He had supported Reagan early on, and in turn, Reagan had cast his first Republican vote for Nixon in 1960, after having campaigned for Nixon as a Democrat. Reagan was one of the few who didn't turn his back on Nixon after Watergate.

After the assassination of Egyptian president Anwar Sadat in 1981, Reagan made sure that Nixon was included in the delegation of former presidents sent to Cairo to represent the U.S. at Sadat's funeral after it was deemed too dangerous for Reagan or Vice President George Bush to attend.[80] Nixon boarded Air Force One along with Gerald Ford and Jimmy Carter, in his first official act since leaving the White House. After his fall from power seven long years before, he was back where it counted, and he took nothing for granted. Aided by a martini or two, Nixon reached out to Ford and Carter and many other VIPs on board the flight. Carter recalled that Nixon "made a great hit," and was himself taken aback by Nixon's "courtesy, eloquence and charm."[81] Kissinger, another member of the delegation, was glad to see Nixon applying the right touch. But as Kissinger would soon discover, he was still the same old Nixon.

Just prior to boarding the flight, Haig, who was heading the delegation as Reagan's secretary of state, had received a cable from the U.S. Embassy in Jidda, Saudi Arabia, inquiring about hosting a dinner for Nixon. They knew that Nixon had planned some sort of a visit after the funeral, but not from the State Department. Haig, as it turned out, knew nothing about it—nor did the White House. Eventually, he wandered back toward the rear of the plane to see if Kissinger knew of Nixon's plans. No, Kissinger told him, but he would quietly ask Nixon about it. When he did, Nixon responded by throwing his hands up in uncertainty. Invitations had been extended, he said, but nothing was definite.[82] It was vintage Nixon, as Kissinger knew all too well, reminiscent of when he had discovered that Nixon would visit China as Ford faced the challenge from Reagan in the 1976 New Hampshire primary.

Nixon did indeed go on to Saudi Arabia, before traveling to other countries across the Middle East and in North Africa to meet with leaders throughout the regions. "To the dismay of some, and the delight of a few," *Time* magazine reported, "Richard Nixon was back in the headlines." Nixon's controversial past got nary a mention. As for the secrecy surrounding the trip—itself controversial—Nixon dismissed it entirely; his mission was more important than that. "We've heard it for years," he told *Time*'s Hugh Sidey, "'the cradle of civilization will be its grave.' Well, now the threat is true."[83] By reaching out to Arab leaders, Nixon was doing what he thought right in containing the threat. Importantly, Nixon's views on the world were being heard, as the press reported not only on his travels but also on his perspectives as well.

Throughout the eighties and nineties, Nixon traveled extensively, visiting the Soviet Union, Eastern and Western Europe, China, Japan, and Southeast Asia. And as he had done after his trip to the Middle East and North Africa, he came to his own conclusions about the nations he saw and their strategic considerations for the U.S. His itineraries were filled with visits to past and present heads of state and government officials, many of whom had never understood his fall from grace. He also spent time touring, walking the markets and bazaars, and meeting ordinary citizens. Upon his return home he would organize the thoughts strewn on yellow legal pads into one more in a series of memos, often unsolicited, to the State Department. In effect, he never stopped being president.[84]

While representing the U.S. with Ford and Carter showed the world that Nixon was indeed a legitimate former president, he did not always appreciate being accorded the same status as his peers. When it came to foreign policy, he felt he was in another league, and hated the notion of being grouped with the others.[85] Prior to a summit with Soviet premier Mikhail Gorbachev, Reagan considered convening Nixon, Ford, and Carter to discuss strategy. After learning of Ford's and Carter's availabilities, Nixon gave the White House a date neither could make, and Reagan soon abandoned the idea.[86]

He distanced himself from other former presidents in other ways, too, refusing to sit on corporate boards or accept honorariums for speeches as the others commonly did, and chiding Ford in particular for "selling the office"—a bit hypocritical given Nixon's own acceptance of money for the

Frost interviews.[87] Nixon claimed that not accepting honorariums allowed him to be more selective about speaking engagements and to speak freely without restrictions. Additionally, in 1985 he gave up his Secret Service security detail, saving taxpayers, he was quick to point out, over $3 million a year.[88]

In April 1986, Nixon achieved one more milestone on his long road to rehabilitation, accepting an invitation to be the keynote speaker at an annual Associated Press luncheon for the American Newspaper Publishers Association in San Francisco, attended by many of the publishers, editors, and writers who had helped precipitate his downfall a dozen years earlier. His speech, which presented a case for American aid for the Contras, delivered a familiar Nixon theme in his post-presidency: "that without the United States playing a responsible role on the international stage, peace and freedom will not survive in the world." His remarks were devoid of bitterness and self-pity, and his only allusion to his past was his reference to "my well-deserved reputation for being controversial."[89] At its close, he drew a standing ovation from an unlikely audience. Just as improbable was the sight of Nixon laughing and ostensibly burying the hatchet with Katharine Graham, the CEO and matriarch of *The Washington Post*, the paper most associated with the reporting of Watergate. After previous incarnations and reinventions during Nixon's long and evolving career, the press proclaimed a "New Nixon," or a "*New*, New Nixon." Here, then, was a "New Nixon" altogether.

Behind the scenes, though, Nixon neither forgave nor forgot. He was the same old Nixon. The anger he spoke about to Kenneth Clawson during his illness in San Clemente was embedded in his character. Eight years after his appearance at the conference, Henry Kissinger held a seventieth birthday party for himself and invited Nixon—and Katharine Graham. Nixon responded with scorn toward both Kissinger and Graham. "Imagine the nerve of [Kissinger inviting her]," he told an aide. "I will not sit in a room with her. I'm a pretty forgiving person, but not when it comes to that crowd."[90]

But the public often saw a carefully crafted image of a benign septuagenarian. This Nixon opened his suburban home to neighborhood trick-or-treaters on Halloween, and took his grandchildren to the circus. He basked in the attention of the public, signing as many as fifty autographs at a single Yankees game, and smiling for pictures. Only rarely was he faced with an unpleasant encounter, though he would occasionally be greeted with a look of surprise as if to suggest he had "risen from the dead."[91]

The headline on the cover of *Newsweek*'s May 19, 1986, issue featured a photo of a smiling Richard Nixon and the headline HE'S BACK! The article contended that Nixon, the "Sage of Saddle River," was "expanding his influence on the White House and Republican Party." In it, John Dean, a former aide who had been among those convicted in the wake of Watergate, said bitterly, "He's running for the office of ex-president—and he's won."[92] If Nixon's comeback was not obvious up to that point, it was now as plain as the unmistakable face on newsstands across America. That same year, Nixon arbitrated a strike among Major League Baseball umpires, ensuring that America's pastime would continue uninterrupted, and further contributing to the softening of his image. In the election of 1988, when Dan Quayle, the callow vice-presidential candidate, debated his heavyweight challenger Lloyd Bentsen, he was asked to identify any work of literature or art of the past two years that had had a "particularly strong effect" on him. Quayle was quick to identify Nixon's book on arms control strategy with the Soviets, *1999: Victory Without War*. Though Bentsen would score an easy knockout against his weaker opponent, invoking Nixon's name and his foreign policy tome only helped Quayle's cause.

For his part, Nixon denied making a conscious attempt at a comeback. In an appearance on NBC's *Meet the Press* in 1988, he said, "What am I coming back to? We already have a good mayor in Saddle River, and we have a very good governor in New Jersey. It isn't a comeback. The purpose is to get a message across and let history judge."[93] But there was little doubt that his moves in getting his message across for the sake of history had been meticulously plotted.

Though Nixon strode admirably toward respectability, the issue of Watergate never completely went away. When interviewed by a former aide, Frank Gannon, in 1984, and asked—not for the first time, or the last—whether he would apologize for the Watergate ordeal, he was adamant. "There's no way you can apologize that is more eloquent, more decisive, more finite, or to say that you are sorry, which would exceed resigning the presidency of the United States," he said. "That said it all. And I don't intend to say anymore."[94] He never went further than that.

One important detail that remained to be worked out in his post-presidency was the building of the requisite presidential library that would enshrine the ambiguous Nixon legacy. Ford and Carter had already erected theirs by the mideighties, but Nixon's had conspicuously yet to materialize. He had approached his law school alma mater, Duke University, as the site of his library, but Duke had rejected the offer. Eventually, he decided on Yorba Linda, California, just twenty miles east of Los Angeles, beside the small white farmhouse his father had built from a Sears and Roebuck kit, and in which Nixon had come into the world. Going his own way again, he obtained the $21 million necessary to fund and operate the library through private sources, making his the only presidential library with no government-funded support. Nixon was still at odds with the government anyway, successfully preventing the release of some 150,000 pages of documents relating to his controversial presidency. The 5,500-square-foot building would contain all of Nixon's congressional and vice-presidential papers, while his presidential papers would remain in legal limbo in a Virginia government warehouse until the 1997 Supreme Court ruling.

Nixon controlled the contents of the library's museum as well, providing visitors with a carefully sanitized glimpse of his life and term in office. Though the exhibits did not exclude Watergate altogether—the curious could listen to three segments of the infamous "smoking gun" tapes—they struck more of the balance Nixon sought in the evaluation of his political career. Dismissing the idea of an Oval Office replica that stands at the center of all the modern presidential museums, Nixon instead re-created the second-floor White House study, where he did much of his writing and thinking. The most impressive room featured life-sized bronze statues of ten world leaders Nixon did business with; De Gaulle, Churchill, Mao, Conrad Adenauer, and others were scattered about as if rubbing elbows at an exclusive UN cocktail party. *Time* essayist Lance Morrow likened it to Nixon "trying to hurry history's judgment by dressing the set with giants, setting the timer, and hurrying to get into the picture himself."[95]

The dedication of the Richard Nixon Library and Birthplace was in keeping with the guarded nature of the place itself. Gerald Ford, Ronald Reagan, President George Bush, and their wives helped the Nixons celebrate its opening on a hot summer day in July 1990. (Jimmy Carter, traveling in an undisclosed country in Africa, sent a note and his regrets, much to Nixon's ire.)[96] The presidential VIPs toured the one-story pink sandstone compound and Nixon's childhood home as a marching band played John Philip Sousa selections and balloons were launched into a cloudless sky. Then they lauded Nixon's accomplishments before a crowd of some 35,000. Only President Bush made brief mention of Watergate as one of the events in the grand sweep of Nixon's career.

By the new decade, the forest of the Nixon administration was beginning to emerge from the trees. But even with the benefit of distance and perspective, historians saw the events surrounding Nixon's resignation as the dominant event in his tenure, dwarfing the opening of China, détente with the Soviets, strides toward peace in the Middle East, and other Nixon achievements. The results of a survey conducted with almost five hundred history professors ranked Nixon in the bottom quintile of American presidents, with such failures as Warren Harding, Ulysses S. Grant, James Buchanan, and Andrew Johnson. In academic terms, Nixon had flunked the presidency.[97]

As always, though, he kept going. He spent the next several years vigorously campaigning for foreign policy initiatives—increased financial aid to Russia in the wake of the collapse of the Soviet Union, and granting China "Most Favored Nation" trading status chief among them—with the unrelenting hope of influencing the last two presidents he would know.

As president, Nixon had appointed George Bush as the chairman of the Republican Committee, contributing to a Bush résumé that rivaled any of his contemporaries, and strongly considered him as his vice-presidential appointee after Agnew's resignation. But he had reservations about Bush's skills as a campaigner, abilities he considered absolutely essential to true leadership, and was wary of his upper-crust Ivy League background, a function of Nixon's own insecurity. Though he and Bush had a cordial relationship, evident in several White House invitations extended by Bush, he felt Bush kept him at arm's length, seldom seeking or adhering to his counsel which, to Nixon, amounted to a great insult. In particular, Nixon lobbied Bush for greater financial support of Russia, which Bush resisted, believing the aid he had allocated was "about right."[98] Nixon thought Bush to be "a good man, but not strong," and worried about his chances in the 1992 election.[99]

He still loved the high-stakes drama of a presidential race. Like a retired quarterback who misses the thrill of playing, he monitored the campaign of 1992 closely from the sidelines, scrutinizing all the action and imagining himself back in the game. His worries about Bush's campaign skills—and his chances of winning—were well founded, particularly in light of the competition. Bill Clinton, the Democratic challenger, was emerging as a force to be reckoned with, a skilled campaigner who connected with the American people despite manifest flaws. Clinton epitomized the antiwar demonstrators who had protested America's involvement in Vietnam when Nixon was president. Nixon found his evasion of the draft and admitted drug use repugnant, and judged him "a phony and a fraud." "If he is elected," Nixon told aide Monica Crowley, "I'll know this country has finally gone to hell."[100]

When Bush lost the 1992 election, as Nixon had predicted, he wrote a handwritten note consoling him. Bush wrote back: "The dust has begun to settle, but we Bushes will do fine. As I contemplate private life, the way in which one Richard Nixon has conducted himself in his post President [sic] private life will serve as a fine example of how to do it."[101] Nixon also wrote another note after the election, this one to the winner. In an attempt to reach out to the president-elect, he congratulated him on a well-fought campaign and assured him he had the "character" to be a strong president.[102] The note opened the door for Clinton to use him as an advisor, but Nixon hedged his bet, showing the new administration he could still play hardball. Through Clinton political advisor Dick Morris, he sent word to Clinton that he could "buy a one-year moratorium" on criticism of the new administration in exchange for a meeting with the president on foreign policy.[103] Whether because of the threat or not, Clinton did call in March 1993, two months after taking office.

Surprisingly, a friendship of sorts developed as Clinton sought Nixon's take on the details of the job that only a former president could understand, such as how he should spend his time during the course of a typical day. Clinton also proffered an invitation to the White House which Nixon accepted, visiting the president a week after the call. Nixon told Monica Crowley that it was "probably the best [visit] I've had to Washington since I left the presidency," and harbored the notion that he could be a foreign policy advisor to Clinton in a greater capacity than he had with Reagan and Bush.[104] In Oval Office calls and lengthy memos to the president, he dispensed advice on Somalia and, in particular, Russia, his greatest concern as the fragile Republic took flight after the Soviet Union's collapse. His counsel was to support Russian president Boris Yeltsin while reaching out to Yeltsin's Democratic political rivals in the hope of forming a united front, even as they sought to divide their ultranationalist and Communist counterparts. He also called for the improvement in the design and administration of Russian foreign aid.[105] Any concerns he may have had about Clinton's foreign policy were alleviated now that he and Clinton had established a dialogue. "As long as he is talking to me," he told Crowley, "he'll be okay."[106]

In June of 1993, Pat Nixon, who had been ailing from lung cancer for three years, died at the Nixons' Park Ridge home. After leaving the White House, she never again spoke to the press, but in a 1968 interview with Gloria Steinem for *New York* magazine, she had said, "I've never had it easy. I'm not like all you . . . all those people who had it easy."[107] Her last years were her happiest; spending time quietly tending to her husband, grandchildren, and garden, far from the harsh political spotlight, may have provided some consolation.[108] At her funeral at the Library and Birthplace, Nixon was visibly shaken as he faced the challenge of moving forward without his partner of fifty-four years.

Though Nixon enjoyed relatively good health after his nearly fatal bout with phlebitis almost two decades earlier, his pace slowed after his wife's death. He had given up on the Clintons, neither of whom made it to Mrs. Nixon's funeral, a slight he couldn't forgive.[109] He also became disillusioned with Clinton's sloppy foreign policy, and not surprisingly, considered Whitewater, the Clintons' pre–White House real estate scandal, to be more egregious than Watergate. "We didn't have profiteering, and we didn't have a body," he told Monica Crowley, alluding to Whitewater's get-rich-quick motivation and the mysterious suicide of White House aide and Clinton friend, Vince Foster.[110] He pinned his hopes on a protégé of sorts, Senate minority leader Bob Dole, to beat Clinton out of the White House in 1996. Dole, he felt, was the most capable of the Republican leadership and the only one who could steer the party in the right direction after Bush's loss. Anticipating the influence he would have in a Dole White House, he actively gave Dole political advice in his bid for the presidency.[111]

But he would not see the next election. Less than a year after his wife's passing, Richard Nixon's turbulent life came to an anticlimactic end. After suffering a massive stroke, he was admitted to New York Hospital on the Upper East Side of Manhattan where, surrounded by his family, he fell into a coma before succumbing to death on the evening of April 22, 1994. For a nation that had watched him "walk on the edge of the precipice" of American politics for almost half a century—winning, losing, and always coming back—it was hard to believe he was really gone. His last and longest campaign, lifting him from disgraced former president to respected elder statesman, may have been his greatest triumph. No other president had gone so far in rehabilitating his image in the course of his post–White House years. *Time* magazine, which featured him on its cover a record fifty-one times, and wrote its first and only editorial urging his resignation, called him "the most important figure of the postwar era."[112]

The epic rises and falls throughout Nixon's political life inevitably drew Shakespearean analogies. Thousands lined Yorba Linda Boulevard as a hearse brought back Nixon's body to the Library and Birthplace through a driving rain. Among those who braved the inclement weather was a thirty-three-year-old nurse who had reviled Nixon, but had come nevertheless to "bring closure" to the Nixon saga. "He strutted his hour on the stage," she said quoting *Macbeth*. "And now he is no more."[113]

Closure may have also been on Nixon's mind when he expressed his wishes about his burial to his two daughters. The Southern California sun returned to Yorba Linda the following day, as four former presidents—Ford, Carter, Reagan, and Bush—and President Clinton came to pay their respects to the thirty-seventh president. Also among the invited mourners was an eclectic mix symbolizing memorable, if infamous, events of the Nixon presidency: G. Gordon Liddy, who had led the Watergate break-in; Archibald Cox, the Watergate special prosecutor Nixon had fired in the "Saturday Night Massacre"; George McGovern, his vanquished Democratic opponent in the 1972 election; Rose Mary Woods, his loyal secretary who was responsible for the eighteen-and-a-half-minute gap in the Watergate tapes; and Spiro Agnew, whose own fall had been overshadowed by

Nixon's. The Reverend Billy Graham presided over the funeral, which included eulogies from California governor Pete Wilson, Henry Kissinger, Bob Dole, and Clinton. Wilson remembered Nixon as "a fighter of iron will"; Kissinger praised his foreign policy, saying, "he achieved greatly and suffered deeply." Dole's most poignant tribute may have been the tears he shed for his friend and mentor upon leaving the podium. But Clinton's sentiments may have most pleased the deceased. While referring to Nixon's "mistakes," he asked for the evenhanded assessment of his predecessor that Nixon himself had campaigned for throughout his post-presidency. "May the days of judging Richard Nixon on anything less than his entire life and career," the president urged, "come to a close."[114]

After the doleful strains of "Taps" sounded from a lone military trumpeter, Nixon's body was lowered into the ground next to his wife, in the shadow of his boyhood home.

In the classic film *Chinatown*, released the year after Nixon left the White House, the villain, played by John Huston, observes, "Politicians, ugly buildings, and whores are all respected if they last long enough." Nixon may have earned the grudging admiration of many former detractors due to his sheer endurance. He could have slowly faded away like the Pacific sunsets he viewed in exile from the cliffs of Casa Pacifica. But like Theodore Roosevelt after the death of his first wife, he "went on." Eventually, he got up every morning with a sense of purpose, and ultimately, made a difference.

In 1986, well into his comeback but eight years before the gauzy halo would be cast after his death, a Gallup poll showed that three-quarters of Americans believed his actions in the Watergate scandal justified his leaving office. But 54 percent believed Ford was right to pardon him—up from just 35 percent after the pardon was announced.[115] Though he stubbornly refused to apologize fully for the sins of Watergate, Americans may have been willing to forgive Nixon, just as they might forgive an unrepentant ex-convict who had nonetheless served his time and contributed to good works. In the end, for many, that was rehabilitation enough.

V.

GERALD R. FORD:
THE GOOD LIFE

Gerald Ford sat on the inauguration platform on the east side of the Capitol with a passive expression on his face, legs crossed, hands folded, and eyes on Jimmy Carter as Chief Justice Warren Burger administered the presidential oath of office. Ford and Carter had done their best to make pleasant conversation as they and their wives, Betty and Rosalynn, drove up Pennsylvania Avenue from the White House to the Capitol together less than an hour before, but Carter noticed a "certain strain there."[1] There was no love lost between the two men. They had faced off in a bitter, sometimes hostile, campaign in which Carter, a one-term governor from Georgia who surprised his own party by securing the nomination, relentlessly reminding voters of the ills of the "Nixon-Ford Administration." The election culminated, as Ford put it, "a long, intense struggle," with Carter winning 49.9 percent of the vote to Ford's 47.9 percent.[2] Just 56 of 538 electoral votes would have changed the election's outcome, making it the closest electoral vote since Woodrow Wilson's narrow reelection victory sixty years earlier.[3] The pardon of Richard Nixon, which Ford had granted just one month into his presidency, almost certainly sealed Ford's fate. The maelstrom of controversy and indignation that came from the press and the American public in its wake had not fully subsided when the polls opened on Election Day. Nearly two-thirds of Americans disapproved of the pardon—and 7 percent of voters cast their ballots for Carter as a direct result.[4] As always, Ford was gracious in defeat but the loss hurt deeply.[5]

After giving Carter the oath, Burger took his seat, leaving the new president at the podium to address the nation. Carter looked out at the audience and paused. "For myself and a grateful nation," he began slowly, "I want to thank my predecessor for all he has done to heal our land." It took

Ford by surprise; no president had ever acknowledged his predecessor in an inaugural speech, much less credited him for his contributions. He bit his lip to hide emotion, nodded at Carter, and said "Thank you." Then, as the crowd's applause swelled, Carter turned toward Ford who rose from his seat and shook the hand of his former rival.

The White House had been Ford's for 895 days, but it was the Capitol where as a congressman from Michigan's fifth district, he had spent more than a quarter of a century. Now, as he and Mrs. Ford walked through the corridors of the House chamber after the ceremony, they saw many of the people they had known during their twenty-eight years in Washington: congressional colleagues, aides, policemen, and doormen. Mrs. Ford held back tears as she and her husband made their way down the steps of the Capitol to Marine One, the new president's helicopter on the Capitol's grounds that would whisk the Fords off to Andrews Air Force Base in nearby Maryland.[6] Many in the crowd, Republicans and Democrats alike, some crying openly, were sorry to see them go.[7]

Jerry and Betty Ford were almost universally liked and respected in the most partisan of towns, and they would be missed. Ford never let politics get in the way of a friendship or in making the right decision. He had clearly done his best for the country, leaving office with an approval rating of 53 percent, and the warmth generated on that cold January day in 1977 may have been as much for him as for his successor.[8] As the helicopter climbed into the air, Ford asked the pilot to circle around the Capitol building. "That's my real home," he said, glancing out the window at the building's massive dome below.[9] As he savored the moment, he may have been satisfied to leave his public life behind. But the thought of reentering politics at the national level and returning to Washington did not leave his mind entirely. The election had been so close . . .

An Air Force jet, a backup to Air Force One, stood ready to take the Fords to Carmel, California, where the former president would golf in the annual Bing Crosby Open, which was already in progress. Then it would be on to Houston where Ford would speak at a dinner honoring the late Vince Lombardi, and finally, to their adopted home of Rancho Mirage, a suburb of Palm Springs, where an abundance of well-watered golf courses served the growing legion of retirees who made the warm California desert their home.

After bidding farewell to many of Ford's aides who had come to see them off, they boarded the plane with their golden retrievers, Misty and Liberty, and thirty-three other passengers, including some friends who would make the journey west with them. The mood was celebratory, charged up in part by Carter's comment as President and Mrs. Ford sipped martinis in their private quarters. An hour and a half into the flight, Ford made his way to the back of the plane in shirtsleeves and a loosened tie to talk with members of the press who accompanied him. "Anything I say isn't of importance any longer," he admitted before taking their questions. Would he consider throwing his hat in the ring for president in 1980, they asked. "I don't want anyone to pre-empt the field without thinking they'll have a challenge from an old-timer who's got the good spirit," he responded. When the subject got back to politics, Ford made it clear he wasn't going to "rule out any options."[10]

Two thousand well-wishers were on hand to greet the Fords as they landed in California.[11] Ford worked the crowd, shaking as many hands as he could, before he and Mrs. Ford climbed into an awaiting limousine that glided them off to private life.

Gerald Ford never thought he would be president and, before his bid to win the White House in 1976, had never wanted the job. Becoming Speaker of the House of Representatives was his sole ambition until fate intervened in 1973. He was elected to Congress in 1948, as a thirty-five-year-old World War II veteran and Yale Law School graduate, with the intent of overcoming the Midwestern isolationism he had known in his Michigan youth. Hardworking and down-to-earth, Ford made friends easily and won the favor of his colleagues on both sides of the aisle. When John Kennedy was assassinated in the fall of 1963, Lyndon Johnson called on him to serve on the Warren Commission. The bipartisan committee, composed of chief justice Earl Warren and five others, probed into Kennedy's death for signs of conspiracy and came to the controversial and frequently challenged conclusion that Lee Harvey Oswald, Kennedy's alleged assassin, had acted alone. In 1964, when a group of young Republican congressmen staged a coup to oust minority leader Charlie Halleck, an older man who they felt was out of touch, it was Jerry Ford they chose to succeed him.

Ford soldiered on as minority leader for eight years, through the Johnson administration and the first term of the Nixon administration, working hard toward achieving the Republican majority in Congress that would promote him to Speaker. When Nixon won reelection by a landslide in 1972, and the Republicans still had not won the House, Ford promised his wife, who had endured years of the congressman's busy travel schedule and late nights on the Hill, that he would retire at the end of Nixon's term in 1977. But when Nixon's vice president, Spiro Agnew, resigned amid revelations that he had taken bribes as governor of Maryland prior to becoming vice president, it was Ford who congressional leaders supported as his replacement. Nixon, already embattled and weakened by Watergate, appeased Congress by appointing Ford to the position. Ford became vice president in early December 1973, the first man to assume the office through the provisions of the 25th Amendment to the Constitution. While he had the confidence of his former congressional colleagues, he wanted to manage the expectations of Congress and the American people. "I am a Ford, not a Lincoln," he told them after taking the vice presidential oath of office at the Capitol.

When Ford was sworn in to Congress in January 1949, the first person to shake his hand and welcome him was a California congressman who had been elected two years before.[12] Ford could hardly have imagined then that that same man, Richard Nixon, would be responsible for putting him in the Oval Office a quarter of a century later. The two men had been friends in Congress and shared a number of things in common. Both were born in 1913, came from modest beginnings, attended elite law schools, and served in the navy in World War II before winning election to Congress where they were looked upon as "comers." When Ford needed a speaker at an annual Lincoln Day Banquet in his district in Michigan, it was Dick Nixon, newly elected to the Senate, to whom he turned. (Ford and Nixon spent the night at the home of Ford's parents who were vacationing in Florida. At Ford's mother's insistence, Nixon slept in her four-poster bed. After Nixon became vice president a year later, she placed a sign on the bed that read THE VICE PRESIDENT SLEPT HERE.)[13] Well before Nixon became president, Ford talked of his "greatness," and, though many agreed with his assessment of Nixon's abilities, was one of the few who actually liked him. Even when Nixon was on the outs politically in the early sixties, Ford kept the faith, staying in touch with the former vice president and failed

Republican presidential nominee when others had turned their back on him as a has-been.[14]

As Nixon's vice president and friend, Ford vigorously defended him against the allegations that he had covered up Watergate, traveling extensively throughout the country with the increasingly dubious message that Nixon was innocent of all charges. As late as July of 1974, as Watergate's cancerous tentacles spread through the Nixon White House, Ford loyally mounted his defense. When the "smoking gun" tapes were discovered that same summer, Ford realized that Nixon had been lying to him and the American people all along and, he wrote, "the hurt was very deep."[15]

A month later, Ford assumed the presidency and the nation breathed a sigh of relief. With his Midwestern openness, he offered the country a much-needed new beginning in the wake of the "long national nightmare" it had endured under Nixon. This president was refreshing in his ordinariness, seemingly as comfortable attending a Lions Club meeting as he would have been presiding over a cabinet meeting. But his short honeymoon with Congress, the press, and the American people came to an abrupt end when he signed Nixon's pardon. "I had to get rid of the son of a bitch some way," he told Don Penny, a consultant on the White House staff. "I just couldn't do the damn job with his political carcass hanging around my neck."[16]

The two and a half years he served as president were filled with crises. Domestically, inflation soared, causing the economy to stagnate. Abroad Ford dealt with the very last of the war in Vietnam, overseeing the harrowing fall of Saigon in 1975. In order to bring closure to the war, which had divided the nation, he extended a limited pardon to those who had illegally evaded military service. Like the pardon of Nixon, it aroused thunderous controversy and, also like the Nixon pardon, Ford defended it as the right thing to do. Ford weathered all the storms of his presidency with aplomb, even surviving two assassination attempts, both in northern California, within a month of each other.

The media often presented Ford as an intellectually challenged, though affable, clod. While he was perhaps the best athlete to occupy the Oval Office, an All-American football player in his college days at the University of Michigan who rejected offers to play professionally, he perpetuated the perception by making a number of high-profile gaffes and falls. (The image of Ford as a bumbler began before he became president. Political adversary Lyndon Johnson jested that Ford played too much football without a helmet and couldn't "fart and chew gum at the same time." Ford was no easier on LBJ, announcing that, "Henry Clay said he'd rather be right than president. Now President Johnson has proved it really is a choice."[17]) His clumsiness provided endless fodder for editorial cartoonists, late-night talk-show hosts, and the new television sensation, *Saturday Night Live*. The show made a star of Chevy Chase, who portrayed Ford as an incompetent klutz who fell—often, it would seem—at inopportune times. Ford went along with it all good-naturedly, even inviting the *Saturday Night Live* cast to the White House and allowing his press secretary Ron Nesson to host the show, but it didn't help his image as president.

Still, he had no doubt that he would prevail in the 1976 election. The last Gallup poll before the ballots came in showed him winning by the thinnest of margins. He expected to remain in the White House, and had not fully prepared for the prospect of another life.[18] The pink slip issued by the American people in the form of votes for his opponent gave him no choice.

In the first weeks after leaving the White House, regrets likely fueled the depression of Lyndon Johnson and the brooding of Richard Nixon. If not for the tragedy of Vietnam, Johnson would almost certainly have coasted to reelection in 1968, and the Great Society may have been a beacon of all that was possible and right in America, giving him a legacy on par with Franklin Roosevelt. If not for the taint of Watergate, Nixon's visionary foreign policy may have given him a place in history alongside Woodrow Wilson. There were many what-ifs for Gerald Ford to ponder as well; things that, if done differently, may have meant that he would have had a shot at achieving the White House for a full term, and a greater chance to contribute to the betterment of the nation like his own hero, Harry Truman.

The pardon, of course, was the big one, but there were others too: What if he had given his appointed vice president, Nelson Rockefeller, the number-two spot on the ticket in 1976 instead of passing him over for Bob Dole? What if Ronald Reagan, who battled him for the nomination, had campaigned for him in swing states like Texas instead of turning his back on Ford? What if he hadn't gaffed in one of the debates with Carter when he said the Soviet Union did not dominate Eastern Europe, reinforcing his image as an intellectual lightweight? If those questions burned in his mind, he didn't let it show. He was comfortable with the decisions he had made and forgave himself for his mistakes.[19] He had not sought the power of the presidency when scandal plagued the Nixon White House, but accepted the reins gracefully; when he had had to give them up, he did so just as easily. What's more, he was confident that history would see his pardon of Nixon as he did—as the price the nation had to pay to move on. In short, Ford did something Johnson and Nixon did not do in their first weeks out of office: he moved on, himself. "I adjusted quickly," he said much later of his transition. "It was easier for me than some of the others."[20]

Betty Ford had only one request of her husband in his retirement: Just don't "come home [for] lunch."[21] She needn't have worried. In his first weeks out of office, Ford kept himself busy, as he would throughout his post-presidency. He returned to Yale, his law school alma mater, where he lectured and hoisted beer with undergraduates; he went to Colorado for a family ski vacation; and he played in three charity golf tournaments. Just two months after leaving Washington, Ford told *U.S. News & World Report* of his new life: "I really enjoy it. It makes a lot of sense for Betty, too, and it's helping to improve my golf game."[22]

The Fords divided their time between a rented villa in Rancho Mirage, their condominium in Beaver Creek (a high-end ski resort town adjacent to Vail in Colorado's Rocky Mountains), and a house in Grand Rapids, Michigan, Ford's hometown and congressional district where his presidential museum would be built. He and Mrs. Ford also oversaw plans for their fifteen-room dream house that would stand next to a Rancho Mirage golf course.

Indeed, golf is the pastime many associate with Ford's life after the presidency. After leaving office, he played four times a week or so, sharpening his game for the dozen Pro-Ams he would play in each year. All the added time spent on his game allowed him to bring his handicap—which was seventeen or eighteen when he was president—to as low as twelve.[23] His

Secret Service detail, shadowing him on some of the finest courses in the country, bragged of having the best jobs in government.[24] His image as a klutz, however, was not helped by his inconsistent game, which was evident in more than a few wild shots. In one of his first Pro-Ams after leaving office, in Milwaukee, an errant tee-shot struck down an unsuspecting spectator just off the fairway. The incident led his friend Bob Hope to quip, "Whenever I play with [Ford], I usually try to make it a foursome—the President, myself, a paramedic, and a faith healer," while Ford himself joked that he knew his game was getting better "because I'm hitting fewer spectators."[25] But Ford's post-presidency was not simply a leisurely retirement spent in golf carts and clubhouses. In fact, up to that point, Ford had been as active an ex-president as any of his predecessors.

While Ford may not have blazed any bold trails as president, he did make unprecedented moves as an ex-president. In effect, he became the first to make a job—a very lucrative one—out of being a former president. Ford wasn't the first to leverage his years in office into a sizable paycheck. The selling of memoirs for tidy sums had become a customary practice among ex-presidents. Ulysses S. Grant, for instance, bankrupt in his twilight years and bankrolled by Mark Twain, hurriedly wrote his autobiography while battling throat cancer in order to keep his family solvent after his imminent death. More recently, Harry Truman and Dwight Eisenhower had sold their stories for sums in the half-million-dollar range. Lyndon Johnson and Richard Nixon landed deals worth well over $1 million, and went one step further by selling TV interviews for six-figure sums. Ford followed suit; he and Mrs. Ford both signed contracts for their memoirs to Harper & Row and *Reader's Digest* for a collective $1 million, and he signed a $1.25 million deal with NBC for his contributions to several documentaries and his participation in global tours for the network.[26]

Ford, however, became the first former president since Theodore Roosevelt to consistently accept honoraria for speaking engagements throughout his post-presidency, initially making upwards of $10,000 to $15,000 per appearance, although the amount would increase over time.[27] To be sure, Ford also spoke free of charge when fund-raising for the party, and, in election years, campaigning for candidates. But often when he made his way to a microphone, almost always speaking on a subject of his choosing, a substantial check came for the privilege of listening to him. Ever gregarious, Ford enjoyed the "mashed potato circuit," shaking hands in receiving lines and posing for pictures, and he had no shortage of offers from corporations, universities, and conventions. Though it wasn't the "bully pulpit" offered by the presidency, it did afford him the chance to express his views as a respected ex-president.

Scores of corporations sought out Ford to sit on their boards of directors. He accepted appointments from Amax Inc., American Express Company, Shearson/American Express, Santa Fe International Corporation, Texas Commerce Bank, Tiger International Inc., Beneficial Corporation of New Jersey, and the 20th Century Fox Film Corporation. He also acted as a paid advisor for two nonprofit organizations, the Aerospace Corporation and the Peabody Institute. Additionally, Ford agreed to endorse a series of collectors' medals commemorating great presidential moments—though it may have been a low for ex-presidents.[28]

All of those endeavors added up to an annual income of between $500,000 and $750,000, climbing up to over $1 million by the early eighties, making his annual pension of just over $100,000 pale in comparison.[29] The big paydays prompted criticism from those who saw him as selling the presidential office, notably—albeit privately—Richard Nixon, the last ex-president not to accept hefty honoraria to significantly enhance annual earnings. Ford himself unabashedly dismissed such accusations. "I'm a private citizen now; it's nobody's business," he said. Bob Barrett, his military aide and administrative assistant, defended his boss, saying that Ford "had been a strong devotee of the free enterprise system for thirty years," and that it wasn't surprising he would want "to serve on boards of directors and practice what he feels."[30] In any case, the business of being a former president made him rich and kept him busy. By the early eighties, he was logging hundreds of thousands of miles on private jets and in first-class cabins on commercial airlines across America and the world.

Ford also spent time his first couple years out of office diligently working on his memoir, appropriately called *A Time to Heal*, which hit bookstores in late May of 1979. A reviewer in *The New York Times Book Review* wrote of the book, "Where is the reader whose heart will leap at the prospect of 454 pages of the autobiography of Gerald R. Ford, a figure destined to afflict schoolchildren yet unborn with the problem of whether it was he or Martin Van Buren who started the French and Indian War?"[31] As the *Times* portended, the book sold poorly. Ford's banality and uncomplicated nature undoubtedly worked against him. There were no sensational revelations or profound insights contained in its pages, and not many were clamoring to hear his story as they had for that of his paradoxical, compelling predecessor, whose book *RN: The Memoirs of Richard Nixon* had been on the best-seller list for months. One of Betty Ford's sixty-third birthday presents to her husband included a customized T-shirt that read BET MY BOOK OUTSELLS YOURS.[32] It proved a good bet. Mrs. Ford's autobiography, *The Times of My Life*, sold briskly, easily outpacing the sluggish sales of *A Time to Heal*.

It was no surprise that America would be captured by the story of Betty Ford. As first ladies went, she was unique. As a young, middle-class girl growing up in Grand Rapids, Betty Bloomer dreamed of becoming a dancer, an ambition she announced to her mother at the age of eight.[33] When her father, a traveling salesman, died in a freak accident when she was sixteen, his insurance policy provided enough money for Betty to attend a two-year dance program at Bennington College in Vermont. Afterward, she pursued her dream by moving to New York, where she was admitted into the prestigious Martha Graham dance troupe, supporting herself by modeling at a Manhattan agency. After two years, when she realized that she would never make it into the starring dance roles in the troupe's major performances, she left the bright lights of Manhattan and returned home to Grand Rapids. Two years after her homecoming, at age twenty-four, she married Bill Warren, a traveling salesman who, like her father, had a penchant for partying. Betty wanted a home and a family; her husband wanted late nights in barrooms.[34] The marriage ended four years later.

Mrs. Warren, aged twenty-nine and not yet divorced from her first husband, wasn't looking for a relationship—and certainly not a husband—when, at Jerry Ford's urging, a mutual friend put him in touch with her. She turned him down flat when he suggested they have a drink. But after witnessing the thirty-four-year-old lawyer's steady persistence, she relented. A friendship developed and love followed. They were married in October 1948, just after Ford was elected to Congress, and they embarked on their Washington journey together. In the course of ten years, they produced three sons, Michael, Jack, and Steve, and a daughter, Susan, raising them in the Alexandria, Virginia, ranch-style home they had built for $34,000, where they would live until their move to the White House in 1974.[35]

As first lady, Betty Ford had her own mind and spoke it freely and openly, regardless of the controversy it aroused. In the midst of her White House reign during the "Swinging Seventies," she was interviewed by Morley Safer on *60 Minutes*. When Safer asked what she would do if her eighteen-year-old daughter told her she were having an affair, Mrs. Ford replied that she wouldn't be surprised if she had. The first lady further raised eyebrows when said she thought her children had "probably" experimented with marijuana and that she "probably" would too if she were their age. She was just as candid in matters relating to women. In the same interview, she proclaimed the Supreme Court's ruling on *Roe v. Wade*, protecting a woman's right to an abortion, a "great, great decision." Her vocal support of an Equal Rights Amendment to the Constitution to protect women from discrimination was in opposition to her husband, who felt the amendment was unnecessary. And when she had a mastectomy after being diagnosed with breast cancer, she dealt with it openly, encouraging women to have regular breast exams. Afterward, clinics and doctors' offices filled up with women who requested examinations for the first time.[36]

Mrs. Ford's independent spirit was evident on her last full day as first lady. Touring the White House for the final time as a resident with family friend and White House photographer, David Hume Kennerly, she confided that she had always wanted to dance on the Cabinet Room conference table. At Kennerly's urging, she kicked off her shoes, hoisted herself up, and performed a perfectly executed pirouette as Kennerly captured the moment through his ever-present lens.[37] Years later when Mrs. Ford and Kennerly shared the resulting photograph with Ford, he said with a laugh, "I never knew you did that." "There were a lot of things you didn't know," she jokingly replied.[38]

Like her footprints on the Cabinet Room table, Betty Ford would leave her mark as first lady—and afterward.

The transition to private life may have been easier for Ford than it was for his wife. Though she put on a brave face for the press, she thought her husband deserved another term in office and left Washington "bitter and depressed."[39] She had enjoyed being first lady and she was good at it. For a woman of admitted low self-esteem, the role offered the immediate gratification that had been lacking in other chapters of her life. Moving from the fast pace of the White House into a life of nights alone as her husband resumed a frenetic travel schedule left her in a state of "emotional shock."[40] As she had in earlier periods of her life, she turned to alcohol and prescription drugs, which she had taken for years to ease a pinched nerve in her neck.

A little more than a year after moving out of the White House, the Fords moved into their newly constructed home in Rancho Mirage. It was everything they had wanted. Fifteen rooms meant plenty of space for family and friends, and Mrs. Ford was looking forward to buying new furniture for the first time in some thirty years. She carefully chose all the new colors for the house with an interior decorator—mostly whites, greens, and blues—and sorted through all the family items that had been in storage from the White House and their house in Grand Rapids to get everything in place. In the hectic weeks leading up to the move, she had led a nomadic existence. With the lease up on their rented house and her husband on the road, she found herself in search of a roof over her head, staying with friends (until their children came for a visit), bunking with Susan in her nearby condominium (until she could no longer tolerate her cat), and finally going to a golf cottage on the grounds of the Thunderbird Country Club.[41]

The Fords finally moved into the house in mid-March, among piles of boxes and unfinished rooms. On April 1, just two weeks after their move, Betty Ford found herself sitting on her new couch in the living room surrounded by her husband and four children, a couple of friends, two doctors, and a nurse. They had all come together in an "intervention" (a relatively new concept at the time) to discuss her dependency on alcohol and drugs. The family had recognized that something was wrong with her during their annual Christmas holiday in Beaver Creek. Over time she had shut out her family and friends, gradually withdrawing into herself. Ford had noticed that she seemed slower, always in "second gear."[42] It was Susan who had insisted that something had to be done. She consulted doctors and came to the conclusion that an intervention—family and medical experts together, confronting her about her problem—was the best course of action to get her to own up to the problem and agree to treatment. After initial denial—"My makeup wasn't smeared, I wasn't disheveled; how could I be an alcoholic? And my drugs were prescribed by doctors, so how could I be a drug addict?"—she agreed to undergo an intensive four-week program at Long Beach Naval Hospital's Alcohol and Drug Rehabilitation Service. This medical facility was located at the nearby navy base; here, she would take the twelve steps toward recovery familiar to countless addicts.[43]

After a week of shaking through detoxification in their new desert home, Betty Ford checked into Long Beach and went to the room she would share with three other women, two young naval enlistees and an admiral's wife closer to her own age. At Long Beach she was no different than any of the other patients. Like them, she attended lectures, meetings, physical therapy, and group therapy, where, in a haze of cigarette smoke, she eventually confessed her worst sins about her condition. She ate in the same cafeteria, wore a name tag stating her first name, and saved quarters for the soda machine. She realized she was very much like the women she met, sharing not only their condition, but also "their hopes."[44] Unlike many, though, she had the support of her family, which "came together like a magnet" over her condition, getting involved in every stage of her recovery, including a week of family therapy.[45] The former president attended for five days, showing up at lectures and therapy sessions that provided him with a better understanding of alcoholism and the role he played in enabling his wife's addiction.

After a month of treatment, Betty Ford left Long Beach, clean and sober, looking forward to settling into her new home and getting back to her life. Her last drink of alcohol was behind her, and happiness with herself and her life were ahead. But she had not spent her last day in a treatment facility. Not by a long shot.

Throughout the late seventies and early 1980, speculation abounded that Ford would reenter the political fray in an election rematch with Jimmy Carter. He remained popular in Washington and across the country, and his presidency was looking better with the passing of years, particularly in comparison with Carter's, which had been undermined by the hostage crisis in Iran.[46] Political pundits spun scenarios about how Ford could win the nomination and recapture the White House, with poll data lending them credence.[47] Ford neither confirmed nor denied his intentions, but spent days on the road sending anti-Carter messages to students and the party faithful.[48]

In his first year out of office, he remained relatively quiet about Carter's performance. "I'm not going to be nitpicking," he told *Newsweek* in the summer of 1977. "A president has got enough troubles without an ex-president beating him over the head every day."[49] But as time went on, he became increasingly vocal in his criticism. In an analogy befitting his post-presidential life, he summed up Carter's performance in 1978 this way: "He's had no birdies, relatively few pars, a number of bogeys, and a heckuva lot of double bogeys."[50]

Only one man, Grover Cleveland, had gone from ex-president back to being president. In 1888, Cleveland, the twenty-second president, lost his bid for reelection to Benjamin Harrison, and came back four years later to beat Harrison to become the twenty-fourth president. Theodore Roosevelt had tried to win back the job after giving it up in 1909, in favor of his chosen successor, his loyal secretary of war, William Howard Taft. When he became disillusioned with Taft, Roosevelt ran against him in 1912, creating the Bull Moose Party to do so. His challenge split the GOP vote, clearing the way for the Democratic nominee, Woodrow Wilson, to beat them both. Since Theodore Roosevelt, no former president had tried to reenter the political arena—although Herbert Hoover had shown interest in securing the presidential nomination of the GOP four years after losing the presidency to Franklin Roosevelt. There were those who wondered why Ford would trade his cushy life to get back into the gritty business of politics. One of them was *Washington Post* writer Carl Rowen, who remarked, "Anybody who is dumb enough to leave the happy and useful life of an elder statesman is not smart enough to be president."[51]

There was some speculation that Ford didn't want the Republican nomination at all, but simply wanted to keep it from Ronald Reagan.[52] Reagan had challenged Ford for the nomination in 1976, beating him in some key primaries and winning over many Republicans, especially conservatives, who saw Reagan—not Ford—as the real future of the GOP. When Ford edged Reagan out of the nomination, Reagan, who considered

Ford a pretender to the throne, gave him a tepid endorsement and little help on the campaign trail. He declined to stump for Ford in pivotal states—Texas, in particular—which Reagan had won handily over Ford in the primaries and where his popularity would have helped drum up much-needed votes for Ford. Ford ultimately lost Texas to Carter, and with it went the election. He was less than pleased with Reagan's lack of support. "They needed a putty knife to get him off the ceiling," a friend recalled.[53] In return, Ford refused to cosign a GOP fund-raising letter with Reagan in 1977. He also didn't help Reagan's cause by telling *The New York Times* in 1980 that, if nominated, Reagan would probably lose the election, a highly unusual statement from a faithful Republican warhorse like Ford. He would rather have seen the nomination go to the next generation of Republican hopefuls, chief among them, George Bush, whom Ford had given a boost as president by appointing him the chief U.S. liaison to the People's Republic of China, and later, the director of the CIA. Bush considered Ford a "father figure," and maintained close contact with Ford after he left office. (Despite forming a well-documented friendship with Bill Clinton in recent years, Ford was Bush's closest friendship among ex-presidents.)[54]

Though some polls put Ford ahead of Reagan in a duel for the GOP nomination, Ford announced in late March that he would not be a candidate. Mrs. Ford called it "one of the happiest days of my life."[55] The only plausible scenario that would have given him the nomination would have been if a deadlocked body of delegates at the Republican Convention turned to him as a compromise candidate. But after Reagan gained momentum in the primaries, there was no doubt that he would have enough delegates at the summer's convention in Detroit to become the nominee. However, speculation about Ford's return to national politics did not end.

Prior to the convention, buzz about a "dream ticket," consisting of Reagan and Ford as his running mate, captured the imaginations of party members—including Reagan himself. Reagan's advisors told him that getting Ford on the ticket would give him a marked advantage in securing a victory over Carter in November.[56] Reagan was wary of the logical choice for his running mate, George Bush, a political moderate who trailed him in the primaries. Ford—popular, proven, and respected—proved the ideal alternative, and there were rumors that he might be receptive to a second spot on the ticket. "These guys say there may be a chance that Ford would accept," he told a group of aides about his advisors. "Maybe we're missing a bet if we don't ask him. What have we got to lose?"[57]

John Quincy Adams, the sixth president and son of the second, was the first of three ex-presidents to come back to politics in a diminished role. After a brief respite upon being defeated for reelection in 1828, the people of his Massachusetts district sent him back to Washington as their representative in Congress—despite the fact that he was not a candidate—a post he would fill with great distinction for twenty years. John Tyler, in sharp contrast, was the second. In 1841, Tyler became the first vice president to assume the presidency when the incumbent, William Henry Harrison, died a month into office. "His Accidency" served out the remainder of Harrison's term before suffering defeat when he made his own run for the presidency. Sixteen years after leaving office, his southern sympathies led him to serve briefly as a member in the Confederate House of Representatives at the outbreak of the Civil War, before his death in 1862. Andrew Johnson, Abraham Lincoln's successor, was the last. Six years after leaving the White House, after dodging impeachment by just one vote, he returned to Congress as a senator from Tennessee before his death in 1875, just several months into his term. But no president had ever considered coming back to the vice presidency, an office Franklin Roosevelt's first vice president, John Nance Garner, once famously likened to (in a cleaned-up version of his colorful vernacular) "a warm bucket of spit."

Reagan had paved the way for asking Ford to share the ticket by taking care to mend the fences that had come apart when he challenged Ford for the nomination in 1976. He and his wife, Nancy, paid the Fords a courtesy call at their house in Rancho Mirage in June, at which time Reagan proposed the idea of a Reagan-Ford ticket. Ford gave him a categorical "no," adding that he would "support" him, but "wouldn't want to be on the ticket."[58] The following month, on the first night of the Republican National Convention in Detroit, the Reagans paid a call on the Fords in their hotel suite as they celebrated Ford's sixty-seventh birthday. Reagan came with an apt gift: a nineteenth-century pipe and tobacco bag from a Montana Crow Indian tribe. "These little traveling smoke kits are rare today, although much revered in pre-reservation days. They allowed two warriors passing on the trail to stop and enjoy a smoke in peace and wish each other good fortune on the dangerous trails that lie ahead."[59] Ford was touched by the gesture, and the hatchet was effectively buried.

That same evening, Reagan formally asked Ford to consider running with him. Ford was noncommittal, remaining unconvinced that sharing the ticket with Reagan would work. Four aides who had served with Ford in the White House—Henry Kissinger, Alan Greenspan, Bob Barrett, and Jack Marsh—wanted to see Ford back in the political spotlight, and sought to convince him otherwise, acting as brokers on his behalf. While Ford left the door open to considering the idea, he made it clear that he was happy with his life and not eager to be relegated to the vice presidency. But the idea of an "expanded" vice presidency—an unprecedented and historical notion—intrigued him. Discussions between the Reagan and Ford camps ensued about how the vice presidency could be tailored for Ford. Ford's advisors proposed that, as vice president, Ford act as "super director of the office of the presidency," with White House staffers reporting directly to him, who would in turn report to Reagan. They also vied for granting Ford "veto" power in the selection of cabinet officers, ensuring that none of the top jobs in the administration would be filled without his approval.[60] The question became, how much power would be acceptable to Ford—and how much would Reagan be willing to give up?

The following day, speculation about seeing Ford on the ticket grew after he gave a scheduled television interview to CBS's Walter Cronkite. Ford confirmed that he was not seeking the vice-presidential nomination, but might entertain it if Reagan were willing to share some of his presidential duties. "A sort of co-presidency," suggested Cronkite. Yes, Ford responded.[61] Reagan, watching the interview in his suite, was concerned that Ford hadn't immediately rejected the concept of the division of presidential authority as inappropriate.[62] Wait a minute, he thought, this is really two presidencies he's talking about here. But he remained intrigued by the prospect of having Ford on the ticket—just as Ford remained on the fence.[63]

Mrs. Ford worried that Ford's reentry into politics would derail her from her life in the desert, which she had come to love.[64] But she supported him, as she always did, in whatever decision he made. "If Jerry wants it . . ." she told Nancy Reagan.[65] As it turned out, he didn't. Several hours after his interview with Cronkite, when his decision was needed, he held to his initial feeling that the situation just wouldn't work. At 11:00 P.M., he put on his suit and went to Reagan's suite to tell him personally.[66] After Ford left, Reagan wasted no time in calling a surprised and delighted George Bush to offer him the number-two spot, ending the prospect of Ford returning to political office and creating the spark that would ultimately ignite the Bush political dynasty.

The bizarre spectacle of the copresidency, though perhaps overblown, lent the convention unexpected drama and created a debate in the press about how such an arrangement would have worked. As *Newsweek* put it, "If a Reagan-Ford ticket had been created and elected, it might have splintered authority in the White House and led to an even greater rivalry and friction than normally exist in any administration. It was a dream ticket that threatened a political morass and a constitutional nightmare."[67]

Reagan and Bush went on to win in a walk in November, with Ford campaigning actively on their behalf, and Ford went back to the good life as an ex-president.

The following April, when asked whether there was any chance of him returning to his former profession, Ford's response was unequivocal. "Absolutely not," he said. "I've got the best of both possible worlds as it is. I've got access and input without the responsibility."[68] The occasion was the dedication of the Ford Library, nestled in the hills of the north campus of his alma mater, the University of Michigan. Unlike all the other presidential libraries, Ford's library was just that: a place of study that housed all of Ford's papers as president, vice president, and congressman. It did not include an attendant museum, which in Ford's case would be built separately on a riverbank in Grand Rapids. Both monuments to the Ford years cost a collective $15.3 million—$4.3 million for the library, $11 million for the museum—and in keeping with Ford's fiscally conservative bent, all the funds were pledged before the yellow ribbons were cut.[69] Like all former presidents, Ford was on the hook to raise the money to build the institutions before handing them over to the National Archives, which assumed all maintenance and operating costs. His relief at leaving politics and the constant need to raise money for campaigns was cancelled out by the laborious responsibility of soliciting funds for the library and museum. "When the last tree is planted, all the bills will be paid," he boasted.[70]

Just over a year later, the Gerald R. Ford Museum opened its doors, with the President and Mrs. Reagan and Vice President and Mrs. Bush in attendance, as well as a number of prominent Democrats including Ted Kennedy, Tip O'Neill, Lady Bird Johnson, and Margaret Truman. The VIPs touring the museum saw an institution very much in keeping with its modest subject. Mrs. Ford described it aptly: "It's not a museum to greatness; it's a monument to the average man. It's a monument to a town where Jerry grew up, the town that knew him as a schoolboy, as a football player, as the son of the middle class who grew up to be president. It sort of says, this can happen to anyone."[71]

In the fall of 1981, tragedy struck in Cairo when Egyptian president Anwar Sadat was gunned down in a spray of bullets from automatic weapons while reviewing a military parade. The attack by three religious extremists, all in the Egyptian military, left eleven dead and forty wounded. Sadat's murder was a severe blow to the prospect of peace in the Middle East.

Diplomatically, Sadat's funeral left the White House in a quandary. Earlier in the year, just sixty-nine days into his presidency, the bullets of a would-be assassin had felled President Reagan and, it would be revealed much later, left him perilously close to death. Cautious officials convinced him that the political climate in Cairo was too unstable for him to attend the ceremonies. But sending an administration official of lesser rank for the funeral of a head of state—particularly one as important to the U.S. as Sadat—would be an egregious breech of protocol. But Reagan's secretary of state, Alexander Haig, devised a solution that would allow the U.S. to save face: He would lead a delegation of all the living former presidents—Nixon, Ford, and Carter, all of whom had known and worked with Sadat while in power—a triumvirate he dubbed "the Presidential Hat-Trick."[72] Reagan loved the idea, and calls went out to the formers from the State Department, asking them to make the trip to Cairo on behalf of the president.

Nixon, who had already planned to attend, accepted readily. Jimmy and Rosalynn Carter also intended to go but, put off by what Carter saw as Reagan's fear in making the trip, chose to go on their own as personal friends of the Sadat family.[73] After numerous calls from friends and aides, and an argument with his staff, Carter was compelled to accept, but he was "really aggravated by it."[74] Ford, on the other hand, had not planned on going, and his family had urged him not to accept when the request to join the delegation was made. They had seen him survive two assassination attempts while he was in office and were not eager to see him back in harm's way. But Ford was nothing if not loyal to his country, and the president was asking . . . He agreed to join the others.[75]

The trip to Egypt was bound to be awkward for the thirty-seventh, thirty-eighth, and thirty-ninth presidents. Ford's relationships with both his predecessor and successor were strained. Not only had Nixon lied to him (and, of course, the country) about his involvement in Watergate when Ford was vice president, but he was also a nuisance for Ford when he became president. He refused to offer a full apology for Watergate upon accepting Ford's pardon, which would have mitigated the political fallout, and he doggedly fought for possession of his presidential papers, which the government wanted in its hands as evidence in possible legal proceedings. In addition, Nixon hadn't done him any favors by making a high-profile trip to China—reminding voters of their connection—just as Ford was battling Ronald Reagan for the Republican presidential nomination in the New Hampshire primary. Now when Ford was invited to parties, aides scoured the list of guests to ensure that Nixon wouldn't be among them.[76]

While in office, Carter had seen Ford a number of times and called him on four or five occasions during his term to consult him on matters of state that Ford had wrestled with, including the recognition of China and the Strategic Arms Limitation Agreement with the Soviets. Carter was particularly grateful for Ford's support of the Panama Canal Treaties.[77] Ford, in turn, had actively lobbied Carter to accept the Helsinki Accords that he, Ford, had negotiated with Soviet premier Leonid Brezhnev. Carter supported the agreement, keeping intact an important part of Ford's legacy, but their relationship was cool at best.[78] Ford simply didn't like Carter, and Carter summed up their relationship as "oil and water."[79]

Carter and Nixon barely knew each other, but their impressions of each other were less than flattering.

Two days after Sadat's assassination, three Air Force jets—two Jetstars and a C-9 Transport—touched down simultaneously at Andrews Air Force Base in Maryland, each carrying a former president. As they discharged their aircraft and walked toward Marine One, the presidential helicopter that would shuttle them to the White House to meet with Reagan before their trip to Egypt, a question of protocol arose: Who should be the first to board? Carter was impressed by Nixon's deference, as Nixon instructed that the man who left office most recently was the most senior member of the delegation. He waited as Carter boarded, followed by Mrs. Carter, and Ford.[80] But despite Nixon's gesture, the tension between the passengers was palpable. Before touching down on the South Lawn, Ford made an attempt to ease the situation. "Look," he said, "for the trip, at least, why don't we make it just Dick, Jimmy, and Jerry?" They all agreed.[81]

The gathering at the White House was a first. Never before had four presidents graced the executive mansion at one time. The normally upbeat Reagan looked unusually somber as he met his three predecessors, though all managed to smile when a White House photographer captured the historic moment as they stood side by side. Carter, the most visibly uncomfortable, thought the resultant photographs were the only reason Reagan had called them to the White House in the first place.[82] After a brief meeting about the trip, Reagan, lifting his coffee cup, closed with a toast to his predecessors: "Ordinarily, I would wish you happy landings, but seeing as you're all navy men, I wish you bon voyage."[83] Then the president escorted them to the South Lawn where Marine One stood waiting to take them back to Andrews to begin the first leg of their twelve-hour journey to Cairo. Before boarding, they flanked Reagan as he paid tribute to the man who had brought them all together. "There are moments in history," he told the world, "when the martyrdom of a single life can symbolize all that is wrong with an age and all that is right with humanity. Anwar Sadat, a man of peace in a time of violence, understood his age. In his final moments, as he had in all his days, he stood in defiance of the enemies of peace, the enemies of humanity. The meaning of his life and the cause for which he stood will endure and triumph."

As the presidential helicopter ascended from the White House grounds, Nixon looked down at the place they had all called home, though not as long as they may have liked. "I kind of like that house down there," he smiled at his peers. "Don't you?"[84]

After the assassination attempt on Reagan, when Reagan had been rushed to the hospital, Alexander Haig, in the ensuing chaos infamously proclaimed, "I'm in charge here"—despite the fact that Vice President

Bush was alive and well in Texas and that, even if he weren't, Speaker of the House Tip O'Neill would have been third in line for the presidency. Haig was no less officious as the leader of the U.S. delegation. The group boarded the Air Force jet that had served as Air Force One for Nixon, Ford, and Carter, and was now employed as Special Air Mission 26000, a backup for the newer, sleeker Air Force One used by Reagan. The spacious, forward cabin they had all enjoyed as president was taken up by Haig, while his staff occupied the next cabin, which had served as the private quarters for their wives or the dignitaries traveling with them. The ex-presidents were relegated to the next compartment—"thrown into the passengers' seats," as Mrs. Carter would recall it—which had been used by the presidents' staffs.[85]

By former presidents' standards, they were flying coach to the Middle East, vying for limited space in close quarters. Initially, they sat at two tables, each seating four, like patrons in the booths of a diner. Nixon and Ford sat across from Henry Kissinger, who had served them both as secretary of state, and Reagan's secretary of defense, Caspar Weinberger. Across the aisle, the Carters faced Ashraf Ghorbal, Egypt's ambassador to the United States, and his wife. The remainder of the plane's fifty-two passengers sat behind them, an eclectic bunch that included Motown artist, Stevie Wonder; U.S. Representative to the UN, Jeanne Kirkpatrick; Sam Brown, a fourteen-year-old South Carolina boy with whom Sadat had corresponded as a pen pal; an array of lawmakers from Strom Thurmond to Jim Wright; and a three-person press pool. Stewards had placed briefing books on the seats of every member of the delegation, along with a classified report on the political dangers in Egypt in the wake of Sadat's death.[86]

It was a restless flight for all the formers, punctuated by the directives Haig continually sent back through chief of protocol Anita Annenberg (the wife of publishing mogul, Lee Annenberg), demanding that they adhere to a choreographed arrival that would have them mutely following Haig out on the tarmac in Cairo as Haig spoke as the voice of the delegation. "He treated us like children," Carter recalled bitterly.[87]

The three formers continued to feel "ill at ease" with each other in the first hours of the trip. Nixon and Carter, Ford noticed, seemed especially awkward with each other.[88] "The truth is that Nixon and Carter were sitting in a little cubbyhole in the plane in a strained atmosphere," Ford recalled, "and I was the middle man between them. Nixon in particular was strained toward Carter."[89] He also got the clear sense that the supercilious Nixon felt he shouldn't have been "subjected to me and Carter for [the trip] halfway around the world."[90] But oddly, somewhere over the Atlantic, it was Nixon who made an effort to bring them all together. As Ford and Carter listened, he flattered Mrs. Carter, complimenting her on her outfit and the color of her eyes, and talked about the new book he was writing and the house he and Mrs. Nixon had just moved into in Saddle River, New Jersey.[91] Despite herself, she actually began warming to Nixon. He also reached out to his presidential peers, pointing out that they had all served their country well, and there was no reason for any residual animosity between them.[92] Eventually, as they settled into the flight, Ford in his shirtsleeves and Nixon and Carter in cardigan sweaters, they huddled together several times and discussed, in addition to their memories of Sadat, the common ground they shared as ex-presidents: the writing of their memoirs, the construction of their presidential libraries, and the transitions they had made from the White House to private lives.[93]

Upon their arrival in Cairo, they climbed into awaiting limousines, armor-plated and imported from Washington for the occasion. The first stop was their hotel in downtown Cairo, followed by an official visit with Sadat's vice president and successor, Hosni Mubarak, who gave the men his assurance that Sadat's policies would be his own, and that he was just as committed to peace and stability in the region.[94] They then visited with other Egyptian leaders and with Sadat's widow, Jihan.

The following day the three formers, stiffened by bulletproof vests, attended the funeral of the fallen leader. Ford was unsettled by the ceremony's lack of coordination and organization—particularly in light of Cairo's unstable political climate—as he and several hundred leaders representing eighty nations marched without direction to the service through the eerily quiet streets of the city.[95] After the service, a number of those who had been with the U.S. contingent split off from the party, traveling on their own to other destinations in the Middle East and Europe. Among them were Nixon, who went on to Saudi Arabia, the first stop on a tour of Middle Eastern capitals, and Haig, who stayed on for meetings with the Egyptian leadership in Cairo.[96]

On the return trip, something unexpected happened for both Ford and Carter. With hours to spend in the air, fewer passengers on board SAM 26000, and the anxiety of entering into a potentially dangerous climate in Cairo behind them, the awkwardness between the two slipped away. As they talked about their political experiences, families, and the monumental and unpleasant task of raising money for their presidential libraries, among other things, the beginnings of an unlikely friendship took root.[97] Their pleasant conversation led to a discussion on "what we could do on joint projects," recalled Ford.[98] Before touching down on American soil, Ford agreed to act as cochairman on several initiatives at The Carter Center, and Carter consented to cohost a conference at the Ford Library.

During the flight, they saw how potent their bipartisan voice could be. In an interview with the three-member press pool accompanying them, around a small table in the president's cabin, the two men held forth on the situation in the Middle East. Speaking informally in shirtsleeves, "Jerry" and "Jimmy" agreed that the recognition of the Palestine Liberation Organization (the PLO) and their grievances with Israel was paramount in achieving peace in the region. "At some point," Ford said, "that has to happen. I would not want to pick a date, but in a realistic way, that dialogue has to take place." Carter restated the point: "There is no way for Israel ever to have an assured permanent peace without resolving the Palestinian issue, so I think Jerry is certainly right in saying these discussions have to take place."[99] The statement immediately aroused controversy among those, including the Reagan White House, who saw the organization as a terrorist group. But with their forward-thinking notion in the papers, Reagan needed to clarify his position on the matter—and he wasn't pleased about it. No, he told the press, he had not ruled out talking with the PLO, but would not invite them into a discussion until they recognized Israel's right to exist.[100]

After the trip, the Palestinian situation continued to be a major foreign policy concern for Ford and Carter, and they worked together to force Israel's reigning prime minister, Menachem Begin, to come to terms with the issue. In a joint article that appeared in the February 1983 issue of *Reader's Digest*, they wrote that Israel, in violation of the Camp David Accords negotiated by Carter, "had shown little inclination to grant real autonomy to the Palestinians in the West Bank and Gaza areas." Ford and Carter reinforced the point and remained critical of Begin at a conference on domestic policy at the Ford Library the same month the article was published. The power of two former presidents who had both dealt with Begin in their tenures, one Republican, one Democrat, speaking out for the rights of the Palestinians, was enough to "create a mild stir in Israel," Carter said.[101]

They also saw eye to eye on the issue of free trade. In 1982, they collaborated on a joint statement condemning protectionism as a threat to world trade and warning of its adverse economic effect.[102] Additionally, along with George Bush, they stood with President Clinton at the White House in 1994, in support of the North American Free Trade Agreement, which would open up further trade opportunities with Canada and Mexico. They would reunite with Clinton at the White House six years later to support the extension of permanent normal trade relations with China, reducing the high tariffs placed on imported Chinese goods. Since World War II, Ford argued, "the expansion of global trade [has been] essential for prosperity and growth for America on a worldwide basis."[103]

The Ford-Carter partnership proved fruitful in other ways too. In 1988, they worked together, backed up by twenty-five bipartisan experts, on "American Agenda: Report to the Forty-First President of the United States of America." The 282-page report outlined the pressing concerns they believed George Bush should address in his term, the most important of which was balancing the burgeoning federal budget. Their work received wide attention, including being selected by the Book of the Month Club as a main selection, and was accepted by Bush in a high-profile ceremony at the White House in November—even though Bush didn't actually implement any of their suggestions. When the 2000 U.S. presidential election exposed flaws in America's antediluvian electoral process, Ford and Carter co-chaired a task force that studied the problem and made recommendations on how to fix it.

Their relationship hit a bump in the road when they both participated in an international delegation to oversee the 1989 Panama election, which threatened to wrest strongman General Manuel Noriega from power.

Noriega was expected to block the democratic process through voting fraud and intimidation, and not surprisingly, he resisted the idea of having foreign observers watching over the election. Carter, who had negotiated the Panama Canal Treaties (which put control of the waterway back into the hands of Panamanians in 2000) talked Noriega into allowing nineteen foreign observers, including himself and Ford, to participate. When Carter concluded that pro-Noriega forces had indeed manipulated the ballot count, preventing opposition candidate Guillermo Endara from taking power, he condemned Noriega for blocking the path of democracy, and successfully appealed to leaders of the Organization of American States to do the same. In a media breakthrough that helped further his image as ex-president, the press heaped praise on Carter for his role in taking on Noriega. Up until that time, he had been celebrated for his post–White House humanitarian contributions, but had yet to be fully recognized for his efforts to foster peace and democracy abroad.[104]

Ford, on the other hand, was denounced for leaving Panama on Election Day—after three days of meeting with pro- and anti-Noriega coalitions—to honor a commitment to attend a celebrity golf tournament in California. *The Washington Post* pointed out what it saw as the wretched excesses of the Ford post-presidency, reminding readers that Ford, in contrast to Carter, "sits on corporate boards and is available as a golf partner for wealthy groupies."[105] Ford felt Carter had overstepped his bounds as an ex-president and was getting in the way of the Bush administration. Carter's activism as an ex-president stood in contrast to the more traditional role Ford had chosen for himself. "I backed off, and he pushed himself forward," he recalled.[106] Ford's ego bruise notwithstanding, the friendship survived intact, and continued to deepen over the years.

When they reunited in December 2000 with fellow-former George Bush and President Clinton at a dinner celebrating the two-hundredth anniversary of the White House, held at the mansion, both of them commented warmly on their unique relationship. "Certainly few observers in January 1977 would have predicted that Jimmy and I would become the closest of friends," Ford told the invited guests, mostly presidential family members and historians. "Yet we have, bonded by our years in this office, and this house." In his turn at the podium, Carter reciprocated. "I challenge any historian here tonight," he said, "to find any former presidents who, after leaving the White House, have formed a closer and more intimate relationship than Gerald Ford and I. I am grateful for that."[107]

While Betty Ford may have lacked a sense of purpose upon giving up her duties as first lady, she soon found one in fighting addiction. After helping a friend and neighbor, Leonard Firestone, with his recovery from alcoholism—a year after beginning her own—she realized that she could make a difference. Afterward, she and Firestone, along with Joe Cruse, another recovering alcoholic, began raising funds for a rehabilitation center to be built on the grounds of the Eisenhower Medical Center in Palm Springs. "[Mrs. Ford] has extracted so much money around here that next year she's going to be a poster child for the IRS," cracked Bob Hope, a contributor and desert neighbor.[108] Mrs. Ford consented to be president of the facility's board, and then agreed, reluctantly at first, to the name her partners had proposed for it after they convinced her it would an asset. On October 3, 1982, President and Mrs. Ford, Firestone, Cruse, members of the Ford family, Vice President and Mrs. Bush, the 15th Air Force Band, the Army Chorale, and some four hundred invited guests showed up in Palm Springs for the dedication of the state-of-the-art Betty Ford Center. A number of people took their turns at the podium, including the former president, who choked up as he addressed his wife: "We're proud of you, Mom . . . we want you to know that we love you."[109]

In her best-selling 1985 book, *Betty: A Glad Awakening*, in which Mrs. Ford describes in detail her struggle with addiction and the creation of the Betty Ford Center, she related a startling statistic: Nine out of ten marriages survive in which the husband is an alcoholic and the wife is not, but only one out of ten survives when the wife is the alcoholic. The Fords not only beat the odds, but they also strengthened their bond—and their family's—through the ordeal. A year into Mrs. Ford's recovery, Ford stopped drinking too, professing to have never much enjoyed it anyway; he just hadn't wanted his wife to drink alone.[110]

As Mrs. Ford happily busied herself at the center that bore her name—raising funds, aiding in administration, and attending meetings and group therapy sessions—Ford continued his busy schedule of speaking engagements, board meetings, golf outings, and various projects. When asked about the role of an ex-president, he responded, "Each of us has different activities and interests. You can't put everybody in the same niche."[111] He, in particular, seemed to be enjoying his. Each year, under the auspices of the World Forum, sponsored by the American Enterprise Institute, Ford put together a reunion of many of the foreign leaders who had served as international counterparts when he was in power. At his invitation, former heads of state—including Great Britain's James Callaghan, France's Valéry Giscard d'Estaing, and Germany's Helmut Schmidt—and one hundred or so foreign policy experts and business leaders convened in Vail to discuss the state of the world. Ford explained it as, "a conspiracy of former world leaders against present world leaders. But thank God none of us has the power to alter anything anymore." They also made a little time to socialize and reminisce at the Fords' $2.5 million home, which they had bought after trading in their ski condo.[112]

In addition, Ford oversaw the annual Jerry Ford Invitational Golf Tournament and The American Ski Classic, featuring the Jerry Ford Celebrity Cup, both in Vail. He even added acting to his résumé. In 1983, he, Mrs. Ford, and Henry Kissinger made brief cameo appearances in the prime-time soap opera and America's guilty pleasure, *Dynasty*, mixing it up at a party with the show's wealthy and troubled Carrington clan. Ford could add the $330 union payment he received for the gig to a burgeoning portfolio of assets, including two Colorado radio stations he had acquired with Leonard Firestone, Mrs. Ford's cofounder at the center, through their joint company, Fordstone.

He continued to keep a watchful eye over the country and the world, not with his own agenda in mind like Nixon or Carter, but to make sure the country's best interests were being served. As the Clinton era progressed, he became increasingly concerned over the "poisonous" political atmosphere that had become the status quo in Washington.[113] When the House of Representatives threatened to impeach Clinton at the height of the Monica Lewinsky scandal in 1998, Ford, in a joint resolution with Jimmy Carter (marking the first time Carter had directly intervened in a political matter as an ex-president), counseled Republican representatives to vote to "censure" the president, stopping short of impeachment but sending a strong message.[114] "History will be the judge of President Clinton," he said later. "And, you can't spin history."[115]

Most Republican House members patently ignored the Carter-Ford recommendation and impeached Clinton anyway, an impetuous move that backfired when the Senate rejected Clinton's expulsion and the president looked like the victim of zealous Republicans who were simply out for blood. This was not the same House that Ford had left twenty-five years earlier, when partisan lines weren't drawn like the borders of battling nations, and political differences were put aside and beers were often lifted after 5:00 P.M. Clinton, as it turned out, also ignored Ford's advice. During the scandal he had phoned Ford for his take on the situation. "Bill, you have to be straightforward on this crisis," he counseled the young president. "You'd better be honest because it's not going to go away." Clinton reiterated what he had told the American people—that he was innocent of all charges, a claim that lacked honesty on an issue that didn't go away.[116]

Two years later, though, it was clear that Ford's impression on the American government had not faded completely. When George W. Bush took office in 2001, he named three of Ford's former White House aides— all young Turks in the Ford years—to key posts in his administration. Paul O'Neill, Ford's chief deputy to the director of the Office of Management and Budget, became secretary of treasury; Don Rumsfeld, whom Ford appointed as the secretary of defense, the youngest ever at forty-two, again took up the post for Bush, as the oldest at sixty-seven; and Dick Cheney, who, while only in his early thirties, had been Ford's chief of staff, now became Bush's number-two as vice president. Additionally, his budget director, Alan Greenspan, remained in the post of chairman of the Federal Reserve Bank, a post he had originally been assigned by Reagan. All told, Bush II looked as much like the Ford administration as Bush I did, showing that the old man had had an eye for talent.

In fact, Ford's presidency continued to look better year by year. Like Harry Truman, whose portrait Ford chose to hang over the conference table in his White House Cabinet Room, he came to be appreciated well after leaving office for the character it took to make the tough decisions of his presidency, in particular his pardon of Nixon. By the nineties, a number of prominent writers and historians had offered new perspectives on him and his presidency. His biographer, Richard Reeves, who wrote *A Ford, Not a Lincoln*, in Ford's first year as president, authored an article in *American Heritage* magazine entitled, "I'm Sorry, Mr. President," in which he contritely suggested he was wrong in his original assessment of the thirty-eighth president. Attending a conference on the Ford years at Hofstra University in 1989, historian Stephen Ambrose said that at the time of the pardon, "I shared the feelings of helpless rage that overcame millions of Americans. My fury knew no bounds. I cursed, I screamed, I swore I'd never ever forgive Ford." But, he confessed, "Over the years, I have come to realize that Ford was absolutely right to do what he did."[117]

Edmund Morris, Reagan's official biographer who won a Pulitzer Prize for his biography of Theodore Roosevelt, maintained that Ford is the "most underrated modern president," and James Cannon offered high praise for Ford in his 1994 book entitled *Time and Chance: Gerald Ford's Appointment with History*.[118] Bob Woodward, who broke the Watergate story with fellow *Washington Post* writer Carl Bernstein, also later agreed with the pardon, a concession Ford was particularly proud of.[119] Even Carter, who reminded voters often during the 1976 campaign of the egregiousness of the Nixon pardon, conceded in hindsight that it was the best thing for the country, and called Ford "one of my political heroes."[120] If Herbert Hoover's best revenge on his critics was that he had "outlived the bastards," Ford's was that he had proven them wrong. The public came around too. In recent opinion polls hearkening back to the pardon, the majority of Americans support the decision, a number that continues to grow over time.

As the lone surviving member of the Warren Commission, Ford also saw the increasing acceptance of the "lone assassin" conclusion he and his colleagues had come to as the explanation of the Kennedy assassination, as conspiracy theories—from Oliver Stone's *JFK* to byzantine plots involving the Soviet Union, Cuba, the mob, the FBI, even Lyndon Johnson—withered away from lack of sustenance.

There was even a certain irony when Chevy Chase became addicted to pain pills prescribed for back injuries he sustained from the falls he did lampooning Ford on *Saturday Night Live*, and was treated at . . . the Betty Ford Center.[121]

The growing appreciation of Ford's leadership was evident when President Clinton awarded him the Medal of Freedom at a White House ceremony in 1999. But the recognition that meant the most to Ford came in 2001, when a bipartisan committee of eleven political and community leaders and historians named him as the recipient of the John F. Kennedy Profile in Courage Award.[122] The committee, which included Kennedy's daughter, Caroline Kennedy Schlossberg, and historian David McCullough, selected Ford for the political selflessness of the Nixon pardon. As Mrs. Schlossberg said, "In an effort to heal a divided nation, he made the very difficult decision that many believe may have cost him the presidency."[123] Ford was touched by the award, which he received in a ceremony at the John F. Kennedy Library on Boston Harbor in May of 2001. Jack Kennedy had been Ford's friend in Congress, and, almost forty years after his death, the luster of the Kennedy presidential legacy gleamed brighter than any of his contemporaries, burnished by the mystique of Kennedy's martyred image, and his family and loyal aides who kept his memory alive and vital. Now the Kennedy glow added light to Ford's own legacy as a self-described "healer and builder."[124] He acknowledged that receiving the award may have been his greatest honor since leaving the White House, and thanked the committee for displaying "its own brand of courage" in selecting him. "To know Jack Kennedy, as I did," he added, "was to understand the true meaning of the word [courage]. President Kennedy understood that courage is not something to be gauged in a poll or located in a focus group. No advisor can spin it. No historian can backdate it."[125]

History, it would seem, had caught up to Gerald Ford.

Less than four months after receiving the Profile in Courage Award, the U.S. faced another dark hour, its worst in two generations or more, when it was struck by the terrorist attacks of September 11. Several days afterward, in a memorial service at the National Cathedral in Washington, Ford and three other former presidents, Carter, Bush, and Clinton, listened as President George W. Bush offered words to comfort and rally the nation. Their presence was symbolic of the unity America enjoys not uniquely but distinctly. Ford, at eighty-eight, the oldest among them by eleven years, had been at the center of more history than anyone in the room: in naval duty in the Pacific during World War II; in Congress during the McCarthy hearings, the Korean and Vietnam Wars, and the worst of the Cold War; on the Warren Commission investigating Kennedy's assassination; in the vice presidency during the height of Watergate; and in the White House after Nixon's resignation and the last days of the Vietnam War and the fall of Saigon. He, perhaps more than any, suggested that America always endured and that it would weather this storm too, as long as we had faith in ourselves.

Three decades have passed since Ford's brief reign as president. He consistently falls in the middle of the pack in rankings of the presidents and will not be remembered among the greats. But there are times in history when greatness is not required. During a time of disquiet and uncertainty, Ford, through his inherent decency, almost single-handedly restored the faith of the American people in their government. Greatness may not have been in Jerry Ford; goodness may have been the best that he could offer. And at that point in time, Jerry Ford may have been best for America.

Jimmy Carter's gracious acknowledgment of Ford in his inaugural address and their resulting handshake portended two things over time: a growing appreciation for Ford's political selflessness in healing the wounds of Watergate and Vietnam, and Carter's indelible role as a peacemaker. Though they couldn't have seen it on that winter's day in 1977, that moment of gratitude and renewal contained the seeds of their legacies.

VI.

JIMMY CARTER:
PEACEMAKER

Plains, Georgia, held little promise for a former president of the United States. A small farm town in the southwest corner of the state that had barely changed since Jimmy Carter sold boiled peanuts on Main Street as a boy during the Depression, Plains was home to 630 souls. Among them was the thirty-ninth president. And it was there that he found himself on Friday, January 22, 1981, upon awakening after almost twenty-four hours of sleep to, as he would later describe it, "an altogether new, unwanted, and potentially empty life."[1]

The last several days had been an exhausting whirlwind of activity and emotion. The previous Sunday morning, he had woken up at the White House, where he would spend the next two days desperately seeking an end to the Iranian hostage crisis that had crippled his presidency. With Ronald Reagan about to succeed him, he and his aides holed up in the Oval Office, negotiating the intricate settlement that would mean the fifty-two U.S. citizens who had been held captive since November 4, 1979, would soon be free. By the time President-elect and Mrs. Reagan arrived at the White House at 11:00 on Tuesday morning to be escorted by the Carters to the Capitol for Reagan's inauguration, Carter had not been to bed for over fifty hours.[2] When he finally left the Oval Office at 10:45 A.M. on Tuesday with the deal not yet confirmed, scrambling to get into his morning clothes before the Reagans' arrival, he glanced in a mirror and wondered, Was it just the exhaustion of the past few days, or had the presidency aged him?[3]

Carter's last year in office may have aged the strongest man in his place. Upon taking office after the euphoria of edging out the incumbent president Gerald Ford in 1976, Carter, in the long wake of Watergate, aimed to create a government "as good as the American people." To show he was one of them, he and Rosalynn Carter, along with their three sons and daughter, walked the 1.2 miles from the Capitol to the White House after his own inauguration in 1977. It was the first time a president had walked from the ceremony since Thomas Jefferson declined a carriage ride and went on foot to his boardinghouse after taking the presidential oath 176 years earlier. The surprised crowd lining Pennsylvania Avenue roared its approval at seeing the new president flashing his now-famous smile and waving with one hand while clutching his wife's hand with the other. Jimmy Carter was going to be a different kind of president.

And he was. This president carried his own bag when traveling, asked that the Marine Band refrain from playing "Hail to the Chief" and "Ruffles and Flourishes" at formal ceremonies, and did a series of radio call-in shows with moderator Walter Cronkite where average citizens could call him directly with their concerns.[4] Those populist gestures and others contrasted him sharply with some of the more imperious men who had held the office before him.

He poured himself into the job—and expected his staff to do the same— immersing himself in the details of even the most minor issues before him, prompting some to criticize his instinct to micromanage. Proud of his outsider status and unwilling to conform to the way things were done in Washington, Carter made few friends in the capital, refusing to court the press and power brokers, and even alienating key members of his own party. With inflation rampant, oil costs escalating, and employment numbers falling to alarming rates, conditions he inherited in part from Ford and Nixon, he struggled to keep the economy on track. Human rights were the hallmark of his administration and a primary determinant in foreign policy. As a reflection of his convictions, Carter boycotted the 1980 Summer Olympic Games in Moscow to protest the Soviet Union's invasion of Afghanistan, a move not popular with either the Politburo or the American people.

Still, he racked up some impressive accomplishments in his first several years in office. Taking on a number of the controversial issues his predecessors had sidestepped, he negotiated and signed the Panama Canal Treaties, which would put the canal back under the control of Panama by 2000, and doubled the size of the U.S. national parks, in an effort to better protect the environment. In answer to the energy crisis, which had driven up gas prices dramatically, Carter enacted a national energy policy and took measures to stimulate domestic petroleum production. Working in secret throughout 1978, he normalized trade relations with the People's Republic of China on the first day of 1979. His crowning achievement, though, was the Camp David Accords, an agreement he brokered during a grueling thirteen-day summit between Israeli prime minister Menachem Begin and Egyptian president Anwar Sadat, paving the way for a peace treaty between the two warring nations. On a perfect spring day in 1979, as Begin and Sadat stood ceremonially with Carter on the White House lawn with their hands stacked upon each other in unity, two bitter enemies overcoming hate to arrive at peace on U.S. soil, anything seemed possible for Jimmy Carter. He even allowed the Marine Band to play "Hail to the Chief" for the occasion.[5]

But no man can fully dictate the events that will define his time. In the fall of 1978, when Iranian revolutionary "students" stormed the U.S. Embassy in Tehran and abducted fifty-two Americans, Carter's presidency was held hostage with them. As days turned into months with no resolution to the crisis in sight, despite the military might of the U.S., the American people grew increasingly demoralized—and the blame fell squarely on the president. When he confronted the country with its "crisis of confidence" in a nationally televised speech in 1979, the "malaise" speech as it would become known, it all seemed his own doing. His fate was sealed in April 1980, when a commando mission to rescue the hostages ended in tragedy. Six C-130 transport planes carrying ninety troops landed in the Iranian desert, where eight helicopters were deployed to storm the U.S. embassy. When only six of the helicopters made it to their rendezvous site, too few to successfully complete the mission, Carter ordered them to pull back. Upon their retreat, one of the helicopters exploded when it hit a transport plane, taking with it the lives of eight servicemen and badly burning four others. The wounded men were evacuated with the remaining troops, but the bodies of the eight who died in the maneuver were left on the ground and later paraded around Tehran and put on display outside the U.S. embassy. As president, Carter never again found favor with the American public after the mission's failure. Reagan coasted to victory in the 1980 election, capturing 51 percent of the electorate to Carter's 41 percent, and Carter faced "involuntary retirement" at the age of fifty-six.[6]

The relief that the hostages had been released after 444 days in captivity came soon after Carter's presidential burden had been lifted. Confirmation that a deal had been struck came to Carter by telephone as he left the ceremonies by limousine en route to Andrews Air Force Base. While the Carters were on an Air Force jet headed for home, the hostages left Iranian air space bound for Algiers and then on to Rhein-Main Air Base just outside Frankfurt, Germany. A driving rain fell when the Carters arrived in Plains, but neighbors and friends, some who had known them their whole lives, greeted them like conquering heroes with a covered-dish supper in the town square.

After the celebration, Carter got a few hours of sleep, then went by helicopter to Robins Air Force Base in Warner Robins, Georgia, and flew eight and a half hours to Wiesbaden, Germany, to welcome the hostages back to freedom along with his vice president, Walter Mondale, and others from his administration. It was the first time Carter and Mondale had been on a flight together, since as government officials they had flown separately in the event of an accident. Once at Rhein-Main, they held a fifty-minute private meeting with the fifty-two Americans whose names and families they had come to know. It was an emotionally draining session that, as Mondale recalled later, "had to be held—but it wasn't happy." Carter spoke briefly, expressing relief that the group was now free, sorrow that their capture had happened on his watch, and pride at their dignity and courage. Then he invited questions, some of which were "tinged with anger" that put him on the defensive, including one about the failed rescue mission. It was clear that while they were glad to be free, many had felt let down by the administration. "This was a damaged group," Mondale said. "They didn't know how to deal with Carter." In a ten-minute Oval Office briefing Mondale would give Reagan afterward, he would characterize the meeting as tense and anxious, adding that "there was a lot of healing that [the] hostages [would have] to go through."[7]

Carter would have to go through a period of healing too. After the meeting, which he described to the press as "emotional and gratifying," he flew back to Plains to sleep off the exhaustion of the past week and get on with the rest of his life.[8]

While Carter may not have known what he wanted to do as an ex-president, he knew what he didn't want to do. He wasn't interested in sitting on corporate boards or making money on the speaking circuit, though he didn't begrudge those who did. Two major universities dangled president's positions before him, but that didn't appeal to him either. Harry Truman, who was his commander in chief while he was in the navy from 1946 to 1953, was Carter's favorite president in his lifetime, and it was Truman whom he most chose to emulate as a former president.[9] Truman, like Carter, left Washington and went back to his own hometown of Independence, Missouri, and the small-town life he had known in all his years before ambition swept him to Washington. Resisting abundant offers to cash in on the presidency, Truman's post-presidential life revolved around the Truman Library, where he estimated he lectured over 200,000 high school students on the presidency through the years.[10] Carter liked that, but he also wanted something that appealed more to "[his] talents, ambitions, and above all, [his] interests."[11] He just didn't know what it was.

The uncertainty of what he would do in the years ahead, and the prospect of raising money for his own presidential library were just two of the anxieties Carter faced in his transition back to private life. There were many others. The Carters' modest ranch-style home on Woodland Street at the edge of town had not been lived in for ten years and had been badly neglected; they had lived in the Georgia governor's mansion in Atlanta from 1971 to 1974, campaigned for the presidency throughout the country from 1975 through 1976, and resided in the White House for the following four years. Boxes shipped from the White House were stacked to the ceiling throughout the house, which lacked proper storage space, and the woods the property bordered had crept up into their yard and needed to be cleared. Thirteen-year-old Amy, the youngest of the Carters' four children by fifteen years, and the only one to live in the White House, wanted nothing to do with the small-town life Plains offered. The Carters, who had enrolled her in public school in Washington while in the White House, made arrangements to send her to Woodward Academy, a private boarding school in Atlanta, two and a half hours north of Plains, making them empty-nesters several years sooner than they had expected.

Then there was the matter of money. The Carters had accrued a debt from the presidential campaign that amounted to $1.4 million, but they would discover shortly after losing the election that the lucrative farming

business they took over from Carter's father in the fifties had been misman-
aged by the blind trust that handled their private business transactions while
they were in the White House. Not only was the business no longer prof-
itable, but they were also in debt by over $1 million, with no cash reserve
to pay it off.[12] Finally, there were the wounds of defeat at the hands of Reagan and the rejection of the American electorate that still hurt deeply.

Carter spent his first weeks out of office turning the events of his presidency around in his perfectionist mind, wondering what he could have
done better. The failed Desert One mission haunted him.[13] "I wish I had
sent one more helicopter on that rescue mission," he said more than twenty-
five years after the fact, a regret he voiced many times in his post-presidency
but likely felt with no greater intensity than in its first stages.[14] He thought
a lot about the hostage crisis and how he could have handled it differently.
But his biggest failure, as he saw it, was losing office to Ronald Reagan, a
man whom Carter saw as not only an intellectual lightweight, but as "im-
moral to the core," according to Carter biographer, Douglas Brinkley.[15]
"When the voters decided to change horses in midstream, not only had they
rejected us, but almost 50 percent of them had chosen a horse determined
to run as fast as possible in the opposite direction," he wrote later. As time
went by, though, he convinced himself that he had done the best he could,
"correctly or not," and his survivor's instinct to move on took hold.[16]

It was harder for Mrs. Carter. "The thing that bothered me most was
that no one knew what Jimmy had done in office. That was the hardest
part," she recalled.[17] Proud of his political courage in the stands he had
taken on controversial issues, she resented the characterization of him as a
failed president, and harbored the hope that he would challenge Reagan to
a second round in 1984, knowing in her heart he would not return to elective office.[18] She wondered how God could have let their defeat happen.
Her dramatic change in circumstance became clear several months after arriving home when she realized that the most important thing in her life
could be whether the brick walkway they were building in front of their
house would be crooked or straight.[19] The former president tried to com-
pensate for his wife's depression in those first weeks by adopting a facade
of artificial cheerfulness, which may only have served to strain their relationship when she felt he didn't recognize the pain she was feeling.[20]

The first thing the Carters set their mind to after arriving home was getting their house back in shape after a decade's worth of neglect. The labor they put into the task turned into a blessing; hours of physically demanding work kept them from thinking of the exalted lives they had left behind. "I was devastated when Jimmy lost the election, and thought that coming home I would be bored for the rest of my life," Mrs. Carter said looking back. "But when we got home it was not as bad as I thought it was going to be because there was so much to do." The former president, a skilled carpenter, spent long, hot hours in the close quarters of their attic, laying down a tongue-and-groove wood floor to store the boxes of White House papers and memorabilia that cluttered the house. He and Mrs. Carter also worked through the winter and spring, clearing the vegetation that had overtaken their property. "By the time we'd get into the house [after a long day], the evening news would be over and I didn't want to see it anyway," Mrs. Carter recalled. As time went on, though, she realized how much things in Washington had changed under the new administration, and felt more comfortable in moving forward with her life.[21] "There were traumatic things that happened back then, but you have to put it behind you and do the best you can," she said. Eventually she did.

Being home in Plains helped too. The townspeople "welcomed us home with open arms," she said. "When we got home we were just Jimmy and Rosalynn Carter like we had always been. It was nice to be back with family and friends who cared about [us]."[22] Plains, a town steeped in religious faith, community, and hard work, defined Jimmy Carter in the same way the Texas Hill Country did Lyndon Johnson. He knew its people by name, and related to their lives and concerns. Though the town held "few job prospects" for an ex-president, he never doubted that Plains was where he belonged.[23] Soon the Carters were once again active in community affairs, showing up at local events and regularly attending services at Maranatha Baptist Church, where Carter taught Sunday school whenever he was in town.

As with Richard Nixon seven years earlier, their financial debts were almost entirely relieved through book deals the Carters signed to write their memoirs. Carter carved out a multimillion-dollar deal with Bantam Books to share the story of his presidency, and Mrs. Carter signed her own lucrative deal with Houghton Mifflin for her autobiography. The execution of those projects would keep them busy long after they got their house back in shape. They further alleviated their financial situation by selling their business, the Carter Peanut Warehouse, which had withered away during their time in Washington. The company was sold for a generous sum to the Archer Daniels Midland Corporation, allowing them to hold on to two thousand acres of farmland outside of Plains that had been in the Carter family for generations.[24]

Carter resolved to do the intensive research and writing for his memoir within the course of a year, a goal Steven Hochman—a professor and presidential scholar from Princeton University who was retained to help with the book—thought "quite unreasonable."[25] For one thing, it meant combing through some six thousand pages of notes from Carter's four-year tenure.[26] But Hochman would soon discover Carter's love of a challenge, and his intensity in meeting it. The former president delved into the project with "enthusiasm and excitement," often outworking Hochman in ten- or twelve-hour workdays that began at 5:00 A.M.[27] The only time Carter's spirit waned was toward the end of the project when they covered the last year of his presidency. Reliving those final twelve months, and all the turbulence and disappointment that had unfolded, was draining. Nonetheless, he worked at a fast, thorough clip, delivering the manuscript for the memoir, to be called *Keeping Faith*, within a year and achieving his goal.

It took Mrs. Carter considerably longer—three years—to deliver her own memoir, *First Lady from Plains*, which spanned her life from her childhood in Plains to her departure from the White House. She worked at a pace decidedly slower than her husband's, although, like him, she enjoyed putting her story down on paper, a process she found "cathartic," further easing her transition back to private life. She also found covering the last year in the White House particularly hard, and encountered similar difficulty in writing a chapter that explored race relations at home in Plains.[28]

Keeping Faith and Mrs. Carter's *First Lady from Plains* were both published to critical and commercial success, boosting the bank accounts and spirits of their authors. As they would write later in their joint book effort, *Everything to Gain: Making the Most of the Rest of Your Life*, a "friendly competition" on whose book would do better ensued. Carter's book sold more copies, but his wife's spent eighteen weeks on *The New York Times* best-seller list, reaching the number-one position, versus *Keeping Faith*, which made the list for thirteen weeks and never made it above the number-three position.[29]

The construction of the Carter Library presented another challenge for Carter. He recognized that raising the money to build a presidential library was an "onerous burden" faced by all modern ex-presidents, but none more so than a self-described "one-term president with no plans to reenter the political arena." Gerald Ford, who was in a similar position, told Carter that drumming up the cumulative $15.3 million for his library and museum was the most difficult task of his life. Even with the money, Carter had no interest in creating a monument to himself, which is how he viewed most of the presidential libraries. He wanted his to be different, more utilitarian and in line with his interests.[30] The question he and Mrs. Carter continually asked themselves was, "How?"

Carter would arrive at an answer late one night in January 1982. Mrs. Carter awoke in their bedroom to find him sitting up in the middle of the bed. She thought he was sick; he usually retired early and slept soundly through the night, even during the most difficult days in the White House.[31] On this night, however, he was struck conscious by an epiphany—he knew what they could do with the Carter Library. "We can make it into a place to help people who want to resolve disputes," he told her. "There is no place like that now. If two countries really want to work something out now, they don't want to go to the United Nations and get one hundred fifty other countries involved . . . We could get mediators that both sides would trust, and they could meet with no publicity, no fanfare, perhaps at times in total secrecy . . . There've been a lot of new theories on conflict resolution [since Camp David], and we could put some of them into use."[32]

In the next several weeks, they further fleshed out the concept, talking excitedly of using the center to address other issues of interest to them: peace and human rights; famine and health issues afflicting the world's poor; and furthering the work Mrs. Carter had done on mental health dating back to 1971, when Carter was governor of Georgia.[33] For the first time since leaving the White House, they were excited by the possibilities their future might hold. But making "The Carter Center" into the kind of organization Carter envisioned was a tall order, particularly for a former president whose agenda had been vetoed by the American voters when they drove him from office. Then again, Jimmy Carter had spent his life achieving his ambitions against all odds, and, as his life's accomplishments reflected, he was nothing if not driven and determined.

As a boy growing up in Plains, the oldest of four children—he had two sisters and a brother—Carter's father nicknamed him "Hot," short for "Hotshot." It was an apt moniker for a smart, talented kid teeming with confidence. He grew up helping out on the family farm and enjoying a Huck Finn–like small-town life in the rural, segregated South which he would later recount in detail in his 2001 book, *An Hour Before Daylight: Memories of a Rural Boyhood*. In 1942, he enrolled in the U.S. Naval Academy in Annapolis, Maryland. While on leave in Plains during his junior year, he met a friend of his sister Gloria's named Rosalynn Smith, a Plains native who was three years younger. Rosalynn grew up working as a dressmaker after school to help her mother earn extra money for her and her three siblings following her father's unexpected death when she was thirteen. Like Carter, she had grown up in Plains, a product of small-town Southern life. She was a freshman at Georgia Southwestern State University in Americus when she and Carter went on their first date. Afterwards, he announced to his mother, "She's the girl I'm going to marry."[34] They courted for a year before wedding in 1946, the same year Carter graduated from the Naval Academy.

Through Carter's career as a naval officer, the young couple was able to cut their Plains roots, and experience life in Virginia, Hawaii, Connecticut, and upstate New York. Along the way, they produced three sons, Jack, Chip, and Jeff from 1947 to 1952, and would later have a daughter, Amy, born in 1967. Recognizing Carter's sharp engineering mind, the navy assigned him to duty working under the legendary nuclear physicist, Admiral Hyman Rickover, who oversaw its nuclear submarine project. But when his father died of cancer in 1953, Carter, against his wife's wishes, chose to quit his promising naval career and return to Plains to be the kind of quiet community pillar he realized his "daddy" had been. Through the years, working together, they built up his father's business, expanding it into a thriving enterprise that sold shelled peanuts, seed, and fertilizer, and settled into a comfortable life in their hometown.

In 1962, Carter ran for the Georgia state senate, winning office only after challenging the election results, which had been rigged by a powerful local political boss. (Carter would later write of the campaign in his 1994 book, *Turning Point*.) He served two two-year terms before running for governor in 1966, in an election he lost narrowly to segregationist candidate Lester Maddox. Crushed by the defeat, he turned to religion, rededicating himself to his Baptist faith by becoming "born again," and embarking on a "new life" by accepting Jesus Christ as his savior. By 1970, he was back in the political arena, vying for the governorship against a liberal opponent, former governor Carl Saunders. Carter exploited race to angle a win over Saunders, using code words as a tactic to sway rural white voters. Upon taking office, however, he announced that "the time for racial discrimination is over," and set a progressive agenda that belied his campaign's racist undertone.[35] That posture gained him his first major national media exposure when he appeared on the cover of *Time* magazine in 1971 as one of a new breed of moderate Southern governors.

Restricted by law from running for reelection to the Atlanta governorship for another consecutive four-year term, Carter set his sights on the ultimate political prize by announcing his candidacy for presidency in 1974, to the indifference of voters, the press, and his own party. Though few noticed, many of those that did asked, "Jimmy who?"—a question that would recur throughout the campaign. With almost no money or name recognition, Carter, along with his wife and a small staff—and later, a dedicated band of supporters called "The Peanut Brigade"—worked feverishly over the next two years, knocking on doors, sleeping in the homes of supporters, and getting to know the most remote corners of Iowa and New Hampshire. Against a field of well-established and well-known opponents, including Hubert Humphrey, George McGovern, and Morris Udall, Carter racked up one Democratic primary win after another—until he had won all fourteen. After becoming his party's candidate, he went on to manage a slim victory over Ford in 1976, pulling off what amounted to a political miracle. To those who had derisively asked "Jimmy who?", the former dark-horse candidate offered a simple, tacit answer on his inauguration day: Carter. President Jimmy Carter.

The only blemish in a lifetime of prodigious achievement was the presidency itself, as reflected in his approval rating upon leaving office, which stood at a meager 34 percent.[36] After leaving Washington, few were left behind to defend him. When he came into office as an outsider, he brought his own troops and resisted cuddling up to the Washington establishment; when he left four years later in defeat, his troops retreated with him, and the establishment was glad to see them go.

"Jimmy Carter's name still comes up in Washington," wrote *The New York Times* in April 1982, "and when it does the reaction typically consists of jokes, winces, shrugs, and frowns." Carter lacked clout and credibility in Washington, and was unlikely to find it in a town that had quickly embraced Ronald Reagan, another outsider who would make the town his own.[37] Even Carter's own party distanced itself from him. In a speech at Washington's annual Gridiron Dinner, a light, bipartisan gathering that drew the town's elite, Morris Udall related how he had been beat by Carter in every primary in 1976. "How would you like that on your record?" he asked ironically to the delight of the audience.[38] Reagan, who also attended the dinner, laughed along with the rest of the crowd. He was no different; his administration made Carter a modern-day Herbert Hoover, FDR's predecessor and Depression-era scapegoat, blaming Carter for the slow economy, America's diminished standing abroad, and, in particular, the declining state of the military. Even outside of Washington, Carter was challenged to find supporters. Most financial backers from the 1980 campaign wanted no part of Carter after his loss. "The people who gave money to President Carter, the winner were not interested in ex-president Carter, the loser," observed Carter aide Hamilton Jordan.[39]

Making The Carter Center work would require Carter to forge his own path once again, just as he had done in the election of 1976. The qualities he would bring to the task—a Christian missionary's philanthropic zeal, an incisive engineer's mind, boundless energy, a tenacious will, and an extraordinarily close partnership with his wife—would prove far more important to The Carter Center's long-term success than immediate political capital.

The first time Carter would make a deep impression on the public's collective consciousness as an ex-president was not for his work at The Carter Center, but by donning a hard hat and wielding a hammer for Habitat for Humanity, a nonprofit organization dedicated to helping struggling, low-income families achieve the dream of home ownership by offering qualified applicants no-interest loans, donated building materials, and volunteer construction labor. Carter knew little about the organization until he agreed to meet with its founder, Millard Fuller, shortly after arriving home.

Fuller, a native Alabaman, had been a successful lawyer and entrepreneur. At his wife Linda's urging, he gave up his prosperous business and material possessions to lead a more Christian life devoted to helping those in need. Habitat for Humanity, based in Americus, Georgia, ten miles from Plains, sprung from Fuller's vision. The formidable energy and initiative he had used to make himself a millionaire in his twenties was channeled toward making Habitat into a successful international venture, spawning local affiliate groups throughout the U.S. and abroad. Carter, after pledging $500 to the organization and putting his carpenter's talents into a day's labor at a Habitat construction site in Americus, developed an enthusiasm for the work and the cause that led to greater involvement, a condition known to frequent Habitat volunteers as *habititus*.[40]

In August of 1984, Carter, along with Fuller and a contingent of Georgian friends and neighbors, boarded a rented Trailways bus in Americus, bound for a derelict, six-floor tenement building on Sixth Street, between Avenues C and D on New York City's Lower East Side. After a twenty-five-hour trip up the eastern seaboard, the group settled in for a week of hard labor that would turn a hollow structure lacking a roof, doors, windows, and in some cases, floors, into a dozen finished apartment units. Braving the fierce summer heat and primitive conditions in "Alphabet City," one of New York's worst slums, the former president and first lady did all the jobs, large and small, required for the transition. Working alongside the other volunteers—including some of the eventual homeowners who were required to put "sweat equity" into the project as part of their agreement with Habitat—they banged nails, scraped paint, hauled two-by-fours, and swept up dust and debris. After long hours on the job, they retired to dormitory-style accommodations set up at Metro Baptist Church in "Hell's Kitchen," sharing rooms with multiple roommates and sleeping in bunk beds. (Mrs. Carter was a bit dismayed to discover she would be sharing a bathroom with twenty other women.)[41]

The Carters' involvement in the project touched off a media blitz. All the major network morning shows devoted segments to the story, and *The*

New York Times made it front-page news. Crowds of New Yorkers stood in front of the building, chanting, "Go, Jimmy, go!"[42] The indelible image of Carter as humanitarian construction worker was unlike anything the public had seen before from an ex-president—and presented a patent contrast to the worst of the Reagan-era zeitgeist, marked by materialism, conspicuous consumption, and Wall Street greed. Just as Jimmy Carter had been a different president, he was going to be, characteristically, a different former president.

The experience in New York proved galvanizing for the Carters—and for Habitat for Humanity, which reaped public relations dividends resulting in unprecedented levels of donations and volunteering. By the following year, Carter would serve on Habitat's board of directors, and dedicate himself to raising $10 million for the organization over two years, shelling out thousands of dollars from his own pocket to make the goal.[43] After their foray in New York, he and Mrs. Carter would make a sustained commitment as Habitat volunteers through the Jimmy Carter Work Project, which would take place annually, alternating between U.S. and international locations. Through the years, weeklong "blitz builds" would be completed in places as far and wide as South Philadelphia, South Africa, South Dakota, and South Korea, where 294 homes were built, a record for a Habitat build.[44] As in New York in the summer of 1984, Carter could always be counted on to be among the first to arrive at the job site in the morning, and among the last to leave at night. Over two decades later, the notion of a former president in dirty work clothes with calloused hands presenting a signed Bible to a new homeowner is no less powerful.

As plans for The Carter Center took shape in the early eighties, its focus became clearer. The Center would be "guided by a fundamental commitment to human rights and the alleviation of human suffering," and "seek to prevent and resolve conflicts, enhance freedom and democracy, and improve health."[45] Carter didn't want a "think tank" involved solely in research, but an action-oriented organization that would take on difficult problems in the U.S. and abroad that were not being adequately addressed by other countries or organizations. Partnering with Emory University, a private institution on the edge of Atlanta, gave the Center an academic affiliation without being reined in by government constraints, as would have been the case in partnering with a state university. Finally, Carter resolved to do only those things that were "not disapproved" by the current administration.[46]

On October 1, 1984, the $26 million Carter Center, including a museum and archive, broke ground in the shadow of downtown Atlanta. Just a day under two years later, President and Mrs. Reagan were on hand with the Carters for its dedication. (Nixon and Ford had begged off, citing pressing commitments and promising future visits.) All political differences between the two former political rivals were put aside for the occasion. Addressing the crowd in attendance, Reagan said of himself and his predecessor, "I can think of no other country on earth where two politicians could disagree so widely yet come together in mutual respect."[47] "For myself," he added, "I can pay you no higher honor than simply this: You gave of yourself to your country, gracing the White House with your passion and intellect and commitment." Responding to the president's gracious remarks, Carter said, "I think I understand more clearly than I ever had before why you won in November 1980, and I lost."

One of the principal purposes of The Carter Center was to take on problems not being adequately addressed by international governments or by other domestic and world organizations, in Carter's own words, "to fill vacuums."[48] In essence, the Center—and Carter himself—filled a void left by the demise of the great American liberal tradition of FDR, Truman, and LBJ, which had gone hopelessly out of fashion by the Reagan era. Though he had governed as a moderate, Carter made The Carter Center a beacon for the world's poor and downtrodden in the same way that FDR gave hope to Americans left behind during the Depression. In the latter years of the twentieth century, that meant focusing on issues affecting the poorest nations of the world, primarily in Africa, that had been plagued by disease, famine, tribal disputes, and political oppression. Like Eleanor Roosevelt before him, Carter spent much of his time after his years in the White House traveling the world and reaching out to those in need. The difference was that he could draw on the resources of The Carter Center to devise long-term solutions to the problems he and others at the organization identified.

As gracious as Reagan's remarks at the opening of The Carter Center were, the administration, for the most part, continued to shut Carter out for the remainder of Reagan's tenure, limiting his diplomatic opportunities.

He was also shut out politically in his own party. When Mondale took on Reagan for the presidency in 1984, he distanced himself from Carter out of political necessity, knowing his association with him would be a liability. Though relations between the two men remained good in and out of the White House—Mondale calls reports that their relationship was strained and that he considered taking himself off the ticket in 1980 "bad history"— Mondale drew on his former boss's support only behind the scenes.[49] Carter's one recommendation was that Mondale refrain from picking a token running mate, though his choice of New York congresswoman Geraldine Ferraro was perceived as just that.[50] Reagan went on to win in a walk, capturing nearly 60 percent of the popular vote and winning every state except Mondale's native Minnesota.

When George Bush succeeded Reagan in 1989, "it was like opening a new door for me," Carter recalled.[51] Not only was the door open, but the new president invited Carter in. Bush was far more receptive to Carter's diplomatic overtures than Reagan had been. Almost invariably when Carter would return from a sensitive overseas mission, he was invited to the White House to brief the president and his advisors, including secretary of state James Baker, with whom he had established a productive collaboration. In a big public relations boost for The Carter Center and the former president, Bush requested that Carter get involved in the democratization of Nicaragua, where the Contra War had raged, with funding for the Contra rebels coming from the Reagan administration. Carter participated in an international delegation to monitor the country's election in 1989, one of many he would oversee under the auspices of The Carter Center. After concluding that the voting had been rigged through fraud and intimidation, leaving the reigning government to remain in power, Carter led efforts in the Americas to pressure incumbent president Daniel Ortega to not block the democratic process. A subsequent election resulted in Ortega's defeat, and Carter was widely praised in the media for righting the wrong.

Not that everything with Bush was smooth sailing. When the U.S. threatened a ground war to drive the invading Iraqi army out of occupied Kuwait after the Bush administration's attempts at a diplomatic solution had been exhausted, Carter sent letters to the leaders of all the nations on the UN Security Council, urging them to vote against the use of force.

(The only exception was the arch-conservative Margaret Thatcher; he didn't want to "waste a stamp" on what was bound to be a futile appeal.)[52] Through his own back channels, Carter had learned that Iraqi leader Saddam Hussein would withdraw from Kuwait if given time. Though Carter had sent Bush a copy of the letter, the administration was not informed that it had also been sent to Bush's counterparts throughout the world. They found out when Canadian prime minister Brian Mulroney tipped off U.S. secretary of defense Dick Cheney, forwarding Carter's letter.[53]

Critics, including those in the Bush administration, eviscerated Carter for his attempt to undermine U.S. policy, which some likened to treason. Bush's national security advisor Brent Scowcroft maintained that "if ever there was a violation of the Logan Act prohibiting diplomacy by private citizens, that was it." Bush himself was "furious," but told Scowcroft to "drop it."[54] However, Bush "never quite got over" the incident, and it adversely changed his perception of Carter. "This guy marches [to the beat of] a different drummer," Bush later recalled thinking at the time. "I wouldn't think of doing that to another president."[55]

It also perpetuated Carter's growing reputation among detractors as a foreign policy meddler with renegade tendencies.[56] *Time* reported in 1994 that Carter later conceded his actions were "perhaps not appropriate," but he claimed in 2005 that he neither remembers making the statement nor harbors regrets for sending the letters.[57] With war on the line, and, from his perspective, a peaceful resolution still possible, he felt strongly it was the right thing to do. Indeed, though his actions often drew fire for being at odds with U.S. policy, Carter never thought better of anything he did in the name of peace.[58]

By the early nineties, Carter's profile had risen substantially. The former president seemed to be everywhere, from the most obscure nations to the most powerful, forging his own relationships with allied leaders and despots alike, and broadening his role as a peacemaker while arousing greater controversy among critics. When he was president, Carter drew cackles in the media when he kissed Leonid Brezhnev's cheek in friendship as the two stood on the Truman balcony of the White House while cameras clicked away during the Soviet leader's state visit. Detractors denounced Carter the ex-president for what they saw as his penchant for coddling dictators. Carter respectfully reached out a hand to some of the world's most reviled tyrants in an effort to not further isolate rogue states from the family of free nations. Establishing a dialogue with a former president of the United States gave them an air of credibility and respect, while giving Carter a chance to advance his agenda for democracy and human rights by appealing to their better nature. Two events in different parts of the world in 1994 proved not only the effectiveness of Carter's tactics, but also, what a potent force on the world stage he had once again become.

In the late spring, sabers rattled between the U.S. and North Korea, perhaps the world's most isolated state under the dictatorship of Kim Il Sung, who had held power since 1946. The U.S. grew increasingly concerned over North Korea's nuclear program in May, when the country withdrew from the International Atomic Energy Agency, and over the objections of the organization, removed 8,000 spent fuel rods from its largest nuclear reactor, sixty miles from Pyongyang, the country's capital.[59] Without the ability to examine the rods, which provided the best evidence of whether grade plutonium was being reprocessed into nuclear weapons, there was no way the international community could be certain that North Korea was not building up an arsenal in direct violation of the Nuclear Non-Proliferation Treaty. North Korea's recalcitrance resulted in the U.S.'s support of a trade embargo against the rogue nation, which the Clinton administration took up with the UN, a move that North Korea made clear it considered an act of war.

Three years earlier in 1991, Kim had extended a rare invitation for Carter to visit North Korea, and twice afterward Carter had been denied requests by the State Department to make the trip. As tensions escalated, though, at Carter's urgent request, Clinton gave him his okay to go to Pyongyang, but, wary of his tactics and keeping him at arm's length from the administration, stressed that he would be going as a "private citizen."[60] With his wife in tow as a note-taker, Carter journeyed to Pyongyang along with a CNN crew that had been granted permission by the North Korean government to cover the trip. In the course of two days, Carter had two lengthy meetings with Kim, bridged by a six-hour cruise on the Taedong River aboard the presidential yacht of the "Great Leader." Carter found the eighty-two-year-old Kim to be "vigorous, alert, and intelligent," and the two struck up an easy, respectful rapport.[61] After making progress in the first meeting by assuring Kim that the White House had "stopped sanction activity with the UN," Carter appeared on CNN urging that "nothing should be done to exacerbate the situation now," a pointed reference to the sanctions. He added, "The reason I came here was to prevent an irreconcilable mistake."[62] The White House, upon hearing Carter's statements, was furious. Not only had the administration not dropped the pursuit of sanctions through the UN, but it also didn't know that CNN had accompanied Carter. They had no idea that he would use the network as a vehicle to express his own views to the world—and the Clinton White House. In response, administration officials quickly took to the air themselves to clarify their position: The U.S. would continue to push for sanctions until North Korea backed down.

The following day Carter emerged from his final meeting with Kim, sanguine that his mission was a success. After hugging the dictator and calling the trip a "good omen," Carter professed confidence through CNN that Kim had abandoned his nuclear intentions.[63] He returned home after exacting promises from Kim to allow international nuclear inspectors back into the country and to use only light water reactor technology, which would lessen its ability to manufacture nuclear weapons. In exchange, the U.S. would be asked for financial and technical aid for the light water reactors and an assurance that it would not wage a nuclear attack against North Korea. In addition, Kim also agreed to return the bodies of three thousand U.S. American soldiers who had died during combat in the Korean War.

Though Carter's peacemaking skills ostensibly eased tensions with North Korea, helping Clinton sidestep a crisis, his renegade tactics further alienated him from the administration. The president stated publicly that he did not share his predecessor's optimism, expressing doubt that North Korea had committed to disarmament when it had established no basis of trust. Several administration officials implied Kim had suckered Carter, and the State Department initially declined Carter's offer to brief them upon his return. The criticism put Carter on the defensive; he called his statement regarding the U.S.'s halt in pursuing sanctions against North Korea a "mistake," and said "I don't feel that I have been duped, but the proof is in the pudding."[64] Eight days later Kim died unexpectedly, but proof would eventually emerge that Carter's mission was in fact successful, as North Korea's belligerent posture simmered over time.

Despite his ambivalence, it would be Carter to whom Clinton would turn three months later as his last hope to ward off a crisis, this time in Haiti, the small Caribbean nation that had suffered a history of brutal regimes. Carter had taken a strong interest in the affairs of the country through The Carter Center, visiting eight times after leaving office. He was there to monitor the voting process when the country held its first democratic election in December 1990, and returned in February to watch the inauguration of a thirty-seven-year-old Catholic priest named Jean-Bertrand Aristide, whom Haitian voters had elected as their president. Shortly after Aristide took office, however, a military coup led by Lieutenant General Raoul Cédras drove Aristide out of the presidential palace and into exile in Washington. In his place the junta appointed as the country's de facto president Emile Jonassaint, the eighty-one-year old chief of Haiti's Supreme Court. The junta's bloody rule resulted in the deaths of over three thousand Haitians. In 1994, Clinton intervened, threatening to take U.S. military action if its leaders didn't willingly cede power.[65] He established a firm deadline of September 19, as well as the terms of their surrender, which included their immediate departure from Haiti. But the ultimatum didn't work. Cédras wasn't budging, despite the threat of a military invasion by U.S. forces.

Fearing unnecessary bloodshed, Carter, who had developed a relationship with Cédras through his involvement in Haiti, had petitioned Clinton repeatedly to act as his diplomatic liaison in the matter, eventually enlisting Georgia senator Sam Nunn and Colin Powell, former head of the Joint Chiefs of Staff, to join him. With his back against the wall and the clock ticking on his ultimatum, Clinton gave Carter the go-ahead.

Early on the morning of September 17, Carter, Nunn, and Powell flew by Air Force jet to Haiti's capital, Port-au-Prince, Carter looking more like a tourist than a U.S. emissary, dressed in khaki pants and a white, open-collared, Latin-style Guayabera shirt. They arrived at 1:00 P.M. with strict instructions from Clinton to leave by noon the next day, deal or no deal. During the course of the next thirty-six hours, the delegation would hold a series of harried meetings with the junta leaders, members of Parliament, and industrialists, in a feverish attempt to prevent a military incursion.[66]

They met with Cédras twice on the day of their arrival, in the afternoon and evening, making clear the inevitability of the attack and providing details on how it would be executed. Powell, the former general, appealed to Cédras's military honor. "What military code calls for the senseless sacrifice of life?" he demanded. "Let me tell you what true honor is. It means having the courage to give up power rather than cause pointless death."[67] Both meetings broke up without a resolution as Cédras balked at the notion of exile, claiming that Haiti's constitution did not allow it.

The following morning at 8:15, the delegation arrived at Cédras's Mediterranean-style villa in the suburbs outside Port-au-Prince, where they had been invited by Cédras to meet his family. At a dinner with Haitian business leaders the evening before, the visiting Americans had been fortuitously told, "If you want to get through to Cédras, his wife [Yannick] is key."[68] "Our ability to convince [her] that [surrender] was proper and honorable was highly important," wrote Carter later.[69] In an incongruous scene, the group forcefully made their appeal to Mrs. Cédras, warning of the danger of the imminent offensive—all of this while she served cookies, and Carter autographed a picture for their fourteen-year-old daughter and gave a Carter Center pocketknife to their ten-year-old son who sat on his knee.[70] Like her husband, the general's wife remained unmoved, telling the delegation she would never accept the "insult" of an American invasion.[71] "We would rather die with American bullets in our chests, than as traitors, with Haitian bullets in our backs," she informed them.[72] Her posture "stunned" Carter, who thought their mission had failed.[73] But the delegation persisted in making their case for surrender. When they left the Cédras home, her position had softened. "My husband will do what is right," she said. "And whatever it is, I will support him."[74]

With time running out on their 12:00 noon deadline, Carter pleaded with Clinton for more time to reach an agreement before Clinton gave the go-ahead for the attack. Clinton relented, extending their deadline to 3:00 P.M., and insisting that this new deadline was firm.[75] "Cédras couldn't have more time to murder children, rape young girls, and slash women's faces," he wrote later.[76]

But the invasion, unbeknownst to the delegation, had already begun. As they seemed to be making headway in striking a compromise with Cédras at his military headquarters, the general's number-two man, Brigadier General Philippe Biamby, stormed into the meeting with a submachine gun slung over his shoulder. "General Cédras, my commander in chief, we have to leave here right now," he shouted as he waved the gun at Carter, Powell, and Nunn. "We have been betrayed. We have intelligence information that the Eighty-second Airborne are getting their parachutes and loading on the planes at Fort Bragg and heading here."[77] Not bad intelligence for a poor country, thought Powell.[78] Biamby was right; the planes were on their way, and U.S. warships loomed just off Haiti's shores awaiting Clinton's order to storm the beaches, a plan set for one minute after midnight on September 19. An exasperated Carter angrily warned Cédras of the futility of his stand-off, insisting that he must take the deal or "your children will be killed. Your country will be burned."[79] But the revelation of the impending invasion was enough to end the meeting.

Emile Jonassaint, the aging Haitian president, thought to be a figure-head, proved to be a decisive force in coming to a resolution. In an eleventh-hour meeting at the presidential palace, well past their 3:00 deadline, Carter took out a hastily written but carefully worded agreement. Before a group that included Jonassaint, members of his cabinet, and Cédras, Carter signed it dramatically, challenging any of the Haitian men to sign on behalf of their country.[80] "I am going to sign the agreement," Jonassaint responded eventually. "I will not let my people suffer further tragedy. I choose peace."[81] Powell asked Cédras if he would abide by the agreement. The general stood erect and looked at Jonassaint. "I will obey the orders of my president," he assured them.[82]

The terms of the agreement Carter carved out were not without their problems. They were considerably less severe than those in the ultimatum Clinton had issued just several days earlier, allowing the dictators to remain in Haiti, and implying general amnesty for all associated with the junta. There was also the question of Jonassaint's legitimacy as the agreement's signatory. Before the delegation left on their mission, Clinton had stated that a signature from Jonassaint, whom the administration did not recognize as president, would not be sufficient, a position he would later have to rescind by admitting he "had the absolutely incorrect impression that Jonassaint was a figurehead."[83] Still, thin as it was, the agreement was enough for Clinton to order a halt to the invasion at 5:45 P.M., two hours after it had begun. The Eighty-second Airborne turned back, and troops aboard the ships were given orders to peacefully go ashore several days later and "cooperate" with the Haitian soldiers. Military action had been averted.

With the agreement in hand, the delegation arrived back in Washington at 3:30 A.M. Carter was immediately taken to the White House, where Clinton had invited him to spend the night, to get a few hours of sleep before a breakfast meeting to brief the president, followed by a joint press conference. But just prior to the breakfast, Carter pulled another wild card. He scheduled a last-minute interview with CNN in which he defended Cédras's human rights to remain in Haiti as part of the settlement, and praised him for his "honor," overlooking the atrocities committed under his bloody reign. Just afterward, in the delegation's Oval Office meeting with the president, Clinton exploded in anger, berating Carter for grandstanding by talking to the media before their briefing, and for warmly defending Cédras. Carter matched his anger in turn, calling Clinton out for putting their lives in jeopardy by giving the green light for the invasion while they were still in Haiti. The presidential shouting match ended as Nunn reminded them of the importance of showing a united front at their impending press conference.[84]

The Haiti episode showed the best and worst of Carter the diplomat. On the one hand was the unyielding peacemaker, willing to throw himself in the path of danger in order to prevent military action that may have resulted in bloodshed among American and Haitian troops. On the other was the loose cannon, making up his own rules as he went along, and self-righteously upstaging the incumbent president he was representing in order to push his own agenda. It also brought Carter to a new level of recognition as a former president. As his image dominated the news coverage, including *Time* and *Newsweek* cover stories, there was no denying his influence on the international scene. Seventy percent of Americans gave Carter credit for resolving the Haiti crisis peacefully, according to a CNN poll, versus just 15 percent for Clinton.[85]

As a result of such positive exposure, Carter's approval rating by the midnineties was 74 percent, well over twice what it had been at the end of his presidential term.[86] Concurrently, The Carter Center had hit its stride, racking up major contributions to the issues it aimed to address. The promotion of democracy became a pivotal part of the Center's efforts as it worked with struggling or fledgling democracies to help ensure free and fair elections. As a former head of state who had been beaten at the ballot box, Carter would often assure other leaders who feared a democratic defeat that there *is* life after politics, as his experience would attest. By early in the new century, The Carter Center had monitored over fifty elections, helping democracy to flourish in many nations throughout the world that had been long oppressed, places like Indonesia, Liberia, Mozambique, Nigeria, and Nicaragua. In the late nineties, The Carter Center secured an unprecedented agreement with China to push democratic reforms in small villages across the country. As the man who had normalized U.S. trade relations with China during his tenure as president, Carter enjoyed a hero's status in the country, and was in a unique position to advance democratic ideals.[87]

The eradication of Guinea worm disease and the control of river blindness, two particularly insidious diseases that had gone largely unchecked among the world's poor, became a central focus of the Center's health programs. In 1986, Guinea worm disease, a parasite carried by water fleas in contaminated drinking water, afflicted some three and a half million people in twenty countries in Africa and Asia.[88] Once consumed, the eggs of the worm hatch and can grow more than two feet long, eventually working its way out of the host's body through blisters in the skin. Victims nudge the worm to exit bit by bit by slowly winding it around a stick, but if the worm is broken off before it fully emerges, its remains can infect the body, sometimes fatally. Even if the worm escapes in tact, the sores can cause crippling among children. By distributing household water filters and larvicides to exterminate the microscopic water fleas that carry the larvae, The Carter Center, in partnership with ministries of health, American corporations, and international health organizations, reduced incidence of the disease by more than 99.5 percent.[89] In 2005, fewer than 12,000 cases remained, creating prospects that Guinea worm might be only the second disease to be eradicated in the world, following smallpox.[90]

River blindness infects 18 million people, mostly in Africa, visually impairing half a million and blinding 270,000. The disease is caused by the

Harry Truman, alone on a morning walk around his home town of Independence, Missouri, 1953. Upon leaving the White House, Truman received no Secret Service protection, staff support, transition or expense budgets, office space, or presidential pension. Five years later, Congress approved a presidential pension and other emoluments, saving him from being "financially embarrassed," though he had no Secret Service protection until Kennedy's assassination in 1963. (Photo courtesy of the *St. Louis Post-Dispatch*)

Truman with Herbert Hoover at the dedication of the Hoover Library in West Branch, Iowa, 1962. As president, Truman rescued Hoover from obscurity, bringing him back into government service. Hoover remained forever grateful and the two became lifelong friends, though their lives were as different as their politics. (Photo courtesy of the Harry S. Truman Library)

Jacqueline and John Kennedy, Lyndon Johnson, Harry and Bess Truman, and Dwight Eisenhower, at the 1962 funeral of Eleanor Roosevelt, Hyde Park, New York. Truman and Eisenhower's relationship had been strained since Ike's 1952 presidential campaign and would remain so through their post-presidencies. The only thaw came temporarily, a year later at Kennedy's funeral. (Photo courtesy of the Associated Press)

Lyndon and Lady Bird Johnson, Hubert Humphrey, and Harry and Bess Truman, at the 1965 signing of Medicare into law, at the Truman Library. Johnson called Truman "the real daddy of Medicare." His Great Society borrowed much from Truman's Fair Deal, further enhancing Truman's growing legacy. (Photo courtesy of the Lyndon B. Johnson Library)

Dwight and Mamie Eisenhower in front of the first and only house they ever owned, in Gettysburg, Pennsylvania, 1965. Eisenhower was eager to shed the burden of power, but constant demands on his time made him think "retirement" was just a word in the dictionary. (Photo courtesy of the Dwight D. Eisenhower Library)

Kennedy consults with Eisenhower (at right and below) at Camp David after the disastrous Bay of Pigs invasion in Cuba, April 1962. Ike privately took Kennedy to task for his mistakes in the matter before voicing his support of the president in a press conference. Kennedy would also seek Ike's advice during the Cuban Missile Crisis the following year. "Something may make [the Soviets] shoot [their nuclear missiles]," he told JFK. "I just don't believe this will." (Photos courtesy of the John F. Kennedy Library)

Johnson and Eisenhower consult aboard Air Force One, 1967. LBJ sought Ike's counsel on every major military decision in the Vietnam War. Ike's hawkish stance on the war was paradoxical; as president, he strongly opposed sending troops into a major war on the Asian mainland. (Photo courtesy of the Lyndon B. Johnson Library)

Johnson at the LBJ Ranch near Johnson City, Texas. After the presidency, LBJ threw himself into the role of rancher. He micromanaged every aspect of the ranch's operation, knew each of his Beresford cattle by name, and demanded memos from his ranch hands on subjects like egg production. (Photo courtesy of the Lyndon B. Johnson Library)

In retirement, Johnson's shaggy hairstyle uncannily resembled the hippie styles of anti-war protesters. Was it the look of a rancher who did "what [he] damned well please," or was it the tacit gesture of a man who desperately wanted to be loved, reaching out to those who most vocally opposed his presidency? (Photo courtesy of the Lyndon B. Johnson Library)

Lyndon and Lady Bird Johnson at the LBJ Library, 1971. Mrs. Johnson was a stabilizing force for her mercurial husband. Vietnam would continue to haunt him in his post-presidency. His early death in 1973 left many wondering whether he simply died as a result of a weak heart, or if disappointment in an unfulfilled destiny played a role. (Photo courtesy of the Lyndon B. Johnson Library)

Richard Nixon leaving the White House after his resignation, August 9, 1974. Nixon left Washington disgraced, returning to his home in San Clemente, California, where he would spend the next four years in self-imposed exile before beginning his slow, steady rehabilitation. (Photo courtesy of David Hume Kennerly)

Nixon on a flight from southern California to Washington for the funeral of former political rival Hubert Humphrey in January 1978. The trip, his first to the capital since his resignation, would mark his emergence from exile. Later the same month, he would rededicate himself to "the causes that had always inspired my actions," striving to once again make his mark on foreign policy. (Photo courtesy of the Associated Press)

Nixon introduces President George H. W. Bush at Nixon's annual foreign policy conference in 1992. Bush's presence was indicative of Nixon's growing influence on foreign policy. Presidents Reagan, Bush, and Clinton actively sought his counsel. (Photo courtesy of the Richard Nixon Library)

Five presidents and first ladies gather for Nixon's funeral at the Nixon Library, April 1994. Twenty years after his resignation, Nixon's rehabilitation hit its peak as he was remembered primarily as a respected statesman. The words of President Clinton may have most pleased Nixon. "May the days of judging Richard Nixon on anything less than his entire life and career," he urged, "come to a close." (Photo courtesy of the Richard Nixon Library)

Ford and Reagan at the 1976 GOP Convention. Ford had nudged Reagan out of the presidential nomination but relations between them remained tense. Four years later, Ford lent the 1980 convention unexpected drama when he considered joining Reagan's ticket in a "sort of co-presidency," an unprecedented notion that collapsed of its own weight. (Photo courtesy of David Hume Kennerly, the Gerald R. Ford Library)

On her last full day as first lady, in January 1977, Betty Ford does a pirouette on the Cabinet Room table. Like her footprints on the table, the unique Mrs. Ford would make her mark as first lady and, through the Betty Ford Center, which opened in 1982, afterward. (Photo courtesy of David Hume Kennerly, the Gerald R. Ford Library)

President Reagan toasts Nixon, Ford, and Carter before sending them off to Cairo to represent the U.S. at the funeral of slain Egyptian leader Anwar Sadat, October 1981. The three very different ex-presidents were "ill at ease" initially, but on the long journey to Cairo, the chill between them lifted. On the return trip, a warm and unlikely friendship took root between Ford and Carter. (Photo courtesy of the Ronald Reagan Library)

Ford with NBC's Brian Williams reviewing pictures of his presidency at an exhibit at the Truman Library, February 1999. Over time historians and the public have seen the wisdom and political selflessness of Ford's pardon of Nixon, the deciding factor in his loss to Carter. Only a third of Americans approved when Ford granted it in 1974, a number that increased to 54 percent ten years later and continues to grow. (Photo courtesy of *Time* magazine)

Jimmy Carter helping to build a Habitat for Humanity home, June 1995. The first time he made a deep impression in the public's collective consciousness as an ex-president was when he donned a hard hat and wielded a hammer for the organization in 1982. Carter continues to give time to Habitat, but considers his "major legacy" to be his work through The Carter Center. (Photo courtesy of The Carter Center)

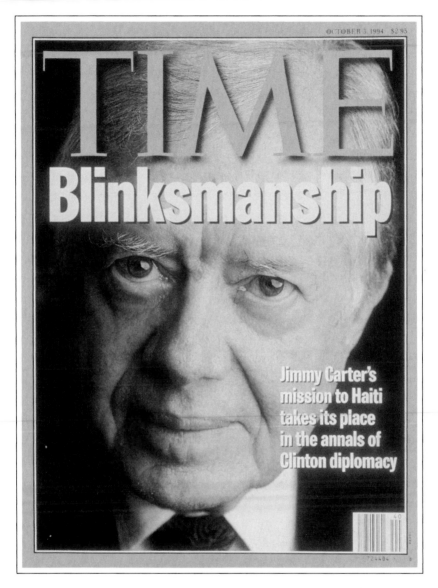

A September 1994 issue of *Time* magazine devoted its cover to Carter after his
dramatic role in staving off a U.S. military invasion of Haiti, bringing him to
a new level of recognition as an ex-president. Afterward, his approval rating among
Americans was 74 percent, more than twice what it had been at the end of his
presidency—though his grandstanding diplomatic tactics alienated Clinton, as they had
with Bush and would later with George W. Bush. (Photo courtesy of *Time* magazine)

Jimmy and Rosalynn Carter in Ethiopia on behalf of The Carter Center, September 2005. The eradication of Guinea worm disease and control of river blindness, two insidious diseases that had gone largely unchecked among the world's poor, became a main focus of the center's health efforts. (Photo courtesy of John Hardman, The Carter Center)

Carter is awarded the Nobel Peace Prize in Oslo, Norway, December 2002. After repeated nominations, Carter won for his "untiring efforts to find peaceful solutions to international conflicts, to advance democracy and human rights, and to promote economic and social development." (Photo courtesy of Knudsen's Fotosenter, Oslo, Norway)

The dedication of the Ronald Reagan Library in Simi Valley, California, in November 1991, brought together five presidents (left) and six first ladies (below), both historical firsts. The occasion befitted the structure's grandiosity, the Reagans' flair for stagecraft, and Mrs. Reagan's ambitions for her husband's legacy. (Photo courtesy of the George Bush Library)

Nancy Reagan covers her husband's half-shaved head, as he leaves the Mayo Clinic after undergoing skull surgery a week earlier, September 1989. During Reagan's fifteen-year post-presidency, Mrs. Reagan's public image would evolve from overprotective Dragon Lady to venerable caretaker as he suffered from the ravages of Alzheimer's disease. (Photo courtesy of the Associated Press)

In a last hurrah for the Reagan-Bush era, Bush, just prior to leaving the presidency in January 1993, awards Reagan the Medal of Freedom. It would be Reagan's last visit to the White House. (Photo courtesy of the George Bush Library)

George and Barbara Bush welcome Bill, Hillary, and Chelsea Clinton to the White House on Clinton's inauguration day, January 20, 1993. The loss to Clinton hurt Bush, who worried that the Americans didn't know his "heartbeat" and wondered about Clinton's character. Family was Bush's greatest solace in defeat. (Photo courtesy of the George Bush Library)

Bush marks his seventy-fifth birthday by making a parachute jump in College Station, Texas, in June 1999. Bush would make three jumps in his post-presidency, including another on his eightieth birthday, an occasion he also used to help raise $56 million for four organizations to which he devoted much of his time: the MD Anderson Cancer Center, the Points of Light Foundation, and the Bush Library and Bush School of Public Service at Texas A&M University. (Photo courtesy of the George Bush Library)

Barbara and George Bush with George W. and Laura Bush, then governor and first lady of Texas, in 1999. The entry of his sons George W. and Jeb into the political arena galvanized Bush, though he rejected the notion of a Bush dynasty. "This is not about vindication or legacy or entitlement," he said. "It's about the love of a father for his son[s]." (Photo courtesy of the George Bush Library)

George W. and Laura Bush, George and Barbara Bush, and Bill, Hillary, and Chelsea Clinton at the September 11th memorial service at Washington's National Cathedral, September 14, 2001. While there has been wide speculation that Bush disagrees with his son over the war in Iraq, Bush has said they "don't dwell on points of difference," and their relationship is, "closer than the public realizes." (Photo courtesy of the White House)

Clinton, Bush, and Laura Bush watch George W. Bush sign a condolence book for the victims of the Asian tsunami at the Thailand embassy in Washington, January 3, 2005. Clinton and Bush paired up to urge Americans to contribute to tsunami relief—and later to raise funds for victims of Hurricane Katrina and Rita—and became friends along the way, a serendipitous development for both of them. (Photo courtesy the White House)

Despite leaving the presidency in a blaze of controversy, Clinton, returning to the White House to visit Bush in 2005, remained enormously popular. While his predecessors left office armed with the prestige of the presidency, Clinton also held the mystique of celebrity. (Photo courtesy of the White House)

Clinton visits Tanzania Zanzibar in 2005 where the Clinton Foundation is supporting government, religious and community leaders to combat the spread of HIV/AIDS. Using Carter's activist post-presidency as a model for his own, he has directed much of the foundation's focus toward the treatment of AIDS throughout the Third World, calling the disease "a preventable holocaust." (Photo courtesy of the Clinton Foundation)

C linton in a strategy meeting for the failed gubernatorial reelection campaign of Gray Davis, Los Angeles, 2004. As Clinton's presidential legacy continues to be debated, his post-presidency has been widely hailed as triumphant. A December 2005 *Esquire* magazine cover story proclaimed him "the most influential man in the world." (Photo courtesy of David Hume Kennerly)

bite of blackflies that breed in rapidly flowing rivers. Like Guinea worm, river blindness is transmitted by flies carrying parasites; multiple bites can mean the victim's body is infested with small worms that infect the body and flock through the skin and eyes, causing profuse itching that can bring on skin discoloration and blindness.[91] While eradication of the disease is currently impossible, it can be eliminated regionally if drugs are administered twice a year to about 85 percent of people at risk. Between 1996 and 2002, The Carter Center provided 70 million treatments in eleven African and Latin American countries.[92] Those health-care accomplishments and others brought The Carter Center enormous acclaim in Africa and other parts of the world, but were far less known in the U.S., partly, in Carter's view, because the diseases are unknown in the United States, and therefore of less interest to the U.S. media.

Additionally, Carter, the former peanut farmer, took a strong interest in improving agricultural conditions and increasing output in Africa as a means of alleviating hunger. In partnership with the Sasakawa Africa Association, The Carter Center trained more than four million small farm owners in fifteen African nations on improved farming methods, resulting in a three- or fourfold boost in grain production and improvement in the quality of maize crops.[93]

Carter's interest in improving living conditions and health-care resources was not limited to the poor on other continents. The Atlanta Project (TAP), which The Carter Center launched in the fall of 1991, was an attempt to make a contribution in his own backyard and to show, in Carter's words, that "in at least one troubled city something can be done about the problem of teenage pregnancy, drug addiction and crack babies, juvenile delinquency, school dropouts, homelessness, and unemployment."[94] The idea was for TAP to work with residents in poor neighborhoods to identify their problems and objectives, and to help them "gain access to the tools they need to improve their own lives."[95] As part of its goal, The Carter Center worked with federal agencies in an effort to cut through the red tape that complicated public assistance.

With $20 million in funding from local corporations, among them Turner Broadcasting, Coca-Cola, and Delta Airlines, and support from President Bush and Georgia congressman, Speaker of the House Newt Gingrich, TAP aimed to be a model for other American cities that faced

similar problems. The program was largely reliant on an extensive volunteer base, and successfully enlisted a regiment of some 100,000 who answered the call. Despite its good intentions, the effort yielded few concrete results. A 1995 report by an Emory professor, based on interviews with over two thousand volunteers and community organizers, concluded that "progress to date toward TAP's goals appears modest relative to the amount of effort and money expended."[96] Carter may have also fallen prey to his own ambition, as resources were spread too thin to make a significant dent in the many problems the program attempted to address. TAP also exposed the racial divide that still prevailed in Atlanta. Much of TAP's executive committee and 90 percent of its volunteers were white, causing some in the black community to cite it as an example of "racial arrogance."[97] TAP's biggest contribution may have been in the show of unity among corporations and local residents who were willing to delve into Atlanta's underlying problems, a development for which Carter was widely and justifiably credited.

While Carter considered his efforts in North Korea and Haiti among his most significant diplomatic achievements, there would be others. Later in 1994 after his triumphant missions in North Korea and Haiti, he and Mrs. Carter traveled to the former Yugoslavia to broker a four-month cease-fire between the Bosnian Serbs and Muslims, helping to bring the warring factions back to the peace table. In 1995, he went to Sudan, which had been torn by civil war since 1983, to talk its Muslim leaders into a two-month cease-fire with Christian and other non-Muslim Sudanese in the country's southern region, and later returned to extend the agreement for another two months. The break in fighting led to efforts to ward off diseases—including Guinea worm disease and river blindness—that threatened the three million refugees resulting from the conflict.[98]

By the new century, Carter had become a revered international figure, as evidenced in an invitation he received from Fidel Castro—who had been a thorn in the side of every U.S. president since Eisenhower, including Carter—to visit Cuba. Castro extended the invitation when the two met at the October 2000 funeral of former Canadian prime minister, Pierre Trudeau.[99] Carter accepted, becoming the first U.S. president, former or otherwise, to visit the country since Castro's Communist revolution overthrew the Batista government in 1959. Members of the Bush administration winced

as the thirty-ninth president embarked on the visit, concerned that it may be interpreted by foreign powers as the legitimization of Castro's dictatorial regime.[100] Predictably, Carter criticized the U.S.'s policy in Cuba, calling for an end to the sanctions in place through the long-standing Helms-Burton Act. At the same time, speaking in Spanish, he openly scolded Castro for his record on human rights in an unprecedented live speech broadcast throughout Cuba, which the aging dictator, knowing Carter might be critical, had allowed. Things had clearly changed for ex-presidents since the days when Eisenhower, upon being invited by the Soviet leadership to visit the Kremlin shortly after he had left office, quickly declined so as not to in any way embarrass the incumbent Kennedy administration.

While many were tempted to canonize Carter for his humanitarian and peacekeeping contributions, he was not without his flaws. Though he made many "friends" in his extensive travels throughout the world, he remained a distant, remote figure, just as he had in his White House days. Even his staff never got too close. His White House assistant, Susan Clough, who remained with him when he returned to Plains, left his service just over a year later, turned off by his lack of warmth—he rarely offered a personal word—and a suggestion that she go to a nearby military base to find male companionship.[101] On a few occasions, he showed lapses in judgment. When Iranian leader the Ayatollah Khomeini sent out death threats to author Salman Rushdie after the publication of *The Satanic Verses*, in which Rushdie blasphemed the Koran, Carter pointed a finger at Rushdie. In a *New York Times* Op-Ed piece, Carter wrote, "It's not right to ridicule another person's religion," blaming the victim and overlooking his right to free speech.[102]

His penchant for grandstanding and following his own diplomatic instincts may have cost him closer official relationships with his predecessors. Carter cited his relationship with George H. W. Bush as the "best" he has had with an incumbent president, but has stated that he "had practically no relationship with President Clinton when he was in office, nor with the current President Bush."[103] Even the elder Bush, who backed off from Carter after his plea to the leaders of nations in the UN Security Counsel not to support military action prior to the Gulf War, became increasingly concerned that Carter "always seem[ed] to be siding with the wrong side when it came to his ostensible support of dictators and despots."[104] He also became incensed in 2006 when, at the funeral of Coretta Scott King attended by himself, Carter, Clinton, and George W. Bush, Carter implied that the governments' inadequate response to Hurricane Katrina was racist, prompting Bush to wonder, "What happened to the guy?"[105] Indeed, while Carter was a full-fledged member of the ex-presidents' club, his renegade tendencies made him an outsider, though his relationships with all its members were cordial. The only one he was close to was Ford, with whom he had struck up a close friendship when the two traveled to Cairo for Anwar Sadat's funeral in 1981.

Ultimately, Carter was less a saintly former president than a remarkable, if enigmatic, international folk hero.

Right-wing critics reliably pointed out Carter's feet of clay. A 2004 book, *The Real Jimmy Carter: How Our Worst Ex-President Undermines American Foreign Policy, Coddles Dictators and Created the Party of Clinton and Kerry*, by journalist Steven Hayward—whose thesis was clearly stated in the book's subtitle—provided a compendium of the vitriol consistently directed at Carter from the right. Author and TV reporter Bernard Goldberg also took note of Carter's radical tendencies when he added Carter to the list comprised in his his best seller, *100 People Who Are Screwing Up America*, slating him at number six. Other conservative voices, like *Newsweek*'s George Will and *The Weekly Standard*'s Fred Barnes, also frequently denounced Carter's post-presidential meddling and liberalism. The latter was evident when Carter happily sat next to extremist right-wing critic, filmmaker Michael Moore, in the VIP section at the 2004 Democratic National Convention.

But the prevailing view was of Carter as ex-president extraordinaire. Historian Douglas Brinkley's definitive account of Carter's years after the White House, *The Unfinished Presidency: Jimmy Carter's Journey to the Nobel Peace Prize* published in 1998, not only detailed Carter's phenomenal post-presidential attainments, but also defended his presidency. "Carter's human rights policy had given the United States moral credibility around the world—no small feat after Vietnam—while putting the Soviet Union on the defensive by exposing the Kremlin as 'evil,' just like Reagan said," Brinkley argued.[106] *Jimmy Carter: A Comprehensive Biography from Plains to the Post-Presidency*, by Peter Bourne, who served as special assistant to Carter in the White House, also provided a highly complimentary portrait.

Like Nixon, Carter told and retold his story and proffered his views through his own prolific efforts as an author of books, among them *Talking Peace: A Vision for the Next Generation*, *The Blood of Abraham: Insights into the Middle East*, and *Why Not the Best*. In *An Outdoor Journal* he explored his passion for fly fishing, which he and Mrs. Carter pursued with great enthusiasm throughout the country in rare moments of downtime, while in *Living Faith* he held forth on the inspiration of God and Jesus Christ in his life and work as he might in one of his weekly Sunday school classes in Plains. He also delved into literary areas heretofore untapped by other ex-presidents, including writing a volume of poetry, *Always a Reckoning and Other Poems*; a novel about the Revolutionary War in the South, *The Hornet's Nest*; and a children's book, *The Little Baby Snoogle-Fleejer*, illustrated by his daughter Amy. In 2005, he wrote *Our Endangered Values: America's Moral Crisis*, a repudiation of the moral values espoused by the religious right, which he contends has led to deep divisions in America during the George W. Bush years.

By 2005, Carter had twenty books under his belt, the bulk of which quickly advanced up best-seller lists after publication, making him the most prolific presidential author. One of them, *Everything to Gain: Making the Most of the Rest of Your Life*, a self-help volume cowritten with Mrs. Carter and published in 1987, tested his marriage as much as anything the couple would face. The intensity of their quarrels about the book's content led to their writing separate passages designated throughout the book under their initials J. and R. For days on end they didn't speak despite inhabiting the same modest-sized home. Brent Scowcroft, as President George H. W. Bush's national security advisor, visited Carter in Plains for a security briefing in the late eighties, when the Carters broke out into an argument over the book while eating the lunch they had prepared for him. Scowcroft sheepishly stood by as verbal volleys were traded over who had contributed more to the work, qualitatively and quantitatively.[107] Ultimately, the marriage survived intact as it had throughout the many trials they faced during their life together, and remained strong. In his book,

Living Faith, the dedication bore testimony to his love for his wife of fifty years. It took the form of a poem by the former president, the last stanza of which read:

With shyness gone and hair caressed with gray,
her smile still makes the birds forget to sing
and me to hear their song.

As Carter pointed out in *Living Faith*, his wife was a "full partner" in all of his efforts, accompanying him on most of his travels, running beside him on early-morning jogs, scribbling notes during his meetings, and sharing her insights into the people they met and situations they encountered. Leading all of The Carter Center's work in the area of mental health, she organized an annual conference that, for the first time, brought together over sixty organizations worldwide to exchange research and ideas.[108] Independent of The Carter Center she was asked by her alma mater, Georgia Southwestern State University in Americus, to head The Rosalynn Carter Institute for Human Development, which would become one of the nation's foremost institutions in the area of patient caregiving.

Despite Carter's monumental efforts to better the world through the years, the Nobel Peace Prize had eluded him. Many felt he was as deserving to win the prize as Begin and Sadat, who were honored in 1979 for advancing the cause of peace between Israel and Egypt through the Camp David Accords. After all, it had been Carter who brokered the agreement. But there had been a technicality: As he would find out years afterward, he hadn't been formally nominated. ("Who knew you needed to be nominated?" asked Mrs. Carter later.)[109] Beginning in 1988, his name had been placed in nomination annually—he had even been an odds-on favorite to receive the award after his missions to North Korea and Haiti in 1994. Each time he was passed up in favor of others.

By 2002 his time had come. On October 12, the Norwegian Nobel Committee recognized him for his "untiring effort to find peaceful solutions to international conflicts, to advance democracy and human rights, and to promote economic and social development," including a retroactive nod for his role in the Camp David agreements as president. Politics, however, played a role in the selection. As the committee saw it, Jimmy Carter the peacemaking former U.S. president stood in marked contrast to the incumbent president George W. Bush, whose military takeover of Iraq they took occasion to repudiate. Their written statement included praise for Carter, coupled with an allusion to "a situation currently marked by threats of the use of power."[110] If there was any doubt that the reference pertained to Bush, the Nobel committee chairman, Gunnar Berge, confirmed that the award "should be interpreted as a criticism of the line that the current administration has taken."[111]

George W. Bush, however, was among those who logged a congratulatory (though brief) call into Carter on the morning the news was announced. The Carters learned he had won the Nobel at 4:30 A.M., when the Secret Service awakened them in their Plains bedroom to let them know that the committee was on the line. The thrill of the moment almost came to an anticlimax when the couple tried to get ahold of their four children to tell them the news—only Amy answered the phone when the call came through.[112] Word spread quickly through Plains that the town's favorite son had finally become a Nobel laureate, and an impromptu celebration was staged on Main Street. Craig Walters, a teacher at Plains' elementary school, got a call from his father at 8:00 A.M. "My daddy was yelling at me, 'Get up! Get dressed! Get downtown! Jimmy won a Nobel,'" he said.[113]

Two months later, Carter went to Oslo, Norway, with eighty friends and relatives to accept his award. Carter, in formal black tie and tails, used his twenty-minute acceptance address in the grand auditorium of Oslo City Hall to bring attention to "the growing chasm between the richest and poorest people on earth." Like the Nobel selection committee, Carter also took a shot at the Bush administration, declaring "global challenges must be met by an emphasis on peace, in harmony with others, with strong alliances and international consensus." Toward the end of the speech, he added a guiding principle: "War may sometimes be a necessary evil. But no matter how necessary, it is always evil, never good. We will not live together in peace by killing each other's children."[114]

While earning the Nobel Peace Prize was a highlight for Carter, it did not mean a deceleration of his efforts. Even as he reached the age of eighty, he kept a schedule that may have exhausted one half his age, and continued to inspire and engage in the work at the heart of The Carter Center. As Carter has stated, the Center is his "major legacy," and how he would most like to be remembered as a public figure.[115] It has exceeded even his massive ambitions, ranking as his and Mrs. Carter's proudest achievement, and with an endowment of over $200 million, and succession plans in place, ones that will last long after the Carters are gone. In their "miserable" first days home in Plains after leaving the White House in January of 1981, the Carters wondered aloud whether they would ever get to a point in their lives where they felt that losing the presidency was actually for the best.[116] Carter got to that point long ago as a result of The Carter Center's phenomenal success—though Mrs. Carter still believes "the country would be better off if Jimmy had been reelected."[117]

Oddly, it is Carter's activities on behalf of Habitat for Humanity that the public most associates with his life after the White House, overshadowing the achievements of The Carter Center—often to Carter's chagrin. As he and members of The Carter Center's staff are quick to point out, Carter devotes just one week a year to Habitat, while he spends the other fifty-one weeks in his work at the Center. But as he has seen repeatedly in his interactions with the public, it is the image of him pounding nails in construction garb that continues to resonate in their minds and to capture their imaginations. "We love the way you build those houses," he is told time and time again.[118] Not a bad legacy in itself.

After winning the Nobel Peace Prize, the Carters were often asked if the award vindicated the Carter presidency. The very question implies that Carter's was a failed presidency, a view the Carters dismiss entirely. "I never felt we had to be vindicated. Even when we came home; I was proud of what we'd done," Mrs. Carter said recently, a view her husband shares.[119] Looking back on his presidency, he remarked, "I don't know of any decisions I made in the White House that were basically erroneous."[120]

The general view among historians, though, is that Carter was a mediocre president—and just as generally, he is applauded for his exemplary deeds out of office. "More than any other ex-president," wrote *The New York Times* after Carter had won the Nobel Peace Prize, "Mr. Carter has stretched the gravitas and the star power of the Oval Office to promote democratic values across the world. Unlike his peers, he never joined corporate boards or went on the lecture circuit."[121] Often Carter has been conferred the title of "the best former president" by admirers, a designation that could be construed as a backhanded compliment, or at least, a consolation prize. But Carter doesn't worry about his place in the presidential pantheon. The things he wants to be remembered for—being a good Christian and a champion for peace and human rights—go beyond any achievement he may have chalked up in the White House alone.[122]

Just a few paces from Carter's glass-encased Nobel Peace Prize in the Jimmy Carter Museum is a collage on a wall, depicting all the presidents of the twentieth century from Theodore Roosevelt through Carter. Each president and his times are captured sequentially through photographs, newspaper headlines, political cartoons, and a quote from the man himself. Only Carter's quote relates to his life after the presidency. Taken from his last address to the nation as president just prior to his return to Plains, it reads: "The only title in our democracy superior to that of president [is] that of citizen."

VII.

RONALD REAGAN:
THE LONG GOODBYE

I t ended about as happily as any movie he had ever made. After eight years as president of the United States, Ronald Reagan was leaving Washington, having changed the city more than any president had since Franklin Roosevelt, the first president he ever voted for. His accomplishments were formidable: He had twice been elected by landslide margins, and as he prepared to leave Washington, his popularity soared with approval ratings at 63 percent.[1] Through his unwavering faith in America, a "shining city upon a hill," he had restored the nation's pride in the wake of the malaise of the Carter years. After establishing a warm but firm relationship with Soviet premier Mikhail Gorbachev—and abandoning the appeasement strategies of previous administrations—the Cold War was in its waning days, with the Soviet Union nearing collapse and the liberation of the Eastern Block not far behind. And he was handing the presidency over to his heir apparent, his vice president, George Bush, the first time an incumbent vice president had won the office since Martin Van Buren succeeded Andrew Jackson 156 years before.

To be sure, the saga had its share of setbacks. He was shot by a would-be assassin just sixty-nine days into his first term, and neared death as doctors scrambled to remove the bullet that came just a quarter of an inch from his heart. The country had lost a barracks of 241 marines in Lebanon during a terrorist bombing in 1983. Budget deficits soared to record-high levels—far greater than those of previous administrations—despite Reagan's heated rhetoric about the dangers of "big government," while the homeless population increased alarmingly and AIDS ravaged the gay community, unacknowledged by the president. The Iran-Contra Affair, in which it was revealed arms had been traded for hostages after White House denials, scandalized the administration and undermined some of his second term. But all told, Reagan was leaving office as well as he and Nancy, his beloved partner of thirty-eight years, could have ever hoped. So there was reason for his infectious optimism when he passed the presidential baton to Bush in January of 1989.

But as he watched Bush go through the inaugural ritual, there may have been some clues to his advanced years and vulnerability. At seventy-six, less than a month from his seventy-seventh birthday, Reagan was the oldest president ever to leave office, just as he had been the oldest to earn the office at sixty-eight. Four years earlier, in his first summit with Gorbachev in Vienna, a vigorous Ronald Reagan waited for the Soviet premier outside their meeting place warmed only by his dark suit in the frigid Austrian air. When Gorbachev's car approached, he emerged, bundled up in a gray topcoat and plaid wool scarf. As a cacophony of press cameras clicked away, Reagan, comfortable and in control of the moment, led Gorbachev into the meeting, looking like the host awaiting his guest, even though Vienna was neutral territory. Advantage: Reagan. Now it was Reagan who was bundled up, shoulders slightly hunched, in a black overcoat and white scarf, as Bush recited the oath and addressed the crowd devoid of winter garb. Reagan's left ring finger was bandaged in white gauze after a sprain, and his hair, usually a dark pompadour helmet belying his years and impervious to wind, blew gently in the January air, revealing a slight touch of gray.

After Bush was sworn into office, he and the new first lady escorted the Reagans through the Capitol to the front of the building and walked them down the steps where they said their goodbyes. As he boarded Marine One, the presidential helicopter, Reagan turned back to Bush, who saluted his friend and mentor. Reagan, smiling a familiar jovial smile, returned the salute, one commander in chief to another. As he and Mrs. Reagan ascended into the heavens, he whispered into his wife's ear the same words he used to end his last speech to the nation as president upon summarizing the achievements accrued during his tenure. "All in all, not bad," he said. "Not bad at all."[2]

Cut. Print. Edit with rolling credits.

On the other side of the country, in the city that made him, the sequel would begin. It would last over fifteen years, and would not be nearly as triumphant. In fact, it would be full of pain and sadness. But ultimately, it would end just as spectacularly.

Ronald "Dutch" Reagan first came to Los Angeles in 1935, during the depths of the Great Depression. Working as a sports announcer for WHO, a Des Moines radio station, Reagan got a reprieve from the endless Iowa winter by convincing his bosses to send him on a ten-day trip to southern California to cover the Chicago Cubs' spring training. While in Los Angeles for the annual sojourn two years later, he looked up a friend from the station who had moved to Hollywood and found work as a singer. She introduced him to her agent, which led to a screen test at Warner Bros.—and a studio contract earning him $200 a week. Reagan soon became the "Errol Flynn of B movies," working on an assembly line of cheap and fast productions. "They [didn't] need 'em good, they need[ed] 'em by Thursday," as Reagan put it later. Reagan obliged, working prolifically—he made thirteen films in his eighteen months at Warner Bros.—in largely forgettable roles.³ But there were exceptions. His performance as George Gipp, "the Gipper," a halfback for Notre Dame fighting a terminal illness in *Knute Rockne All American*, made an impression, as did his role as a small-town Romeo in *Kings Row*. (Reagan had been slated for the lead role as Rick in the 1941 film *Casablanca*, but was moved off the project due to a scheduling conflict. Humphrey Bogart eventually got the part—and a ticket to A-list stardom.)

He met actress Jane Wyman in the late thirties, and a tabloid romance followed. The pair married in 1940, produced a daughter, Maureen, in 1941, and adopted a son, Michael, two years later. By 1947, the marriage had fizzled owing, at least in part, to Reagan's growing interest in politics. A "near hopelessly blind liberal" devoted to FDR, Reagan's views began to change as he got caught up in the union politics surrounding Hollywood.⁴ A decade after inking his contract with Warner Bros., he was elected president of the Screen Actors Guild, presiding over the union as Senator Joe McCarthy's Communist witch hunt was in full swing. Reagan testified in front of Congressman Richard Nixon's House Un-American Activities Committee in 1949. Without naming names, he advocated the practice of blacklisting those in the Hollywood community suspected of politically subversive activity.

His involvement in the guild did nothing for his movie career, which had faded by the early fifties. He worked briefly in Las Vegas as an emcee for lounge acts and dinner shows before getting the pivotal job in his acting career. General Electric contracted him to host *General Electric Theater*, a weekly television series featuring hour-long dramatic productions. But the agreement came with a catch: For ten weeks a year, Reagan would tour GE plants around the country as a morale booster for employees. The experience of touring the country, meeting a cross-section of GE employees, hearing their concerns, and addressing them, set Reagan up for a foray into politics.

Opportunity knocked when Barry Goldwater ran an ill-fated campaign for president against Lyndon Johnson, the popular incumbent, in 1964. Reagan had become a Republican shortly after campaigning for Nixon as a Democrat four years earlier, making an impression on Goldwater benefactors at a speech he gave at a fund-raiser. Goldwater's team asked him if he would give a version of the speech on national television. Reagan agreed and shined in the role, catching the attention of Republican moneymen who hoped to oust Democratic governor Pat Brown, who had squarely defeated former vice president Richard Nixon in a race for the California statehouse in 1962. In 1966, Reagan unseated Brown and became a star of the GOP, holding the governor's office for two terms while harboring presidential ambitions. After two failed attempts for the presidential spot on the Republican national ticket, in 1968 and 1976, he captured the nomination in 1980, and went on to beat Jimmy Carter out of reelection.

Now, after eight years in Washington, he was back home again, trading the White House for a $2.5 million three-bedroom, brick, ranch-style home in tony Bel-Air, up winding hills past gated estates and manicured gardens, less than a mile north of Sunset Boulevard. The address, 666 St. Cloud Road, was quickly changed to 668, so as not to invite any association to the devil (though many liberals had long made the connection). The home was purchased by a collection of longtime Reagan friends who leased it to them for $15,000 a month, with an option to buy the property outright.[5] Though it was 6,500 square feet and boasted a two-bedroom servants' quarters and the requisite heated swimming pool, it was a guesthouse by local standards, dwarfed on one side by a neighboring mansion known to television viewers as the home of *The Beverly Hillbillies*. Just ten minutes away in Century City was the office Reagan had established in the Fox Plaza Building, a reddish marble tower that stood taller than any of the other office buildings on the aptly named Avenue of the Stars. The office suite stood on the thirty-fourth floor, and featured sweeping views of the Pacific Ocean sparkling through smog off the beaches of Santa Monica, just five miles west.

Though he almost surely would have run for a third term as president if not for the confines of the 22nd Amendment to the Constitution, which he opposed, he had little difficulty adjusting to life after the White House. Like Harry Truman and Gerald Ford before him, he had an advantage in making the transition: He was at ease with himself. He knew who he was, and though he had relished the role of president and the power he had wielded, he didn't need it to define who he was. In fact, he found it easy to break away from the seat of power and politics, and from domestic and world events. Unlike many of his predecessors, he didn't feel the need to burden himself with immersion in current affairs. He was content to leave that to others.[6]

He had another advantage too. As he would tell his friend, Canadian prime minister Brian Mulroney (who would step down in similar fashion in 1993, after two terms in office), he had no what-ifs to brood about. He had won the presidency twice by handsome margins, and had had eight years to pursue his agenda and fulfill his mission. His party hadn't rejected him, as would later happen to Margaret Thatcher, nor had an opponent unseated him, as would be the case with Gorbachev and Bush. He had left office on his own terms. Few others would leave so cleanly.[7]

He quickly adapted to his new life. On weekdays when he was in town, he put in banker's hours at the office. Announcing that he refused to retire because "it takes all the fun out of Sundays," he dabbled in a variety of projects, including the writing of his memoirs—for which Simon & Schuster paid $8.5 million as part of a two-book deal that would also include a collection of his speeches—and establishing the Ronald Reagan Library and Museum to be located in Simi Valley, rugged, hilly terrain thirty miles north of Los Angeles, where Reagan had played in Westerns in his acting days.[8] He used office hours to meet with visitors ranging from traveling dignitaries and power brokers—Vice President Dan Quayle and

Henry Kissinger were among those who visited in the first months—to terminally ill children.

When it was time to relax, Reagan often retreated to Rancho del Cielo, Spanish for "Ranch in the Sky," his 668-acre ranch in the mountains overlooking the Santa Ynez Valley, twenty-seven miles above Santa Barbara. The ranch was an informal, low-key affair—including an adobe cottage dating from the 1870s, a small guesthouse and guest-room trailer, a ranch foreman's cottage, a hay barn, and a stable—a place where Reagan could dress down in denim and cowboy boots and indulge his outdoor passions.[9] Horses were one. "There's nothing as good for the inside of a man than the outside of a horse," he often said, and spent hours alone or with Mrs. Reagan or friends, riding through the brown, sun-drenched hills. Time not spent on horseback was often spent working the land with pruning shears or a chain saw, or making home improvements. He put up wooden fencing and built a dock for the ranch's Lake Lucky, more like a pond, and laid a sandstone patio outside the main house. The ranch was a lifeline for Reagan. After he was shot shortly into his presidency, he frequently went there to escape Washington, and got flack from the press for his steady stream of vacations. When his longtime aide Mike Deaver suggested he was taking too much time away from the office, Reagan was unapologetic. The more time he spent on the ranch, he told him, the longer he believed he would live.[10] When Mrs. Reagan was away for any length of time, the ranch was where Reagan was likely to be found.[11]

Though Reagan kept a low profile in his first months out of office, observing an unwritten rule among outgoing presidents to keep out of the headlines for a while as the new president establishes himself, the shadow he cast from Los Angeles was sufficiently long enough to hover over his successor three thousand miles away. George Bush was compared at every turn to his former boss, most of the time unfavorably, particularly by conservative members of the press like columnist George Will, and by the GOP's dominant right wing, which was skeptical of Bush's questionable conservative credentials and wary of his moderate instincts. Bush had moved slightly off the course Reagan had set on many of the programs that had defined the latter's time in office. While he stood behind support for the Contras, Star Wars, and arms control, the programs he proposed became watered-down versions of those Reagan had envisioned. The Bush White House stressed that Bush shared Reagan's vision and goals, but had "his own style," which it hinted was more engaged and less detached than his predecessor's.[12]

In the spring, Bush was among those who paid a courtesy call on Reagan at the office in Century City. The visit was meant to reinforce the "continuity" he and his aides insisted existed between the Reagan and Bush administrations and, implicitly, to seek Reagan's approval of his first months in office. (Bush had also come to tacitly atone for seeking the counsel of Jimmy Carter on Asian policy, asking Reagan to make a trip to the region on behalf of the administration.) When the pair met with reporters after their meeting, Bush, *Time* wrote, looked like "a schoolboy called before the principal to discuss his report card." When Reagan did provide his assessment, he said that Bush was "doing just fine," hardly a rousing endorsement.[13] The visit fueled rumors of Reagan's disapproval of Bush that would grow over time, and add to Bush's political difficulties.

On July Fourth, a small item appeared in the news as the country celebrated its 213th birthday: Ronald Reagan had sustained minor injuries after being thrown from his horse while riding during a hunting trip at a friend's ranch in Mexico. The horse had slipped on a rocky downhill slope, bucking several times before forcing Reagan to the ground where he suffered cuts to his wrists. Soon afterward, he was transported by army helicopter to Fort Huachuca, just outside Tucson, Arizona, where doctors tended his wounds. True to form, Reagan shrugged off the episode with a quip, calling it "my own private rodeo."[14] Though the facts in the news accounts were accurate—the injuries were ostensibly superficial, and Reagan was released after five hours of treatment and examination—the fall was enough to speed up the process of deterioration that had already begun to develop in the former president's brain. Though it would be five years before the disease would be diagnosed, it would become clear that the fall Reagan had taken in the desert hills just below the Arizona border resulted in something far more insidious than a few minor bruises.

The same summer, Reagan put himself back in the spotlight. Along with Mrs. Reagan, he visited the capitals of Europe, taking what amounted to a victory lap, sounding his message on "The Triumph of Freedom" like an aging crooner on a greatest-hits tour. He stopped at Buckingham Palace where Queen Elizabeth made him the fifty-eighth American to receive British knighthood, and went on to Paris to observe the centennial celebration of the Eiffel Tower. He also became the sixth American to be inducted into the French Institute's Academy of Moral and Political Sciences.[15]

It wasn't long before he found himself back on the "mashed potato circuit," taking to the podium and pressing the flesh for honoraria considerably higher than the fees commanded by fellow ex-presidents Ford and Carter. One engagement in particular drew the attention of the press and criticism from those who increasingly accused former presidents of exploiting their years in office for quick and ready cash. In October, the Reagans embarked on an eight-day tour of Japan in exchange for a paycheck of roughly $2 million. Nobutaka Shikanai, a Japanese entrepreneur and owner of the Fujisankei Communications Group, a media conglomerate, sponsored the trip, which required Reagan to deliver several speeches and some media interviews at Fujisankei properties. Some years earlier, ex-president Jimmy Carter had accepted an $80,000 honorarium for a brief tour of Japan, also stirring controversy. The disparity in the amounts owed to the right-wing Shikanai's desire to associate his company with Reagan at a time when Shikanai sought to expand his $5 billion-a-year media empire outside Japan's borders. It also helped the image of the company in Shikanai's own country, where the Japanese public looked upon Reagan admiringly, even heroically.[16]

The Reagans' lucrative trip to Japan wasn't the only thing to stir controversy in the fall of 1989. Mrs. Reagan's tart memoir, *My Turn*, cowritten with William Novak (who had also helped pen Lee Iacocca's best-selling autobiography, *Iacocca*), was published in November, providing plenty of new fodder for critics of the former first lady. As the title suggested, Mrs. Reagan used the book to give her side of the many stories that had surfaced during her years in the White House—and to settle some scores.

Mrs. Reagan was never a press favorite. Her husband was dubbed "the Teflon President" for his uncanny knack of keeping blame from sticking to him. Whether due to his charm, cunning, or luck, he often got soft treatment or a free pass from the media for his mistakes and foibles. Not so Mrs. Reagan, to whom criticism stuck like Velcro. As much as anyone, she was the lightning rod of the Reagan administration, although, to some degree, it was her own doing. Publicly she lacked her husband's warmth and approachability, and chose to openly play the role of his enforcer, the bad cop to his good cop. While he, according to Mrs. Reagan, instinctively "trust[ed] people before they earned that trust," she remained suspicious until they had proven their loyalty.[17] She let nothing get in the way of her husband's presidency and willingly sacrificed her own image to bolster his. "Ronnie" always came first, and Mrs. Reagan's influence on him was indisputable.

"My life began when I met Ronnie," Mrs. Reagan wrote in the pages of *My Turn*, a sentiment she had expressed many times before.[18] In fact, her life began in New York City in 1923, the only child of Edith Lockett, a stage actress, who divorced her car salesman husband shortly after her daughter's birth. The first two years of Nancy's life were spent largely backstage while her single mother plied her trade in the theater, before Nancy was turned over to her aunt and her family in Bethesda, Maryland, for a more stable upbringing. Six years later, she went back to live with her mother after Ms. Lockett's marriage to Loyal Davis, a prominent, well-heeled Chicago neurosurgeon, whose last name Nancy would take as her own.

When she came of age, Nancy Davis chose to follow her mother's path as an actress. Working in New York on the stage and in television productions, she then went on to Hollywood where, aided by family friends like Spencer Tracy, she found minor success as a $250-per-week contract player at MGM. She met her future husband in 1949, after noticing her name in a list of Hollywood Communist sympathizers published in the newspaper, a reference to another actress with the same name. A mutual friend asked Reagan, then the president of the Screen Actors Guild, to help correct the matter on Miss Davis's behalf. A dinner to discuss the problem turned into a romance. They married in 1952.

Soon into their marriage, Mrs. Reagan traded klieg lights for life as a wife and mother. The Reagans had two children, Patti, born just six months into their marriage, and Ron, who arrived four years later in 1958. While being a wife came easily to Mrs. Reagan, motherhood did not. She and the children were often at odds with one another, resulting in tempestuous and distant relationships as they got older. In contrast, she remained a constant support to her husband, weathering the ups and downs of his erratic career as an actor, and championing his move into politics. She began her rough ride with the press as first lady of California, when she refused to live in the governor's mansion in Sacramento due to its state of disrepair. (Reagan benefactors would help fund more suitable housing elsewhere in the city.) But it was in the White House that the real controversy stirred. Mrs. Reagan was taken to task for a grandiose lifestyle that came to epitomize the Reagans' White House reign. Her efforts to spruce up the mansion—through private donations—were looked upon as evidence of her imperiousness, and she was roundly criticized for her fashion excesses. When Don Regan, Reagan's chief of staff and formerly his secretary of the treasury, began to abuse his power by blocking access to the president and thwarting his agenda, Mrs. Reagan actively campaigned for his removal with her husband and others in the administration.

The press eagerly covered the feud between the first lady and chief of staff as Don Regan rode out months on Reagan's benefit of the doubt. His downfall occurred when he hung up on Mrs. Reagan during a heated telephone exchange. After his departure from the White House, Regan, in a tell-all book, reported that throughout her time in the White House, Mrs. Reagan consulted Joan Quigley, a San Francisco–based astrologer recommended to her by longtime friend, Merv Griffin. The first lady, he alleged, often acted on Quigley's advice to alter the president's travel schedule—a desperate ploy to keep him from harm's way after the attempt on his life. The revelation drew howls from the media, and an embarrassed response from the White House.

In *My Turn*, Mrs. Reagan had an opportunity to answer her critics, and to take aim at many of those who had crossed her (and by extension in many cases, her husband) in and outside of the White House. There were few kind words for anyone associated with the Reagan administration, save Reagan himself; Washington insiders took to calling the book, "My Burn."[19] The worst was directed at Regan, to whom she devoted an entire chapter, but even loyal Reaganites were given sharp digs. Jim Baker, who had served throughout the administration first as chief of staff and then as secretary of the treasury, was accused of being too concerned about Jim Baker. Mike Deaver, a friend who had been with the Reagans since their days in Sacramento, came down with a case of "Potomac fever," when they got to Washington. The book did nothing for George Bush, who had labored to overcome the "wimp" label the press had unfairly stuck to him, as Mrs. Reagan implied he could not summon the courage as vice president to tell the president that Regan should resign. When Bush told Mrs. Reagan it wasn't his role to do so, she adamantly disagreed. "That's exactly your role," she told him—but apparently not one Bush chose to play.[20] She also did the sitting president no favors by distancing herself (and by implication, Reagan) from him, informing readers that the president and vice president were on "different schedules" and "different tracks." Further, she wrote that she simply didn't know Bush all that well, a dubious notion given the eight years Bush had spent as Reagan's number-two.[21]

Mrs. Reagan's family wasn't spared in the book's pages either. Her relationship with Patti, she wrote, was "one of the most painful and disappointing aspects of my life," though by recounting her daughter's rebellious exploits in detail, she suggested that the fault was primarily Patti's. She was kinder to Ron, whom she clearly favored, though he also fell prey to his mother's warts-and-all revelations.[22]

Though it did well in bookstores, *My Turn* did little to change the minds of those who saw Mrs. Reagan as a dragon lady—and presumably, did nothing to heal the relationships with those she took aim at.

Mrs. Reagan's image took another hit when she withdrew her support of a plan to build a drug treatment facility in the San Fernando Valley, just above Los Angeles. While first lady, Mrs. Reagan had taken on drugs as her cause, generating awareness about drug abuse among teenagers and urging them to "Just say no." After leaving the White House, she lent her name to a $1,000-a-plate black-tie dinner to raise funds for the project, which would be an extension of the New York–based Phoenix House, an organization committed to fighting drug abuse.[23] When would-be neighbors protested the building of the center, Mrs. Reagan and wealthy friends, who were prepared to write checks in support of the facility, inexplicably backed away, causing great disappointment for the organizers of the project.[24]

While Reagan did not spend much time exerting his considerable political influence out of office, he did pen an Op-Ed piece for *The New York Times* in the spring of 1991, urging the House of Representatives to draft a bill that would require a seven-day waiting period for the purchase of a handgun. His endorsement of the Brady Bill, named for his White House press secretary who had been crippled by bullets in the assassination attempt of Reagan in 1981, represented a blow to the National Rifle Association, one of Washington's most formidable lobbies.[25] It also contradicted his opposition to federal gun-control laws while he was president. Now an ex-president, Reagan was free to express his views without concern that they may not meet with the approval of his conservative base. In March of 1991, he visited Washington to lobby President Bush to support the bill. While conservatives were wary of Bush, Reagan's endorsement of the bill gave the administration an opportunity to reconsider its position with less fear of the political fallout.

Reagan's own memoir, *An American Life*, was published a year after his wife's, in November 1991, reaping poor reviews. Among presidential auto-biographies, Reagan's was a bonbon—light reading, with few passages of substance or note. The pages glistened with Reagan's "Morning in America" optimism, but there was little there to make it a must-read. Like *My Turn*, the book reinforced the more negative aspects of the author's image; in Reagan's case, that he was simplistic and intellectually challenged. "Mr. Reagan remains elusive, a winsome cardboard cowboy," *The New York Times* wrote, "a Rugged Individualist with big romantic dreams and even bigger blind spots."[26]

Another literary endeavor, with the Reagans as subject, was served up six months earlier in the spring of 1991. It would generate more attention than either of their autobiographies, and mark a low in White House tomes. *Nancy Reagan: The Unauthorized Biography*, written by controversial author Kitty Kelley, offered a scathing portrait of the former first couple. Kelley, forty-eight, was already known as a slayer of icons after writing scandalous, popular biographies of Jacqueline Onassis and Frank Sinatra, when she turned her pen on Mrs. Reagan.[27] While her methods and findings as an author were often questioned, she was quick to point out that none of her subjects had ever taken legal action. Despite Kelley's reputation, the book received thunderous media attention, including a front-page story in *The New York Times* and a *Time* magazine cover story just prior to the book's release, and set tongues wagging anew about the exploits—alleged, in this case—of Mrs. Reagan. The book accused her of everything from vanity—lying about her age, and having her nose fixed and eyes lifted—to tricking Reagan into marriage by getting pregnant with their first child, to having an extramarital affair with Sinatra before and during her White House days.

Reagan was also accused of being unfaithful, carrying on an affair with another actress (with whom he had supposedly been at the time of Patti's birth) before and after his marriage to Mrs. Reagan, and having a fling with an eighteen-year-old woman while he was governor of California. As Mrs. Reagan kept a low profile, many rushed to her defense. Among them was Mr. Reagan, who, before attending a Sunday church service at Bel-Air Presbyterian Church, told reporters that the book's "absurd falsehoods clearly exceeded the bounds of decency," and dismissed it as sensationalism intended to "enrich its author and publisher."[28] Even members of the press sympathized with her. But while the book's claims were in many cases suspect, it further damaged the former first lady's image, which had ebbed. The combination of the $2 million Japanese payday, her withdrawal of support for Phoenix House, Kelley's book, and *My Turn*, reinforced the perception many had of her as an emblem of the callous, excessive, vacuous era during which she and her Ronnie reigned in Washington.

The ranking of presidents has long been a parlor game of sorts for Americans, maybe not as popular as barroom arguments on subjects like whether Mantle or Mays was a better center fielder, but often the source of debates and dinner conversations. In the minds of many, Ronald Reagan towered over his contemporaries, and belonged in the pantheon of the greats who had more than made their mark in the country's history. The nation's historians, however, were overwhelmingly not among them. In 1991, five hundred esteemed history professors from universities across the country weighed in on presidential greatness, ranking thirty-seven men who had held office, from Washington to Reagan. (William Henry Harrison and James Garfield, both of whom held office for less than a year, were excluded.) Each man was placed into one of six categories ranging from "great," where Washington, Jefferson, Lincoln, and FDR dwelled, to "failure," inhabited by James Buchanan, Andrew Johnson, Ulysses S. Grant, Warren Harding, and Nixon. It was the first time Reagan had been subject to the collective judgment of historians, who rendered their assessments en masse in a formal survey every ten years or so, a practice that began when Harvard history professor Arthur Schlesinger Sr. polled fifty of his peers in 1948.[29]

Reagan, in his debut outing, did not fare well. The one-time C student and B actor was judged to be a D president, achieving a rank of "below average" that had also been accorded to such forgettables as John Tyler, Millard Fillmore, Franklin Pierce, and Calvin Coolidge. (Reagan may have been pleased to be grouped with the laconic Coolidge, whom he admired and thought to be underrated.) Over 90 percent of the historians polled believed that the American people had overestimated Reagan; they saw him as an intellectual lightweight whose administration was tarnished by corruption. While he got a nod for his hand in ending the Cold War with the Soviets, it was overshadowed by the Iran-Contra scandal and his "inept" policy in the Middle East.[30] How could the majority of Americans, who had twice put him in office by whopping margins, be so wrong about Reagan? Or was it perhaps the historians who got it wrong?

Nancy Reagan was not going to leave her husband's place in history to chance. Long before the historians submitted their rankings, she meticulously led the effort to plot the Reagan legacy. The most important step, one of many to that end, was the planning and construction of the Reagan Library.

At a cost of $56.8 million, the Reagan Library was the most expensive of the nine presidential libraries operated by the National Archives under the Presidential Libraries Act, one for every chief executive since Hoover. Its size, 153,000 square feet, also made it the largest, a sprawling, one-story mission-style structure with an orange tile roof, divided into three wings. The building is perched dramatically on a hilltop with a view of Simi Valley and, in the western distance, the Pacific Ocean.[31] Visitors walk through large iron gates into a courtyard leading to the library's front doors, where they are greeted by a statue of the Gipper himself. The *Los Angeles Times* described the attendant museum, depending on one's point of view, as either "an inspiring tribute to the 'Great Communicator,' or an absurd fun zone of Disneyland homage, an amusing adventure in pomp, circumstance and large deposits of kitsch. Not to mention whitewash."[32]

In an opening ceremony befitting the structure's grandiosity and the Reagans' flair for stagecraft, not to mention Mrs. Reagan's outsized ambition, the event drew a remarkable cast of political and cultural icons. While in office, Reagan had brought Nixon, Ford, and Carter to the White House prior to sending them off as part of the U.S. delegation at the funeral of Anwar Sadat, marking the first time four presidents were under the White House roof at the same time. In Simi Valley, on November 4, 1991, he did one better, uniting five presidents and chalking up another historical first. He, Nixon, Ford, and Carter were joined by George Bush, representing twenty-three years of presidential leadership—and counting. The presidential quintet standing shoulder to shoulder made for a photo op of epic proportions, an image that appeared on front pages throughout the world, and added weight to the occasion.

The presidents were accompanied by their wives, Lady Bird Johnson, and presidential scions Caroline Kennedy Schlossberg, John F. Kennedy Jr., Luci Baines Johnson, and descendants of FDR. Among the other 4,200 invited guests was a mixture of well-known Reagan aides and Hollywood conservatives. Colin Powell, George Schultz, and Jim Baker rubbed elbows with Bob Hope, Jimmy Stewart, Zsa Zsa Gabor, Merv Griffin, Sonny Bono, and Arnold Schwarzenegger. Conspicuously absent were Patti, who did not want to participate in a celebration of her father's presidency "and the Reagan ideology which I obviously didn't embrace," and Reagan officials like Don Regan and Ollie North, who represented low points in the administration.[33]

A graffiti-streaked, 60,000-pound chunk of the Berlin Wall standing next to the library hinted at the image of the fortieth president the library aimed to perpetuate: that of Reagan as the man who won the Cold War. While each of the three other former presidents who took to the podium during the ninety-minute dedication ceremony acknowledged Reagan's role in bringing down the Iron Curtain, they gently dispelled the notion that it was Reagan's deed alone—and protected their own legacies. Nixon invoked his famous "Kitchen Debate" with Nikita Khrushchev in which he, as vice president, had forcefully traded barbs with the Soviet premier on whose political system would stand the test of time. Ford credited the "peace through strength" practiced by every U.S. president since Eisenhower. Carter, who perhaps was most overshadowed by Reagan as a cold warrior, added: "All of us who have been in that office know that to plan, design, test, and produce a weapon system as those used recently in the Gulf War takes several presidential administrations."[34] Bush was careful not to let the aura of power that radiates from an incumbent American president detract from the spotlight on Reagan, though he knew as well as anyone that Reagan was a hard man to upstage.

Reagan, as always, rose to the occasion, delivering a short speech worthy of his "Great Communicator" moniker, taking the crowd back to his childhood in Dixon, Illinois, where the son of an alcoholic shoe salesman began his epic journey to the White House in 1911. "Eighty years is a long time to live," he said, "and yet within the course of a few short years I have seen the world turned upside down and conventional wisdom utterly disproved." While Mrs. Reagan did not take a turn at the microphone, her influence—and perhaps her own legacy—were in evidence. When a reporter shouted a question at Reagan during a photo session with his presidential peers and the first ladies, he asked his wife to repeat the question. "Nothing," she replied. "You can't answer."[35]

Like the Kennedy family, which knew something about creating a lasting legacy, the Reagan Foundation created an award around the Reagan image. For the Kennedys it was the John F. Kennedy Profile in Courage Award, recognizing those who have demonstrated political courage in pursuit of a cause or action despite its political consequences. For President and Mrs. Reagan, it was the Ronald Reagan Freedom Award, given to those who "have made monumental and lasting contributions to the cause of freedom."[36] The first recipient, aptly, was Gorbachev, to whom Reagan himself gave the award during a ceremony in the library courtyard in the spring of 1992. Later recipients included Margaret Thatcher, Billy Graham, Bob Hope, and Rudolph Giuliani.

But even Mrs. Reagan couldn't control everything. The authorized biography of Reagan, written by historian Edmund Morris, was released in 1999. The Reagans had offered Morris the job during Reagan's first term in office after being impressed by his Pulitzer Prize–winning biography of Theodore Roosevelt. After initially declining their offer, Morris eventually accepted in 1985, and thereafter enjoyed almost complete access to President and Mrs. Reagan during his second term. Fourteen years and a $3 million advance later, his efforts resulted in *Dutch: A Memoir of Ronald Reagan*, a presidential biography unlike any other, a fact/fiction hybrid in which Morris created an eponymous character based on himself whom he inserted into the story of Reagan's life.[37] The fictitious Morris, considerably older than the real-life author, had known Reagan since his adolescent days in Illinois, and crosses paths with him throughout his life.

Though at times Morris's Reagan achieved great things, perhaps even greatness overall, he was enigmatic in his complexities. While charming, charismatic, and eminently decent, he is also portrayed as an "airhead," boorish, simplistic in manner and thought (and a man who advocated ketchup as a vegetable in school cafeterias), and largely disengaged as president.[38] One reviewer described the book as "Zelig meets Chauncey Gardiner."[39] Though rich in detail—Does the reader really need to know about the clarity of the Gipper's saliva?—the author seems to conclude that the elusive Ronald Reagan is ultimately a figure too unknowable to be anything less than enigmatic. *Dutch* was a disappointment to critics, and to Mrs. Reagan, who had not gotten the heroic Mount Rushmore–like portrait of her husband she had hoped for, from an important historian with a ringside seat at the Reagan White House. Moreover, she felt Morris had gotten him all wrong; what made him remarkable, she felt, was his uncomplicated nature.[40] Like an overzealous English teacher, Morris may have read more into his subject than was actually there.

After achieving stratospheric approval ratings in the wake of the Gulf War in 1991, George Bush had lost steam by 1992 as the election neared. It became increasingly clear throughout his tenure that Bush lacked Reagan's common touch and his gift for elective politics. His opponent, however, Arkansas governor Bill Clinton, did not. Despite a series of scandals left in his wake, Clinton, like Reagan, resonated with the American people. When Reagan headed to Bush country for the GOP National Convention in Houston that summer, Bush trailed Clinton in the polls and badly needed a lift from the man whose coattails he once rode. In Houston, Reagan gave his last big public speech in perfect pitch. He reminisced about his accomplishments and shared his poetic, sanguine view of America. Alluding to his advanced age and invoking Lloyd Bentsen in his vice-presidential debate with Dan Quayle, he said of Clinton, "This fellow they've nominated claims he's the new Thomas Jefferson. Well, let me tell you something. I knew Thomas Jefferson. He was a friend of mine. And governor, you're no Thomas Jefferson."

Dispelling the rumors that he was disillusioned with Bush, he "warmly, genuinely, wholeheartedly" offered his support. Bush, he said, was "a quiet man, not a showman"—not Ronald Reagan in other words—but he was a trustworthy leader who was respected around the world. Finally, he brought out Nancy and said goodbye to the party he had shaped more than anyone alive.

As it had twelve years earlier when Reagan was elected, America decided on a change of leadership in November, bringing to an end the Reagan-Bush years. A week before leaving office, Bush brought Reagan back to the White House to award him the Medal of Freedom and, in a last hurrah for the era, to reunite many of the players in the Reagan and Bush administrations.

Just after the election, President-elect Clinton paid a visit to Reagan's Century City office. In a December/May presidential scene reminiscent of when Eisenhower passed the leadership torch to Kennedy, the forty-six-year-old Clinton met privately with the sage two-term ex-president who told him stories and offered a few points of advice on the office he was about to take on.[41] Then Reagan gave him a jar of his signature red, white, and blue jelly beans, smiled before the cameras, and sent him on his way. Clinton would keep the jelly beans in his White House office for the next eight years.[42]

Just several years into Reagan's post-presidency, a number of episodes made it clear that his memory was failing him. At a dinner at the library marking his eighty-second birthday in 1993, Reagan rose to toast Margaret Thatcher who was among the guests. After giving the toast to a rousing standing ovation, Reagan remained in place and repeated the words verbatim. Awkwardly, guests rose again in polite applause.[43] A year later, on his eighty-third birthday, Reagan gave his last public speech to a dinner crowd of 2,500 in Washington. This time he got through with no problems, but when he and Mrs. Reagan got back to their hotel he was disoriented. "Well, I have got to wait a minute," he said. "I am not quite sure where I am."[44] The same year, at the funeral of Richard Nixon, where former presidents Ford, Carter, and Bush and their wives joined President and Mrs. Clinton at the Nixon Library to mourn Nixon's loss, Reagan didn't quite seem himself. The "aw shucks" smile and wave he gave to the crowd was vintage Reagan, but many noticed he seemed a bit off-kilter. Ford noticed that he didn't recognize him or Betty, and Bush confided to friends that he was concerned about his old boss.[45]

In the summer of 1994, the Mayo Clinic, after conducting a battery of tests the year before, had made a conclusive diagnosis of Reagan's condition: He was in the early stages of Alzheimer's disease, an incurable degenerative brain disorder that afflicted four million Americans, and a third of Americans over the age of eighty-five.[46] The Reagan family was not surprised by the diagnosis—Reagan himself had stated publicly that he was concerned about the possibility because his mother had been senile in the last years leading up to her death at age eighty—but when they got the news, they chose to keep it private.[47] In a rare show of restraint, the news media held back the story despite widespread speculation about his condition. By the fall, however, the *San Diego Journal* was said to be preparing a piece on his deteriorating health, prompting him to go forward in reporting the news to the public himself. Mrs. Reagan, along with other family members, friends, aides, and doctors, recommended that he tell the American people through his own words, written in his own hand.[48] On November 5, he retreated to his study, where he carefully crafted a two-page letter on simple stationery embossed with a gold presidential seal over his name. "My Fellow Americans," he wrote:

> *I have recently been told that I am one of the millions of Americans who will be afflicted with Alzheimer's disease.*
>
> *Upon learning this news, Nancy and I had to decide whether as private citizens we would keep this a private matter or whether we would make this news known in a public way.*
>
> *In the past, Nancy suffered from breast cancer and I had my cancer surgeries. We found through our open disclosures we were able to raise public awareness. We were happy that as a result, many more people underwent testing. They were treated in early stages and able to return to normal, healthy lives.*
>
> *So, now we feel it is important to share it with you. In opening our hearts, we hope this might promote greater awareness of this condition. Perhaps it will encourage a clearer understanding of the individuals and families who are affected by it.*

At the moment I feel just fine. I intend to live the remainder of the years God gives me on this earth doing the things I have always done. I will continue to share life's journey with my beloved Nancy and my family. I plan to enjoy the great outdoors and stay in touch with my friends and supporters.

Unfortunately, as Alzheimer's disease progresses, the family often bears a heavy burden. I only wish there was some way I could spare Nancy from this painful experience. When the time comes I am confident that with your help she will face it with faith and courage.

In closing, let me thank you, the American people, for giving me the great honor of allowing me to serve as your President. When the Lord calls me home, whenever that may be, I will leave with the greatest love for this country of ours and eternal optimism for its future.

I now begin the journey that will lead me into the sunset of my life. I know that for America there will always be a bright dawn ahead.

Thank you, my friends. May God always bless you.

Sincerely,

Ronald Reagan

On the evening after the letter was released to the public, President Clinton, in Oakland at a political rally, told an audience of supporters that Reagan's letter "touched my heart," a sentiment shared by much of America.[49]

Over the next year Reagan took care to say goodbye to all of the people who had meant something to him. Many received handwritten letters from Reagan, offering his thanks for their friendship and the fond memories they gave him and Nancy. His friend, film producer J. C. Lyles, was told in Reagan fashion through a joke: "Two men are having lunch. One says, 'Joe, I have Alzheimer's, but I met a doctor and he's great. You better go see him because you're getting the same thing.' Joe says, 'Sure; what's the guy's name?' The first guy thought for a long time and said, 'What's that flower that has petals and thorns?' 'A rose,' Joe said. And the man hollered to his wife, 'Hey, Rose, what's the name of that doctor I'm going to?'"[50] The joke had its own poignancy; in the years ahead, Reagan's own wife's name would be the last he would remember long after those of family and friends had faded.

Reagan had survived adversity in his life that may have set others back. In the White House alone he had endured an attempt on his life, his wife's mastectomy, his own skin cancer, Iran-Contra and other scandals—even the dogged Sam Donaldson. His innate buoyancy was a powerful defense mechanism for overcoming the obstacles in his path and moving forward. When the pressure was on, the public often saw a familiar response from the president: a downward twitch of his head, arched eyebrows over a slight smile, and a rakish one-liner, and Reagan was back to being Reagan. But Alzheimer's would attack the mental constitution that gave Reagan his natural ebullience. The Irish storyteller's twinkle in his eyes, gradually supplanted by a dull, blank gaze, provided evidence of the transformation his brain was undergoing bit by bit.

The illness of the beloved former president led to an upturn in the public's perception of Mrs. Reagan. Her fierce, take-no-prisoners protectiveness of her husband, which led to her dragon lady image, was now channeled into being his full-time caretaker as dementia became a daily reality. The public took note of her strength and dedication. She no longer traveled unnecessarily, rarely left the house for any length of time, and cut back on social outings. When she had lunch with friends, it was likely to be on the lush terrace of The Hotel Bel-Air, a five-minute drive away, and then it was right back to the house.[51] The phone was her primary link to her friends. As in the White House, she spent many restless hours awake at night worrying about Ronnie as he slept soundly beside her.[52]

There are no magic cures for the ravages of Alzheimer's. Routines are one way of soothing those afflicted, and Reagan soon settled into rhythms aided by Mrs. Reagan and his staff, who saw to it that he remained active. He regularly put in a few hours a day at his office, sitting behind his oak desk where he would autograph pictures and books, or peruse the comics in the newspaper. On occasion, he would receive visitors. Bush paid a last visit to Reagan well after his Alzheimer's had set in and "could tell that things weren't right." "Do you go up to the ranch much, Ron?" he asked as they talked in Reagan's office. "Let me show you something," Reagan said as he stood at the window pointing to Santa Monica in the distance. "Do you see that line over by those buildings?" he asked. There was no line. "Yes," answered Bush. "That's the ranch," Reagan said.[53]

As with other Alzheimer's victims, some days were better than others. He swam daily in his backyard pool, and could be seen around town, walking on the strand at the Santa Monica beach or sitting in a park in Beverly Hills, robust and bespectacled, in white tennis sneakers and a baseball cap.[54] Occasionally, he would play golf at the exclusive Los Angeles Country Club, which had granted him an honorary membership. Gradually those activities lessened over time. In *Dutch*, Edmund Morris wrote of Reagan raking leaves by the pool at the house for hours at a time, as a means of expending his "slow, unstoppable energy," not realizing that the Secret Service detail would soon collect and replace them to have Reagan rake them up anew.[55]

Reagan's worsening condition was apparent when his ranch was put on the market in 1997 by Mrs. Reagan, who had never quite taken to the strenuous outdoor life favored by her husband. It sold in 1998 to Young America's Foundation of Herndon, Virginia, and Santa Barbara, California, as an historical landmark and education center.[56] Sometime earlier, Mrs. Reagan had realized that he was no longer up to excursions on horseback and charged one of their Secret Service men, John Barletta, who often rode behind Reagan, with the task of telling him. Reagan, with tears streaming down his face, put his own feelings aside, placed his hands on Barletta's shoulders, and said simply, "It's okay, John," trying to comfort Barletta as the bearer of bad news.[57]

As Reagan's condition progressed, Mrs. Reagan found a new role for herself, one that took her from the stage manager and sidekick roles she had played for her husband directly into the spotlight on her own. The legacy of Ronald Reagan, it seemed, could be more than recognition of all he stood for and had accomplished in office; it could live in the form of embryonic stem cell research—the study of human embryos with the keys to the two hundred different cell types that compose the human body—offering the prospect of a cure for Alzheimer's and other diseases, and sparing others the pain she had endured at her husband's side. Mrs. Reagan's role in advocating embryonic research would put her on center stage—and in direct opposition to the incumbent president who, like many conservative members of the GOP, rejected it conceptually on moral grounds. She spent time with medical experts and knowledgeable friends in an effort to better understand how the study of human embryos could unlock the mysteries of human biology.[58]

For supporters of stem cell research, having Nancy Reagan as an advocate was as good as it got, short of having the gold standard for the GOP, Reagan himself. Mrs. Reagan, as a stand-in for her husband, was in a unique position to lobby opponents, including, most prominently, George W. Bush. In 2001, she quietly wrote the president, urging him to push for federal funding of embryonic research, while respectfully but persistently putting the arm on other politicians to do the same, largely behind the scenes. Later that same year, Bush moved toward a middle ground, announcing on national television that the administration would fund embryonic research, but only in cases in which stem cell colonies had already been cultivated in research labs. The stem cells fitting the established criteria, however, were not readily available to scientists, and when they were, their quality was often compromised.[59] To supporters, including Mrs. Reagan, it wasn't enough. In the next several years she would push further and, in May 2004, took a more public stand. At a rare public appearance at a fund-raiser dinner for the Juvenile Diabetes Foundation, Mrs. Reagan told the audience, "Ronnie's long journey has finally taken him to a distant place where I can no longer reach him. Because of this, I'm determined to do whatever I can to save families from this pain. I just don't see how we can turn our backs on this."[60]

Nevertheless, Bush held firm: He would not support science that "destroys life to safe lives." In 2005, he went so far as to threaten a rare veto of legislation reaching his desk that proposed otherwise.[61] To shore up support, he mobilized his own forces, including Laura Bush, who put a softer face on her husband and his administration, and whose father had succumbed to Alzheimer's. "We have to be really careful between what we want to do for science and what we should do ethically," she said, supporting the president's stand in a morning appearance on CBS.[62] Perhaps learning the lessons of his father's presidency, Bush was careful not to take positions that would alienate his conservative base, particularly on moral issues. It was an approach shared by Reagan, whom Bush emulated in his own presidency more than any of his predecessors. One wonders then: Where would President Reagan have stood on embryonic stem cell research?

The stem cell debate raged on, generally split along the same lines as the pro-choice and pro-life camps, and reflecting the ever-widening divisions in red state/blue state America during the George W. Bush years.

Also aiding in the cause of finding a cure for Alzheimer's was Maureen Reagan, Reagan's first child with Jane Wyman. As a board member and spokesperson for the Alzheimer's Association, she worked tirelessly and with great success to raise awareness about the disease and funds to combat it. "Mermie," as she was known to her family, was the most like her father of the Reagan offspring, embracing his political career and party if not all his views, and the most supportive to Mrs. Reagan after his Alzheimer's set in. In 1996, she was diagnosed with melanoma, which had spread to her brain by 2000. Despite radiation therapy and a valiant fight, she succumbed to cancer in August of the following year. In a statement, Mrs. Reagan said, "We will miss her terribly," though her father had ceased to recognize her.[63]

Reagan disappeared from public view entirely in 2001, in his ninetieth year. A fall resulting in a broken hip landed him in the hospital for a brief stay, and after an operation to repair the damage, he returned home, never to leave again. It was somehow strange to think of him behind the gates of 668 St. Cloud Road, unaware of the changes in the world outside; of Twin Towers collapsed and the Pentagon in flames; of a diffuse and unseen enemy, and a new kind of evil. He was of another era, long gone. Yet his heart was still beating strong.

His physical vigor defied the expectations of medical experts, who thought his broken hip would lead to his demise in a matter of months. Even before the hip injury, his own physician predicted he wouldn't live beyond 2000.[64] As Reagan suffered the ravages of Alzheimer's in its last horrible phases, his legend and the public's love of him grew. Monuments to him were proposed in every corner of the country. Washington's National Airport was renamed Reagan National Airport, and an effort was afoot to put Reagan's image on the dime, replacing the profile of FDR that had graced the coin for two generations. When CBS planned a prime-time movie entitled *The Reagans*, which was said to cast him in an unflattering light, the public outcry was such that the network quickly reversed course. Eventually, the movie was relegated to the paid cable channel Showtime, where it aired weeks later to poor reviews. In a piece entitled "Why we've deified the Gipper" in *Newsweek's* last issue of 2003, Jon Meacham explained it this way: "The public's esteem stems not only from respect for the substance of what [Reagan] accomplished in office or from sympathy, but from a subliminal respect for the strength of a man to endure so long . . . [N]o one can gainsay his pure will to live in tragic circumstances."[65]

A number of books also had historians and critics taking a more positive and perhaps a more objective view of Reagan. One, *Reagan, In His Own Hand*, contained the handwritten radio speeches Reagan had drafted and delivered before his presidency, while another, *Dear Americans*, offered some of the more than five thousand letters he had written throughout his life on a variety of different subjects. Additionally, a PBS documentary depicted Reagan as the president who ended the Cold War by suspending détente with the Soviets and outmaneuvering them through his Star Wars gambit, while a *Time* cover story revealed how Reagan had secretly plotted an end to Communism with Pope John Paul II. *When Character Was King*, a best-seller by Reagan speechwriter Peggy Noonan, celebrated Reagan's core values which shaped the era that bore his name. The wealth of new material got the attention of many nonbelievers, who had to concede that the fortieth president was more cerebral, contemplative, and engaged than he had ever been given credit for.

At some point during his remaining years, Reagan failed to recognize even his wife—and slowly, painfully she reconciled herself to his passing.[66] But as she let go, she and her long-estranged family drew closer.[67] When Reagan's condition continued to deteriorate to the point that he was confined to his bedroom, unable to walk, and even the closest of friends were no longer invited to visit to protect the former president's dignity, the family began to fill the void. Patti became a support to her mother, regularly visiting the house and telephoning daily. Gradually they began to overcome the acrimony that had for years driven them apart. Reagan's prolonged illness and Maureen's passing had brought them together.[68] "I hope and pray that before my own life is over, Patti and I will be able to put the past behind us and arrive at the same point. Nothing would make me happier," Mrs. Reagan allowed in *My Turn* over a decade earlier.[69] Ultimately, her wish would be fulfilled, but it came at a price.

Ron rallied around his mother too. Living in Seattle where he free-lanced as a television journalist and producer for, among others, MSNBC, ABC, and Animal Planet, he saw his father as often as his travels took him to Los Angeles, which meant at least several times a year. A liberal with a rebellious streak like Patti, Ron abhorred his father's political leanings, but had never been as bitter toward his parents and enjoyed an easier, less com-plicated rapport with his mother, whom she had favored throughout his childhood. Michael had long ago made his peace with his father. In 1991, he told him for the first time that he loved him, and Reagan said, "I love you too." Rarely demonstrative before, the two hugged every time they saw each other. Even when his father failed to recognize him as his son, he stretched out his arms to embrace him when they were together.[70]

When Reagan finally met his end after battling pneumonia, on the morning of June 5, 2004, Patti and Ron were by Mrs. Reagan's side as he slipped away. Mike, stuck in LA traffic, arrived just minutes afterward. "At the last moment, Patti would write later, "when his breathing told us this was it, he opened his eyes and looked straight at my mother. Eyes that hadn't openend for days did, and they weren't chalky or vague. They were clear and blue and full of love, and then they closed with his last breath. If a death can be lovely, his was."[71]

The news of Reagan's death was no great surprise to the world. The obituaries had long been written. At least five years before the actual event, Mrs. Reagan herself had penned one that would appear in *Time's* memo-rial issue after Reagan's death, when its editor, Walter Isaacson, gently asked for her contribution. Most celebrated Reagan as he had come to be known over time—as a twentieth-century giant who restored America's faith in herself and sped up the collapse of Communism in the Soviet Union and Eastern Europe.

Bidding farewell to the fortieth president would be an elaborate affair befitting European royalty. The details of the ceremony had first been plot-ted while Reagan was in the White House, the information recorded in a book provided by the State Department to all U.S. presidents, and over the years the plans evolved through regular meetings.[72] Reagan's called for a state funeral, America's first since Lyndon Johnson's thirty-one years earlier, that would bring his body back to Washington before returning him to the library in Simi Valley, which would mark his final resting place seven days after his passing. Mrs. Reagan, as always, presided over the planning with a firm hand and an eye for detail. Like Jacqueline Kennedy, she understood not only her husband but her role in putting him to rest, and would stoically attend four public ceremonies with grace and dignity, her black mourning garb contrasting sharply with the signature red she favored and often wore. Her transformation in the eyes of the public from the overprotective dragon lady to the devoted wife and venerable guardian of the Reagan legacy would soon be complete.

Two days after Reagan's death, Mrs. Reagan appeared at the Reagan Library with Patti. Mother and daughter held hands as Patti walked her to the late president's flag-draped coffin. Mrs. Reagan stood alone before it, whispering sentiments unheard before laying her face upon the casket and tenderly kissing it, then running her hand over the flag. The following day, the Reagan family accompanied Reagan's body back to Washington, where it lay in state in the Capitol Rotunda. Tens of thousands, the powerful and the common, filed past to pay their respects.

The memorial service, on the morning of June 11, drew four thousand mourners.[73] Once again, Reagan united five living U.S. presidents. Ford, Carter, Bush, Clinton, and the current President Bush came to pay tribute, along with their wives, officials from the Reagan and current administrations, world leaders, and graying icons from the Reagan era, Gorbachev, Thatcher, and Lech Walesa among them. Thatcher, Brian Mulroney, and the Bush father and son gave eulogies, Mrs. Thatcher's videotaped in advance due to her failing health. Mrs. Reagan had personally asked the elder Bush to speak. His voice broke as he talked about his mentor's enduring influence on him. "I learned more from Ronald Reagan than from anyone I encountered in all my years of public life," he said, giving examples of his kindness, courage, decency, and, of course, humor. When asked, "How did your visit go with Bishop Tutu?" Bush recalled, Reagan replied, "So-so."

"It has been ten years since [Reagan] said his own farewell," George W. Bush said in his turn at the podium. "Yet it is still very sad and hard to let him go."

After the service, the Reagan family boarded an Air Force jet at Andrews Air Force Base and took the former president's body home to his library in the hills of Simi Valley. Midway into the journey westward, the plane tipped its wing as it flew over Tampico, Illinois, while members of the family peered out the window to look at the wooded Midwestern landscape below where Ronald Reagan came into the world.[74] At a final service at the library attended by some 750 relatives and friends, the three surviving Reagan children spoke publicly about their father for the first time since his death.[75] "He is home now, he is free," Ron said as the sun cast its last rays of the day before descending behind the distant western hills and into the Pacific. In a final, heart-wrenching goodbye, Mrs. Reagan broke down beside her husband's coffin, before Ron, Patti, and Michael gathered around her, steadied her, and slowly led her away from the gravesite.

The house was quiet, dark, and empty, and the sun had long set when Mrs. Reagan arrived home in Bel-Air after the funeral. The staff, with the exception of a few Secret Service men, was still at the library. She and her family gathered around the couch in her bedroom and talked until near midnight before she fell into a long, deep sleep.[76]

VIII.

GEORGE BUSH:
PATRIARCH

George Bush couldn't quite understand it. He had done his best for the country, worked hard, cared about the people—didn't they know his "heartbeat"? How could they pass him up for Bill Clinton? Got out of the draft, protested against his country, had a problem with the truth. Where was the man's character? Bill Clinton! How did this happen?

Two years earlier, in January 1991, as he addressed a joint session of Congress after U.S. and allied troops liberated Kuwait from its Iraqi invaders, driving them across the border after a ground war lasting just one hundred hours, George Bush seemed invincible. The House chamber erupted in a series of thunderous ovations for the hero of the Gulf War, the man who resolutely drew a line in the sand for Saddam Hussein and led a fragile coalition of foreign powers to support the U.S.'s position. That triumph was preceded by the fall of the Berlin Wall and the subsequent collapse of the Soviet Union, which Bush couldn't take credit for but oversaw with quiet, keen diplomacy. Against all odds, the Iron Curtain had gone down with a whimper. After the victory in the Gulf, America's position in the world was as solid as it had been since the end of World War II, as reflected in Bush's approval ratings which stood at 91 percent, the highest for a president since Truman's after V-J Day.[1]

But Bush would find that popularity, like military glory, was fleeting. After the parades were over and the confetti had been swept up, Americans went back to worrying about domestic issues at a time when the economy was sagging and crime was on the rise. "Read my lips—no new taxes," Bush pledged in the campaign of 1988, a pledge he could not in good conscience keep as the national debt mounted to unprecedented levels. When he raised taxes in the spring of 1990 as part of a budget compromise, the din among

Democrats and Republicans alike was deafening, and added to Bush's less-than-spectacular record on the economy, which continued to slide. As the months passed, Bush lacked an agenda and looked increasingly out of touch.

Then along came forty-six-year-old Arkansas governor Bill Clinton, smooth (some would say slick), smart, and silver-tongued. Clinton connected with the people. As Bush was asking for "just a splash" of coffee at a New Hampshire diner and insisting incongruously that pork rinds were a favorite snack, Clinton was wolfing down Big Macs and wooing voters like he was one of their own. Ross Perot, the millionaire Texas businessman who had a vendetta against Bush, also joined the fray as an Independent candidate, a development that set Bush back further. As the campaign heated up Bush appeared lethargic, probably owing to a thyroid condition he was being treated for as much as anything, but when he glanced at his watch during a televised debate with Clinton and Perot, it reinforced the impression of indifference.[2] When Election Day 1992 came, Clinton carried 43 percent of the popular vote, with Bush and Perot trailing at 37 percent and 19 percent, respectively. Bush was out, Clinton was in. After the loss, Bush recalled a Kenyan long-distance runner in the Summer Olympics who had run through an injury, crossing the finish line forty-five minutes behind the race's victor. The athlete commented later, "My country didn't send me here to start the race. They sent me here to finish it." Bush's regret was that he didn't finish the race, and that as a result, he had let down his family, friends, and party.[3]

Despite the pain of his loss, Bush, ever the patrician, was nothing if not gracious. He was determined to hand over the White House with dignity and to make the transition smooth. Just several weeks after the election, he met with Clinton at the White House to discuss the office and give his views on the world, telling Clinton he thought the tribal disputes between the Bosnian Serbs and Croats in the former Yugoslavia would be his biggest trouble spot. Afterward, Hillary Clinton joined them for a tour of the residence on the second and third floors as a surprised Barbara Bush greeted them with her "hair practically in curlers."

"Bill," Bush said, as he walked his soon-to-be successor out, "I want to tell you something. When I leave here, you're going to have no trouble from me. The campaign is over and I'm out of here. I will do nothing to complicate your work and I just want you to know that."[4] Mrs. Bush even had nice things to say about Hillary Clinton, though the two women, like their husbands, were as different as their generations.

On his last morning at the White House, Bush left a note for Clinton atop the desk in the Oval Office letting him know he would be rooting for him, and when the Clintons arrived late at the White House for the traditional pre-inauguration coffee with their friends—Hollywood producers Harry Thomason and Linda Bloodworth-Thomason—unexpectedly in tow, the Bushes took it in stride and ordered up two more cups and saucers.[5] In turn, Clinton used a line of his inauguration speech to "salute" Bush "for his half-century of service to America."

Weeks earlier, Tip O'Neill, the Democratic Speaker of the House, candidly told his friend Bush, "You ran a lousy campaign," (a statement Bush thanked him for), but added, "Don't worry; you'll leave this place with a lot of people loving you. You're a good man. You've been a good president."[6] Bush's popularity rating in opinion polls, which, at 56 percent, had climbed since the election, seemed to bear out what O'Neill already knew.[7]

"I've done what I could," said Bush as he left Washington. "Time to get out of town. I intend to do everything I can to honor the office of the presidency . . . I feel good that I have handed over the office so that Iraq is no problem for President Clinton . . . I wish him well."[8] Not everyone in the loyal Bush brood was quite as congenial. Bush's second son Jeb told a *New York Times* reporter at the close of an interview, "Remember, don't stop thinking about tomorrow," a sarcastic reference to the Clinton camp's Fleetwood Mac theme song.[9] It would be an uncertain tomorrow for the forty-first president. What would he do? "I've asked him the question myself and he said 'I don't know,'" his eldest son George W. said on the first day of his father's post-presidency. "I just don't think he's worked it out."[10]

If Bush harbored any bitterness over his loss, he didn't let it show. Disappointment, sure; and he still wondered about Clinton, though not publicly. But the next morning, as he and Mrs. Bush awoke early in the two-story white colonial house they would rent for seven months while their new home was being built nearby in the tony Tanglewood section of suburban Houston, the former president made himself coffee and got on with his life. By 7:30 he had thrown on running shoes and a windbreaker and was out the door on his way to his new office on the ninth floor of a pink granite building at 10000 Memorial Drive. As he exited the building's elevator en route to the eight-office suite, he politely informed a press photographer who accompanied him that he could go no further than his office door. "I've been in public life for more than twenty years," the former president explained. "Now I just want a little time for myself."[11] He had earned at least that. His immediate task was to determine how to answer the seven hundred letters that poured in each day.[12] In the coming days he would busy himself with plans for the $83 million Bush Library and Museum to be constructed at the edge of the campus of Texas A&M University in College Station, two hours from Houston, and doing fundraising work for Houston's M. D. Anderson Cancer Center, where he would eventually become chairman of the board.[13]

Mrs. Bush reacquainted herself with the everyday concerns of suburban living. "On January 20, we woke up [at the White House] and we had a household staff of ninety-three," she recalled of her transition later. "The very next morning we woke up and it was just George, me, and two dogs— and that's not all that bad."[14] Aided by her husband, she bought a car, choosing a blue Mercury Sable wagon that she got used to driving after twelve years of being chauffeured by limousine as the wife of the vice president, and then president. She did her own grocery shopping, often fending off the curious who asked, "Aren't you Barbara Bush?" with a ready answer: "No, she's much older than I am."[15] She and her husband of forty-seven years reacquainted themselves with living on their own. She did the cooking, a skill that didn't come naturally to her, while the former president was "the dish man," rinsing and loading them in the dishwasher. In the mornings, the coffee machine began percolating around 5:00 A.M., and a little later, they had a light breakfast together while reading *The New York Times* and two Houston papers, before walking the dogs. "Along the way we count our blessings," wrote Bush.[16]

The Bushes planned to divide their time between their adopted state of Texas and Walker's Point, the Bush family compound on the rocky coast of Kennebunkport, Maine, two places that were emblematic of Bush's life. The latter reflected Bush as the product of the Eastern Establishment. He was born in Massachusetts in 1924, the second son of his Midwestern parents, who had come east where his self-made father found success on Wall Street. Growing up in Greenwich, Connecticut, his values were learned at the knee of his mother, the former Dorothy Walker, who taught him humility, responsibility, compassion, and the importance of family. He attended Phillips Andover Academy and upon graduation in 1942 enlisted in the navy to join the war effort. At eighteen, he enrolled in the navy and would become its youngest pilot, and at twenty narrowly escaped death and capture in World War II after his plane was shot down by Japanese troops over the Pacific.

Shortly after his arrival home he married his sweetheart, Barbara Pierce, whose first name he had chosen to grace the side of his plane. The two met at a Greenwich Country Club party just after the attack on Pearl Harbor in December 1941, when Bush got up the nerve to ask the "beautiful girl" in the red and green dress to dance.[17] The married couple went on to New Haven, Connecticut, where Bush attended Yale, gaining admittance into the elite Skull and Bones secret society, while his wife played full-time mother to their first son, George Walker, born in 1946. After graduation, Bush took a detour from the traditional Ivy League paths drawn from East Coast privilege; instead of following his father and other family members to Wall Street, he set out for West Texas in a red, two-door Studebaker to make a name for himself in the oil business. The Bush family settled in the boomtown of Odessa in 1948, where they moved into a two-bedroom apartment—sharing a bathroom with a mother-daughter team of prostitutes—and began a new life.[18]

While Bush pursued a prosperous career in oil, the Bush family burgeoned as they moved throughout Texas. A daughter, Robin, was born in 1949 while the Bushes lived briefly in Terrance, California, and was followed by three boys, John Ellis, or "Jeb," in 1950, Neil in 1955, and Marvin in 1956, all born in Midland. Dorothy, "Doro" as she was called, arrived in 1959 after the family settled in Houston. The young couple suffered the loss of Robin to leukemia at age four. "[She was] the epitome of innocence to us, beauty . . . and there was no explanation," Bush reflected later. "But all these things contribute to your life, maybe your character, what you stand for."[19]

In 1965, Bush resigned from Zapata, the successful oil company he had established with several partners, to pursue a life in public service. Bush's father had risen to prominence in Connecticut Republican circles in the early fifties. After losing a race for the U.S. Senate in 1950, Prescott Bush came back to win a seat in 1952, which he would keep for two terms. After serving as Republican chairman in Houston's Harris County, the forty-year-old Bush tried to follow his father to the Senate after challenging the Texas Democratic incumbent Ralph Yarborough in 1964. He lost, but was elected to the House of Representatives two years later. After being defeated in a second bid for a Senate seat, this time by Lloyd Bentsen, President Richard Nixon made him ambassador to the United Nations. When Nixon gained reelection in 1972, Bush took on the role of chairman of the Republican Party, a duty that left him to deal with the toll Watergate had taken on the GOP. After Gerald Ford took over for Nixon in 1974, he appointed Bush as envoy to the People's Republic of China, and then, director of the CIA. Bush took his first stab at the presidency in 1980, running as Ronald Reagan's closest challenger in the Republican primaries and, when Reagan won the nomination, joined the ticket as his running mate, leading to Bush's two terms as vice president. In 1988, Bush followed Reagan into the Oval Office, making him the first incumbent vice president to win the presidency since Martin Van Buren had done it 152 years earlier.

Throughout Bush's rise in business and politics, the Bush family remained strong. The children, though different, shared close relationships with each other and their parents. Bush once said, perhaps partially in jest, that his greatest success was that his children still came home. In fact, they revered him, and despite some stumbles thrived as a result of his example, avoiding the fate of other scions of successful fathers—particularly U.S. presidents—who withered in their shadows. When he was president, the family was his greatest comfort. He wondered how Reagan handled the job without a close family around him to buoy him during the tough times. For Bush there was always a member of the family around to hug or to put things in perspective, like his grandson, Sam, who interrupted an important Oval Office meeting by knocking on the window and pointing out proudly that Millie, the Bushes' dog, had a squirrel in its mouth. "We approach everything as family," Bush said—and they were his greatest solace in the wake of defeat.[20]

Shortly into Bush's post-presidency, the Kuwaiti royal family extended an invitation to visit their country, which the Bushes gladly accepted. Hopping a ride on the royal family's 747 with Neil and Marvin and their wives Laura and Sharon and several friends accompanying them, the Bushes flew in comfort, enjoying five-star hotel amenities that rivaled Air Force One. Upon arrival, Bush was given a hero's welcome by the Kuwaiti people for his momentous role in driving out their Iraqi captors during the Gulf War, along with a number of gifts, including an antique door inscribed with names of the U.S. troops killed in Operation Desert Storm.[21] But just as the Kuwaitis hadn't forgotten Bush's part in the Gulf War, neither had the Iraqis. A day earlier, on April 13, seventeen Iraqis in armed vehicles were taken into custody at the Kuwait-Iraq border. Officials traced materials found in their vehicles back to the Iraqi government, led by a severely weakened Saddam Hussein. Their intent: to assassinate George Bush. The failed plot sparked Clinton's first military action as president as he gave the order to hit Iraqi intelligence quarters in Baghdad with twenty-three Tomahawk missiles as a "proportionate response" and a deterrent to future acts of terrorism.[22]

The attempted assassination of a former president was nothing new. In 1912, four years after leaving the presidency, Theodore Roosevelt had sought the office again as a member of the newly formed Bull Moose Party, challenging his chosen successor, Republican William Howard Taft, and Democratic challenger Woodrow Wilson. At a campaign stop in Milwaukee, as Roosevelt prepared to address the crowd, a would-be assassin shot him in the chest. While the bullet resulted in pain and loss of blood, a copy of his speech and a metal case for his spectacles tucked in his breast pocket prevented it from fatally penetrating his heart. As with Bush, it didn't deter Roosevelt from his plans. He went on with his speech, bravely delivering a fifty-minute oration, before being rushed to the hospital to tend to his wounds.

Mrs. Bush's first year at home was spent "up to her eyeballs" writing her autobiography, which she had been contracted to write by Scribner.[23] She often began work on the book early in the morning, awakening before 5:30 A.M. and remaining in bed while tapping away at the keys of her IBM laptop computer. *Barbara Bush: A Memoir*, a chitchatty book taking the reader from her childhood in Rye, New York, through her White House years, was published in 1994. It quickly became a best-seller, an indication of the former first lady's enormous popularity. Maternal, self-deprecating, witty, and down-to-earth, she topped Gallup's poll for "Most Admired Woman" in 1993, surpassing Margaret Thatcher, Hillary Clinton, and Queen Elizabeth.[24] Though she grew up in relative privilege—her father became president of McCall Corporation, publisher of *McCall's* magazine, and she attended a private boarding school for girls in South Carolina before enrolling at Smith College—she had a common touch and a way of relating to almost anyone.

Bush opted not to write a memoir, the first former president since Woodrow Wilson to forego the chance to tell his story in print. He simply had no interest in writing a self-serving book making his case for the historical record, and was content to leave his political past behind him. As he made clear to Bob Woodward in a letter declining his request to interview him for his book, *Shadow: Five Presidents and the Legacy of Watergate*, "I do not want to direct history."[25] The self-aggrandizement inherent in a typical presidential memoir didn't suit Bush, whose mother's admonitions against bragging were never far from his mind.[26] When he addressed his staff for the last time before leaving the White House, instead of recounting the accomplishments of the administration, he said, "Maybe they'll say we did some good things." But he would leave it up to "them," the historians, to make the call.[27]

What he did not know then was that the historical significance of George Bush had not ended, or even peaked for that matter, with his presidency. Within a year his two eldest sons, George W. and Jeb, aimed to extend their father's legacy beyond the accomplishments of his administration. In 1994, both entered the political arena as candidates for the governorships of their states: Texas for George W., Florida for Jeb.

Jeb was the first to make his intentions known to his family, telling them around Christmastime 1993 that he would take on Florida's incumbent governor Lawton Chiles the following November. His plans came as no great surprise to his family. When older brother George talked as a child of growing up to be Willie Mays, Jeb announced that he was going to be president.[28] He had been plotting his foray into politics for some time, and had carefully taken the right steps in getting there. After establishing himself in

Florida with his wife Columba and their three children, he served in the appointed office of state commerce secretary from 1987 to 1988, worked hard in the real estate development business to ensure his own financial security, and established valuable political contacts. If there was anyone in the family who the Bushes thought would carry on the family political tradition—maybe even back to the White House—it was Jeb.[29]

When George W. announced that he would take on incumbent Texas governor Ann Richards shortly afterward, however, the family's reaction was one of great surprise, even shock.[30] "You can't win," was his mother's response, a view shared by his father. With approval ratings that stood at a mighty 63 percent in mid-year 1993, Richards was a formidable opponent, and an attempt to defeat her seemed quixotic and impetuous. The Bushes had not pinned their political hopes on W., who, if not exactly the prodigal son, was certainly the family rebel with checkered chapters in his past—and possessed of a temperament that didn't always lend itself to a high-flying political career. His tongue could be sharp, his temper volatile, and his manner rough. Though he had largely cleaned up his act from the recklessness of earlier years—giving up drinking around his fortieth birthday seven years earlier after an ultimatum from his wife, Laura, taking up religion, and acting as a valuable aide to his father in the White House—he was not the likely heir to the Bush family's political destiny.

Still, despite marked personality differences between W. and his father, his résumé looked awfully similar: middle school at Phillips Andover; college at Yale and acceptance into Skull and Bones; service in the military as a pilot (albeit in the Texas National Guard, which precluded duty in the Vietnam War); work in the oil business; and an unsuccessful first try to get into elective politics, in his case a failed bid in a run for Congress in 1978. Unlike his dad, he earned an MBA from Harvard and ultimately found financial success not in the oil business but as part owner of the Texas Rangers. But if his father came off as more privileged East Coast patrician than transplanted Texan—which made the Texas electorate slightly wary of him as evident in his two unsuccessful attempts to win a Senate seat—his eldest son was just the opposite. George W. Bush seemed more at home in cowboy boots at a backyard barbecue than in a blue blazer at a country club mixer. When he lost his race for Congress, beaten by an opponent who had "out-countried" him, he vowed never to let it happen again. His country-boy charm and authentic Midland drawl allowed him to play the role of Texan with a genuineness not afforded his father—*The New York Times* described him in 1994 as a man whom "John Ford might have cast as a cowboy if he were a little taller"—and his maverick nature played well in a state known for going its own way.[31]

W.'s mind was made up. He was going to challenge Richards, who he believed was vulnerable on crime and education notwithstanding her poll numbers. And he was just as sure his challenge to unseat her would amount to more than mere folly.

The entry of his sons into the political arena gave Bush a sense of purpose that was lacking in his first year out of office. He threw himself into the task of fund-raising and campaigning for Jeb in Florida. Father and son appeared together on the stump often, an experience that at times proved emotional for both of them. There was less sentimentality between the oldest son and father. W. preferred to go it alone on the campaign trail, and he referred to his father in a campaign speech just once.[32] "I can take care of my own self," he said. "But I hope he raises me a whole bunch of money."[33] He did. Both sons' campaigns were flush with cash, beneficiaries of the old man's drawing power at fund-raisers and his many friends and political connections.

W. did invoke his mother's name often throughout the campaign. In truth, he was more like her than his father. "Dad gives me advice when I ask him for it, my mom when I don't," W. would say later. "She can be blunt, like me. Dad's always gracious."[34] She was also less forgiving, with a long memory for those who crossed the family. While Bush was quick to forgive, she held a grudge, which explained her husband's nickname for her: "the Enforcer."[35] Her role as the family's chief protector belied her benign, matronly image; she often got away with tart-tongued quips about politics and personalities that would have left Nancy Reagan shrouded by controversy.

Watching Jeb and W. in the rough-and-tumble world of politics wasn't easy for Bush. It was one thing when the inevitable slings and arrows from the press and opposition were aimed at him, but it was quite another when they were directed at his sons. There the pain ran much deeper. He realized that while the Bush brand name would be valuable in gaining them initial exposure, it—he—could be a liability for them as well. In the White House he watched helplessly as Neil was dragged down by the Silverado Savings & Loan scandal and was hurt just as much by the toll it took on him. He stayed out of Jeb and W.'s way; "I don't do issues anymore," he told reporter Sam Donaldson.[36] He also knew the pain of losing. And in his heart he worried that one of his sons—George W.—would go down in defeat.[37]

The joint campaigns of the Bush brothers served to strain the relationship between the two.[38] Jeb wasn't thrilled with his brother's quest for a governor's seat at the same time as his. He feared that it would turn his campaign "into a *People* magazine story," not a legitimate run for office based on the issues. He quickly accepted it, but the brothers kept their distance. W.'s cockiness may have eaten away at him too. When asked what they would do at the next meeting of the National Governors Association if they both won, George W. wisecracked, "Jeb's my little brother. He's done what I've told him to all his life."[39]

If Jeb was bothered by his brother's entry into the race, W.'s opponent Ann Richards was downright resentful. At the 1992 Democratic National Convention, Richards famously derided W.'s father as being "born with a silver foot in his mouth," an unkind cut but one that stuck. In the 1994 gubernatorial campaign she scornfully dubbed the younger Bush "Shrub," and at times came off as hostile, even resorting to calling him a "jerk."[40] W. didn't let it get to him. He ran a tight, focused campaign, hammering away at crime and education, the top areas of concern among Texans. He took aim not only at Richards as a champion of the status quo, but at Bill Clinton as well. Citing examples of Clinton's failed leadership in Texas, he declared from the stump, "He's too liberal. And in 1996 you can be sure that Ann Richards will do everything to elect Bill Clinton, and George W. Bush will do the opposite."[41] By winning in Texas he could settle two scores left from his father's failed presidential campaign.

By early November, polls showed both candidates in a dead heat with their opponents. Bush's feeling about his sons throughout the campaigns was one of great pride; he had not pushed them into politics, but was pleased that they had made their way into the arena on their own. On Election Day eve he was a self-described "nervous wreck." On the following day, in two close elections, Jeb went down in defeat in Florida, garnering

49 percent of the vote and losing to Chiles by just two percentage points, while W. prevailed comfortably over Richards in Texas, 53 percent to 46 percent.[42] For their parents watching the returns in Houston, the high of W.'s victory was nearly overshadowed by the pain they felt at Jeb's defeat. "The joy is in Texas," said Bush. "My heart is in Florida."[43]

After the election the Bushes' first stop was in Florida to console Jeb. But two months later on the first day of 1995, the whole family gathered in Austin for the gubernatorial inauguration of George W. Bush. That morning Barbara Bush handed the governor-elect an envelope. It contained a note from his father along with his most precious possession, the cuff links his own father, Prescott Bush, had given him when he went off to war almost two generations earlier as an eighteen-year-old navy pilot. His note ended with the words, "Now it's your turn."[44] George W. had defied his family's expectations—indeed, the low expectations of many—to become the first to carry on the family's political tradition. The author of the note was as surprised as anyone.[45]

In his retirement, Bush sought to "de-imperialize" the post-presidency. The web domain he chose for his office—FLFW, an acronym for "former leader [of the] free world" (with an emphasis on "former")—reflected his self-deprecation and low-key attitude. He was not interested in pursuing an activist post-presidency like Carter's (or later Clinton's); content to be a "point of light in the community," he had given up on "saving the world."[46] Nor was he interested in playing any kind of official advisory role as an ex-president. "Presidents shouldn't be asked to call the guy they defeated or call one of their predecessors unless there's [a specific issue]," was his view. "Many are pressing to get seminars with all the former presidents together. I couldn't care less."[47] Remaining in the limelight held little appeal and he delighted in turning down the media's requests for interviews. He had no interest in serving on corporate boards either—though there were offers aplenty—but that didn't mean he wasn't interested in making money.

When Bush left the presidency, his net worth was $3.2 million, a sum supplemented by a $150,000 presidential pension.[48] By Texas standards that hardly made him rich. That would change as he began to accept paid speaking engagements from corporations, trade associations, and universities.

After just a couple of years back in the private sector, he was accepting fifty or more speaking engagements per year, each one bringing five and even six-figure paydays. Collectively they added up to about $4 million per year.[49] Mrs. Bush got into the act too, and proved just as popular as her husband, while yielding slightly less—$40,000 to $60,000 per engagement.[50] Much of his and Mrs. Bush's time though, was spent giving back. In particular, they devoted much of their effort toward the fight against cancer, a cause close to their hearts since the death of their daughter Robin from leukemia in 1953. In addition to serving on the board at M. D. Anderson, he and Mrs. Bush began serving as co-chairs of C-Change in 1997. Originally known as Dialogue on Cancer, the nonprofit organization brought together, for the first time, all the major players in the cancer field including doctors, researchers, cancer survivors, government officials, and heads of other related nonprofit groups, as well as members of the media, to discuss better ways of curing and treating the disease. Additionally, picking up on one of the themes of his administration, he founded the Points of Light Foundation in 1990, a nonprofit dedicated to the promotion of volunteerism in partnership with the Volunteer Center National Network. Bush's own dedication to the organizations he was associated with went beyond just lending his name. He rarely missed board meetings or an opportunity to contribute in any way he could.

The speaking engagements—"pay the rent speeches," he called them—and board meetings and fund-raisers from his philanthropic activities added to a frenetic travel schedule that also included campaign appearances, dedications, award ceremonies, golf outings, fishing expeditions, vacations, and visits with family and friends. During the course of 1996 alone, Bush spent 143 nights on the road.[51]

But family was Bush's main priority, and being with his thirteen grandchildren was what he enjoyed most. "I really meant it when I said I want to get active with the grandchildren," he said a year out of office. "The big things in the world are better now. But I firmly believe that the biggest danger to us is the disintegration of the American family."[52] In the summers the "grands" all visited the Bushes on the craggy Maine coastline at Walker's Point—the place Bush had always associated most with family—along with their parents and Bush family friends. A private trust Bush funded with part of his prodigious earnings was established to ensure that Kennebunkport would be enjoyed by the grandchildren and generations to come long after he was gone.[53] The role he played as a grandfather was not limited to his own family. He often received letters from kids reaching out to him and he did what he could. When a young boy who was dying of cancer wrote to Bush in 1994, the former president didn't hesitate to travel to his bedside. "Might brighten his life," he thought, and did the same for many others.[54]

While Bush had no interest in writing a memoir, he did sign with Knopf to write *A World Transformed*, a foreign policy book about the dramatic changes the world had undergone on his watch, at least in part because he would coauthor the book with his close friend and former national security advisor, Brent Scowcroft. Bush and Scowcroft wrote separate and joint passages that provided insiders' views of the administration's most important foreign policy strategies, including those around the Gulf War, the Tiananmen Square uprising in China, the reunification of Germany, and the collapse of the Soviet Union. The architecture of the book, according to Scowcroft, was meant to "convey a sense of people working to make decisions rather than providing a homogenized view."[55] It took the team five years to complete *A World Transformed*, a bit longer than Scowcroft's initial projection of two years, but when it was published in 1998 it garnered critical acclaim and commercial success.

Another book from Bush appeared just a year later, this time from Scribner. *All the Best, George Bush* was a collection of Bush's prolific letters, notes, and diary entries made throughout fifty-seven years of his adult life. Bush regretted that while he was president Americans never quite understood his heartbeat, a problem for which he blamed himself. If they had, he felt, the outcome in the '92 election may have been different. But he had no intention of spending long hours on a personal book at a time in his life when he had "never been happier" and was almost as busy as in his White House days. *All the Best* was a good solution, requiring very little writing but mostly rounding up Bush's correspondence through the years and choosing the best examples, a task he left to his chief of staff and friend, Jean Becker. The book, in Bush's words, was "all about heartbeat," providing as intimate a glimpse of Bush as may have come from a memoir.[56] Like Mrs. Bush's book, it quickly achieved best-seller status.

At the not-so-tender age of seventy-two, Bush set an unusual goal for a septuagenarian. After addressing the annual meeting of the International Parachute Association in Houston, describing the terrifying experience of pulling on his chute too early as he bailed out of his plane over the Pacific, he was struck by an epiphany: He wanted to make one more parachute jump.[57] He secured his wife's reluctant approval by announcing, "This is something I must do," and told his children of his plans. "Are you kidding?" was the initial response from George W. "[Just] don't tell anyone about your eighteen-year-old girlfriend."[58]

On March 25, 1997, Bush journeyed to the Arizona desert with his wife by his side. There he boarded a plane that took him into the skies with members of the army's "Golden Knights," who would make the jump with their former commander in chief. Bush pushed himself out of the plane at the target area feeling "a twinge of fear—not panic," and plunged toward the earth at 120 mph, pulling his chute with a jolt at 5,000 feet. As he landed safely in the desert, hugged by his anxious wife, he felt he "had lived a dream. All was right with the world." The following day, pictures appeared throughout the world of the former president hurling through the sky outfitted in his Desert Storm combat boots, helmet, and a white Elvis jumpsuit—"The King would have approved," Bush wrote of his outfit later.[59] However, this experience wasn't quite enough to get parachuting out of his system; despite a fear of falling as he got older, Bush would make two more jumps with the Golden Knights, one to mark his seventy-fifth birthday in June of 1999, and another to celebrate his eightieth five years later.[60] Parachuting became one of Bush's many retirement pursuits, which also included tennis, horseshoes, quail hunting, fishing, speeding off the coast of Kennebunkport in his thirty-four-foot cigarette boat, and playing golf at such a fast clip the Bushes called it "aerobic golf."[61]

On November 6, 1997, twenty thousand people were on hand for the dedication of the Bush Library at Texas A&M. Bush was joined on the occasion by President Clinton and fellow formers Carter and Ford, as well as six first ladies: Hillary Clinton, Nancy Reagan, Rosalynn Carter, Betty Ford, Lady Bird Johnson, and his own Barbara. Bush's children and grandchildren were all in attendance as well. As Bush addressed the crowd, he said with some relief, "Now that my political days are over, I can honestly say that the three most rewarding titles I've held are the only three I have left—a husband, a father, and a granddad." The following week, Bush the father would see his son Jeb climb back in the arena to fight for the Florida governorship once again.

Just as it was no surprise to the Bushes that Jeb would run for governor in 1994, it was no shocker that he would give it another shot in 1998. As George W. had been defying critics by amassing an impressive record in Texas, gaining popularity by working to form coalitions with the opposition on key issues like education, Jeb had been smoothing the way for the next election. He reconnected with his family, converting to Catholicism for his wife after their relationship became strained during the first election, and he retooled his electoral strategy. In battling against lieutenant governor Buddy MacKay for the office, he moderated his conservative message, stressing inclusiveness, and working hard to gain the support of blacks and liberal Democrats.[62]

While Jeb battled for the Florida statehouse and George W. fought for reelection in Texas, their father gave them carte blanche to distance themselves from him as political situations warranted. "At some point you may want to say 'Well, I don't agree with Dad on that point,' or 'Frankly, I think Dad was wrong on that.' Do it. Chart your own course, not just on the issues but in defining yourselves. No one will ever question your love of family—your devotion to your parents."[63] His pride for his boys was unbounded. The evening of the election Bush wrote a letter to his friend, Time's Hugh Sidey. "He is good, this boy of ours," he wrote, describing George W. "He's uptight at times, feisty at other times—but who wouldn't be after months of grueling campaigning. He includes people. He has no sharp edges. He is no ideologue, no divider. . . . All the talk about his wild youth days is pure nuts. His character will pass with flying colors." Of Jeb he wrote, "There is no question in my mind that he will become a major political figure in the country. He is passionate and caring in his beliefs."[64] Still, he feared the toll a loss might have on them. . . .

He needn't have worried. On Election Day the brothers won big: Jeb took 55 percent of the vote in Florida, while Bush carried 69 percent in

Texas, crushing his opponent, Garry Mauro. It marked the first time two brothers had held concurrent governorships since Nelson and Winthrop Rockefeller had done it in New York and West Virginia respectively in 1971. The twin triumphs had pundits chattering about a Bush dynasty, a term with which the family patriarch was uneasy; it implied they were entitled to something, and the family didn't feel that way.[65] George W. commented after the election, "We inherited a great name. It's a great political legacy. It's obviously a political advantage. But to me the election of two sons as governors is a tribute to George H. W. Bush and Barbara Bush."[66]

W.'s landslide also had the press buzzing about him as a presidential contender in 2000. "I hardly ever think about it, except every day when people ask me about it," said W.[67] But if he did not often think about a run for president at that time, he soon would.

Though Bush questioned W.'s political prospects when he ran for governor in 1994, he had come around to appreciating his son's natural political skills and facility as a leader. Still, he had doubts that W. could prevail in a presidential election against the likely Democratic candidate, Al Gore. Bush had initially underestimated Clinton too, but after two terms in office, the U.S. economy was humming, crime rates had plunged, and Americans were sanguine about their future. Times were good. Why would the electorate change horses in midstream?[68] True to form, W. went ahead anyway.

A day after formally announcing his candidacy for the presidency in Iowa, George W. flew to Kennebunkport to be with his family as they celebrated his father's seventy-fifth birthday on Walker's Point. Father and son met with the press on the compound's sweeping lawn in what amounted to an informal ceremony during which the elder Bush effectively passed the torch on to the next generation. "I had my chance," said Bush. "And I got some things right. Maybe I messed some things up. But it's his turn now in the family."[69]

Bush continued to openly reject the notion that the family was a political dynasty. They were not the Kennedys, whose unadulterated ambition flashed as bright as their smiles. "It's not that this is John F. Kennedy's father driving his sons to do something," Bush said. "This is not about vindication or legacy or entitlement. It's about the love of a father for his son, about the love of a mother for her son."[70] As if to prove the point, Bush took care to publicly stay at arm's length of W.'s campaign. W. also made clear that his would not be his father's White House. "This is not going to be George H. W. Bush, Part Two," he would begin almost every meeting with potential political benefactors. "It's going to be George W. Bush, Part One."[71]

Behind the scenes, though, the former president played a pivotal role. Prior to W. announcing his candidacy, Bush had called Republican heavyweights to ask that they refrain from endorsing a candidate until W. had made the decision on his candidacy. Once W. was in the race, he thumbed through his Rolodex, calling his old network of state operatives, drumming up political and financial support, and tapping his former aides and proven Bush loyalists to help out. Brent Scowcroft and Condoleezza Rice, Scowcroft's deputy when he was national security advisor, were brought in to bring W. up to speed on foreign affairs; Andrew Card, Bush's assistant and later, deputy chief of staff, helped run the campaign; and Dick Cheney, Bush's secretary of defense, was brought on to vet W.'s potential vice presidential running mates, a spot that ultimately went to Cheney himself.

When Bush's vice president, Dan Quayle, another candidate for the nomination, called Bush to see if the George W. Bush and Quayle camps could go easy on one another, Bush's dispassionate rejection of the proposal was, "We'll do what we have to do."[72] Ultimately they did, capturing the nomination after a chase from Arizona senator John McCain when W. won the South Carolina primary, at least in part by appealing to the Christian right by accepting an invitation to speak at the racially segregated Bob Jones University. In August, W. accepted his party's nomination for the presidency in Philadelphia, where his acceptance speech included acknowledgments of his well-known Republican parents. Of his mother, he said, "Everybody loves you, and so do I. Growing up you gave me lots of advice—I gave you white hair." He called his father "the most decent man I have ever known," adding, "All my life I have been amazed that such a gentle soul could be so strong."

Staying out of the media wasn't an easy task for Bush. Not necessarily because he wanted the limelight for himself, but because of his natural inclination to defend his son from political assault. At a Democratic fundraiser, Bill Clinton raised doubts about W. by stating, "Nearest I can tell, the message of the Bush campaign is . . . 'How bad can I be? I've been governor of Texas. My daddy was president. I've owned a baseball team.'" The "daddy" then struck back. In an interview on MSNBC, Bush said, "I'm going to wait a month and if he continues that, then I'm going to tell the nation what I think of him as a human being and as a person."[73] When Bush later pulled back, telling ABC News' Charlie Gibson in a joint interview with Mrs. Bush that he would refrain from further quarreling with Clinton, Mrs. Bush got into the action, implying that "unnamed persons" had stained the office of the presidency through scandal. "She went further than she should have," said Bush in an on-air commentary. "I don't care," was her blunt reply.[74] On at least one occasion, Bush also went further than he should have. At a rally the night before the all-important New Hampshire primary, Bush praised "this boy. This son of ours." Afterward, W.'s image took a hit. "That's the way I talk about my sons," he reasoned later, but he knew the consequences of the remark and lowered his profile.[75]

As the race for the White House progressed, Bush's admiration for his son's gifts in the hustings grew, but he worried about Florida. As he sifted through polling data and intelligence gleaned through a constant stream of e-mails, it became clear to him that the contest would be won or lost in the Sunshine State. Jeb knew it too, and he also worried. Winning the state would boil down to his ability to deliver it to his brother. On Election Day eve, the Bush family gathered in Austin to be with the candidate as the returns came in. Bush felt more anxious about the election than he had about his own in 1988 and 1992.[76] The mood was upbeat at a family dinner at the Four Seasons Hotel near the governor's mansion. But when word came in just before 8:00 P.M. that Florida had gone to Gore, they bolted from the hotel to monitor the results at the governor's mansion.

Shortly after they arrived, the networks reversed the call, claiming that Florida was now in the Bush column. Afterward, Gore placed a short call to W. to concede the election. But as Gore made his way to the stage in Tennessee to announce it publicly to supporters, an aide stopped him; the networks now claimed Florida was too close to call. Gore placed another call to the governor's mansion. W. was incredulous as Gore retracted his concession, insisting that Jeb had said Florida's results were firmly in his favor. "Your brother is not the ultimate authority on this," Gore replied tersely.[77]

For the next thirty-six days the electorate's decision hung in the balance as the nation focused on officials in Florida to sort out the mess. The Bush camp chose an old hand, Jim Baker, to lead the fight to recognize George W. as the state's winner. It fell to Baker to surmount the hanging chads, misleading ballots, and revelations of voting irregularities that had gotten in the way and added to the outcome's inconclusiveness.

Baker had not been on the political scene since the Bush administration had folded eight years earlier. A close friend since Bush's days in the oil business in the mid-fifties, Baker was Bush's choice to become his secretary of state at the administration's outset, a post Baker gave up to head up the struggling reelection campaign in 1992 as support for Bush began to slip. Afterward, there were a number of reports that Baker had lost favor with members of the family who had made him a scapegoat for Bush's loss. Rumor had it that Baker resented leaving his exalted post at the State Department for the gritty work of running the campaign and, as the Bushes saw it, had done a lackluster job. But the rumor was just that. Bush never blamed Baker for his loss—if anything he blamed himself—and, to his knowledge, no one else in the family did either. And even if they did, putting the fate of George W.'s presidency largely in Baker's hands would have been a strange way of showing it.

A few years after leaving power, Baker had seen just how quickly the public forgot about former administration officials, however high-ranking, when a man approached him at an airport asking if he was Jim Baker. "Yes, I am," Baker replied, whereupon the man smiled and asked, "How's Tammy Faye?" The events in Florida would put Baker back on the front page and in the public's consciousness—and the stakes couldn't have been higher.

On November 9, the Clintons hosted a dinner at the White House celebrating the two hundredth anniversary of the mansion, bringing together Lady Bird Johnson and three former first couples: the Fords, the Carters, and the Bushes. Presidential grace prevailed over partisanship as the fraternity of presidents and sorority of first ladies waxed nostalgic about their shared privilege of living in "the People's House." But a question about its future hung over the room like a San Francisco fog: Who will be its next resident? "It's the most nervous time in my entire life," Bush told reporters, acknowledging the elephant—or maybe the donkey—in the room. "Whatever happens this week, my pride and Barbara's pride, knows no bounds, and moreover, our democracy will go on."[78]

Nervous he was. "I wasn't getting advice from my dad," Jeb said of his father at the time. "*I* was giving the advice, and that was 'Dad, chill out.' My dad was a living wreck. It was horrible. He was so into this, and to have a son . . . I don't think there would be a way to describe the powerful emotions of pride, anger, love, and all the emotions to the max. And it just stretched out—ebbing and flowing." Mrs. Bush, in the meantime, was cool. She simply turned off the television, stopped reading the newspapers, and let the situation play out. So did W., who retreated to his ranch in Crawford, Texas. The campaign was over and he had done what he could to win the election. Now it was in the hands of others to decide if, in fact, he *had* won.[79]

By mid-December the matter of the Florida election had made its way to the Supreme Court through *Gore v. the United States of America*, with the conservative high court's ruling going in Bush's favor. Bush had lost the popular vote but won the election . . . just barely. Jim Baker's cool, firm leadership was instrumental in the outcome. Jeb was among those who made it official, signing the "Certificate of Ascertainment" as one of Florida's members of the Electoral College once the court's decision came through. He had worked hard for his brother during the legal tussle in Florida with little thought of his own political future, lifting the remnant chill between the two that had lingered since their concurrent gubernatorial campaigns in 1994.[80]

Just over a month later, eight years to the day that his father had surrendered the White House to Bill Clinton, George W. Bush became the forty-third president of the United States.

On September 10, 2001, the Bushes were in Washington, where they attended a number of engagements and spent the night in the White House. Only the first lady, Laura Bush, was on hand that evening, as the president had flown off to Florida to promote his education plan at an elementary school the following morning. The same morning, September 11, the Bushes left Washington early by private jet to make their way back home to Houston via Minneapolis, where they both had speaking engagements. Shortly into the flight word came through the pilots that one of the World Trade Towers in New York had been struck by a commercial plane. When they were ordered to land at the nearest airport after the other tower had been hit in similar fashion, the Bushes knew the U.S. was under attack.

Later that morning the Bushes found themselves in Milwaukee, where they checked into a motel just outside the city. "Like everybody else," Barbara Bush related in *Reflections*, her memoir of her post–White House years, "we spent the day glued to the television. We watched again and again the replay of the attack on the Twin Towers and the Pentagon, and heard rumors of the plane downed in Pennsylvania."[81] Also like everybody else, Bush never could have imagined terrorism of that magnitude occurring on American soil. It was, as he recalled, "traumatic for me and Barbara but no more so than the rest of the country except the president was our son."[82] They were relieved when they talked with George W. several hours after the towers were struck, but they would find out in the days ahead that the attacks had hit close to home. Another son, Marvin, had been in a Manhattan subway car under Wall Street on his way to a meeting when the attacks occurred. After the train was evacuated and orders were given to passengers to walk uptown or across the Brooklyn Bridge as soon as possible, he had trekked seventy blocks through smoke, debris, and confusion to his midtown hotel. Mrs. Bush's nephew Jim Pierce had been scheduled to attend a meeting in a conference room on the 102nd floor of the South Tower, before it was moved to a nearby building. He would find out later that of the twelve people who had been in the original location, eleven had died in the attacks.[83]

W. had not done much to distinguish himself as president in his first seven months. While many previous presidents had done their best to stay in the headlines and lead national television news stories, his approach was to plod along competently and quietly. He had mostly made news for what he didn't do—refusing to sign the Kyoto Protocol, an international agreement to fight global warming that had been ratified by 141 other nations. September 11 would become the defining moment of his presidency. The president had been criticized for not showing greater leadership and resolve in the first hours of crisis as chaos reigned. While his parents were being diverted off course in the Midwest, Air Force One drifted silently across the

U.S., its radio transmissions cut off at the insistence of the Secret Service for security reasons. The president was taken from Florida to secure locations in Louisiana and Nebraska before, on his orders, he was returned to the White House by early evening.

But after a slow start he began to rise to the occasion, demonstrating steely resolve as he visited the downtown New York site of the collapsed towers. He met with firefighters, policemen, and the families of some of the victims in the towers, and toured the wreckage at the Pentagon, rallying workers who had lost colleagues. Four days after the attacks, he led a memorial service at the National Cathedral in Washington that brought together former presidents Ford, Carter, Bush, and Clinton, and his former opponent Al Gore in a show of unity. Toward the end of the service, W. made his way to the lectern to deliver to the congregation, the nation, and the world, the most important speech of his presidency. "War has been waged against us by stealth and deceit and murder," he said. "This nation is peaceful, but fierce when stirred to anger. This conflict was begun on the timing and terms of others. It will end in a way, and at an hour, of our choosing. . . . In every generation the world has produced enemies of human freedom. They have attacked America because we are freedom's home and defender. And the commitment of our fathers is now the calling of our time."

When the president returned to his pew, his own father reached over Laura Bush, who sat between them, and with manifest pride patted his son's arm, whereupon his son clasped his father's hand. The torch had been passed long before, but it may have been at this moment that George W. Bush fully came into his own.

While 2001 saw a new chapter of American history open through tragedy, the following year Bush was able to bring closure to a tragic chapter in his life. In June of 2002, he returned by boat to the spot in the Pacific Ocean off the Japanese island of Chi Chi Jima where his Navy plane had been shot down by enemy fire in 1944. Filled with emotion, he marked it by placing floral wreaths in the water in memory of his crewman—gunner, Ted White, and radioman, John Delaney—who had died when the plane crashed almost fifty-seven years earlier and who he had thought of often in the years that followed.[84] His small act of remembrance, along with his son's moving speech at the National Cathedral the year before, would become two of the most meaningful moments in his post-presidency.[85]

The question for many when W. took office was, How much influence does his father have on matters of state? Bushes "41" and "43," as they took to calling themselves, relating to their order in the presidential chronology, were not the first father and son to hold the presidency, which had also been held by the Adamses, John and John Quincy. The difference was that the presidencies of the Adamses fell almost a quarter of a century apart, with John Adams in far-off Quincy, Massachusetts, and frail with age when John Quincy took the White House in 1825. Proximity and his advanced years prevented Adams from actively influencing his son, the president—and he died at ninety, just a year into John Quincy's tenure. Such was not the case with the Bushes. Only eight years separated their presidencies; distance was all but irrelevant in the communications age, and the elder Bush was a spry seventy-six.

W. said privately during the campaign, "My dad plays a big role in my life as a shadow government."[86] But the consensus among most in the Bush inner circle seemed to be that he didn't have much influence on the president at all.[87] They talked at least several times a week, mostly in early-morning phone calls that W. would make directly to his father's office, circumventing White House operators. Bush didn't want to be "the father calling all the time," and left it to the president to initiate their phone contact.[88] Friends claimed that the subject of the calls was "90 percent family," but there was no way of knowing; Bush was consistently mum about what they discussed and even the closest staffers stayed away during their conversations, giving father and son privacy.[89] As Jean Becker, Bush's chief of staff, put it, "No one should be privy to those conversations."[90] Their dialogues did not include "a lot of analysis of current policy or [talk about] the future or 'What do we do now?'," Bush said. "We don't dwell on points of difference."[91] Andrew Card, the president's chief of staff, saw Bush's influence on his son this way: "He can counsel him to say, 'I hope you're questioning that.' But it's not 'This is what I think you should do.' I know Forty-one practices discipline."[92] By all indications, Bush's duty as first father superseded any role he might have earned as a peer or elder statesman. He was there to offer paternal support, not presidential advice. "What I want to do is support [him] period," Bush said. "And because of that [I don't] get into the depths of these issues as I might otherwise be inclined."[93]

In fact, as president, W. seemed to pull away from his father, at least politically. While he proudly shared his father's name and bore an unmistakable resemblance to him, as his style emerged it was more in the mold of another of his Republican predecessors: Ronald Reagan. Reagan was the cowboy riding into Washington as an outsider to take on the establishment; George H. W. Bush was the quintessential Washington insider complete with Ivy League credentials and an impeccable Washington résumé. Reagan was the archetypal conservative; Bush was a moderate who never quite found favor with the Republican Right. Reagan was a revolutionary; Bush was a steward. Even when it came to his dad's support, W. distanced himself. As he told *Washington Post* reporter Bob Woodward, his father was "the wrong father to appeal to in terms of strength. There is a higher father that I appeal to."[94]

Ideologically the apple fell a ways off from the tree as well. It's anyone's guess what Reagan might have done as president in the early years of the twenty-first century. But W.'s agenda was decidedly influenced by the neoconservative wing of his administration led by Dick Cheney. As Gerald Ford's chief of staff and the elder Bush's secretary of defense, Cheney had been a relative moderate, but after 9/11 he had become something of an ideologue. Brent Scowcroft, who had known Cheney for thirty years, working alongside him in the Ford and Bush administrations, said in 2005, "I don't know him anymore. He's not the same guy."[95] George W. was taken by Cheney's neoconservative notion that as president, he could make history by overthrowing Saddam Hussein's brutal regime and facilitating the democratization of Iraq, a development that could have a transformative effect on the Middle East. The "neocons" believed that foreign policy had suffered in the hands of Bush 41 and Clinton, and looked for a chance to demonstrate U.S. might along with its idealism.[96] Their justification in the post-9/11 world was Saddam's support of terrorism and the "weapons of mass destruction" he was allegedly building up in his arsenal. W., of course, went forward after a vain attempt to get UN backing, achieving a quick military victory followed by a postwar quagmire marked by terrorism and tribal dispute no one in the administration had quite anticipated.

There were rampant rumors inside the Beltway that 41 disagreed with 43 on the war in Iraq, on which W. had staked his presidential legacy. At least one person close to the elder Bush opposed the war: Scowcroft argued in editorials and on the airwaves that toppling Saddam Hussein should not be a U.S. priority in the fight on terrorism, particularly since Saddam and Osama bin Laden were "natural enemies" due to political circumstances.[97] Some suggested that Bush was trying to send a message to W. through Scowcroft. Not likely. It would have been uncharacteristic for Bush to voice dissent on any successor's policies—he had stayed out of Clinton's way as he had promised—let alone his son's. Loyalty was a family trait and was at its fiercest when it came to family, and he knew that "any nuance of difference" between himself and the president, "would be a big story and complicate his life."[98]

But as Bush agreed with Scowcroft on most foreign policy issues, which was clear in *A World Transformed*, it seemed a good bet that he took a similar position on the war in Iraq—albeit privately. After all, Bush endured criticism from the right during the Gulf War for not taking out Saddam upon liberating Kuwait for fear of breaking up the international coalition he had so skillfully assembled. Bush was no unilateralist; he had no intention of alienating the international community. Even Mrs. Bush acknowledged in her book *Reflections* that there was concern among some, though not her, that the war in Iraq would be "another Vietnam."[99] It was also telling that despite his outspokenness about Iraq, Scowcroft remained in good standing with the Bushes, who had pulled away from friends and aides in the past for perceived disloyalty.[100]

If 41 and 43 disagreed on the war, it didn't affect their bond. Jean Becker saw theirs as "the classic father and son relationship—and nothing is going to come between them."[101] They remained, as Bush stated in a rare 2006 interview, "very close. Closer than the public realizes." Any personal feeling he had on the war would probably have been subordinated by concern over the burden it put on the president's shoulders. The most difficult hour of his own presidency was on the eve of the Gulf War. He knew as well as any that "the toughest decision a president makes has to do with sending someone elses' son or daughter into war," and he believed it was no different for his son. At the same time, Bush' relationship with the incumbent vice president, like

Scowcroft's, had cooled. In reflecting on the members of his administration in the same interview, Bush said he had been "very close" to Cheney "in those days," implying they no longer shared the same association.[102]

The war in Iraq was just one of the divisive items on George W.'s agenda as the election of 2004 neared, creating "red state-blue state" chasms on the political landscape, highlighted by the media, as he faced Democratic challenger, Massachusetts senator John Kerry. Bush's approval ratings, which topped out at 82 percent just after September 11, had tumbled to 45 percent, with a disapproval rating of 43 percent just before voters made their verdicts.[103]

The extended Bush family all came together at the GOP Convention in New York in early September to watch George W. accept his party's nomination for president for a second time. Ninety-six attendees crammed into a Bush family dinner held at the Ritz-Carlton, though Bush observed there were a "lot of unfamiliar straphangers" among them.[104] In an effort to soften the conservative image of the GOP, or maybe to give it an edge, the next generation of Bushes, twenty-two-year-old first daughters Barbara and Jenna, took center stage at the convention hall to address delegates after a rousing speech by California governor Arnold Schwarzenegger.

"Thanks to him," the twins giggled, "if one of us ever decides to marry a Democrat, nobody can complain, except maybe our grandmother, Barbara. And if she doesn't like it, we would definitely hear about it. Ganny," they continued, "we love you dearly, but you're just not very hip. She thinks *Sex in the City* [sic] is something married people do, but never talk about." The speech raised eyebrows with some, laughter with others, and prompted *Washington Post*'s Ann Gerhart to write that the twins "seemed to be taking GOP moderation way too far."[105] On balance though, their first big act on the political stage appeared to help their father's cause.

But the political hope for the next generation of Bushes—much in the same way his father had been—was another speaker at the convention: George P. Bush, the twenty-eight-year-old son of Jeb and Columba. George P. had been youth chairman at the previous GOP National Convention, and generated buzz as much for his good looks—*The Austin Chronicle* called him "Gorgeous George," and *USA Today* gushed that he was a "major hottie"—as for his eloquence and family name. His fluency in Spanish, the influence of his Mexican-born mother, was another political asset, and he was now armed with a degree from the University of Texas-Austin, which provided a good foundation for a foray into the family business. At the 2000 convention, his father remarked that the family gave him a hard time, "just to make sure he keeps all this in perspective."[106] The political future of the Bushes, it seemed, was in good hands.

With Florida looking more promising for W. than it did in 2000, the crucial battleground state in the election became Ohio. The former President and Mrs. Bush waited out the election results at the White House with the first couple, with Bush once again as nervous as he was over the previous contests. Once again W. prevailed, managing a narrow win over Kerry as Ohio fell in the red-state tally. And once again he had done what his father couldn't quite muster—winning a second term as president, just as he had won a statewide election in Texas, which had also proved elusive to the old man.

While it's any one's guess how much Bush was called on by his son as an advisor, he was employed by the president for political and diplomatic ends. When Southeast Asia was hit by a tsunami just after Christmas in 2004, devastating coastal towns, killing over 5,000, and injuring over 8,000, the initial U.S. response was to pledge $15 million in relief funds, later upped to $35 million. The miserly contribution—at least, relative to commitments made by other countries—did not help the U.S. image abroad, which had already been tarnished by the war in Iraq. As former president Jimmy Carter often pointed out, the U.S. ranked last among developed nations in foreign aid as a percentage of gross national income, which adversely affected how it was viewed abroad.

Scrambling to show the U.S.'s compassion and generosity, George W. tapped his father and his father's former rival, Bill Clinton, to encourage Americans to donate to designated charities and to tour the regions hardest hit by the disaster. It was a big statement—two former political rivals coming together for a common cause—and a shrewd diplomatic move as Bush and Clinton, symbols of America's compassionate spirit, appeared in news outlets across the world, touring devastated areas together and comforting victims. Though fund-raising was directed toward outside organizations, more than $12 million came directly through Bush and Clinton's offices, money that was redirected to outside organizations like Habitat for Humanity and Catholic Relief Services. Suddenly, the improbable Bush-Clinton duo—"the odd couple," as Bush called them—were fixtures in the media, side by side in Southeast Asia, in commercials for tsunami relief, on CNN's *Larry King Live*, at a charity golf tournament in Florida which raised $2 million for the cause, and in the stands at the Super Bowl.[107] When Pope John Paul II died in April, W. asked his father and Clinton to join him as part of the U.S. delegation at the funeral in Rome, Bush was eager to make the trip with Clinton. "Come on," Bush urged him. "It will be better with you along."[108]

George H. W. Bush and Bill Clinton did not have much in common, as became glaringly obvious to anyone paying attention to national politics in 1992. But a dozen years had passed since Bush called Clinton and Al Gore "bozos" in the heat of the campaign, and winced at the nation's choice for president when the results came in—enough time to heal the wounds of vicious political battle. Their membership in the ex-presidents club was at least enough for the two to form a bond as they flew the world together at the behest of the president, aboard a blue-and-white Boeing 757 emblazoned on its side with UNITED STATES OF AMERICA. Former presidents Ford and Carter had come together under similar circumstances—aloft on an Air Force One backup, making their way to and from Cairo as part of the U.S. delegation for the funeral of Anwar Sadat—and turned a political rivalry into a warm, productive, and enduring relationship. So, it seemed, had Bush and Clinton. But the Bush-Clinton friendship was more potent owing to the clout of their family names, which had dominated the Oval Office since 1989, and counting.

The press was quick to recognize the political benefits of their friendship. For Clinton, an association with the honorable Bush lent him gravitas after a controversial presidential reign marred by impeachment. In the company of Bush, he looked more like a venerable elder statesman who was above party politics, which by extension was helpful to Hillary Clinton as she eyed a run at the 2008 Democratic presidential nomination. Bush could count on a positive historical footnote to his legacy by graciously befriending the man who had driven him out of office. "It always has to be said that Bill Clinton was one of the most gifted American political figures in modern times," he said in 2005. "Trust me. I learned this the hard way."[109] Moreover, Bush's bipartisan friendship had a beneficial rub-off effect on W.

But by all indications, Bush and Clinton had a close relationship that went beyond mere political interests. In addition to their status as former presidents, they bonded over sports and their commitment to help those in need. And their natural differences weren't all bad. Bush said of Clinton's garrulousness, which contrasted with his own reserve, "Suits me. I don't have to do any talking."[110] With twenty-two years between them, just five years less than the age gap between Eisenhower and Kennedy, Clinton was the same age as George W. "Maybe I'm the father he never had," mused Bush of his new friend.[111] To be sure, Clinton treated him with the deference a son accords his father, gestures the old man appreciated. In joint appearances, Clinton let Bush speak first, and on a flight to Asia to visit victims of the tsunami, Clinton insisted that the eighty-year-old Bush take the aircraft's only bunk, despite Bush offering it to Clinton, who at fifty-eight had recently been laid up with quadruple bypass surgery.[112]

When they reunited, they spent long hours huddled in conversation. While shooting a spot for tsunami relief at the Clinton Library and Museum in Little Rock, the presidential duo spent over an hour in private conversation in the museum's mock Oval Office, which had prying tourists likening the scene to an exhibit in a wax museum.[113] "I think he's a genuinely good man," said Clinton of Bush. "I like him. I like his wife. I like his family."[114] The Bush family liked Clinton too, as evidenced by the invitation Clinton accepted to the family compound at Walker's Point for a summer respite of golf and powerboating off the Maine coast. Jeb took to referring to Clinton as "bro," while W. acknowledged the burgeoning friendship in his 2006 State of the Union address when addressing the fact that the first of the baby-boomer generation would be turning sixty, including two of his father's favorite people, "me and President Clinton." Clinton chalked up his adoption into the family as an indication of "the lengths [to] which the Bushes [will] go to get another president in the family," adding "I wish I could get them to adopt Hillary."[115] That may have been pushing it. Bush anticipated that his relationship with Clinton "might get a little more strained when Hillary runs [for president]," adding with understatement, "I won't be her campaign manager."[116]

When Hurricane Katrina struck in late August 2005, the largest natural disaster in American history, George W. was roundly criticized again for his slow and inadequate response, which he initially defended. Once again he went back to the well, enlisting the proven Bush-Clinton duo—the *New York Post* dubbed them "the A-team"—to raise funds for disaster relief, tour devastated areas, and comfort victims. In his late-night monologue, David Letterman quipped, "That's what they do now—whenever there's trouble, they send in presidents Clinton and Bush. Earlier today they arrived on the set of [NBC's struggling sitcom] *Joey*."

This time the two established a fund that donors could contribute to directly. By October it was estimated that their Bush-Clinton Katrina Fund would exceed $120 million with donations from not only the wealthy friends, supporters, and corporations on the former presidents' standard call lists, but from thousands of small donors who contributed up to several hundred thousand dollars a day through the pair's website. Clinton and his Secret Service detail were taken aback at a state fair in Syracuse, New York, when a woman ran up to him with a handful of small bills asking him to give it to Katrina and Rita victims in need.[117] Not only did the ex-presidents help bring in the money, but they also chose where it would be sent, inviting scrutiny on the efficiency and effectiveness of its allocation. Ultimately the Bush-Clinton Katrina Fund would yield more for victims of the hurricane than any philanthropy except the Red Cross and Salvation Army. The potency of the Bush-Clinton partnership was recognized by *Time* in its famed "Person of the Year" issue in 2005, which designated the pair "Partners of the Year," runners-up to its choice of "Persons of the Year," software billionaires Bill and Melinda Gates and rock icon, Bono, named for their own philanthropic efforts. "I think people see George and me, and they say, 'This is how it ought to work,'" said Clinton of their collaboration in a joint interview appearing in the issue.[118]

While a friendship with his immediate successor and erstwhile political rival may yield Bush a positive nod among historians, he didn't spend a minute worrying about his legacy. The very word—"The 'L' word"—was taboo among Bush staffers. "I'm very content as to how history will judge what we did," he said in 2006. In particular, he saw the reunification of Germany, the flourishing of democracy in Eastern Europe and, to a lesser extent, the liberation of Kuwait in the Gulf War, as monumental changes in the world that would ultimately reflect well on his administration—but taking credit for them was not in his nature.[119]

Well after the Berlin Wall fell, Vaclav Havel organized a conference on the Cold War in Prague attended by many of the leaders who had been in power when it ended. The program included a speech by Margaret Thatcher, who began by saying, "Let me be clear from the outset: Ronald Reagan and I won the Cold War." Bush recalled thinking, "What the hell [is she] talking about? Everybody gets a piece of this action. What about the guys [who sat] in jail because of their fight for freedom like Havel and Lech Walesa in this very room. How could [she] possibly [disregard] them that way?" As he stewed over her braggadocio, former German chancellor Helmut Kohl, like a junior high school student during a stern teacher's classroom lecture, passed Bush a note which read simply, "Is this woman nuts?"[120]

A prominent place in history would have been the icing on the cake for Bush in his retirement years, which proved to be the most rewarding of his life. Much of it was playing the roles that meant the most to him: husband, father, and grandfather. It hadn't all been smooth sailing. Jeb and Columba's oldest daughter, Noelle, struggled with substance abuse, which led to troubles with the law including ten days in jail when she was found in possession of crack cocaine while in a court-ordered rehabilitation program; Neil went through a messy public divorce with his wife, Sharon; and he still rode the ups and downs of his son's presidency.

George W. wrestled with problems "much weightier" than those he had faced as president, and his second term had more than its share of troubles.[121] Cheney's chief of staff Scooter Libby resigned when it was revealed that he had lied in a deposition and stonewalled the investigation into the leak of the identity of CIA operative, Valerie Plame. Cheney himself accidentally shot a companion while on a quail-hunting outing in Texas, revealing his penchant for secrecy by keeping silent about the incident for a day and a half. Gas prices soared and the economy limped along. And the war in Iraq continued to divide the country with no exit strategy in place, sending George W.'s approval rating well below the 50 percent mark. Along the way, Bush felt every bump on the road as acutely as the president himself. But he was blessed, and no one knew it more than him.

In his eighty-first year, Bush found himself in hurricane-ravaged Louisiana, visiting with citizens of Cameron, population 1,965. Cameron had a long history of sustaining the angry gales of hurricane season. In 1957, Hurricane Audrey blew through the town, killing 390. Almost fifty years later, in 2005, Cameron had stood largely intact when Hurricane Katrina gripped the Louisiana coast in August, only to be devastated by Hurricane Rita just a month later, which took with it 90 percent of the town including most of its homes. Bush visited Cameron in October with a small entourage that included only his press secretary and a two-man Secret Service detail. After addressing a crowd of residents in the town's courthouse, one of the few structures to remain standing, he greeted them individually. Most had lost almost everything they owned.

One resident, a woman in her late thirties wearing a red sweatshirt, smiled as she shook the hand of the former president—then she wept. At that moment, he was less a symbol of power in a helpless time as he was a father figure, familiar and comforting. Bush embraced her. "Know that you won't be forgotten," he said as he cried too.[122] Tears came more easily in his later years, and more often. He had "gotten over being a sissy about it," and let them flow freely.[123] Thirteen years after losing the White House, at least in part because he was perceived as being out of touch with average Americans, the first father's heartbeat was as plain as the path of Hurricane Rita.

IX.

BILL CLINTON:
LIFE OF THE PARTY

Controversy stuck to Bill Clinton like bubblegum to the tread of a new sneaker. Since he had burst onto the national political scene in 1992—the ambitious, charismatic young Arkansas governor of protean talents—the public had almost come to expect it of him. The long list of scandals left in his wake, whether real or maliciously imagined, had a life of their own. Each could be captured in a name or a word: Gennifer Flowers, Travelgate, Vince Foster, Whitewater, Paula Jones, Monica, impeachment. So, it was altogether fitting that as Clinton left the Oval Office for the last time as president, on January 20, 2001, he courted controversy anew.

Two storms followed Clinton out the White House door and did not let up when he gave the keys over to his successor. The first had to do with reports that the Clintons, Bill and Hillary, had accepted $190,000 worth of gifts in 2000, ostensibly in a frenzied effort to amply provide for themselves as they prepared for life after the White House. Mrs. Clinton was reported to have registered for luxury items at places like Borsheim's Fine Jewelry & Gifts like a soon-to-be bride anticipating her household needs after the honeymoon. And she was allegedly crafty about it, collecting all the loot before swearing in as the junior senator from New York on January 1, 2001, at which time she would be prohibited by U.S. Senate rules from accepting gifts worth more than fifty dollars.[1]

Then there was the second storm, which overlapped a bit with the first. In his last days in office, Clinton issued a flurry of 140 pardons, including one to a fugitive financier named Marc Rich. Issuing pardons was nothing new for an outgoing president; most invoked the privilege given to them in the Constitution on the eve of their departure to right wrongs as they saw them. Their last-minute nature was simply to avoid political consequences.

But Marc Rich, a fugitive who had skipped the U.S. to live between Israel and Switzerland before being indicted on charges of tax evasion, was the former husband of Denise Rich. . . . And Denise Rich was a generous Clinton benefactor, writing checks for $70,000 to Mrs. Clinton's Senate campaign, and $450,000 for Clinton's presidential library fund, and presenting them with $7,000 worth of furniture for their post–White House digs in Chappaqua, New York.[2]

As with earlier scandals, the facts in both cases were a bit cloudy even as the media pounced. When the truth eventually bubbled to the surface, it turned out the Clintons had indeed received $190,000 in gifts, but over their eight years in office, not just the last one, and the value was comparable to gifts accepted by previous outgoing first couples. Mrs. Clinton had not registered anywhere for gifts; however, she was aware that her friends had set up a china registry at an Omaha department store. And the Senate rules would not have prohibited her from accepting the gifts in question. As for Marc Rich, Clinton claimed he had been lobbied by Israeli prime minister Ehud Barak on three occasions to pardon Rich due to his "services to Israel and his help with the Palestinians," though Barak initially denied it, and emphasized that Rich had come to a settlement with the government to pay $200 million in penalties, far exceeding the $48 million he owed in taxes. Further, he insisted he had "based the case on its merits."[3] What he did not point out as readily was that Rich had violated U.S. trade embargoes with Iran during the hostage crisis when he bought Iranian oil at cut rates and unloaded it at a tidy profit, and with Libya after the African nation was implicated in the TWA terrorist bombing over Lockerbie, Scotland.[4] Clinton would later concede in an interview that he regretted the pardon, not because of Rich's actions, which another former president, Jimmy Carter, had condemned as "disgraceful," but because "it was terrible politics" and "wasn't worth the damage to my reputation."[5]

As had happened with earlier scandals, however, it didn't seem to matter. Bill Clinton, the self-proclaimed "Comeback Kid," left the presidency with approval ratings of 65 percent—higher than any president in modern history. Even Ronald Reagan fell just short of Clinton at 64 percent when he left office; so did the martyred John Kennedy with a 63 percent after his assassination. Clinton's outgoing approval rate was significantly higher than his low, which stood at 43 percent just five months into his presidency, suggesting that he had grown favorably in the public mind even as the scandals of his administration piled up. Not that Americans overlooked Clinton's shortcomings—58 percent found him neither honest nor trustworthy—they just didn't think it made him a bad president, or, for that matter, a bad guy.[6]

The public had good reason to like Clinton as president. He presided over the longest period of sustained economic growth in U.S. history and delivered a balanced budget as education test scores and housing ownership rose, unemployment rates and inflation plunged, and peace prevailed. He enacted social programs like the Earned Income Tax Credit, which put $21.2 billion back in the pockets of fifteen million American families in its first year alone.[7] Additionally, he was responsible for a number of smaller initiatives like school uniforms, which the media called "juice-box" politics, based on the product innovation that made life a bit easier and more convenient but wasn't going to change the world. As for the scandals, as Joe Klein put it in his book on the Clinton presidency, *The Natural*, while Clinton "would rub very close to the edge of legality and well past the borders of propriety," the era over which he presided "would likely to be remembered more for the ferocity of its prosecutions than for the severity of its crimes."[8] In fact, after spending $73 million investigating Clinton while he was in the White House, independent counsel Kenneth Starr found no criminal wrongdoing. The questions for historians would be in the legitimacy and impact of the impeachment. How much weight would it be given in the evaluation of his overall record? And as a result of the impeachment, did Clinton, given his prodigious political gifts and powers of persuasion, squander an opportunity to do something bigger—narrow the racial divide, say—with his presidency?

There was no denying that Clinton revived his party, becoming the first Democrat to win a second term since Franklin Roosevelt, and the first to leave the White House favorably since Kennedy. He had an unsurpassed ability to articulate Democratic values and explain complex issues to every cross-section of voters where others had failed—and would continue to fail. And he frequently beat the opposition at their own game, co-opting GOP issues and fending off cartoonish enemies like Starr and Speaker of the House Newt Gingrich, who fell prey to their own zeal to bring him down as he went about doing his job. Had it not been for the 22nd Amendment, preventing his ability to run for a third term, "you'd have [had] to throw me out," said Clinton.[9]

Given his approval ratings as president, it is unlikely it would have come to that. As it stood, he was leaving the White House at fifty-four years of age, the youngest president since Theodore Roosevelt, who retired at fifty in 1909; and like Roosevelt, he was one of the world's most celebrated people. A Gallup poll taken three weeks before his White House departure revealed that he was the "most admired" person in the world, tying with Pope John Paul II, and the majority of Americans thought him to be an "outstanding" or "above average" president.[10] In spite of his excesses and roguish image—or perhaps because of them—he remained enormously likable. Mythologists believe the difference between psychology and mythology is that psychology assumes there is one voice in the human psyche, while mythology assumes a multitude of voices. If so, myth may have been the only means of explaining Clinton, whose outsized intelligence, ambition, lust, compassion, bitterness, forgiveness, self-destructiveness, ego, and love all vied to be heard in the same loud chorus. But his enigmatic nature only served to make him more compelling. While other presidents retired from office armed with the prestige of the presidency, Clinton also held the mystique of celebrity.

Clinton was known to be disappointed by the lost election of his vice president, Al Gore, to George W. Bush—and a bit hurt.[11] Gore had distanced himself from Clinton during the campaign, pridefully going it alone rather than tapping into his boss's star power and getting a lift from his coattails. If he had, Gore, wooden and uninspired on the stump, may well have taken his home state of Tennessee and with it the election. Instead, both men, now somewhat estranged, watched Bush take the presidential oath on Inauguration Day. Afterward, Clinton, along with his wife the senator and their daughter Chelsea, slipped into a government limousine and headed for Andrews Air Force Base, stopping at red lights for the first time in eight years. Loath as always to leave the spotlight—even on the day of his successor's inaugural—he spent over an hour and a half bidding a seemingly endless farewell to supporters who had shown up to see them off. Finally, he boarded a 747 Air Force jet that would take him and his small family to New York where they would retreat to their newly purchased five-bedroom Dutch colonial home in Chappaqua, just under an hour north of New York City. "I'm not going anywhere," he assured supporters before leaving Washington.[12] No one who knew Clinton doubted it for a minute.

"I was always in a hurry," Clinton wrote later of his life, "even when I didn't know where I was going."[13] Throughout his life, Clinton's ambitions matched his abilities. Born William Jefferson Blythe IV in Hot Springs, Arkansas, in 1946, the first child to a single mother who had lost her traveling salesman husband in a car crash just three months before, Clinton seemed destined for big things. He took the last name Clinton when his mother, Virginia, married Roger Clinton, so that it would be the same as his kid brother, Roger junior. A talented saxophonist with a reverence for Elvis, young Bill Clinton first considered a career as a professional musician, then as a doctor. Finally, he decided on a life in public service, a decision he made after taking in the presidential aura of John Kennedy, who he met in a Rose Garden ceremony at the White House as a delegate to Boy's Nation while in high school.

After graduating from Georgetown University in 1968, Clinton accepted a Rhodes Scholarship to Oxford University before going on to Yale Law School. It was in the law library there in the spring of 1971 that he met a fellow student, an Illinois native and valedictorian of her class at Wellesley University, who approached him, saying, "If you're going to keep looking at me, and I'm going to keep looking back, we might as well be introduced. I'm Hillary Rodham."[14] A long walk around the campus later the same spring turned into their first date. They married in 1975, forming a domestic and political partnership that would define the rest of their lives. A year before their wedding, Clinton failed in his first bid for political office when he lost a race for Congress in Arkansas's third district. Two years later, as his wife pursued a private law practice at Little Rock's Rose Law Firm, Clinton was elected as the state's attorney general, and in 1978, at the age of thirty-two, won election as governor. In 1980, the same year Chelsea was born, he lost the office after just one term. Two years later, politically wiser and ever persistent, he was back in the governor's mansion which he would hold until he took the White House from George Bush in 1992.

After eight years of "the ride of my life" in the White House, Clinton said he was "too young" and "too restless" to kick up his feet and take it easy.[15] But while in one sense he felt liberated in leaving the presidency, he also wondered if he would feel "useless."[16] He made headlines when it was revealed that his post-presidential dream job was secretary general of the United Nations, though even he conceded it was not realistic.[17] As models for what he could achieve as an ex-president, he looked to his predecessors: going back into public service like William Howard Taft did as chief justice of the Supreme Court, serving the incumbent administration like Herbert Hoover had as chairman of Truman and Eisenhower's Hoover commissions, or doing good works by pursuing projects independent of the current administration, like Carter. "I didn't want to be a judge. And I wanted to be more active than Hoover. That's why I mainly thought, Carter," Clinton told writer James Fallows.[18] "I've never met anyone who did more with the gifts God gave him than Jimmy Carter," he commented later. "He declared what he was interested in and where he thought he could make a difference." He also liked Carter's flexible agenda, tackling things he had identified well in advance and addressing others as they came up.[19]

Emulating Jimmy Carter might have been setting the bar a bit high. Carter, after all, was a Nobel laureate generally considered to be America's best ex-president—or at the very least, a close second to ex-president-cum-Massachusetts-congressman and abolitionist John Quincy Adams. But, at fifty-four, Clinton was relatively young (Carter left the presidency at fifty-six, Adams at sixty-one), energetic, supremely smart, enormously popular, and imbued with "a lifelong responsibility to use whatever influence I retain to help other people."[20] He would gradually ease into good works and hoped to devote his full energies to philanthropy in five years' time. . . ."[21]

But first there was money to make. About $5 million in legal bills had accumulated in the White House as a result of the Whitewater investigation and the Paula Jones sexual harassment suit; other suits were pending. The Clintons' house in Chappaqua came to $1.7 million, and the Washington mansion they had bought just off Embassy Row for Mrs. Clinton added up to another $2.85 million. Throughout 2001 Clinton quickly began chipping away at the debt and making up for a lifetime of meager earnings as a public servant by accepting fifty-nine of the paid speaking invitations his agent, Don Walker, said were "piling up like airplanes over La Guardia on a foggy day."[22]

The Marc Rich pardon, which hung over Clinton's first weeks out of office and resulted in the cancellation of at least one engagement, barely amounted to a speed bump. The figures he commanded—even for a former president—were staggering: $350,000 from the National Advertising Council; $250,000 to be on hand at a *Fortune* magazine conference in New York; $550,000 for a whirlwind three-day tour through Sweden, Austria, and Poland; and on and on. With one speaking engagement, he could make substantially more than his annual presidential pension of $180,000.[23] In total his 2001 gross earnings on the speaking circuit came to $9.2 million, though only about 40 percent of his speeches were paid; the remainder were gratis.[24] Whether paid or not, Clinton shined in his duties, striking the perfect pitch behind the podium, then working the crowd afterward as though he were in Nashua the day before the New Hampshire primary, shaking every hand, posing for every picture, and signing every autograph—not only to give those writing the checks their money's worth, but because he actually enjoyed it.

The check he drew for his memoirs, however, would dwarf his earnings as a speaker. Reports were that his publisher Knopf had paid a record $12 million for his autobiography—though at least one aide claimed it was more. The advance made Clinton the highest-paid author in history—Pope John Paul II was a distant second at $8.5 million—despite the fact that the memoir would be his debut literary effort.[25] Mrs. Clinton got into the writing business too, earning an $8 million advance for her own memoir. Insiders anticipated that Mrs. Clinton's manuscript, due in 2003, would be submitted on time, while the chronically late ex-president would not meet his own deadline of May 2004. It would turn out to be a good bet.

Like the other members of the former presidents' club, Clinton's dues would come in the form of raising funds for his presidential library. One hundred sixty-five million would be required to build the William J. Clinton Museum over the Arkansas River on the outskirts of Little Rock, which Clinton aimed to make "the first modern museum about our transition into the new millennium—about a new way of working, of relating to each other and the rest of the world," and planning the project would take up much of

Clinton's time.[26] The library's formal name was telling. As an ex-president, Clinton would become increasingly known as William J. Clinton, or William Jefferson Clinton, the name that was used when he was introduced to audiences, and became the one he chose for his William J. Clinton Foundation. No longer in need of votes, he shed the more populist Bill for his full name, which was more in keeping with the gravitas of the elder statesman he hoped to become.

The first year out of office had its rough spots. Clinton spent the first months stewing over the White House gifts and Marc Rich controversies that had dimmed his departure as president. "I was just angry that after I worked so hard and after all that money had been spent proving that I never did anything wrong for money, that I'd get mugged one more time on the way out the door," he complained in an April 2002 interview with *Newsweek*, his first as an ex-president. The political battles he had waged and stinging criticism he had endured for eight years in Washington stuck in his mind. He took solace in the fact that his enemies "think about me apparently a lot more than I think of them now," but those who knew him knew that statement rang hollow—and with time on his hands, he may have had even more time to think about them. During the first year, his press aide Julia Payne was stirred with a 1:00 A.M. phone call from the boss, "ranting and raving about something." "Sir," she responded dispassionately, "are you watching Fox [News] again?"[27] For a man now running for history, it would be virtually impossible to let go.

Shortly into his post-presidency, another controversy erupted, this time over the government-paid office space he had planned on occupying in the high-rent district of midtown Manhattan, on 57th Street just above Carnegie Hall. The rent, at $800,000 a year, was more than those of Ford, Carter, and Reagan combined. After a barrage of criticism, he nixed those plans and, at the suggestion of New York congressman Charlie Rangel, moved his office uptown to the fourteenth floor of a nondescript rectangular building on Harlem's 125th Street, featuring sweeping, unobstructed views of Central Park treetops and midtown in the distance. Clinton felt a special kinship with African Americans who were by and large his most loyal constituency, supporting him by the largest percentages in the wake of the Monica Lewinsky scandal. It made sense that the man author Toni Morrison famously called "our first black president" would "feel at home" in the heart of Harlem. During a very public visit to the new space, the media was filled with images of Clinton being embraced by his new neighbors, though Mrs. Clinton purportedly was put off by the lovefest when the press, distracted by the buzz, all but ignored her first speech on the floor of the Senate.[28]

Clinton would soon find out what it would feel like to be upstaged. On September 11 he watched from the sidelines while the rookie president George W. Bush dealt with his first presidential crisis and the greatest test of leadership of his generation.[29] Clinton had ruled in relatively placid times, a curse for one seeking a lofty place in history, and had no comparable trial during his White House tenure. Nine-eleven would serve to legitimize Bush's presidency as he demonstrated resolute leadership in its wake, dimming the spotlight that, until then, had shined on the more colorful—and by many accounts, more capable—Clinton. Bush, the man who had been lifted into the presidency not by popular vote but by the verdict of a conservative Supreme Court, was now firmly in control. While the forty-second president and megacelebrity would continue to make good copy, September 10 marked an unofficial end to the Clinton era.

When the planes hit, Clinton had been on a speaking tour in Australia. Upon hearing the news he immediately thought: Osama bin Laden did this.[30] A day later he made his way back to New York courtesy of the president, who had dispatched an Air Force jet to bring him home. "I'll give blood; I'll pick up bricks," he promised the president, and he practically did. He visited lower Manhattan with Chelsea, who had been just twelve blocks from the towers when the first plane attacked, assuring the crowds that greeted him, "It will not be that difficult to get bin Laden." He boarded a commercial flight to Chicago, Washington, and back just to show that it was safe to fly again. He teamed up with his former presidential rival Bob Dole to generate a $100 million scholarship fund for the children of 9/11 victims. And he attended funerals, visited schools, and comforted families struck by the tragedy.[31]

But at the same time, Clinton being Clinton, he thought about how the events would reflect on his historical standing. Rationalizing with journalist Jonathan Alter, he maintained that while the attacks were of significance, they weren't "like World War II at all," and that, as Alter wrote in

Newsweek, "they would eventually be seen not through the context of the Bush presidency but of Clinton's global achievements."[32] At the same time, he became defensive about his administration's record on terrorism, which had been maligned by the Bush administration and conservatives looking for a scapegoat.

Clinton took to holding forth at parties and receptions on his administration's superlative record on terrorism, pointing out that it had broken up twenty al-Qaeda cells, thwarted terrorist plots involving the bombings of Los Angeles International Airport and New York's Holland Tunnel timed around the millennium, more than tripled the budget for the government's antiterrorism efforts, and attacked bin Laden's Afghanistan training camp, narrowly missing bin Laden himself.[33] As he would say in 2005, "I always thought bin Laden was a bigger threat than the Bush administration did," and "desperately" wished he had been president when the FBI and CIA confirmed that bin Laden had been behind the USS *Cole* bombing in 1998, at which time he would have driven the Taliban out of Afghanistan. "I don't know if it would have prevented Nine-eleven," he said. "But it certainly would have complicated it."[34] In July 2004, however, when the 9/11 Commission issued its 570-page report on the attacks, it found both the Clinton and Bush administrations culpable of not understanding "the gravity of the threat" from al-Qaeda due to a "failure of imagination." The committee stopped short of blaming the administrations for the attacks, but their reference to "deep institutional failings" were damning to both Clinton and Bush.[35]

Clinton was not a man who liked solitude, but much of the time he found himself home alone in Chappaqua while his wife tended to her duties in the Senate and Chelsea was across the Atlantic doing postgraduate work at Oxford. Though he and Mrs. Clinton spent long weekends together and talked by phone—by his count, six times a day—he would tell friends, "distance does not make the heart grow fonder."[36] In constant need of company, he took refuge on the road where he could bask in the attention he got on the speaking circuit, and often lingered at parties well after others had called it a night. He could be seen in Chappaqua on occasion spending the lonely evening hours by hoisting nonalcoholic beers with locals at a bar and killing at least one free morning by dropping by the auditorium at the Bedford Road Elementary School just up the street to watch its production of *Lost in New York*.[37]

His loneliness and suburban isolation was compounded by the loss of Buddy, his chocolate Labrador, who had been run over by a teenage girl on Route 117, a busy two-lane thoroughfare at the bottom of the Clinton home's cul-de-sac. Buddy's death was, Clinton said, "by far the worst thing that happened in the first year." Mrs. Clinton had bought the dog for her husband while he was president in 1997, shortly before the Monica Lewinsky scandal broke, in anticipation of his transition to empty-nester when Chelsea went off to college at Stanford. In Chappaqua, Buddy became a hiking and running companion, and slept on a large cushion next to his master's bed. Aside from Oscar, his live-in valet, Buddy was the only consistent presence at the Clinton home. His breeder arranged for Clinton to get one of Buddy's nephews, but Clinton, who had had dogs all his life, had never been quite as attached to any of them as he had with Buddy.[38]

"One of the things I've learned that I didn't know before," Clinton said of his first year out of the White House, "is that I think I can be happy and have a full life here not being president. I've learned now that my elective life is basically over, that I'm very glad I did it. I loved it. I loved it. But because I did it full bore, and I gave myself to it and I left it all on the floor, as the basketball players say, I didn't have any lingering regrets about that. And I feel very, very much at peace."[39] It may have helped that while he was gone from the White House, he hadn't been forgotten. In the middle of 2002, he showed up on the *Forbes* "Celebrity 100" list, beating out the Backstreet Boys for the number-eighteen position. As *Forbes* pointed out, he generated more press clips than any other celebrity, and only Britney Spears inspired more hits on the Internet.[40] Marc Rich faded with the other scandals of Clinton's sensational past, while Clinton himself remained bigger than life. His continued popularity was good news for the joke writers of late-night television who could continue to rely on him for easy monologue laughs. Unlike Dan Quayle, also once dependable late-night fodder but now no longer in the spotlight, Clinton was the gift that kept on giving.

In particular, Clinton remained popular within his own party. When he left the White House, the air went out of the Democrats' balloon, and no one in the party ranks was up to filling it in quite the same way as Clinton had. In 2002, he appeared at over a hundred party fund-raisers and campaign events. "I'd like for my direct Party involvement to go way down," he lamented, "but this year [2002], I don't know who would've done it if I hadn't."[41] Or rather, who would have done it as well. No one embodied the Democratic ideal in the same way Clinton did. He remained the life of the party and, for better or for worse, the one who personified it.

The problem was, it didn't help. In fact, if anything, the election proved a repudiation of Clinton and an indication that the George W. Bush era was in full swing. Bucking the usual trend in which the party controlling the White House suffers net losses during the midterms, the 2002 elections proved disastrous for the Democrats. The GOP won back control of the Senate, took three out of four gubernatorial elections, and became the first party of an incumbent president to gain seats in the House in a midterm, picking up two. Three of Clinton's former cabinet members were among the candidates who went down in flames. Erskine Bowles, Clinton's former chief of staff who ran for the Senate in North Carolina, asked his one-time boss to steer clear of the Tar Heel state, though he lost anyway. Sure, Clinton said after the election, a party with a message is always going to beat a party without one, alluding to the Democrats' ideological disarray.[42]

If the party did have a message, it was the wrong one. A month earlier it staged a memorial service for the late Minnesota senator Paul Wellstone, an old-fashioned liberal who had died days earlier in a plane crash. It turned out to be a campaign rally run amok when GOP Senate majority leader Trent Lott, who had come to pay tribute to his Senate colleague, was jeered off stage in an ugly display of intolerance as Clinton, notably in attendance, passively watched the scene unfold. In a post-9/11 political climate, it put the partisan Democrats in a bad light. Even Wellstone's seat was lost to a Republican, former mayor of St. Paul, Norm Coleman, who beat out venerable party elder, former vice president Walter Mondale.

In her first several years in the Senate, Hillary Clinton kept her head down and profile low, focusing on the needs of her New York constituents, serving on the Armed Services Committee, and cultivating a centrist image. The girl from Chicago Cubs country who dubiously claimed to be a longtime New York Yankees fan in her 2000 senate campaign, worked hard to defuse accusations that she was simply a carpetbagger looking for a way back to the White House. Still a lightning rod, she was an easy target for the Republicans. After a number of Democrats, including Mrs. Clinton, demanded that Bush come clean about reports that the government had been tipped off in advance about terrorist activities before 9/11, the White House focused its disapproval on her.[43] A year and a quarter into her Senate tenure, just under half of New Yorkers rated her performance as fair or poor.[44] Rumors abounded about Mrs. Clinton's 2004 presidential intentions, which only hurt her image in her home state. Though it was unlikely that she would throw her hat into the ring for the presidency so soon into her political career, she was by far the most nationally recognized potential Democratic nominee, and she made good copy as pundits looked ahead to the race in 2004.

In the middle of 2003, Mrs. Clinton's profile would heighten when her much-anticipated memoir, *Living History*, made its way into bookstores, giving her account of her life and turbulent days in the White House at the side of her fallible husband. In particular, readers wanted to know about one subject: Monica Lewinsky. The drama that played out around the Clintons' marriage in full view of the public in the summer of 1998, after revelations that Clinton had had a sexual dalliance with the twenty-one-year-old intern, was unlike anything that had ever made it to the front pages, leaving Mrs. Clinton as perhaps the most famous scorned woman in history. Strong, smart, ambitious, and accomplished—the very picture of the liberated feminist—Mrs. Clinton's marriage endured scrutiny that had cynics believing it was a calculated, mutually beneficial political arrangement. However, her report of the ordeal, while guarded, made her a real, flesh-and-blood woman—"dumbfounded, heartbroken, and outraged"—dealing with a "family crisis" like anybody else. "Everyone has to do it at some point in our lives," she wrote, "and the skills required to cope are the same for a First Lady or for a forklift operator. I just had to do it all in the public eye."[45]

"Hillary Clinton's palpable humanity is the pleasant surprise of *Living History*," wrote *Time* magazine in a June cover story. "Unlike her husband, she is not larger than life. She is a recognizable, somewhat overmatched human being in an utterly ridiculous situation."[46] Though she would remain a polarizing figure, Mrs. Clinton's personal reflections made her a more accessible personality—and millions wealthier for having told her story.

As *Living History* sold briskly—200,000 were snatched up in its first day of publication, breaking the record for a nonfiction book—its author's husband labored to write his own book, a struggle that would last throughout much of the following year and would became a story of its own.[47] The former president understood the importance of his memoir to his legacy and to the business of its publisher, but lacking Mrs. Clinton's renowned discipline, he started off writing his book on what White House aides had referred to as "Clinton time." A looming deadline of May 2004 was pushed back to a fuzzy June-July date when it seemed his manuscript would not show up at Knopf on time. The words "book time" began appearing on his daily schedules as though it was an appointment.[48] For those designated hours, he would hole up in the renovated barn next to the house in Chappaqua that served as his study to concentrate on the project, working with the urgency of a C-student cramming for a midterm. No techie—Clinton sent one e-mail during his presidency and did not use a computer in his post-presidency—he filled twenty large notebooks with his written thoughts and talked through others with the help of one of his former speechwriters.[49] Remarkably, he finished the book just after the original May deadline. When it was all over he told a crowd at Harlem's Apollo Theater, "Finishing the book was like a long prison sentence, and I feel like I just got out tonight. I had to finish it—I need my life back!"[50]

"Far from a must-read" was how the St. Louis Post Dispatch judged *My Life* when it came out in late June, which seemed to be the consensus among reviewers. Most also agreed that its 957 pages was excessive.[51] A front-page *New York Times* review excoriated the book as "sloppy, self-indulgent, and often eye-crossingly dull—the sound of one man prattling away, not for the reader, but for himself and some distant recording angel of history."[52] In a sense, *My Life* was two books. The first, about the "fat, uncool" kid growing up poor in Arkansas and rising to the governor's mansion; the second, a verbose, policy-wonk's "diary of what it's like to be president."[53] Generally, reviewers were kinder to the first than the second, but few gave the book as a whole an unqualified thumbs-up.

The estimations of critics hardly mattered to the public; *My Life* flew off the shelves of bookstores. Four hundred thousand sold in its first day of publication, shattering the record Mrs. Clinton had set a year earlier, and by the first week the number had swelled to around a million.[54] Clinton barnstormed the country on a book tour attracting massive crowds who queued up for blocks as he signed copies of the memoir in assembly-line fashion. Sales abroad, where Clinton was revered in almost every corner, were equally impressive. *My Life* was published in over thirty languages, and included special chapters unique to certain regions. The Mexican edition, for instance, included material on The North American Free Trade Agreement that did not appear in other editions. Though sales would taper off by mid-July due to poor word of mouth, the initial boom would ensure that Knopf would make money from the venture and Clinton's take would exceed his hefty advance.[55]

In *Living History*, which Clinton claimed to have read five times, Mrs. Clinton wrote, "Why [my husband] deceived me [in the Monica Lewinsky affair] is his own story, and he needs to tell it in his own way."[56] In *My Life*, he did, in what was, as with Mrs. Clinton's memoir, its most eagerly anticipated content. "I was disgusted with myself for doing it," he wrote of his first encounter with Lewinsky, "and in the spring when I saw her again, I told her it was wrong for me, wrong for my family, and wrong for her, and I couldn't do it anymore." He further admitted he was "deeply ashamed and I didn't want [the affair] to come out," which led to him stonewalling his family, his staff, and the American people.[57] Even he couldn't "fully understand why I had done something so wrong and so stupid."[58]

In the Oprah-age, Clinton's admissions of guilt and heartache fit right in with the zeitgeist that Clinton himself, with his "I feel your pain" New Age sensitivity, helped to define. But they were a marked departure from the pre-Monica presidential archetype. Flawed as they were, it would be difficult to conjure up images of JFK or LBJ serving up talk-show confessionals of *affaires du coeur* with paramours in quite the same way Clinton would. There he was, promoting the book on *60 Minutes*, AOL, *Good Morning America*, *Larry King Live*, *Charlie Rose*, and, of course, *The Oprah Winfrey Show*, revealing he had had the affair with Lewinsky "because I could," reliving the domestic crisis when he literally slept on the couch as the first lady nursed the wounds of his infidelity behind the door of their bedroom, and discussing the year he spent in family counseling afterward.[59] As with the Lewinsky affair itself, Clinton was again breaking new ground.

The unprecedented success of *My Life* in "event publishing" kept Clinton in the news throughout the summer of 2004, as the Democrats' nominee for the presidency, Massachusetts senator John Kerry, was campaigning in earnest to defeat George W. Bush. Inevitable comparisons to Clinton only favored Clinton—and it started early. At a Democratic National Committee dinner in late March, both Clinton and Kerry addressed the gathering. The former president was "folksy, anecdotal, and rhythmic with the cadences of a Southern preacher," said MSNBC's Tim Curry, while the presumptive Democratic nominee's was "slow-paced, halting, and arrhythmic in delivery, with improvisations on the written text that were sometimes awkward and verbose."[60] Both men, in other words, were playing to form.

At the Democratic National Convention in late July, Clinton, introduced by his wife, once again stole the show with a speech praising Kerry for always answering his country's call, employing the refrain, "John Kerry said: 'Send me.'" Clinton said of Kerry's noted service in Vietnam, "During the Vietnam War, many young men, including the current president, vice president, and me, could have gone to Vietnam and didn't. John Kerry came from a privileged background. He could have avoided going too, but instead, he said 'Send me.'" The virtuoso performance only made many in the hall wish they could once again send Clinton to face down the GOP. Fortunately for Kerry, he spoke two days later, as the buzz over Clinton's speech died down, but he didn't do much better at capturing the audience than he had done in March—or at capturing voters at the polls in November, where Bush won a narrow victory to keep the White House. Clinton would attribute the loss to Kerry's weak stand on security. "It was clear even Kerry's supporters weren't clear" on where the candidate stood, he told the Aspen Institute the following summer.[61] It was also clear that the Democratic Party had yet to fill the substantial void Clinton had left when he relinquished the presidency almost four years earlier.

Two months before the election, as Clinton prepared to hit the campaign trail for Kerry, he got a checkup at Northern Westchester Hospital after experiencing chest pains and shortness of breath. The following day, he found himself in New York-Presbyterian Hospital awaiting heart bypass surgery to reroute blood flow around four arteries clogged by fatty deposits. "The Republicans are not the only ones who want four more years," he told CNN's Larry King before undergoing the operation on September 6, which would go successfully.[62] As president, Clinton was often lampooned for his appetite for fast food, an unrequited love that led to a higher-than-normal cholesterol level. But despite falling back to bad food habits on occasion, he had shed twenty pounds since leaving office by adhering to the South Beach Diet, one of a number of trendy, low-carb diets, and by working out with a trainer at his at-home gym in Chappaqua two or three times a week.[63]

After being released by the hospital with a clean bill of health almost two and a half weeks later, Clinton not only stumped for Kerry, but teamed up with the American Heart Association to campaign for healthier dietary habits among Americans, particularly kids. He had also gotten a taste of his own mortality. "I think I take a lot more pleasure than ever in just the stuff that happens every day," he said afterward.[64] It would take Clinton seven months to fully recover from the surgery—including a follow-up procedure in March to clear up minor complications—much of which he spent at home, resting and enjoying books and movies. Far from being depressed or restless, he actually found himself enjoying the respite, "having time off for the first time in thirty-five years."[65]

On November 18, as rain fell in sheets over Little Rock, the newly re-elected President Bush, his father, George H. W. Bush, and Jimmy Carter all gathered with the Clinton family for the dedication of the William J. Clinton Library, which its namesake hoped would teach Americans "what it was like to be president."[66] Clinton had been actively involved in designing the long, rectangular, steel-and-glass structure that resembled a futuristic boxcar and stood on supports over the Arkansas River as a symbol of the "bridge" Clinton had endeavored to build to the twenty-first century. Forty thousand invited guests braved the weather to hear, among other things, the speeches of four U.S. presidents and music of U2 front man, Bono, who was one of a number of celebrity "Friends of Bill" in attendance. Among them was Al Gore, whose strained relationship with his former boss had been patched up just after 9/11, when Gore, grounded in Buffalo, traveled nine hours by car to Clinton's home in Chappaqua, where they reunited at 3:00 A.M. and talked till dawn.[67]

Though he did his part to help Kerry, many Democrats felt Clinton wasn't doing enough to keep the administration at bay. He had become cozy with the Bushes—both father and son—as was evident in the opening ceremonies at the library. Some time before, on June 14, 2004, just over a week before the publication of *My Life*, Bush had invited the Clintons to the White House to unveil their official portraits and had asked his speechwriters to draft something "very praiseworthy, warm, funny, and short" for the occasion.[68] "As chief executive, [Bill Clinton] showed a deep and far-ranging knowledge of public policy, a great compassion for people in need, and the forward-looking spirit that Americans like in a president," said the sitting president of his immediate predecessor at the ceremony. "Bill Clinton could always see a brighter day ahead, and Americans knew he was working hard to bring that day closer."

The bubbly tribute was a far cry from Bush's oft-repeated campaign vow to "restore honor and dignity" to the White House four years earlier.[69] Natural politicians, country boys at heart, and the nation's only living two-term presidents, Clinton and Bush had an easy rapport and affinity that surprised many observers. When Bush asked his father and Clinton to help raise funds to relieve the victims of three natural disasters, 2004's Asian tsunami and 2005's Hurricanes Katrina and Rita, Clinton immediately stepped up to the task, working harmoniously with the elder Bush—with whom he would strike up a warm friendship—and with remarkable effectiveness. He even went further, defending Bush when the administration was roundly criticized for its slow response to those crises.

In fact, Clinton had largely adopted a collegial bearing toward his successor, suggesting that his membership in the exclusive club of U.S. presidents trumped that of his party. "I have to chart my own course, I have to do things that I think are important. I'm not the leader of the opposition anymore," he said in defense of his position.[70] His wife, who actively discredited the administration in the Senate, understood his position. "He is no longer in politics," she said. "He is a former president with an enormous amount of influence and . . . he is willing to serve his country. My role is different. I'm on the front lines."[71] Consequently, her rhetoric was also different. In a 2006 speech in a Harlem church on Martin Luther King Jr. Day, in which she drew fire for accusing GOP leaders of running the House of Representatives like a "plantation," Senator Clinton predicted that the George W. Bush administration would "go down in history as one of the worst that has ever governed our country." To a group of Hurricane Katrina evacuees in attendance, she added an apology "on behalf of a government that left you behind."[72]

While Clinton seemed to give Bush the benefit of the doubt on most issues, he didn't always give him a free pass. He was initially supportive of Bush on the war in Iraq, stating in a June 2004 *Time* interview that he "repeatedly defended Bush against the left on Iraq, even though I thought he should have waited until the UN inspections were over." Furthermore, he rejected the notion that Bush had gone to war for any reason other than his firm belief that Saddam Hussein was stockpiling weapons of mass destruction, while many Democrats maintained that the administration had used them as an excuse to justify the invasion. "You couldn't possibly ignore [the possibility that] a tyrant had those stocks," he said.[73] By the fall of the following year, however, as American support for the war was fast eroding—along with Bush's approval ratings—Clinton called the war "a big mistake." "The American government made several errors," he argued. "One of which is how easy it would be to get rid of Saddam and how hard it would be to unite the country."[74] He also discredited the administration for not sending enough troops to seal off the country's borders from terrorists, and for dismantling the social structure. His remarks, made during a speech to students at the American University in Dubai, United Arab Emirates, drew a standing ovation from the audience—and front-page headlines at home in the U.S.

In the first several years of his post-presidency, Clinton had gotten all the things he needed to do out of the way. He had paid off his debts and become a wealthy man, which gave him some solace; he could buy his wife and daughter anything he wanted, and he knew they would be well taken care of after he was gone. He had also gained "the freedom to speak out against policies that concentrate on wealth and power, which I passionately disagree with."[75] He had given his account of his life and presidency for the historical record, writing one of the most commercially successful nonfiction books in history, if not one that was likely to change opinions about him. And he had built his presidential library. Along the way, he had dabbled in a number of good works, including, among other endeavors, supporting initiatives in Harlem that helped the community and could be rolled out into other urban areas, working with the American Heart Association, establishing the American India Foundation after the Gujarat earthquake rocked India in 2001, and answering President Bush's call to help with disaster relief. But he hadn't done anything to make his mark as an ex-president in any way that made as significant a difference as Carter had.

The culprit, at least in part, was his scattershot approach. Clinton himself noted in 2002 that while an ex-president retains influence after giving up power, "the influence must be concentrated in a few areas."[76] Concentration, however, was not a Clinton strong suit; as a result, his considerable influence had been diluted. "He can't go to a buffet without trying a little of everything. Literally and figuratively," said a former White House aide. "You try everything, so in effect you have nothing."[77] But an entreaty from Nelson Mandela in 2002 impelled Clinton to begin to narrow in on one area that held the promise of rivaling the most prodigious of post-presidential accomplishments.

Clinton first met Mandela when Mandela visited him in his hotel suite before Clinton accepted the presidential nomination at the 1992 Democratic National Convention in New York City. During Clinton's term in office, the two had formed a friendship in which Mandela, twenty-eight years his senior, played the role of mentor. They spoke often by phone, and during their conversations, Mandela would invariably ask about his family, and occasionally even ask the president to put Chelsea on the line.[78] When Clinton was under siege during the Monica Lewinsky scandal, Mandela was among his staunchest defenders. During the thick of it, in March 1998, Clinton took a nine-day trip to Africa, providing a welcome respite from Kenneth Starr's crusade and the pressures of Washington.

When he visited South Africa, Mandela took Clinton to Robben Island Prison where he had spent eighteen of his twenty-seven years in captivity. As they toured the rock quarry where Mandela had worked hard labor during the day and the cramped jail cell where he had spent his nights, Clinton asked him if he hated his captors. "Yes," Mandela said, but he realized that while they had taken everything else from him, they hadn't taken his heart and mind. "Those they could not take away without my permission. I decided not to give them away." Then he smiled at Clinton, and referring to Clinton's political enemies back in Washington, added, "Neither should you." Clinton then asked him if he hated his captors upon his release from prison, whereupon Mandela replied, "Yes, for a moment I did. Then I thought to myself, 'They had me for twenty-seven years. If I keep hating them, they'll still have me.' I wanted to be free, so I let it go." Again he smiled pointedly at Clinton.[79] The visit with Mandela gave Clinton peace of mind for the trials that lay ahead in Washington, and later would help him move past his own ordeal at the hands of oppressors—though at times, his sneering post-presidential comments about his former adversaries belied the absence of bitterness.[80]

So it was difficult for Clinton to say no to Mandela when, at the XIV International AIDS Conference the two men cochaired in Barcelona in July 2002, he asked Clinton to put his time and influence into combating the AIDS epidemic which had devastated Africa, Latin America, and Asia.[81] The challenge was daunting. Mandela was asking Clinton to help not with AIDS prevention, which many Western powers and NGOs had put money and resources toward, but to help save the lives of the millions who had already contracted the virus by providing them with medical treatments that were financially well out of reach. In southern Africa alone, where four million suffered from the AIDS virus, only 50,000 were receiving proper medical treatment.[82] The yearly cost of the drugs and diagnostic testing would come to a minimum of $1,600 per person, adding up to an annual total of $40 billion.[83]

Mandela wasn't the first one close to Clinton's heart to ask him to lend his weight to the cause of fighting AIDS. Chelsea had done her thesis at Oxford on the UN's Global Fund to Fight AIDS, and had told her father he hadn't done enough as president to aid in the cause, urging him to do more as a former president.[84] In fact, Clinton himself had come to the same tentative conclusion before attending the conference in Barcelona. Earlier in 2002, he had asked Ira Magaziner—a former aide who had spent seven years with him in the White House and had worked in vain with Mrs. Clinton toward ambitious health-care reform—to research the causes where

Clinton's focused involvement would do the most good. After several months of study, Magaziner gave Clinton his recommendation: concentrate on the treatment of AIDS in Africa and the Caribbean, the areas hardest hit by the disease. Clinton agreed, but still didn't know how much time he wanted to commit to the effort. While attending the conference with Mandela, his mind was made up. In an address to those in attendance, Clinton promised to "go to Africa and India to lend visibility and support," and urged the audience to "hold me accountable to that commitment and to provide ideas of what else I can do."[85]

In the fall, in a speech at the Woodrow Wilson Center in Washington, Clinton maintained that AIDS was perhaps the most important international challenge of the next decade, and that deaths caused by the disease's fury should be seen as a preventable holocaust.[86] Over the next several years through the auspices of the William J. Clinton Foundation, he would make slow and steady progress toward alleviating the problem. He would become, in his words, "obsessed with the AIDS thing."[87]

As former President and Senator Clinton pursued their own agendas, their marriage carried on in its own inexplicable way. Husband and wife did their best to balance out their hectic schedules and to spend quantity time together as well as quality time—four nights a week when the Senate was in session, and more during recesses. "It's always easier to bag it," Clinton said of marriage during the hard times. "It's harder to stay. But you know, after a certain point it seems like a lot of trouble to start again, too. There's something to be said for sticking."[88] As for the effects of the Monica Lewinsky affair, he pointed out, "Once you've been humiliated in front of the entire world, you've got nothing left to hide. It was kind of a wacko deal for the nation, but it turned out to be kind of liberating for me. It's easier to beat your demons if you let them go, and I have."[89]

He continued to be his wife's most valued political advisor, calling himself "the Westchester County constituent for the junior senator of New York."[90] John Kerry's loss in 2004 boded well for Senator Clinton's presidential prospects, if she chose to pursue them, which most pundits and "insiders" viewed as inevitable. Had Kerry and his running mate John Edwards taken the election, it would have meant that Kerry would have likely been the party's standard-bearer again in 2008—even unpopular incumbent Jimmy Carter won the Democratic nomination again in 1980, despite a challenge from party favorite, Ted Kennedy. And if Kerry had won a second term, Edwards would probably have had the inside track to the nomination in 2012—no incumbent vice president seeking his party's nomination had been denied it since the primaries, not kingmakers in smoke-filled rooms, determined the nominee.

Mrs. Clinton's hard work in the Senate earned her the respect of her colleagues and steadily rising approval ratings among her constituents in New York, and Americans in general. A CNN/*USA Today*/Gallup poll taken in August 2005 showed 68 percent of Americans thought she was a strong and decisive leader, and 60 percent found her likable.[91] And her work on the Senate Armed Services Committee gave her credibility on national security, an area where Democrats had consistently been perceived as weak. Those things, in addition to her unmatched name recognition and her husband's undiminished popularity, meant that she was positioned as well as anyone for a run at the nomination. Though Clinton recommended that she not think about her presidential intentions, let alone talk about them (until her reelection to the Senate in 2006), she had his unconditional support.[92] After all, she had given him, in his words, "all those decades [at my side] and was unbelievably good, in a thousand ways, and made a real difference to my public service. So," reasoned the ex-president and prospective first man, "if she asked me to do anything, I would do it."[93]

As speculation abounded about Mrs. Clinton's future, historians began to take measure of Clinton's past. By 2005, the subject of his impeachment began creeping up in school textbooks, sparing students the unseemly, sensational details of the scandal but covering it as an historical event—even as the cement of the Clinton years had yet to harden. "This is very difficult for everybody, because it's so fresh," said Gilbert Sewall, director of the American Textbook Council, an organization tasked with monitoring scholastic textbooks. "It's easier to nail down history like the transcontinental railroad. With Clinton, you're dealing with material that has by no means been settled." "A sorry mess," was how one high school textbook described the ordeal, while another summed up Clinton's affair with Monica Lewinsky as an "improper relationship with a young White House intern."[94] Middle school textbooks covered it too, though the language was a bit softer.[95]

Addressing the subject of his impeachment at a November 2005 academic conference in New York, Clinton disputed historian Douglas Brinkley's comments that it held back his presidency from greatness. "I completely disagree with that," said the former president. "Now, you can agree with that if you want, but only if you think impeachment was justified. Otherwise, it was an egregious abuse of the Constitution and law and history of our country."[96] The only certainty about Clinton's record as president was that the debate would continue.

Fifteen months after committing himself to facilitating the treatment of AIDS in the Third World, Clinton brokered a breakthrough deal with four pharmaceutical companies in India and South Africa, to sell generic AIDS antiretroviral drugs at less than a third of the cost of brand-name versions. Under the deal's provisions, the companies would allow nine countries in the Caribbean and three in southern Africa to buy daily drug regimens from $1.50 for brand-name drugs, to 40 cents for generic alternatives, a development that would provide treatment for 110,000 people infected in those countries within two years—a number Clinton hoped would climb to two million by 2008.[97] When President Bush invited him to talk about the administration's AIDS policy in an Air Force One chat on the way to the funeral of Pope John Paul II, Clinton was frank. "Well, in the first place," he told the president, "it was terrible because your people thought we were enemies of the drug companies and they didn't want to work with us," upon which the two of them "worked it out."[98] Clinton also leveraged his clout abroad to smooth out other snags relating to AIDS treatment. When the governor of an African nation demanded kickbacks for AIDS treatment, he quickly backed down when Clinton called him to discuss the matter.[99]

The constant travels Clinton made in the name of AIDS and disaster relief had many close to him worried about his health in the wake of his bypass surgery, but there was no slowing him down.[100] Often hopping private jets loaned to him by corporate executives—the loss of Air Force One was generally first among the presidential trappings recent ex-chief executives missed most—Clinton went far and wide to offer compassion to victims spread throughout the world. Visiting a hospital in Kunming, China, he sat at the bedside of a twenty-four-year-old woman suffering from AIDS who told him she was unable to afford the drug protocol needed for

her condition. As he held her hand he said, "Years from now, I want yo to say, 'I remember when that old man came to see me and told me I wa going to be all right."[101] In China, where the epidemic was mostly ignored by the government, the prime minister visited an AIDS clinic after Clinton publicly embraced an AIDS activist.[102]

Clinton was sensitive to criticism that he had spread himself too thin doing other things to make much of a difference on AIDS. He pointed to other important contributions he had made—mostly his work for disaster relief, where his prodigious joint efforts with the elder Bush alone resulted in yielding over $120 million in donated funds for the victims of the tsunami and hurricanes Katrina and Rita. "I cannot honestly say that we'd be further along than we are with AIDS, because there's only so much of the technical stuff I do," he said.[103] Actually, Clinton was doing more on AIDS than most likely realized, but faced the challenge Carter had met when he tried to generate awareness about his efforts in Africa, combating river blindness and Guinea worm disease. Despite his accomplishments in those areas, Carter said, "You can't take a picture of [them]"; therefore, press coverage of his post-presidential efforts often focused on other areas.[104]

Given Clinton's far-reaching ambitions, there were many other things to cover. In mid-September of 2005, he launched the first annual Clinton Global Initiative (CGI), a three-day conference on three floors of the Sheraton Hotel in New York City, convening world leaders, business titans, activists, and high-minded celebrities to discuss four areas Clinton identified as pressing global concerns: extreme poverty, religious conflict, global warming, and obstacles to flourishing democracy. The conference was patterned after the annual World Economic Forum in Davos, Switzerland, but with a twist: each of the eight hundred participants would be asked to make a written commitment toward assuaging one of the areas addressed—in addition to the $15,000 they shelled out to attend. Those who didn't, according to Clinton, would not be asked back the following year.[105] By the end of the conference—which attracted everyone from Condi Rice, Tony Blair, Shimon Peres, and King Abdullah of Jordan to Rupert Murdoch, George Soros, Mick Jagger, and Angelina Jolie—a total of $1.25 million had been pledged, including a $100 million endowment to fight AIDS in Africa through microenterprise development.[106]

The host surprised at least one attendee with his reserve and discipline. Tina Brown wrote in *The Washington Post* that she had expected to leave CGI "begging for mercy" after hearing the voluble Clinton hold forth extemporaneously for three full days; however, he had surprised her by keeping his remarks to a minimum and even making sure the panels stuck to their allotted times. Maybe it was his brush with death, Brown surmised, but "now you feel he's shed the psychic baggage of the impeachment years and with it the toxic rock-and-roll of his constantly roiling reputation."[107] Thinner and with hair that had turned a distinguished silvery gray, Clinton looked better than he had as president. And having cast off—or at least, come to terms with—his demons and become comfortable with himself outside the political arena, focusing on the problems he hadn't quite gotten to while in office, maybe he had grown too.

Almost six years after leaving the Oval Office, with the stain of the Marc Rich pardon on his hands and the lingering whiff of impeachment trailing him out the door, Clinton's post-presidency was being widely hailed as triumphant. A front-page article in *The Washington Post* in June 2005 credited him as succeeding "to a surprising degree in fashioning his ex-presidency to make himself a dominant player on the world stage."[108] A *New York* magazine cover story in August covered his "Plan for World Domination," while *Time* named him and George H. W. Bush "Partners of the Year" in its annual "Person of the Year" issue, a nod to their collaboration on disaster relief. And a December *Esquire* cover story proclaimed him "The Most Influential Man in the World." *Esquire*'s editor, who stressed that the designation was based on Clinton's potential, not just on what he had already accomplished, wrote: "His new freedom, along with the global affection for him, his unmatched capacity for compassion, and his unparalleled access to the world's centers of power and money can combine to make him the most powerful agent of positive change in the world." If Clinton, hampered by scandal, had not reached his full potential as president, he would have his opportunity as an ex-president.[109]

In an address at Indianapolis's Butler University later the same year, Clinton spoke about one of the many privileges of no longer being the leader of the free world. "The great thing about being a former president

is you can say whatever you think," he said. Then he added wryly, "Of course, nobody cares anymore."[110]

Hardly. Now more than ever, what a former president says matters—and what he does can matter even more. Clinton needed only to consider the presidential peers who joined him for the Clinton Library dedication in Little Rock a year earlier. Jimmy Carter, who left the White House with an approval rating thirty-one percentage points lower than his, would go on to win the Nobel Peace Prize twenty-two years later. George H.W. Bush, eight years after losing office to Clinton, would become the nation's first father as his eldest son, who presided over the ceremonies, followed Clinton into the Oval Office. What's more, Clinton's own wife, the junior senator from New York, has a good shot at being next among them.

The library they had all come to christen did not provide the last word on Clinton's legacy. There are chapters in that book yet to be written.

ENDNOTES

INTRODUCTION

1. *Christian Science Monitor*, July 16, 2004.
2. *Mark Twain: A Film Directed by Ken Burns*, 2002.
3. Collier and Horowitz, *The Roosevelts*, pp. 178–9.
4. Freidel, *The Presidents of the United States*, p. 58.
5. Wikipedia.org/wiki/Herbert_Hoover.
6. McCullough, *Truman*, p. 930.
7. Anson, *Exile*, p. 251.
8. Jimmy Carter, interview with the author.
9. George Bush, interview with the author.
10. Smith, "Hoover and Truman," trumanlibrary.org/hoover/intro.htm.
11. Brinkley, *The Unfinished Presidency*, p. 90.
12. George Bush, interview with the author.
13. *Parade*, July 10, 2005.
14. McCullough, *Truman*, p. 928.
15. *Newsweek*, May 22, 1989.
16. Jimmy Carter, interview with the author.
17. The Carter Center, March 2004.
18. Smith, *Patriarch*, p. 301.
19. *Thomas Jefferson: A Film by Ken Burns*, 1996.

I. HARRY S. TRUMAN: BACK TO INDEPENDENCE

1. Hamby, *Man of the People*, p. 618.
2. Miller, *Plain Speaking*, p. 343.
3. Farrell, *Harry S. Truman and the Modern American Presidency*, p. 377.
4. McCullough, *Truman*, pp. 911–2.
5. ABC.com, January 17, 2001.
6. Truman, *Years of Trial and Hope*, pp. 520–1.
7. Hamby, *Man of the People*, p. 618.
8. *The New York Times*, January 22, 1953.
9. Miller, *Plain Speaking*, p. 212.

[10] McCullough, *Truman*, p. 928.

[11] *The New York Times*, January 22, 1953.

[12] Ibid.

[13] McCullough, *Truman*, p. 931.

[14] Ibid, p. 976.

[15] Farrell, *Harry S. Truman and the Modern American Presidency*, p. 385.

[16] McCullough, *Truman*, p. 397 and Farrell, *Harry S. Truman and the American Presidency*, p. 384.

[17] *The New York Times*, January 25, 1953.

[18] McCullough, *Truman*, p. 928.

[19] *The New York Times*, January 28, 1953.

[20] Ibid.

[21] McCullough, *Truman*, p. 963.

[22] Hamby, *Man of the People*, p. 627.

[23] Klapthor, *First Ladies*, p. 74.

[24] Hamby, *Man of the People*, p. 284.

[25] *The New York Times*, Ibid.

[26] McCullough, *Truman*, p. 1031.

[27] Truman, *Off the Record*, p. 292.

[28] Ibid, pp. 297–8.

[29] Miller, *Plain Speaking*, p. 397.

[30] Ibid, p. 395.

[31] McCullough, *Truman*, p. 932.

[32] Truman, *Off the Record*, pp. 298–9.

[33] Ibid, p. 294.

[34] Hill, *Europeans*, p. i.

[35] Truman, *Off the Record*, pp. 306–7.

[36] McCullough, *Truman*, p. 937.

[37] Hamby, *Man of the People*, p. 626.

[38] Truman, *Off the Record*, p. 319.

[39] McCullough, *Truman*, pp. 947–8.

[40] Ibid, p. 947.

[41] Ibid, p. 963.

[42] Truman, *Years of Trial and Hope*, p. 521.

[43] Hamby, *Man of the People*, p. 620.

[44] Ibid, pp. 620–1.

[45] Truman, *Off the Record*, p. 341.

46 Miller, *Plain Speaking*, pp. 219–21.

47 Smith, "Hoover and Truman: A Presidential Friendship,"
    trumanlibrary.org/hoover/intro.htm.

48 Ibid.

49 Herbert H. Hoover, Letter to Harry S. Truman, December, 1962, Harry S.
    Truman Library.

50 Smith, "Hoover and Truman: A Presidential Friendship,"
    trumanlibrary.org/hoover/intro.htm.

51 *The New York Times*, January 24, 1953.

52 Farrell, *Harry S. Truman and the Modern American Presidency*, p. 387.

53 Ibid, p. 388.

54 *The New York Times*, June 30, 1957.

55 Ibid.

56 Ibid.

57 McCullough, *Truman*, pp. 962–4.

58 Smith, "Hoover and Truman: A Presidential Friendship,"
    trumanlibrary.org/hoover/intro.htm.

59 Truman, *Dear Bess*, p. 575.

60 Gelb, Rosenthal, Siegel, *Great Lives*, pp. 632–3.

61 Ibid.

62 Farrell, *Harry S. Truman and the Modern American Presidency*, p. 390.

63 Truman, *Truman Speaks*, p. 67.

64 Truman, *Off the Record*, p. 338.

65 Hamby, *Man of the People*, p. 634.

66 Miller, *Plain Speaking*, p. 186.

67 McCullough, *Truman*, p. 974.

68 Miller, *Plain Speaking*, pp. 178–9.

69 Truman, *Dear Bess*, pp. 575–6.

70 Ambrose, *Nixon: The Education of a Politician*, pp. 582–3.

71 Sidey, *John Kennedy*, p. 36.

72 McCullough, *Truman*, p. 796.

73 Farrell, *Harry S. Truman and the Modern American Presidency*, p. 393.

74 Ibid, p. 391.

75 *Newsweek*, April 4, 1969.

76 McCullough, *Truman*, pp. 982–3.

77 Gelb, Rosenthal, Siegel, *Great Lives*, p.638.

78 *The New York Times*, December 27, 1972.

79 www.icfa.org/7.04_vanbeck.htm.

80 McCullough, *Truman*, p. 988.

81 Miller, *Plain Speaking*, pp. 402–3.

82 Inscription at The Harry S. Truman Library.

II. DWIGHT D. EISENHOWER: ELDER STATESMAN

1 *Newsweek*, April 4, 1969.

2 *National Geographic*, "Eyewitness to the Twentieth Century," p. 203.

3 *Time*, October 20, 1961.

4 *Time*, January 27, 1961.

5 Reeves, *President Kennedy*, p. 22.

6 Sidey, *John Kennedy*, p. 32.

7 Reeves, *President Kennedy*, p. 31.

8 Sidey, *John Kennedy*, p. 32.

9 Schlesinger, *A Thousand Days*, p. 160.

10 Eisenhower, *Strictly Personal*, p. 286.

11 Reeves, *President Kennedy*, p. 23.

12 *Time*, October 20, 1961.

13 Eisenhower, *Strictly Personal*, p. 285.

14 Ambrose, *Eisenhower*, p. 616.

15 Gelb, Rosenthal, Siegel, *Great Lives*, p. 194.

16 Farrell, *The Eisenhower Diaries*, p. 384.

17 Cronkite, *A Reporter's Life*, pp. 236–7.

18 *Time*, October 20, 1961.

19 *The New York Times, Great Lives*, p. 194.

20 Klapthor, *First Ladies*, p. 76.

21 *Time*, April 4, 1969.

22 Ambrose, *Eisenhower*, p. 72.

23 Klapthor, *First Ladies*, p. 76.

24 Eisenhower, *Strictly Personal*, p. 293.

25 Ambrose, *Eisenhower*, p. 617.

26 Gelb, Rosenthal, Siegel, *Great Lives*, p. 194.

27 Ambrose, *Eisenhower*, p. 617.

28 Eisenhower, *Strictly Personal*, pp. 280–1.

29 Gelb, Rosenthal, Siegel, *Great Lives*, p. 194.

30 Ambrose, *Eisenhower*, p. 631.

31 Skidmore, *After the White House*, p. 128.

32 *Time*, April 4, 1969.

33 Sidey, *Portrait of a President*, p. 174.
34 Gelb, Rosenthal, Siegel, *Great Lives*, p. 194.
35 Voss, *Portraits of the Presidents*, p. 117.
36 Hewitt, *Tell Me a Story*, p. 70.
37 *The New York Times*, April 10, 1969.
38 Gelb, Rosenthal, Siegel, *Great Lives*, p. 195.
39 Ambrose, *Eisenhower*, p. 645.
40 Sidey, *Portrait of a President*, p. 174.
41 *Newsweek*, April 7, 1969.
42 Ambrose, *Eisenhower*, pp. 636–7.
43 Ibid, p. 644.
44 Gelb, Rosenthal, Siegel, *Great Lives*, p. 195.
45 Farrell, *The Eisenhower Diaries*, pp. 382–3.
46 Schlesinger, *A Thousand Days*, p. 288.
47 Farrell, *The Eisenhower Diaries*, pp. 382–3.
48 Ambrose, *Eisenhower*, pp. 638–9.
49 Sidey, *John Kennedy*, p. 120.
50 Ambrose, *Eisenhower*, p. 639.
51 Ibid, p. 557.
52 Ibid, p. 640.
53 The White House Tapes of John F. Kennedy, October 22, 1962, The Miller Center, University of Virginia.
54 Ambrose, *Eisenhower*, p. 597.
55 Johnson, *The Vantage Point*, pp. 32–3.
56 Ibid, p. 131.
57 *The New York Times*, March 29, 1963.
58 Ibid, May 2, 1963.
59 Lyon, *Eisenhower*, p. 834.
60 Cronkite, *A Reporter's Life*, pp. 230–1.
61 Ibid, p. 229.
62 *Time*, April 4, 1969.
63 *The New York Times*, July 7, 1963.
64 Gelb, Rosenthal, Siegel, *Great Lives*, p. 194, and *The New York Times*, July 7, 1963.
65 *The New York Times*, July 7, 1963.
66 Eisenhower, *Strictly Personal*, p. 312.
67 *Time*, September 15, 1965.

68 Ambrose, *Eisenhower*, p. 669.
69 *The New York Times*, November 30, 1967.
70 Eisenhower, *Strictly Personal*, p. 329.
71 Ambrose, *Eisenhower*, pp. 655–8.
72 *The New York Times*, November 11, 1967.
73 Lyon, *Eisenhower*, p. 847.
74 *Time*, December 8, 1967.
75 *The New York Times*, November 30, 1967.
76 *Newsweek*, July 7, 1969.
77 Ambrose, *Nixon*, p. 381.
78 Nixon, *RN*, p. 307.
79 Eisenhower, *Strictly Personal*, p. 333.
80 Nixon, *RN*, p. 361.
81 *The New York Times*, March 28, 1969.
82 Nixon, *RN*, pp. 379–80.
83 Eisenhower, *Strictly Personal*, p. 83.
84 *Newsweek*, July 14, 1969, and Nixon, *RN*, p. 376.
85 Nixon, *RN*.
86 *Newsweek*, July 14, 1969.

III. LYNDON B. JOHNSON: EXILE

1 Russell, *Lady Bird*, p. 304.
2 Johnson, *The Vantage Point*, p. 564.
3 Russell, *Lady Bird*, p. 304.
4 Dallek, *Flawed Giant*, p. 599–600.
5 Miller, *Lyndon: An Oral Biography*, p. 530.
6 Tom Johnson, interview with the author.
7 Miller, *Lyndon: An Oral Biography*, p. 530.
8 Whitcomb and Whitcomb, *Real Life at the White House*, pp. 381–2.
9 Goodwin, *Lyndon Johnson and the American Dream*, p. 352.
10 Russell, *Lady Bird*, p. 306.
11 Johnson, *The Vantage Point*, p. 568.
12 Cronkite, CBS interview, 1970.
13 Luci Johnson, interview with the author.
14 Whitcomb and Whitcomb, *Real Life at the White House*, p. 381.
15 Dallek, *Flawed Giant*, p. 601.
16 *Time*, January 31, 1969.

17   Luci Johnson, interview with the author.
18   *Time*, January 31, 1969.
19   Miller, *Lyndon: An Oral Biography*, p. 544.
20   Russell, *Lady Bird*, pp. 12–18.
21   Ibid, p. 20.
22   Miller, *Lyndon: An Oral Biography*, p. 544.
23   *U.S. News & World Report*, September 29, 1969.
24   *Time*, January 31, 1969.
25   Tom Johnson, interview with the author.
26   *Time*, January 31, 1969, and *U.S. News & World Report*, September 29, 1969.
27   *U.S. News & World Report*, September 29, 1969.
28   Caro, *Path to Power*, p. 8.
29   *Time*, January 31, 1969, and *U.S. News & World Report*, September 29, 1969.
30   Goodwin, *Lyndon Johnson and the American Dream*, p. 357.
31   Miller, *Lyndon: An Oral Biography*, p. 545.
32   Goodwin, *Lyndon Johnson and the American Dream*, p. 360.
33   Miller, *Lyndon: An Oral Biography*, p. 546.
34   *Time*, February 4, 1973.
35   *U.S. News & World Report*, September 29, 1969.
36   Goodwin, *Lyndon Johnson and the American Dream*, p. 361.
37   Ibid, p. 355.
38   Ibid, p. xix.
39   Ibid, pp. 358–9.
40   *Newsweek*, January 5, 1970.
41   Cronkite, *A Reporter's Life*, pp. 234–5.
42   Miller, *Lyndon: An Oral Biography*, p. 544.
43   Luci Johnson, interview with the author.
44   Lyndon Nugent, interview with the author.
45   Goodwin, *Lyndon Johnson and the American Dream*, p. 356.
46   *U.S. News & World Report*, September 29, 1969.
47   George Bush, interview with the author.
48   *U.S. News & World Report*, April 12, 1971.
49   Goodwin, *Lyndon Johnson and the American Dream*, p. 7.
50   Cronkite, *A Reporter's Life*, p. 235.
51   Luci Johnson, interview with the author.
52   *Time*, February 5, 1973.
53   *Time*, January 31, 1969.

54 *U.S. News & World Report*, November 29, 1969.
55 *Newsweek*, May 20, 1970.
56 Miller, *Lyndon: An Oral Biography*, p. 549.
57 Graham, *Personal History*, pp. 438–9.
58 Miller, *Lyndon: An Oral Biography*, p. 549.
59 *Newsweek*, May 20, 1970.
60 *Time*, August 27, 1970.
61 Goodwin, *Lyndon Johnson and the American Dream*, pp. 363–4.
62 Ibid, p. 549.
63 *The New York Times*, May 23, 1971.
64 Ibid.
65 Ibid.
66 Goodwin, *Lyndon Johnson and the American Dream*, pp. 263–4.
67 Miller, *Lyndon: An Oral Biography*, p. 550.
68 *Time*, November 8, 1971.
69 Tom Johnson, interview with the author.
70 *The New York Times* magazine, November 2, 1980.
71 Nixon, *RN*, p. 755.
72 Unger and Unger, *LBJ*, p. 510.
73 Nixon, *RN*, p. 337.
74 *Look*, November 1972.
75 Nixon, *RN*, pp. 754–6.
76 Goodwin, *Lyndon Johnson and the American Dream*, p. 365.
77 *Look*, November 1972.
78 Unger and Unger, *LBJ*, p. 527.
79 *Look*, November 1972.
80 Tom Johnson, interview with the author.
81 Miller, *Lyndon: An Oral Biography*, pp. 551–2.
82 Nixon, *RN*, pp. 755–6.
83 Miller, *Lyndon: An Oral Biography*, pp. 551–2.
84 *Life*, December 1972.
85 Miller, *Lyndon: An Oral Biography*, p. 560.
86 *Life*, December 1972.
87 Luci Johnson, interview with the author.
88 *Life*, December 1972.
89 Ibid.
90 Luci Johnson, interview with the author.

91 Miller, *Lyndon: An Oral Biography*, p. 555.
92 Ibid.
93 Goodwin, *Lyndon Johnson and the American Dream*, p. i.
94 *The New York Times*, January 23, 1973.
95 Ibid, January 25, 1973.
96 Miller, *Lyndon: An Oral Biography*, p. 540.
97 *The New York Times*, January 27, 1973.
98 Ibid.
99 Nixon, *RN*, p. 754.
100 *Time*, February 5, 1973.
101 C-SPAN.com.

IV. RICHARD NIXON: REHABILITATION

1 *Time*, August 12, 1974.
2 Ford, *A Time to Heal*, p. 39.
3 Gerald Ford, interview with author.
4 Anson, *Exile*, p. 20.
5 Ford, *A Time to Heal*, p. 39.
6 Nixon, *RN*, p. 1090.
7 Kissinger, *Years of Renewal*, pp. 25–6.
8 Nixon, *In the Arena*, p. 20.
9 *Time*, September 23, 1974, and *Time*, September 16, 1974.
10 White, *Breach of Faith*, p. 342.
11 Woodward and Bernstein, *The Final Days*, p. 434.
12 Kissinger, *Years of Upheaval*, pp. 385–7.
13 Reeves, *A Ford, Not a Lincoln*, p. 42.
14 Anson, *Exile*, p. 39.
15 Ford, *A Time to Heal*, p. 13.
16 *Time*, September 16, 1974.
17 Ford, *A Time to Heal*, pp. 159–68.
18 Gerald Ford, interview with the author.
19 Ford, *A Time to Heal*, pp. 168–72.
20 Ibid, pp. 168–72.
21 Anson, *Exile*, p. 58.
22 Nixon, *In the Arena*, p. 21.
23 Anson, *Exile*, p. 58.
24 Ibid, p. 59.

25 Ford, *A Time to Heal*, pp. 180–1.
26 Anson, *Exile*, p. 20.
27 *U.S. News & World Report*, August 26, 1974.
28 Ibid.
29 Anson, *Exile*, p. 34.
30 Ibid, p. 73.
31 Nixon, *In the Arena*, p. 22.
32 *Time*, September 23, 1974.
33 Nixon, *In the Arena*, pp. 22–3.
34 Ford, *A Time to Heal*, pp. 201–2.
35 Gerald Ford, interview with the author.
36 Ford, *A Time to Heal*, pp. 201–2.
37 *The New York Times*, April 24, 1994.
38 Ibid.
39 Eisenhower, *Pat Nixon*, p. 443.
40 Anson, *Exile*, p. 85.
41 Nixon, *In the Arena*, p. 30.
42 Ibid, p. 30.
43 Ibid, p. 30.
44 *Newsweek*, November 11, 1974.
45 *Newsweek*, May 19, 1986.
46 Eisenhower, *Pat Nixon*, p. 439.
47 *Newsweek*, November 11, 1974.
48 Nixon, *RN*, p. 33.
49 Woodward and Bernstein, *The Final Days*, p. 441.
50 Eisenhower, *Pat Nixon*, p. 439.
51 Anson, *Exile*, p. 150.
52 Ford, *A Time to Heal*, p. 360.
53 *The New York Times*, September 23, 1993.
54 Small, *The Presidency of Richard Nixon*, p. 305.
55 Ibid, p. 43, and Anson, *Exile*, p. 159.
56 David Frost television interview with Richard Nixon, 1977.
57 Anson, *Exile*, p. 169.
58 Ibid. pp. 180–1.
59 Brent Scowcroft, interview with the author.
60 Nixon, *In the Arena*, p. 33.
61 Nixon, *RN* (Revised Edition), p. ix.

62 Anson, *Exile*, p. 43.

63 Nixon, *In the Arena*, p. 33.

64 *The New York Times*, January 16, 1978.

65 *Newsweek*, May 19, 1986.

66 Nixon, *RN*, p. 560.

67 Nixon, *In the Arena*, p. 45.

68 Ibid, p. 47.

69 *New York* magazine, September 9, 1980.

70 Eisenhower, *Pat Nixon*, p. 458.

71 *Newsweek*, May 19, 1986.

72 *New York* magazine, September 9, 1980.

73 Ibid.

74 Ibid.

75 Crowley, *Nixon Off the Record*, p. 9.

76 Nixon, *RN*, p. 1084.

77 *Newsweek*, May 19, 1986.

78 Reagan, *My Turn*, p. 328.

79 Crowley, *Nixon Off the Record*, p. 24.

80 *Time*, May 9, 1994.

81 Jimmy Carter, interview with the author.

82 Anson, *Exile*, p. 254.

83 *Time*, October 2, 1981.

84 Sidey, letter to the author, January 2004.

85 Crowley, *Nixon Off the Record*, p. 59.

86 *Newsweek*, May 19, 1986.

87 Crowley, *Nixon Off the Record*, p. 19.

88 *Time*, November 6, 1989.

89 Richard Nixon, "The Case for Aid to the Contras," Speech to the Annual Associated Press Luncheon for the American Newspaper Publishers Association, April 21, 1986, Richard Nixon Library.

90 Crowley, *Nixon Off the Record*, pp. 19–20.

91 *Newsweek*, May 19, 1986.

92 Ibid.

93 Nixon, *In the Arena*, pp. 74–75.

94 *The New York Times*, April 24, 1994.

95 *Time*, July 30, 1990.

96 Crowley, *Nixon Off the Record*, p. 20.

97 *Time*, April 15, 1991.
98 George Bush, interview with the author.
99 *Newsweek*, May 19, 1986.
100 Crowley, *Nixon Off the Record*, pp. 68–9.
101 Bush, *All the Best*, p. 573.
102 Crowley, *Nixon Off the Record*, p. 131.
103 Small, *The Presidency of Richard Nixon*, p. 308.
104 Crowley, *Nixon Off the Record*, pp. 171 and 159.
105 Clinton, *My Life*, p. 593.
106 Crowley, *Nixon Off the Record*, p. 171.
107 *The New York Times*, September 23, 1993.
108 Eisenhower, *Pat Nixon*, p. 459.
109 Crowley, *Nixon Off the Record*, p. 190.
110 Ibid, p. 211.
111 Ibid, p. 183.
112 *Time*, May 2, 1994.
113 *The New York Times*, April 27, 1994.
114 *Los Angeles Times*, April 27, 1994.
115 *Newsweek*, May 19, 1994.

V. GERALD R. FORD: THE GOOD LIFE

1 Jimmy Carter Library, "The Presidential Inauguration."
2 Ford, *A Time to Heal*, p. 435.
3 Cannon, *Time and Chance*, pp. 408–9.
4 Brinkley, *The Unfinished Presidency*, p. 14.
5 Gerald Ford, interview with the author.
6 *The New York Times*, January, 24, 1977.
7 *Time*, January 31, 1977.
8 Brinkley, *The Unfinished Presidency*, p. 14.
9 Ford, *A Time to Heal*, p. 442.
10 *Newsweek*, January 31, 1977.
11 *The New York Times*, January 21, 1977.
12 *Time*, May 9, 1994.
13 Ford, *A Time to Heal*, p. 69.
14 Reeves, *A Ford, Not a Lincoln*, p. 115.
15 Ford, *A Time to Heal*, p. 6.

[16] New York *Newsday*, April 9, 1989.

[17] Schnakenberg, *Distory.*

[18] Brinkley, *The Unfinished Presidency*, p. 68.

[19] Gerald Ford, interview with author.

[20] Ibid.

[21] *The New York Times*, January 24, 1977.

[22] *U.S. News & World Report*, March 21, 1977.

[23] Van Natta Jr., *First Off the Tee*, p. 99.

[24] *Newsweek*, August, 1, 1977.

[25] Van Natta Jr., *First Off the Tee*, pp. 94, 80.

[26] *Newsweek*, August 1, 1977.

[27] *Newsweek*, May 22, 1989.

[28] Ibid.

[29] Ibid.

[30] *The New York Times*, December 19, 1983.

[31] *The New York Times Book Review*, May 30, 1979.

[32] *Newsweek*, August 1, 1977.

[33] Cannon, *Time and Chance*, p. 46.

[34] Ibid, pp. 46–7.

[35] *The New York Times*, January 24, 1977.

[36] Ibid.

[37] Kennerly, *Photo Op*, p. 103.

[38] David Hume Kennerly, interview with author.

[39] Ford, *Betty: A Glad Awakening*, p. 39.

[40] Ibid, p. 39.

[41] Ibid, p. 43.

[42] Ibid, p. 22.

[43] Ibid, p. 7.

[44] Ibid, p. 69.

[45] Ibid, p. 69.

[46] *The New York Times*, March 5, 1980.

[47] *The New York Times*, May 4, 1978.

[48] *The New York Times*, February 1, 1980.

[49] *Newsweek*, August 1, 1977.

[50] *The New York Times*, May 21, 1978.

[51] *The New York Times*, March 3, 1980.

[52] *U.S. News & World Report*, March 21, 1977.

[53] *Newsweek*, August 1, 1977.

[54] George Bush, interview with the author.

[55] Ford, *A Time to Heal*, photo caption.

[56] Reagan, *An American Life*, pp. 14–15.

[57] *Newsweek*, July 28, 1980.

[58] Gerald Ford, interview with the author.

[59] *Newsweek*, August 1, 1977, and Ford, *Betty: A Glad Awakening*, pp. 95–96.

[60] *The New York Times*, July 20, 1977.

[61] Cronkite, *A Reporter's Life*, p. 238.

[62] *Newsweek*, July 28, 1980.

[63] Reagan, *An American Life*, pp. 214–5.

[64] Ford, *A Time to Heal*, pp. 95–6.

[65] *Newsweek*, July 28, 1980.

[66] Ibid.

[67] Ibid.

[68] *The New York Times*, April 28, 1981.

[69] Ibid.

[70] Ibid.

[71] Ford, *Betty: A Glad Awakening*, p. 102.

[72] Anson, *Exile*, p. 251.

[73] Carter, *Keeping Faith*, pp. 270–2.

[74] Ibid, pp. 270–2, and Brinkley, *The Unfinished Presidency*, pp. 66–70.

[75] Anson, *Exile*, p. 255.

[76] *Newsweek*, August 1, 1977.

[77] *Atlanta Journal-Constitution*, February 21, 2005, and *The New York Times*, October 12, 1981.

[78] Gerald Ford, interview with author, and *The New York Times*, October 12, 1981.

[79] Brinkley, *The Unfinished Presidency*, p. 67, and Anson, *Exile*, p. 255.

[80] Jimmy Carter, interview with the author.

[81] Anson, *Exile*, p. 82.

[82] Brinkley, *The Unfinished Presidency*, p. 67.

[83] Ibid, p. 67.

[84] Ambrose, *Nixon: Ruin and Recovery*, p. 544.

[85] Rosalynn Carter, interview with the author.

[86] *Time*, October 19, 1981.

[87] Brinkley, *The Unfinished Presidency*, p. 67.

[88] Jimmy Carter, interview with author.

[89] Gerald Ford, interview with the author.

[90] Ibid.

[91] Carter, *Keeping Faith*, pp. 270–2.

[92] Brinkley, *The Unfinished Presidency*, p. 67.

[93] *Time*, October 19, 1981.

[94] Brinkley, *The Unfinished Presidency*, p. 68.

[95] Gerald Ford, interview with the author.

[96] *The New York Times*, October 12, 1981.

[97] Brinkley, *The Unfinished Presidency*, pp. 68–9, and *Atlanta Journal Constitution*, February 21, 2005.

[98] *The Boston Globe*, November 3, 1989.

[99] *The New York Times*, October 12, 1981.

[100] Brinkley, *The Unfinished Presidency*, p. 69.

[101] Ibid, pp. 103–4.

[102] CNN.com, May 9, 2000.

[103] *The New York Times*, December 17, 2000.

[104] Bourne, *Jimmy Carter*, p. 493.

[105] Brinkley, *The Unfinished Presidency*, p. 287.

[106] Gerald Ford, interview with the author.

[107] White House Historical Association, *The White House*, pp. 52 and 60.

[108] Ford, *Betty: A Glad Awakening*, p. 2.

[109] Ibid, p. 1–3.

[110] Ibid, p. 265.

[111] *The Boston Globe*, November 11, 1989.

[112] *The New York Times*, August 29, 1983.

[113] Gerald Ford, interview with the author.

[114] Brinkley, *The Unfinished Presidency*, p. 480.

[115] Gerald Ford, Truman Library, Independence, MO.

[116] Gerald Ford, interview with the author.

[117] New York *Newsday*, April 9, 1989.

[118] Cannon, *Time and Chance*, p. 415.

[119] Gerald Ford, interview with the author.

[120] *The Atlanta Journal-Constitution*, February 21, 2005.

[121] New York *Newsday*, April 9, 1989.

[122] Gerald Ford, interview with the author.

[123] JFK.com, May 21, 2001.

[124] Gerald Ford, interview with the author.

[125] JFK.com, Ibid.

VI. JIMMY CARTER: PEACEMAKER

[1] Carter and Carter, *Everything to Gain*, pp. 3–4.

[2] Carter, *Keeping Faith*, p. 3.

[3] Ibid, p. 13.

[4] Hugh Sidey, *The Presidency*, p. 97.

[5] *Time*, April 9, 1979.

[6] Jimmy Carter, interview with the author.

[7] Walter Mondale, interview with the author.

[8] *The New York Times*, January 22, 1981.

[9] Jimmy Carter, interview with the author.

[10] Farrell, *Harry S. Truman and the Modern American Presidency*, p. 390.

[11] Jimmy Carter, interview with the author.

[12] Brinkley, *The Unfinished Presidency*, p. 35.

[13] Ibid, p. 42.

[14] Jimmy Carter, interview with the author.

[15] Brinkley, *The Unfinished Presidency*, p. 3.

[16] Carter and Carter, *Everything to Gain*, p. 16.

[17] Rosalynn Carter, interview with the author.

[18] Jimmy Carter, interview with the author.

[19] Carter and Carter, *Everything to Gain*, p. 15.

[20] Ibid, p. 8.

[21] Rosalynn Carter, interview with the author.

[22] Ibid.

[23] Ibid, and Brinkley, *The Unfinished Presidency*, p. 39.

[24] Rosalynn Carter, interview with the author.

[25] Steve Hochman, interview with the author.

[26] Jimmy Carter, interview with the author.

[27] Steve Hochman, interview with the author.

[28] Rosalynn Carter, interview with the author.

[29] Carter and Carter, *Everything to Gain*, pp. 28–9.

[30] Jimmy Carter, interview with the author.

[31] Rosalynn Carter, interview with the author.

[32] Carter and Carter, *Everything to Gain*, p. 31.

33 Ibid, p. 32 and Rosalynn Carter, interview with the author.

34 Klapthor, *First Ladies*, p. 87.

35 Beschloss, *American Heritage Illustrated History of the Presidents*, p. 465.

36 CBS.com, June 7, 2004.

37 *The New York Times*, April 12, 1982.

38 Ibid.

39 Ibid.

40 Brinkley, *The Unfinished Presidency*, p. 77.

41 Carter and Carter, *Everything to Gain*, p. 37.

42 Brinkley, *The Unfinished Presidency*, p. 184.

43 Ibid, p. 42.

44 Habitat for Humanity International.

45 CarterCenter.org.

46 Jimmy Carter, interview with the author.

47 Brinkley, *The Unfinished Presidency*, p. 48.

48 Jimmy Carter, interview with the author.

49 Walter Mondale, interview with the author.

50 Brinkley, *The Unfinished Presidency*, p. 129.

51 Jimmy Carter, interview with the author.

52 *Time*, October 3, 1994.

53 Brian Mulroney, interview with the author.

54 Bush and Scowcroft, *A World Transformed*, pp. 413–4.

55 George Bush, interview with the author.

56 Brinkley, *The Unfinished Presidency*, p. 339.

57 *Time*, October 3, 1994 and Jimmy Carter, interview with the author.

58 Jimmy Carter, interview with the author.

59 *The New York Times*, June 17, 1994, and Bourne, *Jimmy Carter*, p. 503.

60 *The New York Times*, June 19, 1994.

61 Carter, *Talking Peace*, p. 174.

62 *The New York Times*, June 17, 1994.

63 Ibid, June 19, 1994.

64 Ibid, June 20, 1994.

65 *Time*, October 3, 1994.

66 Bourne, *Jimmy Carter*, p. 64.

67 Powell, *My American Journey*, p. 599.

68 Ibid, p. 599.

69 Carter, *Talking Peace*, p. 177.

70   *The New York Times*, September 17, 1994.
71   *Time*, October 3, 1994.
72   Powell, *My American Journey*, p. 600.
73   *Time*, October 3, 1994.
74   Powell, *My American Journey*, p. 600.
75   Ibid, p. 601.
76   Clinton, *My Life*, pp. 617–8.
77   Brinkley, *The Unfinished Presidency*, pp. 426–7.
78   Powell, *My American Journey*, p. 601.
79   Ibid, p. 601.
80   *Time*, October 3, 1994.
81   Powell, *My American Journey*, p. 601.
82   Ibid, p. 601 and *Time*, October 3, 1994.
83   *Time*, October 3, 1994.
84   Brinkley, *The Unfinished Presidency*, pp. 432–3.
85   *The New York Times*, September 21, 1994.
86   *Time*, October 3, 1994.
87   Jimmy Carter, interview with the author.
88   Carter, *Talking Peace*, pp. 82–3.
89   The Carter Center, "Highlights of 20 Years of Achievement," 2002.
90   WBS News Channel 4, Atlanta, Georgia, *Jimmy Carter*, 2002.
91   CarterCenter.org.
92   Ibid.
93   The Carter Center, "Highlights of 20 Years of Achievement," 2002.
94   Bourne, *Jimmy Carter*, pp. 500–1.
95   Carter, *Talking Peace*, pp. 162.
96   Brinkley, *The Unfinished Presidency*, pp. 262–3.
97   Bourne, *Jimmy Carter*, pp. 500–1.
98   Carter, *Talking Peace*, pp. 183–5.
99   BBC.com, May 17, 2002.
100 TIME.com, May 11, 2002.
101 *The New York Times*, April 12, 1982.
102 Skidmore, *After the White House*, pp. 147–8.
103 Jimmy Carter, interview with the author.
104 George Bush, interview with the author.
105 George Bush, interview with the author.
106 Brinkley, *The Unfinished Presidency*, p. 101.

[107] Brent Scowcroft, interview with the author.

[108] Carter, *Living Faith*, p. 136.

[109] Rosalynn Carter, interview with the author.

[110] *Time*, October 12, 2002.

[111] *The New York Times*, October 12, 2002.

[112] Rosalynn Carter, interview with the author.

[113] *The New York Times*, October 12, 2002.

[114] Ibid, December 11, 2002.

[115] Jimmy Carter, interview with the author.

[116] Rosalynn Carter, interview with the author, and Brinkley, *The Unfinished Presidency*, p. 12.

[117] Rosalynn Carter, interview with the author.

[118] Jimmy Carter, interview with the author.

[119] Jimmy Carter, interview with the author.

[120] Jimmy Carter, interview with the author.

[121] *The New York Times*, October 12, 2002.

[122] Jimmy Carter, interview with the author.

VII. RONALD REAGAN: THE LONG GOODBYE

[1] CBS.com, June 7, 2004.

[2] *Time*, June 14, 2004.

[3] Reagan, *An American Life*, pp. 88–9.

[4] *Time*, June 14, 1989.

[5] *The New York Times*, January 2, 1989.

[6] *The New York Times*, June 10, 1989.

[7] Brian Mulroney, interview with the author.

[8] WSJ.com, August 8, 2001.

[9] *American Spectator*, September/October, 2002.

[10] A&E Television, *Biography: Ronald Reagan*.

[11] Morris, *Dutch*, p. 656.

[12] *Time*, May 8, 1989.

[13] Ibid.

[14] *The New York Times*, July 4, 1989.

[15] *Time*, June 26, 1989.

[16] *The New York Times*, October 19, 1989.

[17] Reagan, *My Turn*, p. 110.

[18] Ibid, p. 94.

19 *The New York Times*, November 18, 1990.
20 Reagan, *My Turn*, p. 315.
21 Ibid, p. 369.
22 Ibid, p. 161.
23 *The New York Times*, January 5, 1989.
24 Ibid, March 22, 1990.
25 Ibid, March 28, 1990.
26 Ibid, November 18, 1990.
27 Ibid, April 7, 1991.
28 Ibid, April 9, 1991.
29 *Time*, April 15, 1991.
30 Ibid.
31 *Los Angeles Times*, November 28, 1991.
32 Ibid.
33 Ibid, November 18, 1991.
34 Ibid, November 5, 1991.
35 Ibid.
36 ReaganFoundation.org.
37 *Time*, October 4, 1999.
38 *Time*, September 29, 2003.
39 *Time*, October 4, 1999.
40 Nancy Reagan, conversation with author, November 3, 1999, Bel-Air Hotel, Los Angeles, California.
41 *Newsweek*, June 21, 2004.
42 Clinton, *My Life*, pp. 450–1.
43 Morris, *Dutch*, p. 656.
44 *Newsweek*, June 21, 2004.
45 *People*, June 21, 2004, and *Time*, November 11, 1994.
46 *The New York Times*, November 7, 2005.
47 Ibid, November 8, 2005.
48 Morris, *Dutch*, pp. 665–6.
49 *Time*, March 25, 2005.
50 *People*, June 21, 2004.
51 Ibid.
52 *Newsweek*, June 21, 2004.
53 George Bush, interview with the author.
54 *Time*, March 24, 1997.

55 Morris, *Dutch*, p. 52.
56 *American Spectator*, September/October 2002.
57 *Newsweek*, June 21, 2004.
58 Ibid.
59 *The New York Times*, June 7, 2004.
60 Ibid, May 23, 2005.
61 Ibid.
62 Ibid.
63 CNN.com, August 9, 2001.
64 *People*, March 13, 2000.
65 *Newsweek*, December 29, 2003.
66 Ibid, June 21, 2004.
67 *People*, December 15, 2003.
68 Ibid.
69 Reagan, *My Turn*, p. 169.
70 *People*, December 15, 2003.
71 *People*, June 21, 2004.
72 *The New York Times*, June 12, 2004.
73 Ibid.
74 *Time*, June 21, 2004.
75 *New York Times*, June 12, 2004.
76 Davis, *The Long Goodbye*, p. 198, and *Newsweek*, Ibid.

VIII: GEORGE BUSH: PATRIARCH

1 CBS.com, March 21, 2003.
2 Brent Scowcroft, interview with the author.
3 Bush, *All the Best*, p. 578.
4 Ibid, pp. 575–6.
5 Ibid, p. 583.
6 Ibid, p. 578.
7 ABC.com, January 23, 2001.
8 *Time*, February 1, 1993.
9 *The New York Times*, January 20, 1993.
10 Ibid, January 22, 1993.
11 Ibid.
12 Bush, *A Memoir*, p. 544.
13 Kilian, *Barbara Bush*, p. 209.

14 Bush, *Reflections*, p. 6.
15 Bush, *A Memoir*, pp. 546–7.
16 Ibid, p. 586.
17 McGrath, *Heartbeat*, pp. 267.
18 Bush, *A Memoir*, pp. 34–5.
19 McGrath, *Heartbeat*, pp. 270–1.
20 George Bush, interview with the author.
21 Schweizer and Schweizer, *The Bushes*, pp. 410–11.
22 Clinton, *My Life*, pp. 526–7.
23 Bush, *All the Best*, p. 587.
24 Kilian, *Barbara Bush*, p. 206.
25 Bush, *All the Best*, pp. 609–10.
26 Brent Scowcroft, interview with the author.
27 McGrath, *Heartbeat*, pp. 292–3.
28 Schweizer and Schweizer, *The Bushes*, p. 320.
29 Brent Scowcroft, interview with the author, and Brian Mulroney, interview with the author.
30 Schweizer and Schweizer, *The Bushes*, p. 413.
31 *The New York Times*, November 5, 1994.
32 Schweizer and Schweizer, *The Bushes*, p. 425.
33 Ibid, p. 420.
34 *Time*, August 8, 2000.
35 George Bush, interview with the author.
36 *The New York Times*, November 5, 1994.
37 Brent Scowcroft, interview with the author.
38 Schweizer and Schweizer, *The Bushes*, p. 420.
39 *The New York Times*, Ibid.
40 Ibid, November 4, 1994.
41 Ibid, November 5, 1994.
42 Ibid, November 6, 1994.
43 *Time*, August 7, 2000.
44 Ibid.
45 Brent Scowcroft, interview with the author.
46 George Bush, interview with the author.
47 *Time*, March 28, 1994.
48 Schweizer and Schweizer, *The Bushes*, p. 441.
49 Ibid, pp. 444–5.

50 George Bush, interview with the author, and Kilian, *Barbara Bush*, p. 207.

51 Ibid, p. 209.

52 *Time*, March 28, 1994.

53 Schweizer and Schweizer, *The Bushes*, p. 441.

54 *Time*, March 28, 1994.

55 Brent Scowcroft, interview with the author.

56 Bush, *All the Best*, pp. 21–2.

57 Ibid, p. 598.

58 Ibid, p. 601.

59 Ibid, pp. 601–2.

60 George Bush, interview with the author.

61 George Bush, interview with the author, and *Time*, June 7, 2004.

62 *The New York Times*, November 11, 1998.

63 Bush, *All the Best*, p. 615.

64 Ibid, pp. 618–19.

65 *The New York Times*, June 14, 1999.

66 Ibid, November 4, 1998.

67 Ibid.

68 Schweizer and Schweizer, *The Bushes*, p. 458.

69 *The New York Times*, June 14, 1999.

70 Schweizer and Schweizer, *The Bushes*, p. 485

71 Schweizer and Schweizer, *The Bushes*, p. 486.

72 Ibid.

73 Kilian, *Barbara Bush*, p. 214–5.

74 Schweizer and Schweizer, *The Bushes*, p. 459.

75 Kilian, *Barbara Bush*, pp. 214–5.

76 George Bush, interview with the author.

77 *Newsweek*, November 20, 2000.

78 *The New York Times*, November 9, 2000.

79 Schweizer and Schweizer, *The Bushes*, pp. 493–4.

80 George Bush, interview with the author.

81 Barbara Bush, *Reflections*, p. 386–87.

82 George Bush, interview with the author.

83 Barbara Bush, *Reflections*, pp. 386–7.

84 James Bradley, *Flyboys*, p. 333, and Jean Becker, interview with the author, and George Bush, interview with the author.

85 George Bush, interview with the author.

86 *Time*, August 7, 2000.

87 *New York Times*, September 16, 2002.

88 George Bush, interview with the author.

89 George Bush, interview with the author.

90 Jean Becker, interview with the author.

91 George Bush, interview with the author.

92 *The New York Times*, September 16, 2002.

93 George Bush, interview with the author.

94 *The Guardian*, July 1, 2005.

95 Brent Scowcroft, interview with the author.

96 Packer, *The Assassins' Gate*, pp. 36–8.

97 Brent Scowcroft, interview with the author.

98 George Bush, interview with the author.

99 Bush, *Reflections*, p. 190.

100 Brent Scowcroft, interview with the author.

101 Jean Becker, interview with the author.

102 George Bush, interview with the author.

103 CBS.com, October 31, 2004.

104 *Time*, September 13, 2004.

105 *The Washington Post*, September 2, 2004.

106 *USA Today*, July 28, 2000.

107 *Time*, December 26, 2006.

108 TIME.com, April 23, 2005.

109 *San Diego Union-Tribune*, February 19, 2005.

110 TIME.com, April 23, 2005.

111 Ibid.

112 *The Guardian*, July 1, 2005.

113 *Time*, December 26, 2005.

114 *The Guardian*, July 1, 2005

115 *San Diego Union-Tribune*, February 19, 2005.

116 George Bush, interview with the author.

117 *The New York Times*, October 10, 2005.

118 *Time*, December 26, 2005.

119 George Bush, interview with the author.

120 Ibid.

121 Ibid.

[122] Tom Frechette, interview with the author.

[123] McGrath, *Heartbeat,* p. 270.

IX. BILL CLINTON: LIFE OF THE PARTY

[1] Salon.com, February 9, 2001.

[2] Ibid.

[3] Clinton, *My Life,* pp. 940–1.

[4] *Vanity Fair,* June 2004.

[5] Ibid, and *Newsweek,* April 8, 2002.

[6] *The Washington Post,* January 23, 2001.

[7] Klein, p. 56–7.

[8] Ibid, pp. 159 and 88.

[9] *Vanity Fair,* June 2004.

[10] Bloomberg.com, December 30, 2000, and ABC.com, January 17, 2001.

[11] *New York,* September 22, 2005.

[12] *The New York Times,* January 21, 2001.

[13] *Time,* June 28, 2004.

[14] Clinton, *Living History,* p. 52.

[15] *The New York Times,* January 21, 2001, and *The Atlantic Monthly,* March2003.

[16] *The Atlantic Monthly,* March 2003, and *Esquire,* December 2005.

[17] *The Washington Post,* January 1, 2005.

[18] *The Atlantic Monthly,* March 2003.

[19] *Esquire,* December 2005.

[20] *The Atlantic Monthly,* March 2003.

[21] *Newsweek,* April 8, 2002.

[22] *The Atlantic Monthly,* March 2003.

[23] Ibid.

[24] Ibid, and *Newsweek,* April 8, 2002.

[25] *Vanity Fair,* June 2004.

[26] *The Atlantic Monthly,* March 2003.

[27] *Newsweek,* April 8, 2002.

[28] *Newsweek,* February 26, 2001.

[29] *Newsweek,* April 8, 2002.

[30] CBS, *60 Minutes,* June 20, 2004.

[31] *Vanity Fair,* June 2004.

32 *Newsweek*, April 8, 2002.

33 Ibid.

34 *New York*, September 22, 2005.

35 "The Independent National Commission on the Terrorist Attacks Upon the United States Report," July 2004.

36 *Ladies' Home Journal*, November 2005, *Vanity Fair*, June 2004, and *Newsweek*,

    April 8, 2002.

37 *Vanity Fair*, June 2004.

38 *Newsweek*, April 8, 2004.

39 Ibid.

40 Forbes.com, June 25, 2002.

41 *The Atlantic Monthly*, Ibid.

42 *Time*, November 11, 2002.

43 BusinessWeek.com, June 10, 2002.

44 Ibid.

45 Clinton, *Living History*, p. 473.

46 *Time*, November 11, 2002.

47 *Seattle Times*, June 24, 2004.

48 *Newsweek*, February 2, 2004.

49 *Seattle Times*, June 24, 2004.

50 *New York Post*, May 13, 2004.

51 *St. Louis Dispatch*, June 27, 2004.

52 *The New York Times*, June 20, 2004.

53 *Time*, June 28, 2004.

54 *Seattle Times*, June 24, 2004, and *New York Post*, July 22, 2004.

55 *New York Post*, July 22, 2004.

56 *Vanity Fair*, June 2004, and Clinton, *Living History*, photo caption 61.

57 Clinton, *My Life*, pp. 773–4.

58 Ibid, p. 800.

59 CBS, *60 Minutes*, Ibid.

60 MSNBC.com, March 26, 2004.

61 Aspeninstitute.com.

62 CNN, *Larry King Live*, September 3, 2005.

63 *Ladies' Home Journal*, November 2005.

64 Ibid.

[65] *Esquire*, December 2005, and *Ladies' Home Journal*, November 2005.

[66] *The New York Times*, November 20, 2004.

[67] *Newsweek*, February 2, 2004.

[68] Ibid, January 8, 2005.

[69] CBS.com, June 14, 2004.

[70] *Esquire*, December 2005.

[71] *The New York Times*, September 6, 2005.

[72] CNN.com, January 17, 2006.

[73] *Time*, June 28, 2004.

[74] *USA Today*, November 16, 2005.

[75] *People*, September 26, 2005, and *Esquire*, December 2005.

[76] *The Atlantic Monthly*, March 2003.

[77] *Vanity Fair*, June 2004.

[78] Clinton, *My Life*, pp. 417–8.

[79] Ibid, pp. 782–3.

[80] *Newsweek*, April 8, 2002.

[81] *Esquire*, December 2005.

[82] BBC News, October 24, 2003.

[83] *Esquire*, December 2005.

[84] *People*, September 26, 2005, and *Vanity Fair*, June 2004.

[85] *Vanity Fair*, June 2004.

[86] *The Atlantic Monthly*, March 2003.

[87] *Esquire*, December 2005.

[88] *Ladies' Home Journal*, November 2005.

[89] *People*, September 26, 2005.

[90] *Vanity Fair*, June 2004.

[91] CNN.com, August 8, 2005.

[92] *People*, September 26, 2005.

[93] *New York*, September 22, 2005.

[94] AOL.com, December 27, 2005.

[95] Ibid.

[96] CBS.com, November 11, 2005.

[97] *The Washington Post*, June 1, 2005.

[98] *Esquire*, December 2005.

[99] *New York*, September 22, 2005.

[100] *People*, September 26, 2005.

101 Ibid.

102 *New York*, September 22, 2005.

103 Ibid.

104 Jimmy Carter, interview with the author.

105 *U.S. News & World Report*, September 19, 2005.

106 *The Washington Post*, September 16, 2005.

107 Ibid, September 22, 2005.

108 Ibid, June 1, 2005.

109 *Esquire*, December 2005.

110 Clinton, Butler University, November 6, 2005.

BIBLIOGRAPHY

INTERVIEWS

Becker, Jean. Houston, Texas, March 22, 2006.

Bush, George. Office of George Bush, Houston, Texas, March 22, 2006.

Carter, Jimmy. The Carter Center, Atlanta, Georgia, March 22, 2005, and February 28, 2006.

Carter, Rosalynn. The Carter Center, Atlanta, Georgia, March 22, 2005 (phone), and Atlanta, Georgia, April 15, 2005.

Ford, Gerald R. Office of Gerald R. Ford, Rancho Mirage, California, November 30, 2004.

Frechette, Tom. Kennebunkport, Maine, and Houston, Texas, 2005 (phone).

Hardman, John. The Carter Center, Atlanta, Georgia, March 22, 2005.

Hochman, Steve. The Carter Center, Atlanta, Georgia, March 22, 2005.

Johnson, Luci. Austin, Texas, April 13, 2005 (phone).

Johnson, Tom. March 2004 (e-mail).

Kennerly, David Hume. New York, New York, and Los Angeles, California, 2004–2006.

Mondale, Walter. Minneapolis, Minnesota, November 17, 2004 (phone).

Mulroney, Brian. Montreal, Quebec, Canada, February 2004 (phone).

Nugent, Lyndon. San Antonio, Texas, March 12, 2004 (phone).

Scowcroft, Brent. Washington, D.C., October 6, 2005.

Sidey, Hugh. Washington, D.C., 2003–2005.

BOOKS

Aiken, Jonathan. *Nixon: A Life*. Washington, D.C.: Regnery, 1993.

Ambrose, Stephen. *Eisenhower: Soldier and President*. New York: Touchstone, 1990.

Ambrose, Stephen. *Nixon: The Education of a Politician 1913–1962*. New York: Simon & Schuster, 1991.

Ambrose, Stephen. *Nixon: Ruin and Recovery: 1973–1990*. New York: Simon & Schuster, 1991.

Anson, Robert Sam. *Exile: The Unquiet Oblivion of Richard M. Nixon*. New York: Simon & Schuster, 1984.

Beschloss. Michael, ed. *American Heritage Illustrated History of the Presidents*, New York: Crown Publishers, 2000.

Boller Jr., Paul F. *Presidential Anecdotes*. New York: Oxford University Press, 1981.

Bourne, Peter. *Jimmy Carter*. New York: Lisa Drew Books/Charles Scribner's Sons, 1997.

Bradley, James. *Flyboys*. New York: Little, Brown, and Company, 2003.

Brinkley, Douglas. *The Unfinished Presidency: Jimmy Carter's Journey to the Nobel Peace Prize*. New York: Penguin Books, 1999.

Bush, Barbara. *A Memoir*. New York: Lisa Drew Books/Charles Scribner's Sons, 1994.

Bush, Barbara. *Reflections: Life After the White House*. New York: Lisa Drew Books/Charles Scribner's Sons, 2003.

Bush, George. *All the Best, George Bush: My Life in Letters and Other Writings*. New York: Scribner, 1999.

Bush, George and Brent Scowcroft. *A World Transformed*. New York: Alfred A. Knopf, 1998.

Cannon, James. *Time and Chance: Gerald Ford's Appointment with History*. Michigan: University of Michigan, Reprint edition, 1998.

Caro, Robert. *The Years of Lyndon Johnson: Path to Power*. New York: Alfred A. Knopf, 1997.

Carter, Jimmy. *An Hour Before Daylight: Memories of a Rural Boyhood*. New York: Simon & Schuster, 2001.

Carter, Jimmy and Rosalynn Carter. *Everything to Gain: Making the Most of the Rest of Your Life*. New York: Random House, 1987.

Carter, Jimmy. *Keeping Faith*. New York: Bantam Books, 1982.

Carter, Jimmy. *Living Faith*. New York: Times Books, 1996.

Carter, Jimmy. *Talking Peace*. New York: Puffin Books, 1993.

Clinton, Bill. *My Life*. New York: Alfred E. Knopf, 2004.

Clinton, Hillary. *Living History*. New York: Simon & Schuster, 2003.

Collier, Peter and David Horowitz. *Roosevelts: An American Saga*. New York: Simon & Schuster, 1994.

Cronkite, Walter. *A Reporter's Life*. New York: Alfred A. Knopf, 1996.

Crowley, Monica. *Nixon Off the Record*. New York: Random House, 1996.

Dallek, Robert. *Flawed Giant: Lyndon Johnson and His Times 1961–1973*. New York: Oxford University Press, 1998.

Davis, Patti. *The Long Goodbye*. New York: Alfred E. Knopf, 2004.

Eisenhower, John. *Strictly Personal*. New York: Doubleday, 1974.

Eisenhower, Julie Nixon. *Pat Nixon: The Untold Story*. New York: Simon & Schuster, 1986.

Farrell, Robert H. *Harry S. Truman and the Modern American Presidency*. Boston: Little, Brown & Company, 1983.

Ford, Betty. *Betty: A Glad Awakening*. New York: Doubleday, 1987.

Ford, Gerald R. *A Time to Heal*. New York: Harper & Row, 1979.

Freidel, Frank and Hugh Sidey. *The Presidents of the United States*. Washington, D.C.: The White House Historical Association in cooperation with The National Geographic Society, 1964.

Gallen, David, ed. *The Quotable Truman*. New York: Carroll & Graf Publishers Inc., 1994.

Gelb, Arthur, A. M. Rosenthal, and Marvin Siegel, eds. *New York Times Great Lives of the Twentieth Century*. New York: Times Books, 1988.

Goodwin, Doris Kearns. *Lyndon Johnson and the American Dream*. New York: St. Martin's/Griffin, 1991.

Graham, Katharine. *Personal History*. New York: Alfred A. Knopf, 1997.

Greene, Bob. *Fraternity: A Journey in Search of Five Presidents*. New York: Crown Books, 2004.

Hamby, Alonzo L. *Man of the People: A Life of Harry S. Truman*. New York: Oxford University Press, 1995.

Hayward, Steven F. *The Real Jimmy Carter: How Our Worst Ex-President Undermines American Foreign Policy, Coddles Dictators, and Created the Party of Clinton and Kerry*. Washington, D.C.: Regnery Publishing, 2004.

Hewitt, Don. *Tell Me a Story: Fifty Years and 60 Minutes in Television*. New York: Public Affairs, 2002.

Hill, Richard. *Europeans: An Alternative History of Europe*. Brussels: Europublic, 2000.

Johnson, Lyndon B. *The Vantage Point: Perspectives of the Presidency 1963–1969*. New York: Holt, Rinehart and Winston, 1971.

Kennerly, David Hume. *Photo Op*. Texas: University of Texas Press, 1995.

Kilian, Pamela. *Barbara Bush: Matriarch of a Dynasty*. New York: St. Martin's Press, 2002.

Kissinger, Henry. *Years of Renewal*. New York: Simon & Schuster, 1999.

Kissinger, Henry. *Years of Upheaval*. Boston: Little, Brown & Company, 1982.

Klapthor, Margaret Brown. *The First Ladies*. Washington, D.C.: The White House Historical Association with the cooperation of the National Geographic Society, 1975.

Klein, Joe, *The Natural: The Misunderstood Presidency of Bill Clinton*. New York: Random House, 2002.

Lyon, Peter. *Eisenhower: Portrait of a Hero*. Boston: Little, Brown & Company, 1974.

McCullough, David C. *Truman*. New York: Simon & Schuster, 1992.

McGrath, Jim. *Heartbeat: George Bush in His Own Words*. New York: Citadel Press Books, 2003.

Miller, Merle. *Lyndon: An Oral Biography*. New York: Putnam, 1980.

Miller, Merle. *Plain Speaking: The Oral Biography of Harry S. Truman*. New York: Berkley Publishing Corporation, 1974.

Morris, Edmund. *Dutch: A Memoir of Ronald Reagan*. New York: Random House, 1999.

Nixon, Richard. *Six Crises*. New York: Doubleday, 1962.

Nixon, Richard. *RN: The Memoirs of Richard Nixon*. Touchstone, 1978, 1990.

Nixon, Richard. *In the Arena: A Memoir of Victory, Defeat, and Renewal*. New York: Simon & Schuster, 1990.

Packer, George. *The Assassins' Gate: America in Iraq*. New York: Farrar, Straus and Giroux, 2005.

Powell, Colin with Joseph E. Perisco. *My American Journey.* New York: Random House, 1995.

Reagan, Nancy. *My Turn.* New York: Random House, 1990.

Reagan, Ronald. *An American Life.* New York: Simon & Schuster, 1990.

Reagan, Ronald, Annelise Anderson, and Martin Anderson. *Reagan, In His Own Hand: The Writings of Ronald Reagan that Reveal His Revolutionary Vision for America.* New York: The Free Press, 2001.

Reeves, Richard. *A Ford, Not a Lincoln.* New York: Harcourt Brace Jovanovich, 1975.

Reeves, Richard. *President Kennedy: Profile of Power.* New York: Touchstone, 1993.

Russell, Jan Jarboe. *Lady Bird: A Biography of Mrs. Johnson.* Taylor Trade Publishing, 1999.

Schlesinger Jr., Arthur M. *A Thousand Days: John F. Kennedy in the White House.* Boston: Houghton Mifflin, 1965.

Schnakenberg, Robert. *Distory: A Treasury of Historical Insults.* New York: St. Martin's Press, 2005.

Schweizer, Peter and Rochelle Schweizer. *The Bushes: Portrait of a Dynasty.* New York: Anchor Books, 2005.

Sidey, Hugh. *Hugh Sidey's Portraits of the Presidents: Power and Personality in the Oval Office.* New York: Time Inc., 2000.

Sidey, Hugh. *John Kennedy, President.* New York: Atheneum, 1963.

Sidey, Hugh (text) and Fred Ward (photographs). *Portrait of a President.* New York: Harper & Row, 1975.

Sidey, Hugh. *The Presidency.* New York: Thornwillow Press, 1991.

Skidmore, Max J. *After the White House: Presidents as Private Citizens.* Houndmills, Basingstoke, Hampshire, England: Palgrave Macmillan, 2004.

Small, Marvin. *The Presidency of Richard Nixon* (Reprint Edition). Kansas: University of Kansas, 2003.

Smith, Richard Norton. *Patriarch: George Washington and the New American Nation.* Boston: Houghton Mifflin, 1993.

Truman, Harry S. and Robert H. Farrell, ed. *Dear Bess: The Letters from Harry to Bess Truman, 1910–1959.* New York: W. W. Norton, 1983.

Truman, Harry S. *Mr. Citizen*. New York: Bernard Geis and Associates, 1960.

Truman, Harry S. and Robert H. Farrell, ed. *Off the Record: The Private Papers of Harry S. Truman*. New York: Harper & Row, 1980.

Truman, Harry S., edited by Columbia University. *Truman Speaks*. New York: Columbia University Press, 1969.

Truman, Harry S. and Margaret Truman, ed. *Where the Buck Stops: The Personal and Private Writings of Harry S. Truman*. New York: Warner Books, 1989.

Truman, Harry S. *Year of Decisions* (Vol. 1 of Memoirs). New York: Doubleday, 1955.

Truman, Harry S. *Years of Trial and Hope* (Vol. 2 of Memoirs). New York: Doubleday, 1956.

Truman, Margaret. *Harry S. Truman*. New York: William Morrow & Co., 1973.

Unger, Irwin and Debi Unger. *LBJ: A Life* (Revised Edition). New York: Wiley, 2000.

Van Natta Jr., Don. *First Off the Tee*. New York: Public Affairs, 2003.

Voss, Frederick. *Portraits of the Presidents: The National Portrait Gallery*. New York: Rizzoli International Publications, 2000.

Whitcomb, John and Claire Whitcomb. *Real Life at the White House: 200 Years of Daily Life at America's Most Famous Residence*. London: Routledge Publishing, 2002.

White, Theodore. *Breach of Faith: The Fall of Richard Nixon*. New York: Atheneum, 1975.

White House Historical Association, The. *The White House: Celebrating Two Hundred Years, 1800–2000*. Washington, D.C.: The White House Historical Association, 2002.

Woodward, Bob and Carl Bernstein. *The Final Days*. New York: Simon & Schuster, 1976.

WEBSITES

ABC.com

AOL.com

Aspeninstitute.com

BBC.com

Bloomberg.com

BusinessWeek.com

CarterCenter.org

CBS.com

CNN.com

C-SPAN.com

Forbes.com

JFK.com

MSNBC.com

Newsweek.com

ReaganFoundation.org

Salon.com

TIME.com

Trumanlibrary.org/hoover/intro.htm

Wikipedia.org

WSJ.com

Yahoo.com

TELEVISION/VIDEOTAPES/AUDIOTAPES

Biography: Ronald Reagan: The Role of a Lifetime. A&E Television.

Jimmy Carter. WBS News Channel 14, Atlanta, Georgia, 2003.

The John F. Kennedy White House Tapes. The Miller Center, The University of Virginia.

The Presidential Inauguration. Jimmy Carter Library, 1988.

60 Minutes. CBS. The White House Tapes of Dwight D. Eisenhower, October 22, 1962, The Miller Center, University of Virginia.

MAGAZINES AND PERIODICALS

American Heritage

American Spectator

Atlanta Journal-Constitution

The Atlantic Monthly

The Boston Globe
Christian Science Monitor
The Cleveland Plain Dealer
The Dallas Morning News
The Economist
Esquire
The Guardian
The Houston Chronicle
Idaho Falls Register
Ladies' Home Journal
Life
Look
Los Angeles Times
National Geographic
Newsweek
New York magazine
New York *Newsday*
New York Post
The New Yorker
The New York Times
Parade
People
San Diego Union-Tribune
The St. Louis Dispatch
Seattle Times
Time
USA Today
U.S. News & World Report
Vanity Fair
The Wall Street Journal
The Washington Post

SPEECHES

Bill Clinton, Butler University, Indianapolis, Indiana, November 6, 2005.

Gerald R. Ford, The Harry Truman Library, Opening of "*Time* and the Presidency" exhibit, February 23, 2000.

Richard Nixon, "The Case for Aid to the Contras," Speech to the Annual Associated Press Luncheon for the American Newspaper Publishers Association, April 21, 1986, Richard Nixon Library.

INDEX